P9-CDV-765

TO THE PEOPLE WHO MADE THIS BOOK:

To the clients and popular movements
that exercised their human rights effectively,

To the lawyers, jurors, and judges
who broadened the impact
of human rights law,

AND

To the rising generations
who follow in their footsteps.

Other Books by Ann Fagan Ginger

The Relevant Lawyers

Minimizing Racism in Jury Trials

Civil Liberties Docket

Human Rights Casefinder: The Warren Court Era

M01 40010 05876

The Law, the Supreme Court, and the People's Rights

by Ann Fagan Ginger, LL.M.

President, Meiklejohn Civil Liberties Institute
University of California,
Hastings College of the Law (Adjunct Faculty)

Barron's Educational Series, Inc.

Woodbury, New York 1973

RENNER LEARNING RESOURCE CENTER
ELGIN COMMUNITY COLLEGE
ELGIN, ILLINOIS 60123

Gloria M. Barron Editions
Books bearing this imprint represent
a distinguished contribution to
scholarship and to world understanding.
Their purpose is to help people learn
to live together in peace.

© Copyright 1974 by Barron's Educational Series, Inc.

All rights reserved.
No part of this book may be reproduced in any form, by photostat, microfilm,
xerography, or any other means, or incorporated into any information re-
trieval system, electronic or mechanical, without the written permission of
the copyright owner.

All inquiries should be addressed to:
Barron's Educational Series, Inc.
113 Crossways Park Drive
Woodbury, New York 11797

Library of Congress Catalog Card No. 73–7465

International Standard Book No. 0–8120–0502–3

PRINTED IN THE UNITED STATES OF AMERICA

CONTENTS

PREFACE

Suddenly, in the 1970s, the governmental system of the United States is under close scrutiny. There is a deepening interest in how the system works in general, how the electoral and presidential systems work, how (and whether) the judicial system works. More people are studying law than ever before, to become lawyers, legal workers, investigators and paraprofessionals, or simply to become more effective citizens. Others are studying in order to propound theories of law based on the disciplines of political science, philosophy, anthropology, and sociology.

This is an exciting development for practicing lawyers who share an interest in legal theory, and was my reason for taking time out to write this book.

There are many possible places to start learning about the realities of the law. A careful study of the operation of Congress or of a state legislature will provide one set of valuable insights. An analysis of the functioning of the executive branch, at the federal or state level, will provide another piece of the picture, as the Watergate hearings demonstrate. Focusing on the litigation that is taken to the United States Supreme Court seems to provide a broader canvas than either of the other two methods because many cases require consideration, not only of the judicial system, but of the actions of Congress and of the executive branch leading to the litigation. That is the approach chosen for this book.

Within the field of Supreme Court litigation, many areas can be used as the focal point for a study of the law. Perhaps more could be learned about the operation of the United States governmental system (and its significant relationships with the economic system) by studying cases in tax, antitrust, and labor-management law than by selecting other fields. The difficulty with this approach is that many important cases in these fields are settled before they reach the Supreme Court, and the ones that are appealed to that body are usually argued on such narrow, technical grounds that the average reader—whether layman or lawyer—is quickly bored or confused. One cannot easily see the forces at work or the ultimate significance of the decisions.

The most interesting cases reaching the Court in the past quarter of a century have been those dealing with the rights of the people. Litigants have taken the Bill of Rights seriously, have insisted that it protects human values that were not specifically spelled out in that document—values that suggest the broader term "human rights." This book describes landmark human rights cases reaching the Supreme Court while Earl Warren was Chief Justice, in order to illuminate the underlying relationships between the law, the judicial system, and the people's rights.

In selecting landmarks in human rights law, one quickly focuses on the Warren Court era as the first, and only, era to date in which the United States Supreme Court has considered a significant number of cases in this field. The cases discussed in this book were selected on a number of grounds, not simply on the importance of the decisions. If the parties were particularly colorful and the incidents leading to the lawsuits were exciting, the cases went in unless the opinions were so narrowly technical and difficult to follow that they would not be of interest to the general reader. The process of selection is necessarily highly colored by subjective preferences, but the cases here include most of those listed as important by other constitutional law specialists.

A word of caution: I have taken the word "landmarks" to

include only victories for the proponents of human rights law. When an important issue was decided against the proponents, I have not given the case major treatment, although it may be discussed briefly. The theory is not that every important case was won, even during the Warren Court era, because that is patently false. But issues lost by the advocate of human rights will probably be raised again in later court cases, before legislative bodies, in administrative hearings, or at elections. The selection process, in other words, followed the old maxim: Nothing is settled until it is settled right.

It was easy to decide to start with the Warren Court era in a book focusing on the law and the rights of the people. It was necessary to stop with the end of that era because there is no other logical place to stop. The great danger in writing books about law is that significant new decisions will be handed down after the manuscript has gone to the printer. The author cannot conscientiously leave them out of the text if the book is to be labelled "up-to-date." Yet no matter how many changes are made, a book on the law is always dated. This book, therefore, concludes its major consideration of the law with the end of Warren's term on the Supreme Court. Some comments have been made at the ends of chapters incorporating Burger Court decisions that may have a permanent effect on precedents set by the Warren Court, but the reader should not assume that every significant change has been mentioned. Hopefully reading this book will lead to a determination to keep up with new Court decisions as they are reported in the media.

There were several logical ways to organize this book. All of the cases based on the Bill of Rights could have been put in part one, all those based on the Reconstruction Amendments in part two, and all those arising out of New Deal law in part three. Or the cases could have been placed in simple chronological order according to the dates of decision, which would have emphasized the political and social settings in which the justices worked. I also thought of placing all of the opinions by a particular justice together to provide fascinating studies of Black, Douglas, Harlan, Warren, and the other justices who wrote many opinions, indicating how their attitudes on some constitutional questions changed through the years.

The decision to divide the cases into three broad categories based on constitutional principles seemed, in the long run, most helpful to the reader. The repeated discussions of First, Fifth, and Fourteenth Amendment rights to freedom, justice, and equality will assist the reader in understanding the human rights issues that develop throughout his life.

Each chapter contains four types of material: (1) the historical background and social setting of the cases; (2) the facts in the specific case and descriptions of the parties, their attorneys, the judges, and the trials; (3) the history of the lawsuit, with quotations and summaries of trial and lower appellate court opinions; and (4) direct quotations and paraphrases of the opinions of the United States Supreme Court justices. The easiest material to read is the statement of the facts in the case, and some people may find this the best place to start each chapter. If a reader gets interested enough in the facts and the parties, he or she will be motivated to go back to the background material and then to struggle through some unfamiliar words and turgid prose in the Court opinions. When an unfamiliar legal word or phrase is used, I have tried to follow it with a synonym or definition in the text. Most legal terms are also defined at some length in the Glossary.

The Bibliography lists many kinds of materials written on many levels of complexity. The collections of American literature may be of particular interest to humanities students.

The biographies of important figures in the continuing struggle for human rights will probably be of broader interest. Other reference works suggest the richness of the subject and how much has had to be left out of this book.

Zipporah Collins participated in the research and write-ups of many of the cases in this book. She also provided valuable criticisms, comments, and editorial suggestions about the rest of the manuscript. Both of us struggled to provide clear, accurate descriptions of sometimes complex legal questions, in order to produce a book that a nonlawyer could understand and even enjoy. Although I sometimes rejected her particular suggestions for reasons that seemed legally necessary, many happy turns of phrase and common sense insights into issues previously confused by legal verbiage are hers.

Loralee Lowe and Elizabeth Sklut also assisted in drafts of cases. Brian Beckwith, John Bishop, John McCullough, Paul Silver, Michael Solomon, and Carol Vanairsdale checked the legal research. I benefitted from the comments and criticisms of parts of the manuscript by Janet Bailey, Clark Coleman, Jim Ginger, Tom Ginger, Daisy Goodman, Siegfried Hesse, Frances Herring, Regina Minudri, Manuel Nestle, Katharine Rich, Dennis Roberts, Samuel Rosenwein, and Stefan Rosenzweig. Madeleine Bratt, Jean Hom, Pamela Riley, and Linda Rageh turned the messy drafts into cleanly typed manuscript.

Going to Court to Protect Human Rights

You are living in a house with several people. You are the only one home when the police arrive, search the place, and arrest you for possession of illegal drugs, which you didn't know were there. What are your rights?

You are buying a car on time, but after making a few payments, you break your leg. The medical bills eat up the money for the payments, and your boss tells you he was just ordered to hold back part of your wages in favor of the finance company. Is there anything you can do about it?

A power company is planning to build an atomic power station in a wilderness that you think should be a recreation area. How can you make an effective protest?

Your sister got high grades in school but now employers turn down her applications for jobs or apprenticeship programs. You think her race and sex are the reasons. How can you help her prove it?

Problems like these come up almost every day in almost every part of the United States. You can try to solve them by going to court, by writing a letter to your congressman, or by appealing to an administrative official. But these raise general policy questions as well as problems for the individuals. In order to change present policies in these areas of law, or to make policy where none exists, you can vote for candidates for judge, prosecutor, legislator, president, or governor. Or you can run for office yourself. Before making up your mind what to do to solve such specific and general problems, you will probably explore each alternative, pursuing the one that lets you participate most effectively in the final decision.

Decision-making is the real issue: who makes the decision and on what grounds. Many of the factors in decision-making by the legislative and executive branches of the federal government have been brought to public attention by the Watergate investigations. This book will focus instead on decision-making by the judicial branch, which necessarily includes analysis of executive and legislative action. The problems just mentioned point to a study of human rights law as the most interesting area for concentration.

It is significant that, for the first time in our national history, while Earl Warren sat as Chief Justice from 1953 to 1969, the United States Supreme Court played a major role in developing human rights policy while deciding a great many cases based on similar facts. Its decisions will have a profound effect on your life. They will influence your actions in protecting your rights and those of your friends. They will influence the behavior of policemen, school superintendents, college presidents, power companies, judges, landlords, and employers when you protest their actions.

The courts did not stop handing down decisions on human rights cases when Earl Warren stepped down from the Supreme Court, and it is too early to gauge the degree to which these later decisions may erode the landmarks carved out by the people and the courts during the Warren Court era. But it is clear that the Warren Court decisions provide an exciting text for believers in human rights and that they will withstand many efforts to move backward or sideward, or simply to return to the policy of ignoring this field of law.

This book is not a text for lawyers or a manual for clients

on self-defense in the courts. It simply tries to provide accurate information on how our legal system operates, using as examples the human rights cases decided recently by the Supreme Court.

Equally important, it tries to ask questions that will help you figure out whether you agree with the Court's decisions or whether you have good grounds for disagreement. This country is a democracy based on the consent of the governed, so it matters what you think about the law. Our history shows that the law must ultimately reflect the will of the people. If a majority of the people agree with or accept a Supreme Court decision it will remain the law. If a majority actively disagree with a decision, it will be eroded by disuse or eventually will be changed (by Congress, the President, a later Supreme Court decision, or occasionally by a constitutional amendment).

After you read and think about the *Court's* answers to the questions raised in the cases in this book, it may take you just as long to work our *your own* answers to the questions.

The answers worked out by the Court are more than words on paper, however. They are the product of disputes between litigants or parties who raised legal questions before an institution, the Supreme Court, operating in a particular manner because of its composition at the time. It is necessary to analyze each of these many elements—the parties, the issues, the times, the sources of law, the law as previously stated, the role of the Court in general, and its role under Chief Justice Warren. Then it may be possible to decide whether the Supreme Court has proved its ability to settle significant disputes, or whether we need to try another approach to solving the many problems pressing in upon our lives.

The Parties

People get arrested and people file lawsuits but they are often ignored in books about the law. The emphasis is on what their lawyers argued and what the judges decided. This book tries to describe the people who went to court, on both sides, and to let them tell in their own words why they acted as they did. It is not possible to give every detail in any case, but I try to give an accurate summary of the exciting struggles that led to these Supreme Court decisions.

The Issues

After the judge or jury decides the case, one side may appeal. If so, the issues that go to the appellate (appeals) court are not based on the actual events. They are limited to the written record of the testimony of witnesses about those events, the objections to testimony by trial lawyers, and the rulings and instructions of the trial judge. If a case is appealed two or three times, the statement of facts begins to sound like an old story; it has been polished and simplified until it appears smooth and logical.

In our system, all the legal questions that will ever be raised in a case must be raised at the trial level. Otherwise an appellate court can refuse to consider them. To be on the safe side, lawyers raise all the legal questions they can think of at trial, even if some may be mutually exclusive or contradictory ("My client was not present and did not do it, and moreover he had every right to be there and do it"). After trial, the losing side carefully selects and frames the questions to raise on appeal.

The Lawsuits

How does a case reach the United States Supreme Court? A case that concerns state law usually begins in a city or county trial court. The case usually must be appealed through the state court system—often two appellate courts after the trial court—before going to the United States Supreme Court. On a federal question, a case is usually filed in the federal district court, is appealed to the federal court of appeals, and appealed again to the United States Supreme Court. The Supreme Court can agree to hear any state or federal case or can refuse to hear it without stating a reason.

Out of the thousands of cases it is asked to hear each year, the Court decides which hundreds to hear, according to the significance and timeliness of the questions presented to it by the attorneys. These legal questions, too, have been refined and smoothed until they fit together as precisely as a jigsaw puzzle. They give the impression that the case was carefully constructed from start to finish by specialists in litigation architecture. But the justices are master architects, too. They can often select two or three issues from a complex case, decide them, and leave to another case and time the solution to other issues with broader social implications.

The Human Rights Cases

Usually people go to court to take care of a personal problem—to obtain a divorce, to get damages for injuries received in an accident, or to settle the estate of a deceased relative. But, in the United States, people also can go to court to challenge the way something is being done by the government. Our judicial system is equipped to provide a forum for debate on many social questions. This is not true in most countries, and, even in the United States, this does not make it possible to win if the point is new or unpopular. But the *chance* of winning sends many citizens to court to seek social change. In such a lawsuit, victory for the individual will result in victory for many others who do not go to court. (The same is true for defeat.)

Frequently in disputes about human rights, each side feels deeply that it is in the right and that it cannot afford to let the other side win. The side that loses in the trial court will take an appeal to the next higher court. The side that loses the appeal will appeal to the court above that, and so on to the Supreme Court, unless the losing side loses heart or runs out of money to pay court costs and attorneys' fees at some stage, or both sides give in a little and reach a settlement.

By the time a human rights case gets to the Supreme Court, three to five years have usually passed since the events that started the lawsuit. The noisy demonstrations of students, the tumult of police officers arresting masses of people, the statements of government officials have faded from hearing, and seldom echo loudly through the neatly printed pages presented to the Court.

The Supreme Court's Role

Over the years, the questions that started the case may have been settled by other events. The children whose parents wanted them to attend a desegregated school have graduated or dropped out. The man fired for his political beliefs has long since found another job, moved to another city, or decided to keep his mouth shut in the future. Other participants may have become ill, retired, or died. (Often the government attorney in the original case is a judge by the time the Supreme Court hears the case.)

What is left for the Supreme Court to do, now that the crisis is past? It cannot put things back where they were before the case began, and it cannot create the situation that would have existed if the law had been enforced properly at the very beginning.

But the Court can lay down the rules for all future cases. It can describe the history of illegal practices and proclaim a warning to all citizens, companies, organizations, and government officials: the Constitution means what it says about the law and cannot be ignored without serious consequences.

Sometimes the Court can act quickly enough to save a prisoner from execution, to release a person who has been unfairly convicted, to stop an official threatening to deprive citizens of their right to free expression, or to prevent some other injustice. Often the best it can do is to order one side to pay money to the other side to help make up for a wrong.

The Court is not an elected body responsible to the voters; its members are appointed for life so that they will have the perspective to make immediate decisions that will have sound long-term effects. But their distance from the people and the realities of life is often exaggerated. The Court does not act in a vacuum. It consists of nine human beings who read the newspapers and ride through the streets and talk to their friends. They are selected by the President with the advice of the American Bar Association and the consent of the Senate, and they usually come from positions in government or political parties.

They are sworn to uphold "the law" and to keep this "a government of laws, not of men."

Precisely what is the law they are sworn to uphold? Who formulated it? Where can you find it?

The Law

The law in the United States is neither boring nor mysterious. It is often couched in language that seems foreign, but a few keys will unlock its meaning.

Our law can be found in four kinds of documents. The most fundamental is the United States Constitution and its amendments. The other three are the statutes enacted by the legislative branch, the orders and regulations issued by the executive branch, and the court decisions rendered by the judicial branch.

Each of these kinds of documents is issued by our federal government and by fifty state governments. To know the law on a question, you must look to the constitutions, statutory law, administrative law, and court case (or common) law in your jurisdiction.

The court system in the United States is governed by rules limiting its power in some respects and leaving it virtually unlimited in others. Whenever there is a relevant statute or regulation, the courts must analyze and apply it in order to reach a decision in a lawsuit. However, when there is no valid statute or regulation to help reach a decision, the courts must follow precedent, that is, each decision must have a basis in some past decision. Therefore, the parties to a lawsuit must seek to prove that the practice being followed today is (or is not) authorized by the law of the past. For this reason, suing to protect the rights of the people today always requires studying the history of the rights of the people in the past.

The Sources of Law

The acts of individuals and groups of Americans are the basic source of law. When a colonial editor insisted on printing attacks on the colonial government and the British king, he was writing an early draft of the First Amendment to the

United States Constitution. When the first person arrested in the New World demanded to know the reason for his arrest, he was helping to write the due process clause of the Fifth Amendment. When the first black man escaped from slavery he was preparing the first version of the Thirteenth Amendment.

The "underground" leaflets written by members of the Committee of Correspondence to rouse the colonists to fight King George III, official documents like the Declaration of Independence, the constitutions adopted by the thirteen new states, and reports of the debates at the Constitutional Convention—all of these contributed ideas and phrases to our basic document, the United States Constitution.

The actions of Americans continue to provide the basis for our law. When a person seeks to change the law through a court case, his success does not depend solely on the logic of his position or its historic validity. In practice, he will succeed in making a change in the law if he can convince a particular judge or jury or appellate court that he is right. By and large, and in the long run, he will succeed if the change he proposes has roots in our traditions and if enough people agree that the change is necessary at this time. If the majority of the people want and need a new rule based on precedent, a change will come about—although it will often be partial, usually slow, and sometimes too late to help the person who raised the issue. The change may not come through a court decision, but through the act of a president or governor, Congress or a state legislature, or even through constitutional amendment.

The Sources of Human Rights Law

Almost before the ink was dry on the Constitution, ten amendments were added to set forth the basic United States law of human rights. The members of the Convention at Philadelphia had been primarily concerned with establishing the power of the federal government. But the people eligible to vote for or against the Constitution saw that it was also necessary to guarantee that this strong central government would not become as tyrannical as the royal government just overthrown.

At the time it was written, the American Bill of Rights was the most complete statement of human rights law ever adopted, guaranteeing freedom of expression (discussed in part I of this book) and a fair method of deciding civil and criminal cases (discussed in part II). It crowned the first of five major periods in the development of laws protecting the rights of the people.

After a period of consolidation of federal power, the nation faced a second American revolution, although it was not given that name and many did not agree that the change was that profound. The struggles against the extension of slavery and for its abolition led to innumerable petitions to Congress and to much litigation. After the Supreme Court in 1857 upheld the constitutionality of slavery in the *Dred Scott* decision (discussed in part III), the voters elected Abraham Lincoln, the South seceded, and the Civil War began. The victory of the federal government made possible the adoption of the Thirteenth, Fourteenth, and Fifteenth Amendments. These major additions to our human rights law were to end slavery and all of its trappings, to extend the constitutional protections against government interference with the rights of citizens to include protection against *state* government interference, and to insure citizenship and voting rights to the freedmen.

The third major period became the Dark Ages of human rights law. From the Tilden-Hayes compromise in 1876 (discussed in part III) until the depression of the 1930s, few gains were made in spelling out the rights of the people, and the Supreme Court permitted many of the rights won by black citizens in the Reconstruction period to be snatched away. As giant corporations like Standard Oil were established, the Court used the new Fourteenth Amendment to protect their corporate rights, but denied its protection to the black citizens for whom it had been written. The Court ruled that corporations would not have to obey state laws safeguarding the health of workers and fixing railroad rates. At the same time, it ruled that members of minority groups would have to obey state laws requiring racial segregation. "Separate but equal" was declared constitutional in the case of *Plessy* v. *Ferguson.*

Around the beginning of the twentieth century, a populist movement of small farmers, small businessmen, and working people pushed through constitutional amendments authorizing a tax on income and direct election of senators; in this period woman suffrage was finally won. Some antitrust and labor laws were passed, and the Supreme Court required the states to follow some federal due process standards. But big business dominated government, and these measures did not increase the political power or economic position of the powerless as much as had been hoped. World War I soon followed, leading to passage of repressive state and federal laws and Attorney General Palmer's Raids against aliens and naturalized citizens (discussed in part I).

A new major spurt of human rights activity occurred during the Great Depression, and flowered in President Franklin D. Roosevelt's New Deal programs. Although no constitutional amendments were proposed, a major amendment took place in the attitude of Americans about government responsibility for the citizens' well-being. With one-third of the nation ill-housed, ill-clothed, and ill-fed, Congress passed a series of laws touching the economic needs of the people, including the right to protection from low wages and long working hours, the right to form trade unions and to bargain collectively with employers about job conditions, the right to receive payments in the event of unemployment, disability, and old age. In addition, Congress provided funds for low-cost government-built housing, for public works and conservation programs putting millions of Americans back to work, and for price-support programs for some agricultural crops. The people rejected dog-eat-dog philosophy when this meant some Americans would literally starve to death; they rejected the doctrine of "survival of the fittest" when it doomed many Americans to serious deprivations. For the first time in this country, people accepted the notion that the *government* must provide people with money and services to alleviate acute poverty. In practical terms, this meant that people could be taxed to support public services to the less fortunate. So many of the taxpayers in the late 1930s had just been in the category of "the less fortunate" that they welcomed this idea.

FDR coined the phrase "freedom from want and freedom from fear" to describe two of the most important needs of the American people in that period. The justices of the Supreme Court tried to overrule nearly every statute designed to give the federal government power to protect some of the economic interests of small businessmen, wage earners, and farmers at the expense of the free enterprise system. They eventually had to give way before a broad movement supporting the President's programs.

The United States economy was slowly pulling out of the depression when our participation in World War II catapulted the country into an economic boom. Suddenly most people could find jobs, and were able to turn their attention in other directions. When Germany, Japan, and Italy became our enemies, men were drafted into the armed forces and women were encouraged to get jobs previously held by men only. In order to build morale to defeat the enemy, it was necessary to define the differences between the three fascist nations and our own democratic system. It was necessary to make good on some old civil rights pledges. After hard prodding from the black community and its white supporters, FDR finally called for an end to segregation in the armed forces and established the first Fair Employment Practices Commission. Wartime labor boards accepted the rights of labor unions to improve the wages of working people, and local and federal governments established child-care centers and other community services for working mothers.

Many veterans returning home after the defeat of fascism assumed this kind of human rights activity would continue. They elected congressmen who wrote a law requiring the President to establish a board of economic advisers to help him keep people employed. Although the Full Employment Act of 1946 was watered down before passage, it attempted to prevent a recurrence of the high unemployment rates of the 1930s. Congressmen proposed guaranteed medical care for all Americans, fair employment practices acts, and an anti-lynching law. None of these bills passed Congress. The American ambassador to the United Nations, Eleanor Roosevelt, took the lead in promulgating a new international bill of rights that would include all the political guarantees in our Bill of Rights and Reconstruction amendments and would add the economic rights spelled out in our New Deal period and in the constitutions of many social democratic and socialist countries abroad. The United States delegation voted for the resulting Universal Declaration of Human Rights of the

United Nations adopted on December 10, 1948. Since then it has been largely ignored; few of its provisions for protecting the living standards of our people have been implemented by Congress or the President.

The New Deal-World War II period, like the Reconstruction period, was followed by a severe backlash against human rights gains. This started in 1947 with the requirement that all government employees take an oath of loyalty to the federal government and swear they were not members of loosely defined "subversive" organizations. It led to passage of the Taft-Hartley Act, which curbed union political activity, and then to a wide range of Cold War actions.

When President Eisenhower appointed Earl Warren to the Supreme Court in 1953, the country was in a period of severe political repression and hysteria about alleged subversive activities (the Joe McCarthy anti-Communist witch-hunts). Our socialist ally in World War II was now considered an insidious menace to democracy, to be ringed by Winston Churchill's Iron Curtain. We were fighting the Red menace abroad in a "police action" in Korea, and at home by investigations, criminal prosecutions, political persecutions, and economic reprisals against a variety of progressive-minded citizens. Long-cherished constitutional rights and protections were rudely cast aside in the name of "internal security." The New Deal programs were denounced as "creeping socialism"; militant labor leaders were said to be Red agents planning "political strikes" to create chaos in the economy; atomic spies were alleged to be lurking everywhere; and teachers were accused of indoctrinating the young to overthrow the "American way of life."

In this atmosphere, where do Supreme Court justices go to find answers to the human rights issues posed in cases coming before them?

The Law of Human Rights

The justices base their decisions mainly on legal research, rather than research in history as such. Like all lawyers, they turn to constitutional documents.

The justices are concerned with three elements of human rights—freedom, justice, and equality. The legal phrases describing these rights are "civil liberties," "due process," and "civil rights," and they are protected in a series of constitutional amendments:

(1) Protections of *freedom and civil liberties* from interference by government are found mainly in the First Amendment (discussed in part I of this book);

(2) Provisions for *fair trial and due process of law* in the courts and before administrative agencies are found mainly in the due process clauses of the Fifth and Fourteenth Amendments (discussed in part II);

(3) Guarantees of *civil rights and equal protection of the laws* for all Americans—regardless of race, creed, color, nationality, religion, or sex—are found mainly in the Thirteenth, Fourteenth, and Fifteenth Amendments (discussed in part III).

The Supreme Court

Supreme Court justices must always decide whether they will hear and decide important cases, or refuse to hear them and leave the law as stated by the President, Congress, lower courts, and other officials. If they reject the law as stated by others, and agree to hear a case, they must also decide whether to rule only on the very narrow issue raised, leaving the general law unclear, or to formulate new, definite standards for use in many future cases. They can exercise a judicial courage that has been quite rare in our history by explicitly overruling bad previous decisions.

The Court often looks to history for guidance. Should it reject some congressional enactments and executive orders and look back to the law of the Revolutionary War and Bill of Rights period? Should it ignore almost 100 years of decisions and read the amendments and statutes of the Reconstruction Period according to their words and the spirit of their framers? Should it hold that black and white are entitled to equal protection in every sphere of life? Should it limit corporate power to protect the public interest? Should it recognize and extend the economic rights that were won during the New Deal but never written into the Constitution? Should it find a constitutional basis for providing equal protection for the poor, as well as for the black? Should it follow Justice Black's lead and decide that all of the protections against federal power spelled out in the first ten amendments also apply against state power through the due process clause of the Fourteenth Amendment (discussed in chapter 20)?

These are the underlying questions facing every Supreme Court justice and lower court judge in this era. They were the major issues facing the justices making up the Warren Court.

The Warren Court

Earl Warren joined eight justices on the Supreme Court, five appointed by President Roosevelt as New Dealers, and three appointed by President Truman in the backlash period. Many changes took place on the highest bench during Chief Justice Warren's sixteen-year tenure, and he was ultimately joined by four justices appointed by President

Eisenhower, two by President Kennedy, and two by President Johnson.

Yet with all the changes, with all the divergence in views of the justices, with all the in-fighting evident in some opinions, the Warren Court came to have a style and meaning unique in American history. Unlike some of his predecessors, Earl Warren evoked a friendly atmosphere in which lawyers could engage in sharp oral arguments. Chief Justice Warren frequently joined three colleagues to make the necessary four votes required for the Court to hear controversial cases. As a result, the Warren Court undoubtedly heard more human rights cases than all previous Supreme Courts combined. While every decision was not a victory for the side raising a human rights issue, almost every decision was informed by an awareness of the revolutionary principles of the Bill of Rights and the egalitarian principles of the Reconstruction Amendments and New Deal legislation. Chief Justice Warren and many of the other justices had studied our history in depth and prefaced their discussions of legal questions with references to the significant people's movements that have shaped our law.

The Court listened to arguments by hundreds of lawyers representing large movements of people demanding their rights. The people persecuted by Senator Joe McCarthy and his "Communist conspiracy" witchhunts demanded reversal of criminal convictions; they wanted decisions giving back their jobs. The civil rights movement insisted on an end to all segregation, violence, and racism. Poor people insisted on equal treatment from the judicial system, including the right to assistance of lawyers. The peace movement insisted on its right to petition the government by a variety of methods, since Washington seemed so hard of hearing. More than most of their predecessors, the justices of this Court not only listened, but actually seemed to hear what the parties were talking about and to understand that the slums, as well as the suburbs, were listening for its answers.

The Best Court

In many ways, however, the Supreme Court is the worst place to win a human rights case—even when an Earl Warren is sitting as Chief Justice. It takes a large amount of money and a long time to get a case to the Court. Even when a party wins, he may not come out with a clear victory. The decisions are seldom unanimous, and a five-to-four or six-to-three split tends to weaken the impact of the majority opinion. A Supreme Court decision may have a tremendous effect in the long run, but it seldom brings about immediate major changes.

Most cases do not get to the Supreme Court anyway. This is especially true of human rights disputes, where the parties usually cannot afford to appeal, and their lawyers will never get paid even if they win because a monetary award seldom goes with a victory on principle.

Most disputes never even become lawsuits. People don't tend to go to a lawyer when they think they have been treated unfairly. They may not know a lawyer they trust; they may not have the money to pay a fee; and they don't think it will help to go to court anyway.

This means that for most people the highest court, the supreme court of the land, is the policeman on the beat, the highway patrolman, the landlord, the boss, the creditor, or the voter registrar. A decision by the Supreme Court guaranteeing human rights has no meaning until these people around the country know about and decide to follow it.

Of course, all the courts and government agencies in the

country are required to follow Supreme Court decisions, too. But "the Court's authority—possessed of neither the purse nor the sword—ultimately rests on sustained public confidence in its moral sanction," as Justice Frankfurter put it so succinctly. And compliance with Warren Court opinions was certainly not automatic, as several cases in this book illustrate.

Studying the development of human rights law through the landmark decisions of the Warren Court can lead to increased respect for our legal system. At the same time it can lead to the opposite conclusion: that the best time to win a human rights case is at the beginning, the best place is where the case starts, the best judge and jury are the participants, and the best method is without a lawsuit. In other words, the best protectors of human rights are not the courts but rather citizens who know and insist on their own rights and who act to guarantee the rights of others to freedom, justice, and equality.

Citizens concerned about human rights who were raised during the Warren Court era came to depend on the Court to right the wrongs created by acts of Congress, executive orders, and lower court decisions, and by the actions of government officials, private citizens, and groups. The Court did not always fulfill this function, but it did so more often than any previous Supreme Court—and perhaps more often than any Court of the near future. To the extent it followed and advanced the development of human rights law, it was the Camelot of courts. To the extent it disarmed the people by suggesting reliance on the courts rather than on their own collective action, it led to disillusionment when Earl Warren stepped down. It is necessary now to reassess the opportunities for progress through the judicial system.

The value of studying landmark human rights decisions of

the Warren Court lies in the nature of those decisions. Because so many of them were based on fundamental law—the Constitution and its amendments—and on historic struggles of the American people, the decisions will stand firmly against petty attacks by government officials and private interests. These broad, basic rulings should be of great service to Americans, even if a later Supreme Court, Congress, or President seeks to limit their scope or to modify their impact. Their validity rests on their adherence to both the wording of our fundamental law and the spirit in which it was developed. They represent a high point in Supreme Court affirmance of the law that protects the people's rights.

PART I

FREEDOM

FIRST AMENDMENT:
Congress shall make no law respecting an establishment of religion, or prohibiting the free exercise thereof; or abridging the freedom of speech, or of the press; or the right of the people peaceably to assemble, and to petition the Government for a redress of grievances.

NINTH AMENDMENT:
The enumeration in the Constitution, of certain rights, shall not be construed to deny or disparage others retained by the people.

FOURTEENTH AMENDMENT, Section 1:
. . . nor shall any State deprive any person of life, liberty, or property, without due process of law. . . .

ARTICLE 1, Section 9:
. . . No bill of attainder or ex post facto law shall be passed. . . .

First Things First

When a group of Des Moines high school students wanted fellow students to know their views on the war in Southeast Asia, they put on black armbands. Before they could get around to discussing the war, the school authorities sent them home for wearing the armbands. This shifted the question from what was wrong with the war to their right to discussion on campus. The same thing happened when a Connecticut doctor wanted to discuss birth control techniques with his patients. He was arrested for violating a Connecticut law prohibiting the use of contraceptives. Before he could talk about family planning, he had to fight for the right to talk about it.

This experience is repeated dozens of times on important issues. Some agency of government or some group of private citizens attacks the right of people to speak or remain silent, to read or write, or to organize together. Then the activists have to discuss the right of discussion before they can discuss the subject that concerns them.

When the right of discussion wins, the questions that need debate can be aired and the public can form opinions and eventually take action. When repression wins, the public is deprived of the opportunity for informed debate and is forced to accept the action or inaction of its leaders without analysis. Frequently lack of information leads to lack of action at many levels, causing the pressing problems to reach crisis proportions before they are dealt with. Many commentators say that this happened in the 1960s to questions of racial discrimination and conditions in the ghetto, that it happened in the 1970s to questions of the treatment of prisoners. In both instances, violence erupted, which shifted the discussion from the underlying problems to the need to end the violence. This put another stumbling block in the way of finding reasoned answers to very complex problems.

These events explain why it is so appropriate that freedom of expression comes first in the list of people's rights, set forth in the First Amendment. The first point that must be settled is that "I have a right to say this!" Before the speaker can discuss the subject itself, people in authority must agree with his right of expression. If they refuse him the right to rent a hall or arrest him for speaking on a soapbox, he must go to court for an order protecting his rights. As a result, those with new ideas must also be prepared to fight for the age-old ideas expressed in the First Amendment.

Why was the First Amendment written in the first place? If we understand this, we can use the amendment better in our own lives and see why clients and lawyers use it in Supreme Court cases.

It was 1787, and the American people had just achieved an exciting victory over a foreign government headed by a hereditary king with almost absolute power. They wrote a constitution establishing an entirely different system of government, with no hereditary or absolute rulers. The president would be elected by the voters for a limited term, and his power would be checked and balanced by a Congress and a Supreme Court. However, this new and democratic form of government could not exist without an informed electorate, and this required a guarantee that everyone would have the freedom to hear and to express all kinds of views concerning public questions.

"Those who won our independence believed that the final end of the State was to make men free to develop their faculties; and that in its government the deliberative forces should prevail over the arbitrary. They valued liberty both as an end and as a means. They believed liberty to be the secret of happiness and courage to be the secret of liberty. They believed that freedom to think as you will and to speak as you think are means indispensable to the discovery and spread of political truth; that without free speech and assembly discussion would be futile; that with them, discussion affords ordinarily adequate protection against the dissemination of noxious doctrine; that the greatest menace to freedom is an inert people; that public discussion is a political duty; and that this should be a fundamental principle of the American government."

This series of truths defined the meaning of the First Amendment according to Justice Louis Brandeis, writing 140 years after its adoption, in the case of *Whitney* v. *California.*

Brandeis believed that the founding fathers "recognized the risks to which all human institutions are subject. But they knew that order cannot be secured merely through fear of punishment for its infraction; that it is hazardous to discourage thought, hope and imagination; that fear breeds repression; that repression breeds hate; that hate menaces stable government; that the path of safety lies in the opportunity to discuss freely supposed grievances and proposed remedies; and that the fitting remedy for evil counsels is good ones.

"Believing in the power of reason as applied through public discussion, they eschewed silence coerced by law—the argument of force in its worst form. Recognizing the occasional tyrannies of governing majorities, they amended the Constitution so that free speech and assembly should be guaranteed."

What happened to these lofty ideals in practice? The first serious challenge to freedom of political expression came early. In 1798, only seventeen years after defeating the British, the United States seemed to be on the verge of war with France, and the ideas of the French revolution aroused fear and hostility among conservative members of the Federalist Party. Some Federalists saw in the opposition Republican (or Jeffersonian) Party not a group of political opponents, but a subversive association that intended to take over the government by force of arms, as soon as it gathered enough strength, and to make the United States subservient to the interests of the French government (for perspective, see the description of Communism in the Subversive Activities Control Act, quoted in chapter 6). In Jefferson's words, the primary difference between the two parties was that "one fears most the ignorance of the people; the other, the selfishness of rulers independent of them."

The Federalists used their position of power in 1798 to pass statutes against aliens and "alien ideas." They vigorously enforced their Sedition Act against Republican Party members, newspapermen, lawyers, preachers, and a variety of others who dared to speak or write critically of Federalist officials. A prime example was made of Congressman Matthew Lyon of Vermont, who published material less critical of President John Adams than much political comment published today. Lyon was arrested, convicted, fined $1,000, and sent to jail for four months. His constituents triumphantly reelected him to Congress while he was still in jail (see Julian Bond's similar situation in *Bond* v. *Floyd*, discussed in chapter 2.)

The Federalists' Naturalization Act, extending the residency requirement to fourteen years, and their Enemy Alien Act, permitting enemy nationals to be jailed in the event of war or threatened war, served their function without ever being enforced, causing many liberal aliens to flee or keep silent.

The Supreme Court was never asked to rule on the constitutionality of the Sedition Act (although several justices expressed their view that it was constitutional). Jefferson and Madison led the campaign against these acts, Madison, the father of the Constitution, explaining that the United States might well have continued to be "miserable colonies, groaning under a foreign yoke," if such a sedition act had been in effect before the Revolution. The voters were profoundly shocked by these laws and defeated the Federalists in the election of 1800. The acts expired automatically in March 1801, and the new president, Jefferson, promptly pardoned all those convicted under the Sedition Act. (Eventually Congress even repaid most of the fines charged against its victims.)

This experience kept Congress out of the thought-control business for a century, but it did not end all problems under the First Amendment.

Freedom of expression is important when there are issues that cannot be settled without freewheeling debate. When almost everyone agrees about a subject, people often (although not always) are willing to be tolerant of a few dissenters. But when two very strongly opposing views are seeking adherents, and the issue is critical to each group, the right of freedom of expression of one group or the other may be attacked.

Freedom of expression suffered many attacks in the nineteenth century for this reason. The century opened with major questions that had to be decided concerning the status of various classes of working people, and there were always some who preferred a physical free-for-all to free debate on the issues. Should the First Amendment protect speakers who stirred popular feelings, sometimes to the point of physical encounters? Should the First Amendment protect discussion of questions like the rights of emancipated blacks? Even more critical, should the government protect discussions about the constitutional rights of workers held in slavery?

The passage of years did not settle these questions, and new questions came to the fore about immigrants from Ireland and China, who came in response to advertisements by employers seeking cheap labor. Could these newcomers be kept in an inferior status to the English who had arrived a little earlier? Would they destroy the new trade unions being built with so much difficulty? And these substantive questions led to the First Amendment questions: What limits should be placed on debates about the rights of aliens? Should the government protect aliens against antialien attacks by the so-called Know-Nothing Party? The last third of the century saw several economic panics (depressions) and violent strikes in major industries. Could employers get judges to issue injunctions preventing workers from talking about unions and stopping them from striking? Would such injunctions violate the First Amendment guarantee of freedom of expression?

Each of these questions affected the pocketbooks of the people, and a bitter debate on any of them could be started on a moment's notice almost anywhere in the country. Often a verbal debate led to fisticuffs, sometimes to a riot. Did the First Amendment mean the police should arrest the unpopular speaker or the unruly audience?

Looking more closely at the early nineteenth century, we can see that the problem of freedom of expression became acute in the southern states as some slaves staged revolts against the barbaric behavior of their employer-masters, and as northern propaganda for abolition of slavery increased. Before 1830, the South allowed a limited amount of free discussion, although it was already sensitive to antislavery talk from within and from without. But when the abolitionists became more aggressive, the dominant slaveholding group found it imperative to prevent the dissemination of antislavery doctrines. The South could be self-critical, and slaveholders themselves recognized that slavery had its faults, but they intended to retain political and economic control of the South, and, to do so, frank discussion of slavery must be forbidden and nonslaveholding southerners must be brought around to this view.

Every southern state (except Kentucky) eventually passed laws controlling and limiting speech, press, and discussion. In 1849, Virginia punished by one year's imprisonment and $500 fine any person who "by speaking or writing maintains that owners have no right of property in slaves." Louisiana set punishments ranging from twenty-one years at hard labor to the death penalty for conversations "having a tendency to promote discontent among free colored people, or insubordination among slaves." These limitations on speech and press were justified by their proponents as preventing slave revolts stirred by abolitionists.

These statutes hampered free expression of antislavery opinion, but they did not fully suppress it. Southern courts usually meted out light sentences for conviction, not wanting the defendants to appeal because the statutes were badly drawn and might not stand up under constitutional attack. When the legal process against southern abolitionists seemed too slow and ineffective, citizen mobs developed, as they had on the frontiers. Mobs were not uncommon in the North as well, particularly from 1833 to 1840. In one week in 1835, an editor noted five hundred items on mob violence in the national press. In Boston, William Lloyd Garrison, outstanding abolitionist editor, was mobbed and dragged through the streets. In Alton, Illinois, a mob destroyed the offices and printing presses of Reverend Elijah P. Lovejoy and then murdered him. This spirit receded in the North after 1845, but continued in full force in the South until the Civil War.

None of the legal issues related to the right to debate the slavery question reached the Supreme Court. This strange result occurred because the Court decided in 1833, in *Barron* v. *Baltimore,* that the Bill of Rights guarantees were limited to protection against the *federal* government and did not protect a person against actions by state or local authorities, or against private individuals or groups. Since these were the agencies permitting or causing the repression, antislavery forces had no court to turn to.

In the North, the right to freedom of speech, press, and assembly became linked with the antislavery movement. The campaign of suppression failed, and arguments about freedom strengthened the theory and practice of First Amendment rights. But in the South, the refusal to allow freedom of discussion on the slavery question continued, and many commentators believe it was disastrous. Intelligent southerners were frightened into silence, instead of playing a constructive role as critics of some actions in their region. The trend toward sectionalism and insularity in the South found no corrective, and the institution whose supporters could not permit discussion or criticism was more certainly doomed.

In this tense period, a few followed the openly courageous path of the martyr, Lovejoy, and the Grimké sisters, who had to move from their beloved South in order to continue their work against slavery unmolested. Others, feeling hemmed in by narrow-minded neighbors who criticized their political beliefs or unconventional life styles, took the path charted by Henry David Thoreau, who left society without walking a dozen miles. Still others simply went West. There they might find more tolerance, or even support for their views. At the very least, they could be let alone in the unpoliced, ungoverned territories. These independent spirits seldom considered going to court to stop repressive conduct by their local governments or vigilante groups, since local judges had done nothing to demonstrate concern for protecting free debate.

This period of intense nondiscussion of the most critical question facing the country ground to an end when the South fired on Fort Sumter. President Lincoln took a series of executive actions to meet the military emergency, recognizing that freedom of speech and press by secessionists was intertwined with overt acts of rebellion. (His executive actions to limit attacks on the federal government were never reviewed by the Supreme Court during the Civil War, and, although interesting historically, are not part of the mainstream of First Amendment problems in the period since that bitter war.)

The spirit of free discussion returned to both North and South with the Reconstruction period (described in chapter 21). Ultimately it led one Civil War veteran to provide a memorable explanation of the need for freedom, in a Supreme Court case, *Abrams* v. *United States*. This, like much of the philosophy of Justice Oliver Wendell Holmes, grew out of his participation in that unexpectedly long and costly war.

"Persecution for the expression of opinions seems to me perfectly logical. If you have no doubt of your premises or your power and want a certain result with all your heart you naturally express your wishes in law and sweep away all opposition. To allow opposition by speech seems to indicate that you think the speech impotent, as when a man says that he has squared the circle, or that you do not care wholeheartedly for the result, or that you doubt either your power or your premises.

"But when men have realized that time has upset many fighting faiths, they may come to believe even more than they believe the very foundations of their own conduct that the ultimate good desired is better reached by free trade in ideas—that the best test of truth is the power of the thought to get itself accepted in the competition of the market, and that truth is the only ground upon which their wishes safely can be carried out. That at any rate is the theory of our Constitution. It is an experiment, as all life is an experiment.

"Every year if not every day we have to wager our salvation upon some prophecy based upon imperfect knowledge. While that experiment is part of our system I think that we should be eternally vigilant against attempts to check the expression of opinions that we loathe and believe to be fraught with death. . . ."

This view was not expressed until 1919—fifty years after the end of the Civil War. The failure of the United States Supreme Court to say that the First Amendment concept of freedom of expression was relevant to the debate on slavery while that issue was raging left the struggle over that question out of the courtroom and in the streets. Meanwhile the Court did take a position on the legality of the institution of slavery, in 1857, holding that the founders of the country had intended to deny all rights to black Americans, whether free or slave. (See the discussion of the *Dred Scott* case in chapter 21.) This decision, reversed by the Civil War, limited the prestige of Court decisions on all questions for many years.

Some questions debated in the early twentieth century have been similar to those in the nineteenth: What can be done to change the distribution of wealth in this country? Is an income tax constitutional? What rights, if any, does a workingman have against his employer, individually and as a member of a trade union? What rights, if any, does a person have who was born abroad and came to the United States as an alien? These issues were strongly debated in election campaigns from 1896 on. After 1916, a key question was, What rights does an alien, a voter, or a juvenile have to oppose United States participation in war?

People seeking to organize workers into unions found that freedom of speech and press was essential to their task. Employers opposing them sometimes resorted to the courts for injunctions forbidding their activity; sometimes resorted to legislative bodies for statutes forbidding their activity; and sometimes resorted to "frontier-type justice" through shootings, evictions of striking workers, and use of spies in labor unions. Free speech became an open issue when a group of workers formed the Industrial Workers of the World (IWW) —the Wobblies—seeking to organize transportation and factory workers in the Midwest and migrant laborers in the West. When a Wobbly organizer was thrown in jail during a strike, he would send out a call, and Wobblies throughout the country would hitch rides to that town. They would take to the soapbox to talk about the workers' rights until they too were arrested. These "free speech fights" were given wide publicity, jamming the jails in several cities and opening up discussion on unions and on the values of free speech. None of these cases reached the United States Supreme Court either.

In 1916 the voters reelected Woodrow Wilson to the presidency, partly because he had kept the country out of the war in Europe; the United States then entered World War I and drafted men to fight overseas. Congress passed the Espionage Act in 1917, a statute reminiscent of the hated Alien and Sedition Acts of the late eighteenth century. When antiwar speakers and leaflet distributors were charged with violations of the Espionage Act, they turned to the First Amendment for protection.

That same year, the Russian people overthrew the Czar and established the first socialist economic system, confiscating the land and property of feudal and capitalistic owners in the process. As in 1798, this resulted in an antialien, anti-"Red" hysteria and the Palmer Raids—dragnet arrests of ten thousand aliens and naturalized citizens (described briefly in chapter 6).

These events led the United States Supreme Court, almost for the first time in its history, to determine exactly what protections the First Amendment provided and exactly what the First Amendment meant when it said, "Congress shall make no law . . . abridging the freedom of speech, or of the press."

It is difficult to remember that the amendment had almost never been defined and discussed by lawyers and judges up to that point. And in several World War I cases the Supreme Court majority held, in effect, that American participation in the war permitted the Court to ignore the First Amendment. As a result, Justice Oliver Wendell Holmes was hailed as a great liberal when he said the First Amendment was relevant to the cases, even though he also said that the words "Congress shall make *no* law" really meant that Congress could make *some* laws restricting freedom of expression. Justice Holmes, who wrote the stirring defense of the concept of freedom of expression in *Abrams* quoted earlier, also wrote the first significant language limiting the amendment.

At the end of that defense, Holmes added an "unless" clause that made all the difference: "I think that we should be eternally vigilant against attempts to check the expression of opinions that we loathe and believe to be fraught with death, *unless* they so imminently threaten immediate interference with the lawful and pressing purposes of the law that an immediate check is required to save the country. . . . I had conceived that the United States through many years had shown its repentance for the Sedition Act of 1798 by repaying fines that it imposed. Only the emergency that makes it immediately dangerous to leave the correction of evil counsels to time *warrants making any exception* to the sweeping command, 'Congress shall make no law . . . abridging the freedom of speech.'" [Italics added.]

With this language, Holmes put his interpretation or gloss on the First Amendment, and his prestige is such that every lawyer from then until now has had to deal with him. Many commentators today feel that he clouded, distorted, limited, or changed the meaning of the amendment. Others maintain that he turned it from an impossible ideal into a workable, though limited, tool. Many Americans since Holmes have argued that the language of the First Amendment contains an *absolute* prohibition against repression. They have insisted on their right to absolute freedom of expression rather than to some limited form, and have asked the courts to reverse their convictions for speaking, picketing, or otherwise disturbing the status quo.

Throughout the 1920s and into the 1930s, First Amendment people fared badly in the courts. In 1940, just before American entry into World War II, antialien hysteria developed again, and Congress passed the Smith Act. It was intended primarily to make it easy to "deal with" radical aliens—deport them, prevent their naturalization, or take away their U.S. citizenship after naturalization. With less than an hour's debate, Congress also inserted a clause making it a crime for anyone—alien or citizen—to organize a group advocating overthrow of the government by force and violence. The clause was aimed at the Communist Party, which, during the Great Depression, had attracted many people looking for explanations of their poverty and the country's economic failure.

In World War II, the United States and the Communist government of the Soviet Union were military allies in a struggle to defeat the Fascist governments of Germany, Italy, and Japan. During this period, the United States Supreme Court decided several cases filed by the federal government against aliens in the 1930s. Its decisions in favor of the foreign-born defendants harked back to the Revolutionary War concepts and discussed the need for protection of the individual against government interference with his freedom of expression. Even then, few considered filing *affirmative* suits to obtain rights based on the First Amendment. The amendment was used mainly by defendants arrested for making speeches or participating in demonstrations.

Within two years of the end of the hot war against fascism abroad, the cold war against communism began at home and abroad. The years from 1947 to 1953 were bleak ones for an amendment that says "Congress shall make no law" abridging freedom of expression, for in this period Congress made several such laws, which the presidents gladly signed, and the presidents issued several executive orders that could not be squared with the amendment. The government launched attacks on the Communist Party, its members, and those sympathetic to it. In 1947, President Harry Truman issued an executive order prohibiting "disloyal" people from working for the federal government, and his attorney general, without notice or hearings, listed eighty-two organizations that a government employee must not join. In the same year, the United States government indicted thirteen national leaders of the Communist Party, under the 1940 Smith Act, charging them with conspiracy to organize the Party with the intention, at some time in the future, of advocating the overthrow of the government by force and violence. (See the description of *Dennis* v. *United States* in chapter 6.)

In 1950, while the nation was engaged in the Korean War, Congress passed the Internal Security Act of 1950, also known as the McCarran Act. The act assumed as a starting point that there was a cohesive, worldwide "Communist movement" seeking to overthrow the governments of every capitalist country "by treachery, deceit, infiltration, espionage, sabotage, terrorism, and any other means deemed necessary." The McCarran Act then established a procedure for identifying members and groups of this "Communist movement" in the United States and imposing severe restrictions and penalties on them, including lifetime prison sentences (for failure to register themselves as Communist Party members). (See the discussion of the *Communist Party* cases in chapter 6.)

Other statutes were passed by Congress, many state legislatures, and some city councils requiring citizens to take a "loyalty" oath swearing that they were not members of "subversive" organizations in order to get a government job, rent a public hall, get a passport, or carry on many other activities.

While this repressive spirit was rising nationally, those who opposed civil rights took the offensive in the South. They had started organizing right after the Supreme Court's decision in *Brown* v. *Board of Education* (see chapter 22), requiring desegregation of the nation's public schools. Their attitude toward the National Association for the Advancement of Colored People (NAACP) was similar to Senator Joe McCarthy's attitude toward the Communist Party: if it could not be outlawed directly, it must be attacked by harassment, intimidation, economic pressure, and other methods. Civil rights groups and their leaders were investigated by state un-American activities committees and ordered to register as subversive (see *Dombrowski* v. *Pfister* in chapter 6). NAACP officials were ordered to give state officials the lists of all their members (see the *NAACP* and *Bates* cases in chapter 6).

The "anti-Red" and "anti-Black" laws passed during this period required Americans to register or take oaths or do something else before they would be allowed to express their opinions or associate in organizations. They are therefore called "prior restraints" on the exercise of First Amendment liberties, and are forbidden by this amendment.

A prior restraint prohibits a person from speaking his mind or showing a movie or publishing a book or renting a hall until he has passed the "censorship board" set up to screen communications. Sometimes the censorship is absolute, as when statutes forbade people to work for government agencies if they were Communist Party members, even if they were willing to take an oath that they would not use unlawful methods to change the form of government. Other statutes set up partial censorship, as when a person was permitted employment if he disavowed certain views. Either type of restraint violates the First Amendment concept that no one shall be punished for or prohibited from expressing his views. (It also violates Justice Holmes's more limited position that a person could be punished for certain words or acts but not for merely holding beliefs.)

A great number of individuals and organizations decided

to express their views within a few years after Earl Warren was appointed Chief Justice. People demanded civil rights for racial, national, and religious minority groups; they protested the war, insisted on freedom of classroom teachers and students, and tried to improve the status of prisoners. Such diverse groups as the foreign-born, welfare recipients, and booksellers felt they were under attack by the government, and asked the Supreme Court for protection.

This gave the Court responsibility to examine the validity of prior restraints. It was faced with the old question: does the First Amendment mean exactly what it says or can it be modified just a little to prohibit certain kinds of conduct that someone in authority opposes?

Lawyers for the government argued that the absolute language of the First Amendment was simply not meant to be absolute, that the Court should balance the citizens' interest in their freedom against the government's interest in stability and order. For example, the national security must be balanced against the needs of a conscientious objector applicant or a Marxist teacher; and, the lawyers contended, in this balance, "security" must win out over "freedom."

How is it possible to limit language that says, "Congress shall make *no* law respecting" certain forms of expression? Government lawyers and some judges have found several ways. One way has been to say that a particular subject is not covered by the First Amendment. For example, some argue that the amendment protects freedom of speech and press about political questions but not speech or publications that are "obscene." Constitutional lawyers differ about whether this is really what the framers of the First Amendment intended. But even if we accept the view that obscene material can be restrained, it is no easy matter to establish what is obscene.

Another way to limit the First Amendment is to say that

particular groups of people are not covered—for example, public school students, legislators, prisoners, draftees, or teachers.

Still other limitations have been attempted by saying that certain places are not part of what Justice Holmes considered the free marketplace of ideas. The Supreme Court has been asked to decide whether the marketplace extends to a prison, a draft board, a schoolroom, and a doctor's office.

Some have argued that expressions lose their First Amendment protection when they become too boisterous or vigorous, when they are so controversial that they stimulate the audience to become unruly, or when they defame others untruthfully. The Court has been asked to distinguish free speech from rioting, disturbance of the peace, incitement to unlawful action, and libel.

Lawyers urge the Court to define the word "speech" narrowly, excluding expressions that could be called "actions." The 1940 Supreme Court had ruled, in *Thornhill* v. *Alabama,* that peaceful picketing in a labor dispute was a form of free speech and was therefore protected by the First Amendment. The Supreme Court is often asked to decide whether free speech also includes marching in a demonstration, organizing a union, joining a political action group, burning or turning in a draft card, filing a lawsuit, buying a contraceptive, or wearing an armband.

Finally, some lawyers argue that citizens brought to *state* courts for violations of *state* statutes are not entitled to invoke the First Amendment protections that might be appropriate against the federal government. A different standard could be applied by state governments from that applied by the federal government. The Court examined this argument in several cases, and often the justices disagreed strongly with each other about it (see chapter 20).

What, if anything, could opposing lawyers say in reply?

July 25, 1963: High-pressure fire hose turned on civil rights marchers at a demonstration in Birmingham, Alabama.
Credit: Wide World Photos

They hold the key card—the broad language in the amendment itself. Then, they have the reasoning behind the language: that freedom of expression is essential in a democracy. Alexander Meiklejohn, the First Amendment scholar, explained it this way in *Political Freedom* (1960):

"When men govern themselves, it is they—and no one else—who must pass judgments upon unwisdom and unfairness and danger. And that means that unwise ideas must have a hearing as well as wise ones, unfair as well as fair, dangerous as well as safe, un-American as well as American. Just so far as, at any point, the citizens who are to decide an issue are denied acquaintance with information or opinion or doubt or disbelief or criticism which is relevant to that issue, just so far the result must be ill-considered, ill-balanced planning for the general good. *It is that mutilation of the thinking process of the community against which the First Amendment to the Constitution is directed.* The principle of the freedom of speech springs from the necessities of the program of self-government. It is not a Law of Nature or of Reason in the abstract. It is a deduction from the basic American agreement that public issues shall be decided by universal suffrage."

The First Amendment spells out eight basic rights of the people against government interference. These rights are guaranteed to both individuals and groups. For example, freedom of speech and of the press includes the right of the individual to speak and write, and also of the group to read and hear. Freedom of assembly is the right of individuals to meet together in a group, and the right to petition is based on the cooperation of many individuals. Freedom of religion includes the right of an individual to worship and of each church to exist as an organization (without government approval on the one hand or assistance on the other).

From these specific rights, we have fashioned the "right of association" to include all of the others. Americans have long known that "in union there is strength." And our governments have long known that the quickest way to break up challenging activity by individuals is to attack their organizations and their leaders. Such a two-pronged attack immobilizes the organization and its leadership and frightens individual members into silence or submission. For this reason, the hardest fought battles under the First Amendment have been on freedom of association, as you will notice in chapter 6.

The cases discussed in part I have been selected because they deal most explicitly with issues of freedom of expression. However, often when parties raise First Amendment issues the Court declines to decide them, instead relying on the doctrine of fairness ("due process") or equality ("equal protection") to rule in favor of the party claiming First Amendment rights. Thus you will find First Amendment questions at the heart of many of the cases in parts II and III of this book, and some of the cases in part I were actually decided on other grounds. Freedom, fairness, and equal treatment are the three basic principles in the amendments to the Constitution, and they are frequently intertwined in cases where freedom of expression is at stake.

The Warren Court, sitting for sixteen years, agreed to hear more First Amendment cases than all previous Supreme Courts put together. The number of such cases increased markedly during the Warren era. This was probably due, in part, to the fact that the Court ruled in favor of the First Amendment party in many cases, and against several government agencies. But this was not the main reason for the increase in First Amendment cases. Many groups of individuals decided that the time had come to insist upon their rights, and very often this put them into confrontation situations with the police or other government agencies. In other words, the ferment in the land required free and robust debate on important questions, and this led to disputes about the right to discuss those questions. Once the right to debate was assured, the society of the 1970s moved into extensive consideration of problems hidden or forbidden in the 1960s—birth control, abortion, and overpopulation; pollution, consumerism, and ecology; the status of women, young people, and senior citizens; and questions forced into prominence by government actions: war, the draft, unemployment, civil rights, control of the media, and honesty in politics.

The Supreme Court faces three common attitudes about freedom of expression and the proper interpretation of the First Amendment. One group says, in effect: "Shut that guy up; he's telling lies!" They heckle speakers they disagree with so that others will not hear and possibly be convinced by them. They say, "Look, these things should be left to the authorities. They know how to make the right decisions. The general public doesn't have the experience or the common sense. Just look how they voted in the last election! If we let the men in charge decide these things, we'll all save a lot of time."

Other citizens are firmly convinced that authoritarian regimes inevitably break down, and in the long run democratic processes are the most effective and least costly. They believe that ultimately people refuse to carry out decisions of an authority when they didn't participate in making the decisions and don't approve of them. These advocates claim that this kind of refusal can be labeled anything from "inefficiency" to "rebellion," depending on the number of people who participate in the refusal and how deeply they refuse to go along. It crops up at all levels in an authoritarian system, from the typist who thinks her boss has made the wrong choice to the people's movement that deposes a dictator.

A third group of citizens feels that the idea of freedom of expression is no longer workable today because the population is so large, and political and social questions are so complex. "What's the use of trying to argue about these things one way or the other?" they ask. "What difference does the opinion of one person make?"

Some who feel this way have tried to "drop out" of every relationship with the political-economic-social system. Usually they discover that some agency of government pursues them tenaciously, to collect taxes or deliver a tax refund, inspect the safety of their apartments or require them to install a better sewage system on their rural communes. Most Americans feel the hand of "the system" touching their personal lives too frequently for them to abdicate the chance to participate in governing it. Laws passed by Congress or state legislatures, regulations and orders from executive branches of government, and decisions handed down by courts daily require citizens to do certain acts and forbid them from doing others. In many cases the citizen does not understand or agree with the reasons for or methods used in these legal commands. Rather than running away from these conflicts, citizens tend to plunge into the arena and battle for more, and more effective, participation in government.

During the Warren Court era the Supreme Court became a significant theater of these battles. In the minds of many, it became the first line of defense of the Bill of Rights. But a closer look shows that the Court can never truly play this role. It can act on an issue only *after* people have exercised their rights and gone (or been brought) to court to justify their actions. The activists are thus the first line of defense.

Those few who become litigants in court form a second line. Their lawyers and defense committees may be considered a third defense line. Perhaps the media, exercising communication skills to inform public opinion, are the fourth line. And the courts then become the fifth line of defense.

Even when that fifth line has been reached, and the Supreme Court has ruled that the people legitimately exercised constitutional rights, the matter is not always settled for everyone then and there, as some of the following cases illustrate. Sometimes the decision comes too late and sometimes it is not obeyed by the individuals who have the power to either protect or infringe rights at the time they are exercised. Again, the crucial line of defense, the crucial decision maker is the individual choosing to act—you.

If the decisions discussed here make sense to you, you may follow them in your daily activities and will see how they apply to new agencies and procedures devised to thwart the Bill of Rights. You may want to contest efforts to limit the application of some of these Warren Court decisions. You may be able to use them to prevent Watergate-type actions seeking to limit the flow of accurate information to the general public on matters of importance in policy-making.

RENNER LEARNING RESOURCE CENTER
ELGIN COMMUNITY COLLEGE
ELGIN, ILLINOIS 60123

CHAPTER 2

Freedom of Speech

Critics say Americans like to argue politics almost as much as they like to describe their favorite all-time great football team or trade the best recipe for apple pie.

Throughout American history, a variety of groups have cared deeply about political questions. They have made speeches and gathered crowds of admirers. Of course, proponents tend to draw opponents, and many political debates have turned into fights, riots, or demonstrations. The name you attach to such a happening often depends on your point of view.

If you think freedom of speech is a great idea, you may not mind a little heckling while your side is speaking and you'll also be incensed if someone throws rotten eggs at the other side. If you feel that people usually don't vote intelligently and need to be told what to do by the people in authority, then giving everyone a chance to "shoot his mouth off" may seem unnecessary and even unwise to you.

Not many cases on freedom of speech get to the Supreme Court of the United States. Usually the first step is taken by the local police. They arrest someone for speaking or demonstrating, and the local court convicts him. Then the defendant must decide whether he can afford to hire an appellate lawyer and pay all the costs of appeals to several courts before reaching the Supreme Court. As a result, Supreme Court decisions on free speech usually involve organizations and their leaders. During World War I, for example, the head of the Socialist Party, Eugene Debs, was arrested for making a speech against American involvement in "an imperialist war in Europe." He was convicted of violating the Espionage Law and sentenced to ten years in prison. The Supreme Court affirmed his conviction in *Debs* v. *United States,* and Debs went to jail. In the 1930s, labor organizers were often arrested in northern industrial cities for holding rallies and demonstrations. The CIO took one of these cases, arising in Jersey City, New Jersey, to the Supreme Court, and in *Hague* v. *Committee for Industrial Organization* free speech won.

By the 1950s and 1960s, free speech battles had moved South. Although the issue remains significant in all parts of the country among people of all ages, the particular cases discussed here all happen to have occurred in the South.

"You may jail our bodies but not our souls"

Edwards v. *South Carolina* (1963)
372 U.S. 229, 83 S. Ct. 680, 9 L. Ed. 2d 697

In the spring of 1961, all over the South groups of black people, particularly students, began organizing to get equality. They knew they had a right to equal service. They had learned in American history classes about the struggles for freedom and equality from colonial times to the present. In church they had read stories from the Bible telling how oppressed people gained the right to be free and equal. Since 1954, the newspapers had carried almost daily stories about the decision by the Warren Court in *Brown* v. *Board of Education* that public schools must be desegregated to stop discrimination against blacks (see chapter 22). But these black citizens had also seen how slowly the establishment moved to make the changes ordered by the United States Supreme Court.

Militant blacks went to restaurants, lunch counters, swimming pools, and other public places, demanding admission and service. When they were denied service, they didn't hire a lawyer to file a lawsuit for money damages to compensate for the denial of their civil rights. They sat in or they sat down. They used self-help, as northern workers had done during the Great Depression of the 1930s when they were trying to organize their unions. When the students could not even get into a public place to sit down, they marched and picketed on the outside.

Although their idea was to get what they were entitled to without going to court, the students often wound up in court despite themselves. They had rejected the idea of starting a lawsuit as plaintiffs, but when they were arrested, they became defendants, whether they liked it or not. When they saw all the newspaper stories about their arrests, they realized that they might help the cause of freedom more by the publicity they got from the arrests than by their peaceful picketing. Nonviolence and no arrests seldom make news. So, sometimes civil rights groups held general protest marches to publicize their demands for equal treatment. One of the first places young black people were arrested for marching was in the capitol of South Carolina.

Late in the morning of March 2, 1961, a group of almost two hundred Negro high school and college students gathered at the Zion Baptist Church in Columbia, South Carolina. They were going to march to the State House "to submit a protest to the citizens of South Carolina, along with the Legislative Bodies of South Carolina," to demonstrate "our feelings and our dissatisfaction with the present condition of discriminatory actions against Negroes, in general, and to let them know that we were dissatisfied and that we would like for the laws which prohibited Negro privileges in this state to be removed."

Around noon they began walking in separate groups of fifteen to the State House grounds, coming in through a horseshoe-shaped driveway. The demonstration had been announced beforehand, so some thirty law enforcement officers were there waiting for them.

The police told them, "You have a right, as a citizen, to go through the State House grounds as any other citizen has, as long as you are peaceful."

The demonstrators proceeded to walk through the grounds in an orderly line, some single file and some two abreast. Their signs proclaimed: "I Am Proud to Be a Negro," "Down with Segregation," and "You May Jail Our Bodies but Not Our Souls."

As the noontime march went on, spectators gathered. The area became crowded at times, and a policeman was sent to direct traffic at one intersection, where cars were slowing down. Now and then officers asked the crowd and the demonstrators to move on and to clear the sidewalk. At one time it was blocked by thirty or forty people, spilling over into the street of the horseshoe. The people complied with the police requests.

City Manager McNayr was keeping a close watch on the scene. He noted that there were some "possible troublemakers" in the crowd, but he didn't have the police take any action against them "because there was none to be taken. They were not creating a disturbance, those particular people were not at that time doing anything to make trouble."

After about forty-five minutes of the march, the crowd of spectators had swelled to around three hundred. The City

Manager decided that this now constituted an imminent danger to peace and safety. He approached Dave Carter, a leader of the demonstration, and told him, "Tell each of the groups and the group leaders that they must disperse."

Then he added, "Warn them that I will give them fifteen minutes from now to disperse and if they have not dispersed, I will direct my Chief of Police to place them under arrest."

Carter went from group to group with McNayr's message, but instead of advising the students to follow the City Manager's instructions he delivered a "religious harangue," according to McNayr.

The demonstrators responded with shouts and singing. They sang, "We Shall Not Be Moved," "The Star-Spangled Banner," and other patriotic and religious songs.

"They became boisterous. They stomped their feet," said McNayr. "They sang in loud voices to the point where, again, in my judgment, a dangerous situation was really building up."

When the fifteen minutes had passed, he ordered the police to line up the students, arrest them, and march them off to jail. The police arrested 187 demonstrators.

The defendants decided they needed good lawyers to represent them in court, lawyers who believed in civil rights and who would explain to the judge why they had been picketing. They didn't have much hope of winning in the trial court, but they wanted their community to understand why they had permitted themselves to get arrested.

The prosecutor decided to try the 187 defendants in four groups on a charge of breach of the peace. All were found guilty. The judge did not give them all the same sentences. He sentenced some to a ten-dollar fine or five days in jail and others to a hundred-dollar fine or thirty days in jail.

Some people in the community felt the students had wanted to get sent to jail and had got what they expected, so that should have been the end of it. But the lawyers for the defendants explained that the case was a very important one and could have effects all over the country. The NAACP Legal Defense and Education Fund would pay the lawyers' fees and the court costs if the defendants wanted to appeal. The young people decided to go on fighting through the courts. They contended there was a complete lack of evidence that they had broken the peace. Therefore their convictions could not be upheld or it would be a denial of fair procedure, that is, due process of law.

When the case reached the South Carolina Supreme Court, the court defined the offense of breach of the peace as "a violation of public order, a disturbance of the public tranquility, by any act or conduct inciting to violence." The court said, "It includes any violation of any law enacted to preserve peace and good order. It may consist of an act of violence or an act likely to produce violence. It is not necessary that the peace be actually broken to lay the foundation for a prosecution for this offense. If what is done is unjustifiable and unlawful, tending with sufficient directness to break the peace, no more is required. Nor is actual personal violence an essential element in the offense." The court upheld all of the convictions.

The United States Supreme Court agreed to hear the case and decided to make an independent examination of the whole record, since this case clearly raised the question: What is free speech?

Who do you think is to be protected under the First Amendment? Should the police protect an unpopular speaker from a crowd and arrest members of the crowd, if that is necessary in order to let the speaker finish? Or should the police protect the crowd from the speaker by arresting the speaker so he does not make the crowd angry? Do the police have a greater duty to protect the crowd, because there are more of them? Or should the police protect the speaker, because the audience is free to stop listening and leave, without denying the speaker his First Amendment freedom of speech or endangering anyone?

After hearing and considering the arguments, the Supreme Court voted eight to one. Justice Stewart delivered the majority opinion. "The state courts have held that the petitioners' conduct constituted breach of the peace under state law, and we may accept their decision as binding upon us to that extent," he said. But after making "an independent examination of the whole record," the Supreme Court found it clear "that in arresting, convicting, and punishing the petitioners under the circumstances disclosed by this record, South Carolina infringed the petitioners' constitutionally protected rights of free speech, free assembly, and freedom to petition for redress of their grievances.

"It has long been established that these First Amendment freedoms are protected by the Fourteenth Amendment from invasion by the States," Justice Stewart noted. "The circumstances in this case reflect an exercise of these basic constitutional rights in their most pristine and classic form."

"These petitioners were convicted of an offense so generalized as to be, in the words of the South Carolina Supreme Court, 'not susceptible of exact definition.' And they were convicted upon evidence which showed no more than that the opinions which they were peaceably expressing were sufficiently opposed to the views of the majority of the community to attract a crowd and necessitate police protection."

Justice Stewart went on, "This, therefore, was a far cry from the situation in *Feiner* v. *New York* [a 1951 case], where two policemen were faced with a crowd which was 'pushing, shoving and milling around,' where at least one member of the crowd 'threatened violence if the police did not act,' where 'the crowd was pressing closer around petitioner and the officer,' and where 'the speaker passes the bounds of argument or persuasion and undertakes incitement to riot.' And the record is barren of any evidence of 'fighting words.' "

"The Fourteenth Amendment does not permit a State to make criminal the peaceful expression of unpopular views," Justice Stewart continued, and he quoted Justice Douglas in *Terminiello* v. *Chicago,* saying that "a function of free speech under our system of government is to invite dispute. It may indeed best serve its high purpose when it induces a condition of unrest, creates dissatisfaction with conditions as they are, or even stirs people to anger. Speech is often provocative and challenging. It may strike at prejudices and preconceptions and have profound unsettling effects as it presses for acceptance of an idea."

Thus, freedom of speech must be "protected against censorship or punishment, unless shown likely to produce a clear and present danger of a serious substantive evil that rises far above public inconvenience, annoyance, or unrest."

Justice Stewart also quoted former Chief Justice Hughes in *Stromberg* v. *California:* "The maintenance of the opportunity for free political discussion to the end that government may be responsive to the will of the people and that changes may be obtained by lawful means, an opportunity essential to the security of the Republic, is a fundamental principle of our constitutional system. A statute which . . . is so vague and indefinite as to permit the punishment of the fair use of this opportunity is repugnant to the guaranty of liberty contained in the Fourteenth Amendment."

"For these reasons," Justice Stewart summed up, "we conclude that these criminal convictions cannot stand."

Justice Clark dissented. He argued that the Court's opinion

did not accurately describe the facts and that the situation was actually much more threatening. This justified the arrests, he felt. As in other cases, he relied not only on previous Supreme Court opinions but also on folk sayings: "to say that the police may not intervene until the riot has occurred, is like keeping out the doctor until the patient dies. I cannot subscribe to such a doctrine," he declared.

The Court gave strong protection to the exercise of First Amendment freedoms of speech and assembly in the *Edwards* case. It did so at a time when increasing numbers of people were finding their voices again after the "silent fifties," described in chapter 6. This decision encouraged further exercise of First Amendment freedoms on civil rights questions and on all other public issues.

Of course, getting a chance to speak in public without arrest is only the very first step. It does not guarantee that the public will listen. And it certainly does not guarantee that the government will listen or make any changes. There is no assurance that even a loud, vigorous, and continued cry for a change in government policy will be effective.

But the reverse is certainly true: If the Supreme Court had affirmed the criminal convictions of people who made statements to audiences that did not agree with them, it would have been easier for the government to ignore the demands of the speakers and their followers.

Soliciting members without a permit

Staub v. *City of Baxley* (1958)
355 U.S. 313, 78 S. Ct. 277, 2 L. Ed. 2d 302

Rose Staub and Mamie Merritt came into Hazelhurst, Georgia, in February 1954. They were organizers for the International Ladies' Garment Workers Union, and some of the employees of a company there invited the women to their homes. They talked union, saying the workers would gain a lot by joining; union dues would be only sixty-four cents a week and the workers wouldn't have to start paying until enough employees had signed up to call for an election at the company, which would be conducted by the National Labor Relations Board.

Organizing unions has always been hard work. During most of the history of the United States, it was even illegal. It wasn't until 1933 that organizing unions was declared a legal right of working people in FDR's National Recovery Act. But passage of that federal law did not stop cities, counties, and states from passing local laws making it very difficult to organize. For example, Alabama passed a statute making it a crime to picket a place of business. Picketing was considered similar to loitering, and both were made misdemeanors, that is, crimes for which a person could be sent to jail for a year or less. The United States Supreme Court declared this statute unconstitutional in *Thornhill* v. *Alabama,* in 1940.

Many other statutes remained on the books as late as 1954, particularly in the South, where government officials usually agreed with employers that union organization was a threat to industrialization and prosperity. After all, many local governments had wooed northern industries to come south with promises of exemptions from local taxes and a large and low-paid work force. If the workers organized into unions and demanded higher wages and better working conditions, the companies that had moved from New England could just as well move further south, to Latin American countries, for example.

All of these factors were below the surface, as Ms. Staub and Ms. Merritt went to the city of Baxley (near Hazelhurst) on February 19, 1954, to talk to company employees who lived in the town. They made the traditional arguments for unions: "Unless you get together, you will never get better wages. How do you think the workers got paid vacations, time-and-a-half for overtime, the eight-hour day, and company payments for medical care? And how do you think workers have gotten some recognition that they are human beings and not simply machines to be pushed around by a boss?"

Some of the workers were skeptical. They were afraid they would lose some favors from their supervisor and would get nothing in return. They were wary about labor bosses, and they feared they would end up paying dues to a union that would do nothing for them. The organizers explained that the company had built its plant in Hazelhurst to get cheap labor and that the union had to fight these runaway shops to keep up wages and working conditions as much as possible.

As the two organizers were sitting in a restaurant later that day, the chief of police came up to them and asked what they were doing in Baxley.

Ms. Staub explained that she and Ms. Merritt were "going around talking to some of the women to organize the factory workers."

While the two went on to a meeting at the home of one of the employees, the chief of police went back to his office and soon had a summons for the two women to appear before the Mayor's Court three days later to answer "to the offense of Soliciting Members for an Organization without a Permit and License."

The organizers realized they needed legal help. Their union lawyers checked with the city and learned that Baxley had a city ordinance requiring any paid organizer for "any organization, union or society of any sort" that collected dues to get a city permit to solicit members. The mayor and city council had to pass on the permit application to "consider the character of the applicant, the nature of the business of the organization for which members are desired to be solicited, and its effects upon the general welfare of citizens of the City of Baxley." If they granted the permit, it cost $2,000 a year plus $500 for each new member.

The lawyers for the union immediately took the offensive. They moved to "abate" (wipe out) the summons to the Mayor's Court on the ground that the city ordinance, on its face, violated the First and Fourteenth Amendments, because it restricted freedom of speech, press, and assembly at the discretion of the mayor and city council. They also charged that the permit fee was discriminatory and unreasonably high, and therefore violated the First Amendment.

Obviously if the ordinance was unconstitutional, it didn't matter how low or high the permit fee was. If the permit fee were lowered, the defendants would still have the same First Amendment objections to it. But lawyers often have to make arguments that are inconsistent in whole or in part. They cannot know which argument will convince a court so they raise all the issues they can find and hope that one will convince the judge.

The union lawyers also brought a suit in the superior court of the county, asking for an injunction to stop the city officials from enforcing the ordinance because it violated freedom of expression. The superior court decided against the organizers and the Supreme Court of Georgia affirmed this decision, saying that the organizers would have to stand trial in the Mayor's Court—if they were right, they would win there; but they couldn't skip this criminal trial. (See what happened in a similar situation in Louisiana a few years later, in *Dombrowski* v. *Pfister*, page 161.)

So the two organizers lost in their efforts to take the offensive and had to come back to the Mayor's Court for trial as defendants under the city ordinance. They asserted the First Amendment as their defense, but the judge found them guilty and sentenced each of them to thirty days or $300 fine.

The union appealed to the superior court, which upheld the convictions, and held that the ordinance was valid. When the defendants took the case to the Georgia Court of Appeals, it affirmed the convictions on a different ground: Ms. Staub had never applied for a permit and had not attacked a particular section of the ordinance; therefore, it was not necessary to decide any other issues.

Ms. Staub then appealed to the United States Supreme Court, raising the issue of the constitutionality of the ordinance. The city of Baxley claimed that the Supreme Court did not have jurisdiction to hear the appeal. It was a state issue that had been decided properly by a state court, the city argued, and the federal courts should bow to state court practice and abstain from reviewing the matter.

Do you think this is a question of state's rights versus federal rights? Or is there an underlying right to talk about organizing unions? Is this the kind of case in which the federal courts should abstain from considering claims of federal constitutional rights? Is there ever such a case? Or is there a significant First Amendment question here?

The Supreme Court, in a seven-to-two opinion by Justice Whittaker, first held that it did have jurisdiction to consider the appeal, because "failure to apply for a license under an ordinance which on its face violates the Constitution does not preclude review in this Court of a judgment of conviction under such an ordinance."

The state also complained that Ms. Staub had failed to specify the sections of the ordinance that she claimed were unconstitutional. The Court replied: "The several sections of the ordinance are interdependent . . . and constitute but one complete act for the licensing and taxing of her described activities. For that reason, no doubt, she challenged the constitutionality of the whole ordinance, and in her objections used language challenging the constitutional effect of all its sections . . . , though not by number. To require her, in these circumstances, to count off, one by one, the several sections of the ordinance would be to force resort to an arid ritual of meaningless form."

Then the Court came to the heart of the appeal: "It will be noted that appellant was not accused of any act against the peace, good order or dignity of the community, nor for any particular thing she said in soliciting employees of the manufacturing company to join the union. She was simply charged and convicted for 'soliciting members for an organization without a Permit.' This solicitation, as shown by the evidence, consisted solely of speaking to those employees in their private homes about joining the union."

Justice Whittaker found that the ordinance did not set any "definitive standards or other controlling guides governing the action of the Mayor and Council in granting or withholding a permit."

He concluded: "It is undeniable that the ordinance authorized the Mayor and Council of the City of Baxley to grant 'or refuse to grant' the required permit in their uncontrolled discretion. It thus makes enjoyment of speech contingent upon the will of the Mayor and Council of the City, although that fundamental right is made free from congressional abridgment by the First Amendment and is protected by the Fourteenth from invasion by state action. For these reasons, the ordinance, on its face, imposes an unconstitutional prior restraint upon the enjoyment of First Amendment freedoms and lays 'a forbidden burden upon the exercise of liberty protected by the constitution.' "

Justice Frankfurter, who had been pro-union in his law professor days, wrote a dissent, in which Justice Clark, a former attorney general, joined. In effect, Justice Frankfurter argued state's rights; he did not want the United States Supreme Court to interfere with the decision of the Georgia courts. So he said, "There is nothing frivolous or futile (though it may appear 'formal') about a rule insisting that parties specify with arithmetic particularity those provisions in a legislative enactment they would ask a court to strike down." He admitted the possibility "that with little expenditure of time and effort, and with little risk of misreading appellant's charges, a court could determine exactly what it is about the Baxley ordinance that allegedly infringes upon appellant's constitutional rights. But," he admonished, "rules are not made solely for the easiest cases they govern. The fact that the reason for a rule does not clearly apply in a given situation does not eliminate the necessity for compliance with the rule," as long as the state rule is not used as a means for abridging people's federal rights. "There is no indication whatever in the case before us that the Georgia Court of Appeals applied this well-established rule of pleading arbitrarily or inadvisedly."

The decision for Ms. Staub and Ms. Merritt did not organize the workers of Baxley into the ILGWU or any other union. It may not have changed the minds of the city councilmen who had passed the licensing law. But the decision did begin to bring to some small towns in the South, North, and West the law passed by Congress twenty years before. It set the stage for a promised southern organizing drive by northern-based unions, although the large cast needed to organize the South is only now beginning to be assembled.

The legislator's duty to take a stand

Bond v. *Floyd* (1966)
385 U.S. 116, 87 S. Ct. 339, 17 L. Ed. 2d 235

Julian Bond was a handsome black student from a highly educated professional family in Atlanta. In his college years he became active in the Student Non-violent Coordinating Committee, fighting for desegregation and Negro voting rights in the South. The struggle became so important to him that he dropped out of school, to his family's dismay, and became a full-time staff member of SNCC (usually pronounced "snick").

In 1965, the voting districts for the Georgia state legislature were redrawn, to make them more equal in population as the Supreme Court had required in its "one-man-one-vote" decisions in *Wesberry* v. *Sanders* and *Reynolds* v. *Sims* (see chapter 23). A new district was created in Atlanta, with approximately 6,500 voters, of whom 6,000 were black.

Julian Bond was then twenty-four years old and Communications Director for SNCC. He decided to run for the new legislative seat, and he won handily—2,320 to 487.

The election was held in June 1965, and the representatives were to be sworn in the following January 10. On January 6, SNCC issued a policy statement opposing United States involvement in the Vietnam War, because the government was not guaranteeing the freedom of its own black citizens and could not be trusted when it claimed concern for the freedom of colored people in other countries.

"We ourselves have often been victims of violence and confinement executed by United States government officials.

We recall the numerous persons who have been murdered in the South because of their efforts to secure their civil and human rights, and whose murderers have been allowed to escape penalty for their crimes," SNCC charged. "We recall the indifference, suspicion and outright hostility with which our reports of violence have been met in the past by government officials."

Noting the voting rights struggle in this country, SNCC questioned "the ability and even the desire of the United States government to guarantee free elections abroad. We maintain that our country's cry of 'preserve freedom in the world' is a hypocritical mask behind which it squashes liberation movements which are not bound, and refuse to be bound, by the expediencies of United States cold war policies."

SNCC then announced: "We are in sympathy with, and support, the men in this country who are unwilling to respond to a military draft which would compel them to contribute their lives to United States aggression in Viet Nam in the name of the 'freedom' we find so false in this country."

SNCC noted the high percentage of Negroes being drafted to defend a "democracy" they did not enjoy at home. "We therefore encourage those Americans who prefer to use their energy in building democratic forms within this country. . . . We believe that work in the civil rights movement and with other human relations organizations is a valid alternative to the draft. We urge all Americans to seek this alternative, knowning full well that it may cost their lives—as painfully as in Viet Nam."

The press went wild. Reporters began calling Bond for a statement. Although he had not participated in drafting the SNCC paper, he told a radio reporter that he endorsed it, because he was a pacifist and because he agreed with the facts and reasoning it set forth.

Asked about his responsibility to support the government, he replied: "I think my responsibility is to oppose things that I think are wrong if they are in Viet Nam or New York, or Chicago, or Atlanta, or wherever."

The reporter then suggested that the war was a question of stopping Communism.

Bond responded, "I'm not taking a stand against stopping World Communism, and I'm not taking a stand in favor of the Viet Cong." He explained, "I'm against all war. I'm against that war in particular, and I don't think people ought to participate in it. Because I'm against war, I'm against the draft. I think that other countries in the world get along without a draft—England is one—and I don't see why we couldn't, too." He added, "I'm not about to justify that war, because it's stopping International Communism, or whatever."

The interviewer then asked whether Bond thought he could take the oath of office required of Georgia legislators— swearing loyalty to the state and federal constitutions. Bond saw nothing inconsistent between his statements and the oath.

Other Georgia legislators did, however. In the next three days seventy-five House members filed petitions challenging Bond's right to be seated. They charged that his statements gave aid and comfort to the enemies of the United States and Georgia, violated the Selective Service laws, and tended to bring discredit and disrespect on the House. They felt his endorsement of the SNCC statement was "inconsistent with the mandatory oath" for Georgia legislators, and that he could not swear to uphold the United States Constitution.

On January 10, 1966, the clerk refused to swear Bond in until the matter of the challenges was resolved. Bond filed a response, asserting his willingness and ability to take the oath in good faith, and charging that the challenges denied his First Amendment rights and were racially motivated. Great pressure was put on him to withdraw his support for the SNCC statement, but he remained firm in his position and cool and collected in his manner.

The issues first went to a special investigatory committee of the legislature, which heard testimony and tapes of Bond's statements, and then Bond himself.

"I stand before you today charged with entering into public discussion on matters of National interest," he said. "I have chosen to speak my mind and no explanation is called for, for no member of this House, has ever, to my knowledge, been called upon to explain his public statements for public postures as a prerequisite to admission to that Body."

He did clarify for the benefit of his constituents that he had "not counselled burning draft cards, nor have I burned mine," as the newspapers implied. "I have suggested that congressionally outlined alternatives to military service be extended to building democracy at home. The posture of my life for the past five years has been calculated to give Negroes the ability to participate in formulation of public policies. The fact of my election to public office does not lessen my duty or desire to express my opinions even when they differ from those held by others." And he offered to take the oath, saying, "that will dispel any doubts about my convictions or loyalty."

Nevertheless, the committee upheld the challenges, and the legislature adopted the committee's report by a vote of 184 to 12. By this action, it refused Bond his seat.

Bond then went to court for an injunction against the denial of his seat. He was represented by SNCC's attorney (Bond's brother-in-law) Howard Moore, a militant black Atlanta lawyer. The three-judge federal district court split two to one. The majority upheld the legislature's power to determine whether to seat its members, and held that Bond's statements went beyond protected free speech to the point where he could not take the oath of office in good faith. His right to dissent, the two judges stated, was limited by his decision to become a legislator.

Bond appealed to the United States Supreme Court, while the governor called a special election to fill his seat. Bond entered the election and was easily reelected, since no one was willing to oppose him. The House, of course, again refused to seat him, despite the protests that poured in from around the country.

By November 1966, when the Supreme Court heard the issues, Bond's term of office was over. The regular election for the next term had been held in June. Again Bond had run and won by an overwhelming majority.

Do you think this was a free speech question? Does an elected state official have less freedom to speak than a voter? Is there some limit on freedom of speech during an undeclared war, like the one in Vietnam? If so, where is this written down? Is there a line between a statement opposing the war and a statement urging people to oppose the draft? Who drew that line? In view of all these issues, how would you decide this case?

The Court's unanimous opinion was delivered by Chief Justice Warren. He said the issue was not whether a legislator must take a loyalty oath or must take it in good faith. Such provisions clearly did "not violate the First Amendment. But this requirement does not authorize a majority of state legislators to test the sincerity with which another duly elected legislator can swear to uphold the Constitution. Such a power could be utilized to restrict the right of legislators to dissent from national or state policy or that of a majority of their colleagues under the guise of judging their loyalty to the Constitution."

The Chief Justice continued, "Certainly there can be no question but that the First Amendment protects expressions in opposition to national foreign policy in Vietnam and to the Selective Service system." But the state argued that Bond "went beyond expressions of opposition, and counseled violations of the Selective Service laws," and that a stricter standard applied to legislators than to private citizens in determining whether their speech violated the law.

"We do not agree," Chief Justice Warren responded. He found no evidence in Bond's statements that he was inciting people to violate the law, and he rejected the argument "that a State is constitutionally justified in exacting a higher standard of *loyalty* from its legislators than from its citizens. Of course, a State may constitutionally require an oath to support the Constitution from its legislators which it does not require of its private citizens. But this difference in treatment does not support the exclusion of Bond, for while the State has an interest in requiring its legislators to swear to a belief in constitutional processes of government, surely the oath gives it no interest in limiting its legislators' capacity to discuss their views of local or national policy."

On the contrary, "legislators have an obligation to take positions on controversial political questions so that their constituents can be fully informed by them, and be better able to assess their qualifications for office; also so they may be represented in governmental debates by the person they have elected to represent them. We therefore hold that the disqualification of Bond from membership in the Georgia House because of his statements violated Bond's right of free expression under the First Amendment," Chief Justice Warren concluded.

On January 9, 1967, Julian Bond took the oath of office and was seated in the Georgia legislature. Since then, he has become a leading figure in political reform in his state, and played a key role in challenging the state delegation to the Democratic National Convention in 1968. That challenge resulted in a split of Georgia's votes between the regular delegation and Bond's "freedom" delegation. Bond himself was put in nomination for the vice presidency at that convention, as an expression of respect by liberal delegates, but he declined, noting that he did not meet the age requirements.

In March 1967, the United States House of Representatives tried to exclude another black legislator. The House voted not to seat veteran Harlem Representative Adam Clayton Powell, for alleged improper conduct. Powell had been both militant in fighting for the rights of black people and workers, and extravagant in taking advantage of his privileges as a congressman. This matter, too, came before the United States Supreme Court, which ruled in 1969 that this exclusion was illegal as well (*Powell* v. *McCormack*). "Our examination of the relevant historical materials leads us to the conclusion that the petitioners are correct," said Chief Justice Warren, "and that the Constitution leaves the House without authority to *exclude* any person, duly elected by his constituents, who meets all the requirements for membership expressly prescribed in the Constitution."

Freedom of speech becomes an issue only when it is challenged. During periods of relative stability in society, anyone is permitted to "shoot his mouth off" in almost any direction on almost any issue. The significance of Warren Court decisions on free speech was, first, that the Court agreed to hear the cases, although they arose out of important unsettled social questions (civil rights, value of trade unions, opposition to war) and, secondly, that the opinions encouraged wide-open discussion, even in the face of vocal opposition.

January 9, 1967: Julian Bond takes his seat in the Georgia legislature right after his Supreme Court victory, a year and a half after his election.
Credit: Wide World Photos

It is increasingly clear that the exercise of First Amendment rights in the twentieth century requires microphones or television cameras. Efforts to discourage investigative reporting by the media limit public access to the facts necessary to form opinions, and public speakers in lecture halls and on street corners lack the necessary impact on debates that must take place if citizens are to reach reasoned decisions on basic public questions.

While the First Amendment guarantee of freedom of speech is a staff to fend off repression and a shield against prior restraint on speech, and while the Warren Court opinions added new strength to the staff and shield, this chapter seems to call for a moral: Opposition to free speech is never killed; the people who cherish the right to speak must always be prepared to fight for it, whether the cause in question is fashionable or not. They must not be frightened into silence by vague allusions to "threats of national security" or "information leaks."

CHAPTER 3

Freedom of the Press

Freedom of the press is so much a part of the American heritage that the reading public is shocked when anyone openly suggests, "You can't print that!"

Of course, a good deal of censorship occurs in the office of the editor of any magazine, newspaper, or book publishing company. Writers are discouraged from writing on certain subjects because "The public won't buy that kind of stuff." Some publications don't want to print stories that are "too highbrow"; others reject "hippie rhetoric"; but there are so many periodicals that ultimately a writer usually can find some market for his work, even if it is unpaid. Still, the person who wants to write for a living learns to tailor his work to fit his market.

This kind of self-censorship works in reverse, as well. When a lot of underground newspapers spring up and publish material that previously was self-censored, writers begin to use words and to discuss incidents that they had previously deleted from their work. When slick magazines begin to publish the kinds of pictures and stories that previously were published only in pulp magazines, authors begin to write for the new market.

These aspects of self-censorship and the market approach

to literature actually determine most of what is offered to the reading public.

However, criminal statutes, licensing laws, and court decisions also affect freedom of the press. Many cities and states have passed laws making it a crime to sell obscene literature. Police officers arrest booksellers, theatre owners, and art dealers, who become defendants in criminal cases and claim their activities are protected by the guarantee of freedom of the press. Sometimes the police search a store for obscene materials and seize books they say are obscene. The bookseller goes to court to complain about the search without a warrant, and to get his books back. In this instance, he becomes the plaintiff, bringing a suit on the civil side.

The idea of freedom of speech and of the press now includes freedom of radio and television stations and of movie producers. Here there is often a licensing problem. Because there are a limited number of air frequencies for broadcasting, the federal government decides who will get licenses. The Federal Communications Commission can refuse to issue a license to a radio or TV station if it fails to meet certain standards, including standards of morality. This gives the federal government the opportunity to censor what goes over the air. Congress also passed a law requiring equal time for all candidates for public office. If a candidate objects that a particular station denied him equal time, his complaint goes first to the FCC and, after its ruling, may end up in court.

This chapter describes two fairly common free press cases: obscenity charges against two booksellers, and libel charges against the *New York Times* and several ministers arising out of an ad taken by a civil rights group. When these cases reached the Supreme Court, they gave the justices an opportunity to reiterate the basic American commitment to a free press set forth in the First Amendment in unequivocal terms, and then to decide the specific cases before them.

Is obscenity as easy to spot as poison ivy?

Roth v. *United States* (1957)
354 U.S. 476, 77 S. Ct. 1304, 1 L. Ed. 2d 1498

Punsters have long claimed that the only difference between obscenity and great art is the price tag. Selling a nude on a postcard can get you arrested, while selling a nude in marble weighing a ton may put you on the cultural pages as an outstanding art dealer.

Samuel Roth and David Alberts raised some of these questions of definition before the Warren Court. Roth was charged with mailing obscene circulars, obscene advertising, and an obscene book in violation of a federal statute. He was convicted after a jury trial and sentenced to five years in prison plus $5,000 fine. Alberts ran a mail-order book business and was convicted under a California obscenity statute. Both lost on appeal and the U.S. Supreme Court agreed to hear their cases together.

The defendants contended that obscenity was protected under the First Amendment. It did not present any clear and present danger of inciting antisocial behavior. It was alleged to stimulate only impure *thoughts*, and freedom of thought was the essence of the First Amendment.

They also maintained that the obscenity statutes were too vague to give a person a clear understanding of what was prohibited and what was not. This was a denial of due process, they said.

Roth also argued that the federal statute violated the Ninth and Tenth Amendments, by encroaching on an area of legislation reserved for the states and the people. Alberts argued the other side of the coin—that the state statute was void because the federal statute preempted or covered the field.

The Court did not look at the materials the defendants had mailed, but decided the case solely on these legal questions.

How would you vote on the First Amendment question? Is obscene speech or writing protected because political speech and writing are protected? Or should people be jailed for selling books that blatantly appeal to the reader's base instincts? What happens when community standards change? Can the federal government pass legislation against obscenity? Can states pass such legislation? Can federal courts rule on the constitutionality of such state legislation?

The Supreme Court, in the majority opinion by Justice Brennan, first noted that this was the first time the question of obscenity as a protected form of expression had been "squarely presented to this Court." The Court split six to two, with Justice Harlan concurring in part and dissenting in part. Chief Justice Warren concurred in the majority result but on different grounds, which he described in a separate opinion. Justice Douglas wrote a dissenting opinion, joined in by Justice Black. Clearly this was a controversial case. Previously, the Court had decided many obscenity cases by reading the books or watching the movies and ruling on whether the particular work was obscene, without making broader statements. This time, however, the opinions dealt with the standards and constitutionality of obscenity law.

Justice Brennan began by tracing the history of enactment of the First Amendment and pointing out that freedom of expression was never absolute. Libel had from the beginning been criminal, and the first fourteen states had also made blasphemy or profanity criminal. "In light of this history," he said, "it is apparent that the unconditional phrasing of the First Amendment was not intended to protect every utterance."

He went on, "The protection given speech and press was fashioned to assure unfettered interchange of ideas for the bringing about of political and social changes desired by the people." To achieve this, "all ideas having even the slightest redeeming social importance—unorthodox ideas, controversial ideas, even ideas hateful to the prevailing climate of opinion—have the full protection of the guaranties, unless excludable because they encroach upon the limited area of more important interests. But implicit in the history of the First Amendment is the rejection of obscenity as utterly without redeeming social importance." He concluded: "We hold that obscenity is not within the area of constitutionally protected speech or press."

"However, sex and obscenity are not synonymous," Justice Brennan pointed out. "Obscene material is material which deals with sex in a manner appealing to prurient interest. The portrayal of sex, *e.g.*, in art, literature and scientific works, is not itself sufficient reason to deny material the constitutional protection of freedom of speech and press. Sex, a great and mysterious motive force in human life, has indisputably been a subject of absorbing interest to mankind through the ages; it is one of the vital problems of human interest and public concern."

Justice Brennan then carefully limited the scope of the Court's opinion, stating: "The fundamental freedoms of speech and press have contributed greatly to the development and well-being of our free society and are indispensable to its continued growth. Ceaseless vigilance is the watchword to prevent their erosion by Congress or by the States.

The door barring federal and state intrusion into this area cannot be left ajar; it must be kept tightly closed and opened only the slightest crack necessary to prevent encroachment upon more important interests. It is therefore vital that the standards for judging obscenity safeguard the protection of freedom of speech and press for material which does not treat sex in a manner appealing to prurient interest."

The test of obscenity was "whether to the average person, applying contemporary community standards, the dominant theme of the material taken as a whole appeals to prurient interest." This standard, said Justice Brennan, "provides safeguards adequate to withstand the charge of constitutional infirmity," and since the trial courts had properly applied the standard, their decisions were valid.

On the question of vagueness of the statutes in defining the improper conduct, Justice Brennan said: "The thrust of the argument is that these words are not sufficiently precise because they do not mean the same thing to all people, all the time, everywhere.

"Many decisions have recognized that these terms of obscenity statutes are not precise. This Court, however, has consistently held that lack of precision is not itself offensive to the requirements of due process." He found that the wording of the statutes did "give adequate warning of the conduct proscribed."

Taking Roth's contention that the federal government was encroaching on states' rights, the court found that this argument depended on a holding that obscenity was protected by the First Amendment. Since the Court held it was not protected, "that argument falls." In response to Alberts's contrary argument that the California statute was void, the Court found that the California prohibition of "keeping for sale" or "advertising" obscene matter did not duplicate the federal prohibition against "mailing." Therefore, the state statute was valid.

Both convictions were affirmed.

Chief Justice Warren agreed with the result reached in these cases, "but, because we are operating in a field of expression and because broad language used here may eventually be applied to the arts and sciences and freedom of communication generally, I would limit our decision to the facts before us and to the validity of the statutes in question as applied."

He noted that "the line dividing the salacious or pornographic from literature or science is not straight and unwavering. Present laws depend largely upon the effect that the materials may have upon those who receive them. It is manifest that the same object may have a different impact, varying according to the part of the community it reached.

"But there is more to these cases. It is not the book that is on trial; it is a person. The conduct of the defendant is the central issue, not the obscenity of a book or picture." In this case, the defendants "were plainly engaged in the commercial exploitation of the morbid and shameful craving for materials with prurient effect." On that ground, the Chief Justice concurred in affirming their convictions.

Justice Harlan disagreed with the majority's grounds also, "because I find lurking beneath its disarming generalizations a number of problems which . . . leave me with serious misgivings as to the future effect of today's decisions."

He elaborated: "The Court seems to assume that 'obscenity' is a peculiar *genus* of 'speech and press,' which is as distinct, recognizable, and classifiable as poison ivy is among other plants. On this basis the *constitutional* question before us simply becomes . . . whether 'obscenity,' as an abstraction, is protected by the First and Fourteenth Amendments, and the question whether a *particular* book may be suppressed becomes a mere matter of classification, of 'fact,' to be entrusted to a fact-finder and insulated from independent constitutional judgment."

In Justice Harlan's view, on the contrary, the obscenity of each work must be examined individually by the appellate courts, because "the question whether a particular work is of that character involves not really an issue of fact but a question of constitutional *judgment* of the most sensitive and delicate kind. Many juries might find that Joyce's *Ulysses* or Bocaccio's *Decameron* was obscene, and yet the conviction of a defendant for selling either book would raise, for me, the gravest constitutional problems, for no such verdict could convince me, without more, that these books are 'utterly without redeeming social importance.' "

In addition, Justice Harlan felt the two cases could not be lumped together, partly because federal courts have a "very narrow" function in reviewing state judgments under the Fourteenth Amendment.

In the *Roth* case, however, Justice Harlan found that the federal government had no business legislating in the area of obscenity. "Congress has no substantive power over sexual morality," he said. Rather the states "bear direct responsibility for the protection of the local moral fabric." Moreover, "the dangers of federal censorship in this field are far greater than anything the States may do." Justice Harlan found comfort in the fact that if one state banned a book others might allow it, whereas the federal government's ban would cover all.

Finally, viewing the case in light of the First Amendment, Justice Harlan said, "I do not think that this conviction can be upheld. The petitioner was convicted under a statute which, under the judge's charge, makes it criminal to sell books which 'tend to stir sexual impulses and lead to sexually impure thoughts.' I cannot agree that any book which tends to stir sexual impulses and lead to sexually impure thoughts necessarily is 'utterly without redeeming social importance.' Not only did this charge fail to measure up to the standards which I understand the Court to approve, but as far as I can see, much of the great literature of the world could lead to conviction under such a view of the statute. Moreover, in no event do I think that the limited federal interest in this area can extend to mere 'thoughts.' The Federal Government has no business, whether under the postal or commerce power, to bar the sale of books because they might lead to any kind of 'thoughts.' "

Justice Douglas also dissented, joined by Justice Black: "When we sustain these convictions, we make the legality of a publication turn on the purity of thought which a book or tract instills in the mind of the reader. I do not think we can approve that standard and be faithful to the command of the First Amendment, which by its terms is a restraint on Congress and which by the Fourteenth is a restraint on the States." Using the trials courts' standards, "punishment is inflicted for thoughts provoked, not for overt acts nor antisocial conduct. This test cannot be squared with our decisions under the First Amendment."

"The tests by which these convictions were obtained," Justice Douglas went on, "require only the arousing of sexual thoughts. Yet the arousing of sexual thoughts and desires happens every day in normal life in dozens of ways. Nearly 30 years ago a questionnaire sent to college and normal school women graduates asked what things were most stimulating sexually. Of 409 replies, 9 said 'music'; 18 said 'pictures'; 29 said 'dancing'; 40 said 'drama'; 95 said 'books'; and 218 said 'man.' "

Justice Douglas found that "any test that turns on what is offensive to the community's standards is too loose, too capricious, too destructive of freedom of expression to be squared with the First Amendment. Under that test, juries can censor, suppress, and punish what they don't like, provided the matter relates to 'sexual impurity' or has a tendency 'to excite lustful thoughts.' This is community censorship in one of its worst forms. It creates a regime where in the battle between the literati and the Philistines, the Philistines are certain to win."

"I assume there is nothing in the Constitution which forbids Congress from using its power over the mails to proscribe *conduct* on the grounds of good morals. No one would suggest that the First Amendment permits nudity in public places, adultery, and other phases of sexual misconduct."

Rejecting both the "appeal to prurient interest" definition and the "no redeeming social importance" standard, Justice Douglas concluded: "Freedom of expression can be suppressed if, and to the extent that, it is so closely brigaded with illegal action as to be an inseparable part of it. . . . As a people, we cannot afford to relax that standard. For the test that suppresses a cheap tract today can suppress a literary gem tomorrow. All it need do is to incite a lascivious thought or arouse a lustful desire. The list of books that judges or juries can place in that category is endless.

"I would give the broad sweep of the First Amendment full support. I have the same confidence in the ability of our people to reject noxious literature as I have in their capacity to sort out the true from the false in theology, economics, politics, or any other field."

The *Roth* decision upholding obscenity statutes has been followed in a series of federal and state prosecutions against producers, advertisers, and sellers of books, movies, magazines, photographs, and works of art. But it is obvious from a quick check of any paperback and comic book collection and of any hard cover bestseller list that community attitudes about sex literature are very different from those in another time, and differ from place to place at the same time. With this fact in mind, the Burger Court decided to try its hand at fashioning clear and definite standards for use in cases involving allegedly obscene written matter and films, whether for public distribution or for private use only. Four cases decided in the spring of 1973 yielded four 5–4 votes and 15 written opinions. The Court reaffirmed the *Roth* holding that obscene material is not protected under the First Amendment; held that such matter is not protected by any constitutional doctrine of privacy, and set the following guidelines for the jury or judge deciding cases in state or federal court: 1) whether the average person, applying contemporary standards of his own community (not national standards) would find that the work, taken as a whole, appeals to the prurient interest; 2) whether the work depicts or describes, in a patently offensive way, sexual conduct specifically defined by the applicable state law, and 3) whether the work, taken as a whole, lacks serious literary, artistic, political, or scientific value.

Uninhibited, robust, and wide-open debate

New York Times Company v. Sullivan (1964)
376 U.S. 254, 84 S. Ct. 710, 11 L. Ed. 2d 686

In the late 1950s and early 1960s, several civil rights groups working in the South launched voter registration campaigns. Efforts to desegregate schools, lunch counters, swimming pools, restaurants, and other facilities continued, but new efforts were made to register the thousands of black people who had been refused and discouraged from seeking the right to vote (see part III).

The Southern Christian Leadership Conference, under the leadership of Reverend Martin Luther King, was one of the groups active in these movements, and King became a focus for white southern antagonism. In 1959 he was arrested on a perjury charge and faced up to ten years in jail. A defense organization was formed to muster support for King, for militant black students also facing harassment, and for voter registration. On March 29, 1960, the group took a full-page ad in *The New York Times* to ask for funds.

The ad described the southern civil rights efforts and said that they were being met by "an unprecedented wave of terror." It related some incidents: students sitting in at a lunch counter "were forcibly ejected, tear-gassed, soaked to the skin in freezing weather with fire hoses, arrested en masse and herded into an open barbed-wire stockade to stand for hours in the bitter cold."

Dr. King's peaceful protests brought him "intimidation and violence. They have bombed his home almost killing his wife and child. They have assaulted his person. They have arrested him seven times—for 'speeding,' 'loitering' and similar 'offenses.' "

"In Montgomery, Alabama," the ad said, "after students sang 'My Country 'Tis of Thee' on the State Capitol steps, their leaders were expelled from school, and truckloads of police armed with shotguns and tear gas ringed the Alabama State College Campus. When the entire student body protested to state authorities by refusing to re-register, their dining hall was padlocked in an attempt to starve them into submission."

Mr. L. B. Sullivan, one of three elected city commissioners of Montgomery, filed suit against *The Times* and against four

Negro clergymen whose names appeared among those endorsing the appeal for funds. Mr. Sullivan was the commissioner in charge of Public Affairs and the Police Department of Montgomery, and he claimed he had been libeled in the ad. He contended that in using the word "police" in describing events in Montgomery, the ad referred to him as the commissioner supervising the police; that the use of the word "they" elsewhere in the ad would be read to refer to the police; and that people reading the ad would impute to the police and therefore to him the acts of ringing the campus, padlocking the dining hall to starve the students, arresting Dr. King seven times, using intimidation and violence against Dr. King, bombing his home, assaulting his person, and charging him with perjury. Mr. Sullivan asked for $500,-000 damages.

Four other libel suits were filed against *The Times* and the clergymen (all leaders in the civil rights movement) by other Montgomery city commissioners and by the governor of Alabama, asking damages totaling $2.5 million. Shortly afterward, the mayor and city commissioners of Birmingham sued *The Times* for libel for an article it had published about the city's race relations. They asked $1.5 million damages. The city commissioners of Bessemer, Alabama, filed a similar suit asking $500,000 damages apiece. A series of five suits, totaling $1.7 million in damages, was filed against the Columbia Broadcasting System.

In the *Sullivan* case, the clergymen denied all knowledge and endorsement of the ad before its publication. *The Times* readily admitted that some of the ad's statements were inaccurate. For example, the students had sung the National Anthem, not "My Country 'Tis of Thee" at the capitol; they had boycotted classes, not refused to register, as a protest; and Dr. King had been arrested three, not seven, times before the perjury charge.

But the defense maintained that none of the statements referred to Mr. Sullivan, and therefore the ad did not libel him. In response to a demand for retraction, *The Times* wrote to Mr. Sullivan that it was "somewhat puzzled as to how you think the statements in any way reflect on you." Nevertheless, Sullivan brought suit and produced six witnesses to testify that they had read the ad as referring in part to him.

After three days of trial, the judge instructed the all-white jury that the ad was "libelous per se," that legal injury to Mr. Sullivan was implied by the law "from the bare fact of publication itself," that "falsity and malice are presumed," that "general damages need not be alleged or proved but are presumed," and that "punitive damages may be awarded by the jury even though the amount of actual damages is neither found nor shown."

The defendants objected among other things that the judge's rulings abridged freedom of speech and of the press. The judge rejected this contention.

The jury came back with a verdict for Mr. Sullivan and awarded him the full $500,000. He proceeded to attach the cars, property, salaries, and savings of the four ministers, which tied them up in legal battles to free their assets. *The Times* was able to post the $1 million bond (twice the amount of damages) required under Alabama law for appeal.

The Alabama Supreme Court affirmed the judgment, holding that the judge's rulings were correct under Alabama law, that it was possible for the jury to find that the libelous statements had been made about Sullivan, and that malice could be inferred from *The Times*'s "irresponsibility" in printing the ad when it "in its own files had articles already published which would have demonstrated the falsity of the allegations in the advertisement." It dismissed the appellants' constitutional arguments stating, "The First Amendment of the U.S. Constitution does not protect libelous publications," and

"The Fourteenth Amendment is directed against State ac tion and not private action."

The Times sought review by the U.S. Supreme Court. In January 1963, the Court agreed to hear the case. Finally, in March 1964, it rendered its judgment.

Do you think the time element in this instance was important? Do you think the Court should have found some way to decide the case more quickly than it did? Do libel laws and damage suits for libel protect individuals from false statements of their enemies? Or is the main purpose to protect the public from untrue statements? How would you have decided this case?

Justice Brennan announced, for the unanimous Court: "We hold that the rule of law applied by the Alabama courts is constitutionally deficient for failure to provide the safeguards for freedom of speech and of the press that are required by the First and Fourteenth Amendments in a libel action brought by a public official against critics of his official conduct." In addition, he noted that even if the Alabama courts had used "proper safeguards" of constitutional rights, "the evidence presented in this case is constitutionally insufficient to support the judgment."

The Alabama court's rulings on the First and Fourteenth Amendments were erroneous, Justice Brennan stated. The Fourteenth Amendment applies to actions by any part of the state government. Here a state court applied a state rule of law in a manner alleged to be unconstitutional. That is enough to bring it under the Fourteenth Amendment even though it was applied in a civil action between private parties rather than in a criminal action prosecuted by the state.

The First Amendment applied as well, because "libel can claim no talismanic immunity from constitutional limitations. It must be measured by standards that satisfy the First Amendment," Justice Brennan ruled.

"Thus we consider this case against the background of a profound national commitment to the principle that debate on public issues should be uninhibited, robust, and wide-open, and it may well include vehement, caustic, and sometimes unpleasantly sharp attacks on government and public officials. . . . The present advertisement, as an expression of grievance and protest on one of the major public issues of our time, would seem clearly to qualify for the constitutional protection. The question is whether it forfeits that protection by the falsity of some of its factual statements and by its alleged defamation of respondent."

Tracing the answer to that question through the Supreme Court's past decisions and the history of the Sedition Act of 1798, "which first crystallized a national awareness of the central meaning of the First Amendment," Justice Brennan found that "the constitutional protection does not turn upon 'the truth, popularity, or social utility of the ideas and beliefs which are offered.' . . .

"The fear of damage awards under a rule such as that invoked by the Alabama courts here may be markedly more inhibiting than the fear of prosecution under a criminal statute," he noted. "The judgment awarded in this case—without the need for any proof of actual pecuniary loss—was one thousand times greater than the maximum fine provided by the Alabama criminal statute, and one hundred times greater than that provided by the Sedition Act." He concluded, "Whether or not a newspaper can survive a succession of such judgments, the pall of fear and timidity imposed upon those who would give voice to public criticism is an atmosphere in which the First Amendment freedoms cannot survive."

"The state rule of law is not saved by its allowance of the defense of truth," Justice Brennan continued. "A rule compelling the critic of official conduct to guarantee the truth of all his factual assertions—and to do so on pain of libel judgments virtually unlimited in amount—leads to . . . 'self-censorship' " comparable to that the Supreme Court had already condemned.

Justice Brennan now announced a broad ruling: "The constitutional guarantees require, we think, a federal rule that prohibits a public official from recovering damages for a defamatory falsehood relating to his official conduct unless he proves that the statement was made with 'actual malice'—that is, with knowledge that it was false or with reckless disregard of whether it was false or not."

On the theory that Mr. Sullivan might seek a new trial following the Supreme Court's decision, the Court then examined the record in the case to discover whether the evidence could constitutionally support the verdict against *The Times* and the clergymen. It found that there was no proof of the clergymen's knowledge or approval of the ad, that there was no adequate showing of malice on the part of *The Times,* that there was no reasonable ground to infer that the ad referred to Mr. Sullivan, and that there was no ground for considering criticism of a government agency libelous personal criticism of the official in charge unless actual malice were proved.

The Court's southern Justice, Hugo Black, wrote a concurring opinion taking an even stronger position. "I vote to reverse exclusively on the ground that *The Times* and the individual defendants had an absolute, unconditional constitutional right to publish in *The Times* advertisement their criticisms of the Montgomery agencies and officials." He noted that the size of the judgment and the factual background of civil rights struggle involved in the case supported the inference that Mr. Sullivan's reputation may have been enhanced rather than damaged by the ad in the segregationist community of Montgomery. The numerous similar suits then pending constituted a "harassing and punishing" technique of "deadly danger to the press" and "by no means limited to cases with racial overtones."

He concluded: "An unconditional right to say what one pleases about public affairs is what I consider to be the minimum guarantee of the First Amendment.

"I regret that the Court has stopped short of this holding indispensable to preserve our free press from destruction." (Justice Douglas joined in this opinion.)

Justice Goldberg's concurrence (also joined in by Justice Douglas) similarly stressed that "the First and Fourteenth Amendments to the Constitution afford to the citizen and to the press an absolute, unconditional privilege to criticize official conduct despite the harm which may flow from excesses and abuses."

He noted that "if newspapers, publishing advertisements dealing with public issues, thereby risk liability, there can also be little doubt that the ability of minority groups to secure publication of their views on public affairs and to seek support for their causes will be greatly diminished. . . . To impose liability for critical, albeit erroneous or even malicious, comments on official conduct would effectively resurrect 'the obsolete doctrine that the governed must not criticize their governors.' "

Justice Goldberg explained, "This is not to say that the Constitution protects defamatory statements directed against the private conduct of a public official or private citizen," because "purely private defamation has little to do with the political ends of a self-governing society."

But "vigorous criticism by press and citizen of the conduct of the government of the day by the officials of the day will soon yield to silence if officials in control of government agencies, instead of answering criticisms, can resort to friendly juries to forestall criticism of their official conduct."

"I strongly believe," Justice Goldberg concluded, "that the Constitution accords citizens and press an unconditional freedom to criticize official conduct."

The *New York Times* decision virtually abolished the libel suit as a method of frightening newspapers into not publishing information about public officials. It opened up a whole spectrum of public criticism of government officials at all levels without fear of damage suits.

But it must be noted that the organizations and individuals attacked by libel suits during the hot summers of civil rights activity were not saved by the Court's opinion. They had learned to depend on themselves, not on the courts that finally upheld their First Amendment rights. They had also learned that the First Amendment is not self-executing and that fighting this kind of litigation takes a considerable amount of time, effort, and money from the struggle for civil rights and desegregation.

The Warren Court decision did not mark the end of the era of our history that began in feudal England when no person could make a statement critical of the king without fear of being sent to the Tower of London for beheading. New types of attacks are often launched—sometimes against publication of "secret" government documents, sometimes to limit the application of the Public Information Act of 1968 (5 U.S.C. §552), or to punish reporters for refusing to reveal the names of informants.

The *New York Times* found itself before the Supreme Court again early in the 1970s when it published excerpts from the so-called Pentagon Papers prepared by the Defense Department as secret documents concerning United States involvement in the Southeast Asia war. The Court held the federal government could not enjoin publication of the documents and upheld the First Amendment in *New York Times* v. *United States.* With the dismissal of charges against Ellsberg and Russo for making the Pentagon Papers available to Congressmen, that threat to First Amendment liberties abated, even though the ground for dismissal was the dirty tricks used by government agents (including breaking into the office of the psychiatrist to one of the defendants in order to obtain material about the defendant without his knowledge).

CHAPTER 4

Freedom of Assembly and Petition

Since the early sixties, the right of the people to assemble and petition the government for a redress of grievances has been exercised almost to the point of exhaustion. Newspapers daily report marches to city halls, draft boards, federal buildings, courthouses, state capitols, and public officials' offices and homes by such diverse groups as antiwar protesters, welfare mothers, civil rights groups, farm workers, college and high school students, GIs and veterans, and parents of school children.

Often the petitioners are expressing views unpopular in their communities, and face hostility from onlookers. The police are sometimes hard pressed to protect the demonstrators; at other times they appear to have no desire to protect them, or they allege that the spectators are the ones needing protection from the protesters.

Hundreds of these assemblies have resulted in arrests; many have been appealed to the Supreme Court. The issues in each revolve around the same basic questions: Is the particular case of sufficient importance to warrant consideration by the busy Supreme Court? If so, is the First Amendment an absolute, requiring that all these convictions be reversed? Or must each case be considered on its own facts? Is this case one of protected activity—people peaceably assembling to petition for redress of grievances? Were the demonstrators, the spectators, or the police correct in their actions?

The Warren Court, unlike all of its predecessors, decided to find the time to hear a great many of these cases. Its decisions constructed a framework for future courts to build on. Even more, they helped establish a climate in which diverse groups with grievances would take to the streets to open public debate on public questions.

Many of these demonstration cases, like *Edwards* v. *South Carolina* (see chapter 2), arose in the South, but some in the North, such as the protest resulting in the case of *Gregory* v. *Chicago,* also brought the issues of the First Amendment sharply into focus.

Chicago's meat-ax ordinance

Gregory v. *Chicago* (1969)
394 U.S. 111, 89 S. Ct. 946, 9 L. Ed. 2d 697

Dick Gregory was one of the first black comedians to start making racial jokes to white audiences that put down white people instead of black people. When the civil rights movement started, Gregory thought he would stick to being funny. But before long he found himself marching and picketing and getting arrested in this or that southern city.

At a certain point in the 1960s, Gregory and a lot of other black people began to feel that the South was coming along, but they weren't "taking care of business" up North. Segregation and discrimination were rampant in every large northern city, and pressure for action began to mount from these ghettos.

In 1965, Chicago became a target of civil rights demonstrations, chiefly demanding desegregation of the schools and open housing. The windy city was notoriously friendly to Jim Crow in both fields.

Dick Gregory lived in Chicago, and in the summer of 1965 he planned to lead a demonstration there. Marchers were to picket the home of Mayor Richard Daley, demanding that Superintendent of Schools Benjamin Willis be removed because he had not moved to desegregate the public schools.

The mayor technically had no authority to fire Willis, but the black people in Chicago understood the city's power structure well enough to know that if the mayor wanted Willis out, he would be out, and if the mayor wanted Willis in, no amount of pressure applied to the board of education would get him out.

The demonstrators gathered at Grant Park about 4:00 in the afternoon. Gregory made a speech, saying, "First we will go over to the snake pit," meaning city hall. "When we leave there, we will go out to the snake's house," meaning Daley's house. And the demonstrations would continue, he said, at "Mayor Daley's home until he fires Ben Willis."

At 4:30 the marchers started out, two by two, carrying placards—"Daley Fire Willis," "Defacto, Desmacto, It Is Still Segregation." It was five miles from city hall to the mayor's house. The demonstrators got there around 8:00 and began marching around the block. Their ranks had swelled to about 85. At one street corner there were some 35 spectators. There were about 180 police accompanying the march and spread around the block.

The demonstrators chanted, "Ben Willis must go, Snake Daley, also."

"Ben Willis must go!"

"When?"

"Now!"

April 2, 1963: Dick Gregory is moved along by a police officer in Greenwood, Mississippi, after accompanying blacks to the court-house to register to vote.
Credit: Wide World Photos

They sang "We Shall Overcome" and "We Shall Not Be Moved."

The police tried to keep spectators across the street from the march. People came out of their houses, and some turned lawn sprinklers on their sidewalks. The marchers walked around the water. As the crowd grew and began shouting at the marchers, Gregory went down the line saying, "Don't stop and don't answer anyone back. Don't worry about anything that is going to be said to you. Just keep marching. If anyone hits you or anything, try to remember what they look like, but above all means, do not hit them back. Keep the line straight and keep it tight."

The marchers had promised to stop singing and chanting at 8:30 that evening, and they marched quietly after that. By 9:00, the spectators had grown to a few hundred, and 100 or 150 tried to start a line in front of Gregory's line. The civil rights demonstrators moved their march to the next block to separate it from the spectator's line. After 9:00 the crowd swelled rapidly to a thousand or more, people streaming in from every direction. Neighbors hung out of windows and yelled at the marchers. Threats were shouted from the crowd on the street: "Get out of here, niggers—go back where you belong or we will get you out of here." Some spectators had Ku Klux Klan signs. Cars stopped and blew their horns.

Rocks and eggs were thrown at the marchers. Small groups of teenagers broke out of the crowd and rushed at the line, but the police forced them back. The police tried to catch the spectators who were throwing things.

Around 9:30, the policeman in charge told Gregory the situation was becoming riotous. He asked the demonstrators to leave and offered police escort out of the area. The line kept marching. He repeated the request several times. He offered police escort to any individual marchers willing to leave. Three accepted.

The rest of the marchers were then arrested and taken away in police vans. They were charged under a Chicago ordinance reading: "All persons who shall make, aid, countenance, or assist in making any improper noise, riot, disturbance, breach of the peace, or diversion tending to a breach of the peace, within the limits of the city; all persons who shall collect in bodies or crowds for unlawful purposes, or for any purpose, to the annoyance or disturbance of other persons; . . . shall be deemed guilty of disorderly conduct. . . ."

At the trial, the marchers maintained that they had been engaged in peaceful picketing protected by the First Amendment, and that the spectators were the ones who should have been controlled or arrested by police. The judge, however, instructed the jury (over defense objections) that "the fact that persons other than these Defendants may or may not have violated any laws or may or may not have been arrested should not be considered by you in determining the guilt or innocence of these Defendants."

The jury found Gregory and thirty-nine others guilty, and the defendants appealed to the Illinois Supreme Court. They argued that the ordinance was so broad that it prohibited acts protected by the First Amendment, and therefore it was invalid. But the court interpreted the ordinance narrowly. It "does not authorize the police to stop a peaceful demonstration merely because a hostile crowd may not agree with the views of the demonstrators," the court said. "It is only where there is an imminent threat of violence, the police have made all reasonable efforts to protect the demonstrators, the police have requested that the demonstration be stopped and explained the request, if there be time, and there is a refusal of the police request, that an arrest for an otherwise lawful demonstration may be made." The court affirmed the convictions.

The defendants then went to the United States Supreme Court.

What is your opinion? Is there a point where the First Amendment stops and civil disorder begins? Can police be expected to protect a small group of orderly demonstrators against a large unruly mob? Are they permitted to act to avoid a dangerous situation, if this infringes some people's rights to assemble peaceably?

The Court's unanimous opinion was delivered by Chief Justice Warren. "This is a simple case," he began. "Petitioners' march, if peaceful and orderly, falls well within the sphere of conduct protected by the First Amendment." The Chief Justice cited as authority the Supreme Court's opinions in a series of southern civil rights cases involving peaceful demonstrations. "There is no evidence in this record that petitioners' conduct was disorderly. Therefore, under the principle first established in *Thompson* v. *City of Louisville* [discussed in chapter 11], convictions so totally devoid of evidentiary support violate due process."

Chief Justice Warren found error in the Illinois Supreme Court's opinion because if the demonstrators were found guilty "for their refusal to disperse when requested to do so by Chicago police," as the Illinois Supreme Court seemed to suggest, this was not what they had been charged with. "However reasonable the police request may have been and however laudable the police motives, petitioners were charged and convicted for holding a demonstration, not for a refusal to obey a police officer." It was a denial of due process to convict them on a charge that was never made.

In conclusion, the Chief Justice found that "the trial judge's charge permitted the jury to convict for acts entitled to First Amendment protection," and this, too, "requires reversal of these convictions."

Justices Stewart and White concurred on the last point only.

Justice Black, joined by Justice Douglas, concurred separately, stating, "This I think is a highly important case which requires more detailed consideration than the Court's opinion gives it. It in a way tests the ability of the United States to keep the promises its Constitution makes to the people of the Nation."

"In 1954," Justice Black recalled, "our Court held that laws segregating people on the basis of race or color in the public schools unconstitutionally denied Negroes equal protection of the laws." He summarized the nature and emotional tone of the desegregation demonstrations and struggles that followed, and the problems they had presented to the courts. The Supreme Court had "pointed out in many cases that the States and their subordinate units do have constitutional power to regulate picketing, demonstrating, and parading by statutes and ordinances narrowly drawn so as not to abridge the rights of speech, press, assembly, or petition," Justice Black noted. But "neither Chicago nor Illinois at the time these petitioners were demonstrating had passed any such narrowly drawn laws."

Examining the facts of the case, Justice Black found that both police and demonstrators had done their best to maintain order, but had ultimately failed. This pointed "unerringly to one conclusion, namely, that when groups with diametrically opposed, deep-seated views are permitted to air their emotional grievances, side by side, on city streets, tranquility and order cannot be maintained even by the joint efforts of the finest and best officers and of those who desire to be the most law-abiding protestors of their grievances."

"It is because of this truth, and a desire both to promote order and to safeguard First Amendment freedoms, that this Court has repeatedly warned States and governmental units that they cannot regulate conduct connected with these freedoms through use of sweeping, dragnet statutes that may, because of vagueness, jeopardize these freedoms." Justice Black found that the Chicago ordinance, far from being narrowly drawn, "might better be described as a meat-ax ordinance, gathering in one comprehensive definition of an offense a number of words which have a multiplicity of meanings, some of which would cover activity specifically protected by the First Amendment." The phrase "diversion tending to a breach of the peace" might be broad enough to "authorize conviction simply because the form of the protest displeased some of the onlookers." This infringed constitutional rights.

Although the Illinois Supreme Court interpreted the ordinance narrowly to avoid unconstitutionality, the trial judge's charge to the jury was very broad, and thus, Justice Black agreed with Chief Justice Warren, the jury may have convicted the demonstrators on unconstitutional grounds.

Justice Harlan concurred with Justice Black on the basis of the broad or "ambulatory sweep" of the ordinance and the possibility that the jury convicted on unconstitutional grounds.

The reversal of these convictions came in 1969, four years after the demonstration. In the interim, Dick Gregory had run (unsuccessfully) against Richard Daley for mayor of Chicago in 1966, and had been arrested and jailed in the midst of the campaign on an assault charge arising out of another demonstration against School Superintendent Willis.

In 1968, young people had poured into Chicago to the Democratic Party Convention to demonstrate their views on the war in Vietnam, civil rights, machine politics, the draft, lifestyles, and other social issues, even though many were not old enough to be elected delegates. Mayor Daley's handling of these demonstrators brought him into the limelight nationally. Many citizens were outraged at what they considered to be police brutality unleashed against unarmed young people. Some were outraged at the behavior of the demonstrators. In that same year, Dick Gregory ran for president of the United States on a third party ticket, and the next year eight political activists were on trial in Chicago before federal Judge Julius Hoffman for their actions at the 1968 convention.

The mood of civil rights demonstrations shifted in those four years, too. Instead of turning the other cheek, marchers North and South began adopting policies of self-defense. The frustrations of black people in the North erupted in revolts in Watts, Detroit, Newark, Washington, and elsewhere in the late 1960s. A few cities are electing black mayors. But the white power structures seem generally unmoved. Chicago's schools and housing remain segregated. Urban renewal projects in that city have received federal funding, despite evidence of de facto segregation, and higher-priced apartments have systematically replaced low-rent housing, forcing ghetto residents into more crowded living conditions. The city's schools continue to follow its segregated housing patterns.

The *Gregory* decision came after the tactic it protects was partially abandoned by the civil rights movement, but its strong affirmation of the right to assemble peaceably and petition the government for redress of grievances has been used effectively by the antiwar and other movements in fighting restrictive statutes and ordinances across the country. The impact of public demonstrations cannot be gauged accurately at the time they are held, but testimony in the Watergate investigations suggests that government officials pay close attention to these actions by groups of people, even when they express lack of concern or ignorance of their occurrence.

CHAPTER 5

Freedom of Religion

Everyone has many questions about religion and morality. Is there a God or Supreme Being? What is the origin of mankind? What is the responsibility of each man toward his fellow men? Toward his God? Is it better to go to church on Sunday and pray and work with others of similar faith, or to commune with nature individually? Is there one answer for all men, or are there different answers for each man?

The American colonists, fresh from religious persecution in England, were determined to protect freedom of religion in this country. They knew what trouble had been caused in England when Henry VIII decided to stop being a Catholic with allegiance to the Pope in Rome and to become head of a new independent Anglican church. The church and state became intimately connected because the king of England became head of the Anglican church. From then on, attacks on the church could be considered attacks on the state; differences over religious doctrine could be called treason against the monarch. In such a society, freedom of religion could not flourish.

The men who wrote the Constitution were also aware that arguments over religious doctrine had split several colonies. People who came to the New World to practice their own religions freely often became as narrow-minded as those in the Old World about the religious freedom of their neighbors. They wanted everyone to join their church, which was natural, but many were prepared to force everyone to do so. The politicians of 1789 knew that religious differences would make it difficult to achieve the unity necessary to establish a new national government. And they had to be sensitive to the religious beliefs of powerful individuals and groups such as the Pennsylvania Quakers, who believed in pacifism, and the Catholics in Maryland.

The authors of the First Amendment therefore wrote three guarantees of religious freedom: first, that the government cannot establish an official state religion; second, that it cannot give any one religion preference over others; and third, that it cannot inhibit people from worshipping according to their religious preferences.

These guarantees served their purpose in part, and few people have been prosecuted in criminal trials because of their religious belief, or lack of it. On the other hand, there has been a great deal of persecution of religious minorities by society as a whole, by institutions, and by employers. Anti-Catholic sentiment was visited upon immigrants from Ireland in the middle of the nineteenth century, particularly in eastern cities. Latter-Day Saints (Mormons) were persecuted in the Midwest and West. Antisemitism led to discrimination in admission of Jews to colleges, graduate schools, and many occupations. Members of other religious groups have been made to feel different, unwelcome, alien.

Questions of freedom of religion come up in many ways. The Warren Court heard Daniel Seeger, a religious pacifist who didn't believe in a Supreme Being; they heard parents of the Jewish, Unitarian, and Ethical Culture faiths who were against prayers in New York schools; they heard Susan Epperson, a teacher who wanted to teach Darwin's theory of evolution, even though it contradicted the Book of Genesis; and they heard Thomas Cooper, a Black Muslim serving two hundred years in prison who wanted to read publications by his sect and to consult with ministers of his faith. Many other religious freedom cases were appealed to the Court but the Court heard few of them.

The Court's decisions in these four leading cases express the law of religious freedom for the fifties and sixties, and are showing the path to the law of the seventies and beyond.

A parallel belief

United States v. *Seeger* (1965)
380 U.S. 163, 85 S. Ct. 850, 13 L. Ed. 2d 733

Daniel Seeger was eighteen years old in 1953, as the United States withdrew from its "police action" in Korea. He registered for the draft and was classified I-A. In 1955, he asked for a student deferment and was classified II-S. This status was renewed in 1956 and 1957. In July 1957, he wrote to his draft board that he had been examining his conscience and beliefs and now felt bound to refuse to serve in the army because he was opposed to war in any form. The draft board accordingly sent him Form 150 (the application for conscientious objector status).

The Military Training and Service Act of 1948 was much broader than the World War I draft law. It provided an exemption from combatant service in the armed forces for any young man "who, by reason of religious training and belief, is conscientiously opposed to participation in war in any form. Religious training and belief in this connection means an individual's belief in a relation to a Supreme Being involving duties superior to those arising from any human relation, but does not include essentially political, sociological, or philosophical views or a merely personal moral code."

The C.O. application form asked, "Do you believe in a Supreme Being?" Seeger did not check either yes or no, and on a separate sheet wrote, "Of course, the existence of God cannot be proven or disproven, and the essence of His nature cannot be determined. I prefer to admit this, and leave the question open rather than answer 'yes' or 'no.' However, skepticism or disbelief in the existence of God does not necessarily mean lack of faith in anything whatsoever." He expressed his "belief in and devotion to goodness and virtue for their own sakes, and a religious faith in a purely ethical creed."

In answer to a question about the nature of his belief and whether it involved duties to a Supreme Being that he considered were higher than any owed to a human relation, Seeger wrote a three-page explanation. He felt "men do far more harm and inflict far more injury on one another by attempting to prevent evil by violence than if they endured evil." War is ineffective. Moreover it destroys the values it ostensibly is trying to preserve. The cold war arms race will inevitably result in war. "I cannot participate in actions which betray the cause of freedom and humanity," he concluded.

The draft board denied the application and classified Seeger I-A in 1958. He appealed to the Selective Service Appeal Board. At that point, the FBI made its routine investigation for the Justice Department. It concluded that Seeger "had a good character and reputation and that no one who was aware of his views questioned their sincerity." But the FBI characterized his beliefs as "probably based upon ethical and philosophical grounds."

Seeger protested the FBI investigation, because he was not

allowed to see the report and because he felt the FBI had asked the wrong people the wrong things. They asked his business acquaintances and apartment house neighbors about his religious and philosophical beliefs, but they had not interviewed his friends, the people with whom he had worked on the school newspaper, or his associates in disarmament and nonviolence movement groups. These were the people he was most likely to talk to about his beliefs.

(Another C.O. applicant, Britt Peter, who later joined in the Seeger case, remarked that the FBI went around trying to prove that the C.O. claimant was insincere, a liar, cowardly, and disreputable in his business and social life—all in order to show that he should be classified I-A, meaning he was fit for military service.)

Seeger at this time was also interviewed by a hearing officer, who became fully convinced of his sincerity and felt his beliefs qualified him for the exemption.

The Appeal Board was thus faced with two opposing recommendations. Seeger asked to appear before the board, but was refused. He submitted a nine-page statement to clarify his beliefs to the board. His mother, too, wrote to the board at this time, saying that she knew her son's beliefs well, and "I think he is wrong in his stand, but I do know he is sincere." She said they had had many arguments about questions of war and peace and about religion (his family was Catholic, although he no longer belonged to the church), and he was firmly committed to his position.

The Appeal Board denied the appeal, and upheld Seeger's I-A classification. He was ordered to report for induction on October 20, 1960, and on that date he refused induction.

The FBI arrested him and charged him with violating the draft law, a felony punishable by five years in prison or $10,-000 fine, or both. He was released on bail while waiting for trial in the federal district court, where he waived a jury.

Seeger argued that his claim for C.O. status had been wrongfully denied, that the requirement of belief in a Supreme Being was an unconstitutional favoring of one religious belief over another, and that he had been denied due process of law when the FBI's report was not shown to him.

The Justice Department answered that there was no constitutional right to C.O. status, and that Congress had specifically stated the beliefs that qualified for C.O. status so that draft boards would not act arbitrarily or discriminate in granting or denying C.O. applications. Seeger did not meet the standard because, though sincere, he did not express an allegiance to a Supreme Being that took precedence over earthly commitments.

The federal judge ruled against Seeger on these questions, convicted him, and sentenced him to one year and one day in prison. He appealed to the court of appeals. In 1964, that court reversed his conviction, stating, "We feel compelled to recognize that a requirement of belief in a Supreme Being, no matter how broadly defined, cannot embrace all those faiths which can validly claim to be called 'religious.' " The judges went on, "While we are, therefore, most reluctant to find that Congress, in a sincere attempt to balance the personal rights of a minority with the insistent demands of our national security, has transgressed the limits imposed by the Constitution, we are compelled so to hold."

The Justice Department then sought review by the U.S. Supreme Court. The Court agreed to hear the case along with those of two other young men who had been denied C.O. status and had refused induction. Both had expressed their beliefs in individual terms rather than the formal terms of established churches. One, Arno Jakobson, expressed belief in an "ultimate cause" or "Supreme Reality," which he called "Godness." It was to be approached by dealing directly with the "givens" of existence—life, death, health, love, time—as they were found in oneself and others. The other draft refuser, Britt Peter, had expressed a conviction that taking human life was a violation of moral law that overrode his obligation to the state. He felt his belief in the sacredness of human life and human spirit was religious in the sense of religion as "the supreme expression of human nature." Jakobson's conviction had been reversed and Peter's had been upheld by different courts of appeals.

The Constitition gives Congress the power "to raise and support armies." The First Amendment says Congress cannot interfere with "the free exercise of . . . religion." Are these two provisions inconsistent for men whose religious beliefs tell them not to participate in war? Does this mean Congress cannot pass a law drafting everyone, including pacifists? Can Congress exempt pacifists who go to church and believe in God and draft pacifists who stay home and practice their religion in some other way? Or does national security require every able-bodied American to serve his country regardless of his religion? Should the Supreme Court have the power to decide these questions?

Justice Clark delivered the opinion of a unanimous Court, in 1965, before U.S. involvement in Vietnam became heavy. He traced the history of exemption of conscientious objectors from military service, which had started before the Civil War and expanded with every subsequent conflict. After examining the 1948 statute, the Court "concluded that Congress, in using the expression 'Supreme Being' rather than the designation 'God,' was merely clarifying the meaning of religious training and belief so as to embrace all religions and to exclude essentially political, sociological, or philosophical views.

"We believe that under this construction, the test of belief 'in a relation to a Supreme Being' is whether a given belief that is sincere and meaningful occupies a place in the life of its possessor parallel to that filled by the orthodox belief in God of one who clearly qualifies for the exemption. Where such beliefs have parallel positions in the lives of their respective holders we cannot say that one is 'in a relation to a Supreme Being' and the other is not. We have concluded that the beliefs of the objectors in these cases meet these criteria. . . ."

The Court opinion recognized that the modern religious community embraced a "broad spectrum of religious beliefs." Justice Clark quoted passages from Dr. Paul Tillich, Dr. David Muzzey, and other religious philosophers to demonstrate different ways in which expressions about belief in "God" might be worded, and concluded that it would be wrong to put "too narrow a construction" on the statute.

Justice Douglas, in a concurring opinion said, "The legislative history of this Act leaves much in the dark. But it is, in my opinion, not a *tour de force* if we construe the words 'Supreme Being' to include the cosmos, as well as an anthropomorphic entity." He explained the many forms and expressions used for the concept of "Supreme Being" in Buddhism and Hinduism, to illustrate the breadth of the concept. He also listed the Buddhist sects in America and their membership figures.

"When the Congress spoke in vague general terms of a Supreme Being I cannot, therefore, assume that it was so parochial as to use the words in the narrow sense urged on us. I would attribute tolerance and sophistication to the Congress, commensurate with the religious complexion of our communities."

This decision was critically important to young men increasingly facing the draft for the Vietnam war, but it received scant publicity.

Nevertheless, the nonviolent teachings of the civil rights movement combined with an unpopular Asian war led many young men in the late 1960s to examine their consciences and find themselves opposed to participation in war.

The Selective Service System did not change the C.O. application form until August 1968, three years after the Supreme Court enunciated the "parallel belief" test. So for three more years applicants were led to think that belief in a "Supreme Being" was a requirement for C.O. status, and many thought they could not qualify as C.O.'s, although their consciences forbade them to participate in the war. Increasing numbers went to prison for draft refusal and some fled the country.

Others, who sought help from counselors or lawyers, did apply for C.O. status, only to find that their local draft boards apparently did not know of the *Seeger* decision and would not apply it.

More and more draftees were tried all over the country. A few, like Seeger, had their fate decided by the Supreme Court on basic questions. More won or lost on procedural grounds—because the procedure used in classifying or drafting them was unconstitutional in some respect (see the *Oestereich* case discussed in chapter 19). For example, Joseph Mulloy, a young organizer for the Southern Conference Educational Fund, described in *Dombrowski* v. *Pfister* (see page 162), submitted a C.O. application after being classified I-A, and his local board declined to reopen his case and consider his C.O. form. In 1970, the Supreme Court, in *Mulloy* v. *United States,* held that the board had to reopen the question of a man's classification if he presented a claim that was not "frivolous." This means that if the man presented new facts that were not before the board when they gave him his present classification, and if these facts appeared on their face to be sufficient grounds for sustaining his claim, the board must reopen his case and consider whether the new facts are convincing.

Many procedural points have been decided, and many are still pending. To date, the Supreme Court, under Chief Justices Warren and Burger, has assumed the constitutionality of a peacetime draft law; the Court has declined to rule on the legality of the Vietnam war and the relevance of the Nuremberg Judgment.

The need for draft counseling became more and more apparent, and the number of counselors multiplied. An antidraft movement developed along with the antiwar movement. Debate continues about the need for and legality of the draft, raising several basic constitutional issues. Whether these questions about national defense, aggression, and nonviolence will be pressed after the war in Southeast Asia is over will depend on whether this country is then engaged in other international conflicts, whether Congress abolishes the draft permanently, and whether the young people of the country feel as deeply committed to these issues after the crisis passes.

School prayers

Engel v. *Vitale* (1962)
370 U.S. 421, 82 S. Ct. 1261, 8 L. Ed. 2d 601

The First Amendment guarantees that the government cannot establish an official state religion, or give any one religion preference over others. Yet religious phrases abound in government rituals and symbols. Since 1954, by act of Congress, we have pledged allegiance to "one nation under

God." Congress begins each daily session with a prayer, and appropriates salaries for chaplains in the armed forces. Our coins are stamped "IN GOD WE TRUST." The crier of the Supreme Court opens each session with "God save the United States and this honorable Court." Most Americans seemed to feel that these phrases were a proper expression of the religious feelings of our citizens, as long as they were put in nondenominational general words that did not suggest a particular religion or sect.

In 1951, during the Korean war and the so-called Cold War, the Board of Regents governing the New York State public schools issued a "Statement on Moral and Spiritual Training in the Schools," suggesting that each school day begin with an "act of reverence to God" following the salute to the flag. The Regents recommended the following prayer: "Almighty God, we acknowledge our dependence upon Thee, and we beg Thy blessings upon us, our parents, our teachers and our Country."

The Board of Education in New Hyde Park, New York, adopted the Regents' recommendation in 1958, and directed that the prayer be said in each class, although no child was to be required or encouraged to join in it against his wishes.

To most of the teachers, parents, and children, the prayer was a simple, innocuous statement of general faith. But to some, it was a distasteful imposition of a ritual contrary to their religious beliefs. The Christian majority had difficulty imagining how their neighbors found it offensive. They could not turn the tables and imagine themselves daily being called on to pray in the Moslem or Buddhist style, for example.

Five parents brought suit against the school board to stop the practice, contending that it violated both the First Amendment prohibition against "establishment of religion" and the "free exercise" of their religious practices and beliefs. Two were Jewish, one a Unitarian, one an Ethical Culturist, and one a nonbeliever.

The school board maintained that the prayer did not constitute establishment of religion, but was merely an expression of "an integral part of our national heritage."

The trial judge held that the prayer did not violate the "establishment" clause of the First Amendment, but that in order not to violate the "free exercise" of religion clause, the school board must inform each parent of the practice and ask whether or not his child was to participate. The school board must also insure against embarrassment of or pressure on nonparticipating children by instructing that no teacher was to comment on participation or suggest that any particular posture or dress or language be used. The judge suggested that nonparticipating children whose parents wanted them excused from the room might go to an assembly instead or come to school a little later or go to separate classes for opening exercises or follow some other procedure "which treats with equality both participants and non-participants."

The petitioning parents were not satisfied with these measures, and appealed the case. As the controversy continued, it illustrated the depth of emotional feeling around questions of religion for many people, particularly parents. The parents demanding an end to the prayer practice were labeled atheists, antireligionists, and un-American. They in turn accused their opponents of lawless disrespect for the Constitution and attempting to cram the majority religion down the minority's throats. The prayer proponents responded that the minority was limiting the freedom of religion of the majority. Educators made speeches demanding *more* moral and religious instruction in the schools to combat juvenile delinquency. Other educators denounced this approach as simplistic as well as unconstitutional, and said the schools were not the proper institution to do the job the churches and parents had failed to do.

The intermediate state appellate court affirmed the trial judge's decision, and the petitioners appealed to New York's highest court. This court, too, affirmed the decision by a vote of five to two in 1961. The parents then sought review by the United States Supreme Court. By the time the Court heard the case, twenty states had appeared as "friends of the Court" (amici curiae) urging retention of the prayer, and the American Civil Liberties Union and several religious and other groups had appeared as "friends" arguing against keeping the prayer.

Do you feel that this prayer violates the First Amendment? Can children who don't participate really be treated equally? Is it possible to formulate a prayer that will not offend someone's beliefs? If not, must prayer be totally banned from schools and other state institutions?

Justice Black wrote the opinion for the six-to-one majority; two justices did not participate in the decision. "It is a matter of history," said Justice Black, "that this very practice of establishing governmentally composed prayers for religious services was one of the reasons which caused many of our early colonists to leave England and seek religious freedom in America." He traced the intense disputes among religious sects that had occurred in both England and the Colonies, which led to the First Amendment position on freedom of worship and separation of church and state. Under that amendment, "as reinforced by the provisions of the Fourteenth Amendment, government in this country, be it state or federal, is without power to prescribe by law any particular form of prayer which is to be used as an official prayer in carrying on any program of governmentally sponsored religious activity," the Court ruled.

"There can be no doubt that New York's state prayer program officially establishes the religious beliefs embodied in the Regents' prayer. . . . Neither the fact that the prayer may be denominationally neutral nor the fact that its observance on the part of the students is voluntary can serve to free it from the limitations of the Establishment Clause," the Court held.

"When the power, prestige and financial support of government is placed behind a particular religious belief, the indirect coercive pressure upon religious minorities to conform to the prevailing officially approved religion is plain. But the purposes underlying the Establishment Clause go much further than that. Its first and most immediate purpose rested on the belief that a union of government and religion tends to destroy government and to degrade religion." Another purpose of the clause "rested upon an awareness of the historical fact that governmentally established religions and religious persecutions go hand in hand."

The Court concluded that, "by using its public school system to encourage recitation of the Regents' prayer, the State of New York has adopted a practice wholly inconsistent with the Establishment Clause."

Anticipating that the decision would provoke criticism of the Court, Justice Black was careful to say, "It is neither sacrilegious nor antireligious to say that each separate government in this country should stay out of the business of writing or sanctioning official prayers and leave that purely religious function to the people themselves and to those the people choose to look to for religious guidance." He went on, "To those who may subscribe to the view that because the

Regents' official prayer is so brief and general there can be no danger to religious freedom in its governmental establishment, however, it may be appropriate to say in the words of James Madison, the author of the first Amendment: '[I]t is proper to take alarm at the first experiment on our liberties.' "

Justice Stewart dissented on the ground that the prayer was no more an establishment of religion than the many religious phrases in other government rituals, such as the Pledge of Allegiance. By using a voluntary nondenominational prayer, the schools were simply following "the deeply entrenched and highly cherished spiritual traditions of our Nation."

Justice Douglas, too, felt that the school prayer did not differ from prayers at the opening of Congress or of the Supreme Court or at other government functions. He found "in each of the instances given the person praying is a public official on the public payroll, performing a religious exercise in a governmental institution." In each case the prayer is given before what is "in a sense a 'captive' audience."

"I cannot say that to authorize this prayer is to establish a religion in the strictly historic meaning of those words," Justice Douglas continued. "A religion is not established in the usual sense merely by letting those who choose to do so say the prayer that the public school teacher leads. Yet once government finances a religious exercise it inserts a divisive influence into our communities."

Justice Douglas, in an uncommon move, said he had come to disagree with his former stand in *Everson* v. *Board of Education,* a 1947 case holding that public finds could be used to pay bus fares for parochial school students as well as for public school students. He now agreed with the dissenting opinion by Justice Rutledge in that case, stating that the church should neither participate in nor receive largesse from the state, for the good of both.

Justice Black was correct in anticipating strong public reactions and attacks against the Court because of this decision. Southern Congressmen voiced their objections immediately, one commenting that the justices had first "put the Negroes in the schools and now they've driven God out" (referring to the school desegration case, *Brown* v. *Board of Education*, discussed in chapter 22).

Controversy about the case ran high. Groups such as the John Birch Society were so incensed that they began a campaign to impeach Earl Warren as Chief Justice. Beneath the storm, however, almost unnoticed, parents and organizations representing a wide variety of religious beliefs wrote quiet tributes to the Court for relieving their children of an onerous daily practice that grated upon their souls. And the Burger Court seems to be carrying forward the careful construction of the line between church and state spelled out in the First Amendment.

Evolution in the schools

Epperson v. *Arkansas* (1968)
393 U.S. 97, 89 S. Ct. 266, 21 L. Ed. 2d 228

Darwin's theory of evolution created quite a stir at its publication in 1859 and for many years afterward. The crux of the controversy, as with Galileo's seventeenth-century theories of planetary movements, was that these new explanations of the universe contradicted the Bible. With Darwin's ideas there was the added insult of suggesting that man had common ancestry with the undignified and much ridiculed ape. Human egos did not accept this blow to self-esteem with aplomb.

During the 1920s, bills prohibiting the teaching of evolution were introduced in twenty states in America. Some passed, among them the Tennessee "monkey law" that gave rise to the famous *Scopes* case, in which Clarence Darrow defended a young man prosecuted for teaching the theory. Scopes's conviction was reversed in 1927 on a technicality, so the validity of the "monkey law" was not destroyed, although it was lampooned from H. L. Mencken's columns in the twenties to the play and movie *Inherit the Wind* in the sixties.

In 1928, Arkansas enacted a version of the Tennessee law, probably with the *Scopes* decision in mind. It forbade "any teacher or other instructor in any University, College, Normal, Public School, or other institution of the State, which is supported in whole or in part from public funds derived by State and local taxation to teach the theory or doctrine that mankind ascended or descended from a lower order of animals"; it also forbade the use of books that taught the theory. The penalty for violating the law was loss of job and up to $500 fine.

The statute had been a popular initiative measure, passed by vote of the citizens of Arkansas. During the campaign, proponents of the law characterized it in these terms: "THE BIBLE OR ATHEISM, WHICH? All atheists favor evolution. If you agree with atheism vote against Act No. 1. If you agree with the Bible vote for Act No. 1." Their literature asked, "Shall conscientious church members be forced to pay taxes to support teachers to teach evolution which will undermine the faith of their children?" The theory of evolution was associated with "Russian Bolshevism" as well as atheism in advertisements advocating passage of the statute.

Several of the states that had enacted monkey laws eventually repealed them. Tennessee did not repeal its statute until

1967. Arkansas left its statute on the books but did not prosecute anyone under it.

Susan Epperson was raised in Arkansas. She got a master's degree in zoology from the University of Illinois and then came back, married, and started teaching tenth grade biology at Central High School in Little Rock. A year later, in 1965, the school got new biology textbooks, which had a chapter on Darwin's theory. Mrs. Epperson, faced with an "illegal" textbook, decided to test the constitutionality of the law. A parent of two high school boys joined her in seeking a court declaration that the law was invalid and an injunction against prosecuting those who violated it. They filed an affirmative suit, seeking to get a ruling on the civil side without violating the law and facing a possible criminal charge. (See *Dombrowski* v. *Pfister,* page 163.)

The Arkansas Chancery Court ruled in Mrs. Epperson's favor, holding that the law interfered with First Amendment freedom of speech and thought and thus violated the Fourteenth Amendment, which prohibits states from such interference. The judge said the "truth or fallacy of arguments on each side of the evolution debate does not either contribute to or diminish the constitutional rights of teachers and scientists to advance theories and discuss them." He found that the statute "tends to hinder the quest for knowledge, restrict the freedom to learn, and restrain the freedom to teach."

The Arkansas Attorney General appealed the decision to the state supreme court. The court opinion was a single paragraph:

"Upon the principal issue, that of constitutionality, the court holds that [the statute] is a valid exercise of the state's power to specify the curriculum in its public schools. The court expresses no opinion on the question whether the Act prohibits any explanation of the theory of evolution or merely prohibits teaching that the theory is true; the answer not being necessary to a decision in the case, and the issue not having been raised."

The lower court's decision was reversed. One justice concurred in the first sentence only of the supreme court's opinion, and another justice dissented without opinion.

Mrs. Epperson appealed to the United States Supreme Court. She contended that the statute denied due process of law, because it was too vague to give teachers clear notice of what was prohibited (the point the Arkansas Supreme Court had refused to clarify), that it violated the First Amendment's protections of speech and thought, and that it violated the "establishment clause" by favoring biblical doctrine over other doctrine on the subject of the origin of man.

The state stood behind the holding of its supreme court.

Should the voters of 1928 determine the school curriculum for students in 1965? What is at stake here—the rights of the teacher or the students or the general public? Is there a constitutional right to get a broad education in the public schools? Is the theory of evolution antireligious?

The Supreme Court's decision was unanimous, although the justices' reasons differed. Justice Fortas, speaking for the Court, first said, "We do not rest our decision upon the asserted vagueness of the statute." He went on, "It is of no moment whether the law is deemed to prohibit mention of Darwin's theory, or to forbid any or all of the infinite varieties of communication embraced within the term 'teaching.' Under either interpretation, the law must be stricken because of its conflict with the constitutional prohibition of state laws respecting an establishment of religion or prohibiting the free exercise thereof. The overriding fact is that Arkansas' law selects from the body of knowledge a particular segment which it proscribes for the sole reason that it is deemed to conflict with a particular religious doctrine; that is, with a particular interpretation of the Book of Genesis by a particular religious group."

Justice Fortas traced the Court's previous decisions on establishment of religion, and the Court concluded, "These precedents inevitably determine the result in the present case. The State's undoubted right to prescribe the curriculum for its public schools does not carry with it the right to prohibit, on pain of criminal penalty, the teaching of a scientific theory or doctrine where that prohibition is based upon reasons that violate the First Amendment." It was clear to the Court that the reason for the prohibition in this case was the "fundamentalist sectarian conviction" that "the Book of Genesis must be the exclusive source of doctrine as to the origin of man." The case was reversed.

This reason was by no means clear to Justice Black, however. He suggested other possible motivations for the prohibition, and stated, "It is not for us to invalidate a statute because of our view that the 'motives' behind its passage were improper; it is simply too difficult to determine what those motives were."

Justice Black felt the Court's opinion might be infringing the religious freedom of orthodox believers by forbidding states to forbid evolutionary teaching. "Unless this Court is prepared simply to write off as pure nonsense the views of those who consider evolution an anti-religious doctrine, then this issue presents problems under the Establishment Clause far more troublesome than are discussed in the Court's opinion."

And he considered Darwinian theory simply a subject matter in the realm of science that a state could select or reject for its curriculum. However, he found the Arkansas statute to be so vague in its prohibitions that it had to be invalidated for failure to specify what was illegal.

Justice Stewart agreed that the statute was void for vagueness, but he reached that conclusion from a different path. He felt that the state had every right to set its own curriculum but no right to "make it a criminal offense for a public school teacher so much as to mention the very existence of an entire system of respected human thought." Since the vague statute might be doing just that, it was invalid.

Justice Harlan deplored the Arkansas Supreme Court's apparent attempt to "pass the buck" to the U.S. Supreme Court in this case. He agreed with Justice Fortas' opinion only as to the unconstitutionality of the statute because it violated the establishment clause. He regretted the majority's explorations of the vagueness and free speech issues.

Mrs. Epperson apparently left the state before the case reached the Supreme Court, and the controversial book was used in Central High School even while the suit was going on.

The decision, however, seems to have ended the long struggle over the teaching of evolution in American public schools. Perhaps Clarence Darrow smiled down on (or up at) the Court from wherever his spirit may now reside.

Religion behind bars

Cooper v. *Pate* (1964)
378 U.S. 546, 84 S. Ct. 1733, 12 L. Ed. 2d 1030

Thomas Cooper was found guilty of murder and given two 100-year terms in state prison to be served consecutively, not simultaneously. Sent to the maximum security state prison at Joliet, Illinois, he allegedly attacked some guards in 1957, and was put into isolation as punishment. After that he was kept in what was called "segregation" and not allowed to mingle with the general prison population.

Cooper was defiant and intelligent—not a happy combination for a prisoner or his jailers. In addition, he was black and a follower of Elijah Muhammad's Nation of Islam (known popularly as the Black Muslims). Prison officials considered the Muslims to be a serious threat to order and discipline in the penitentiary, which housed 4,700 inmates—white, black, and brown. The Intelligence Division of the Chicago Police Department reported in 1962: "Federal and State prisons continue to have serious problems involving Muslim inmates. The State Prison in Fulton, New York, has a 50% Negro population. Twenty-five percent of this number claim Muslim membership insisting on religious recognition and special privileges which would obviously break down discipline. Muslim violence also took place at Federal prisons in Terre Haute, Indiana, and at Atlanta, Georgia. Stateville and Joliet penitentiaries in Illinois continue to have some Muslim activity amongst their inmates. This situation is being closely observed to contain any incident that could arise. . . ." Although no specific incident in an Illinois prison is related in this report, its ominous tone conveys a vague fear of the Muslims by the police and prison authorities.

Many blacks in prisons throughout the United States, especially those in segregated facilities, were attracted to the Muslim faith and its approach for blacks living in a country ruled by whites. Cooper considered Islam his religion. He demanded a copy of the Quran (the Muslim bible); he asserted his right to consult with ministers of his faith, and he asked to buy copies of Arabic and Swahili language books to study Islamic materials in their original languages. The warden denied all these requests.

Cooper had access to some law books in the prison library. He read them and decided he had a good case. In 1962, he wrote out in longhand a "Petition for Relief under the Civil Rights Act," against Warden Pate and Illinois Director of Public Safety Ragen. He sent it to the federal district court, where it was treated as the complaint needed to start a lawsuit.

He charged that he had been denied permission to buy religious books, to receive Muslim literature, and to see or write to his minister; that he was kept isolated from his fellow prisoners; and that these were acts of discrimination against him because of his religion. He said this discrimination was unconstitutional abridgment of freedom of religion and denial of equal protection of the laws, since other prisoners were accorded the treatment he was denied.

Pate and Ragen filed a motion to dismiss Cooper's complaint. In effect, they admitted that Cooper's statement of the facts was correct, by not denying it. But they said he did not state any claim for relief that the court could grant. The federal judge dismissed the complaint without stating why.

Cooper was not so easily daunted. With almost two hundred years of prison life ahead of him, he had time to pursue his case and the incentive to get his prison routine enlarged to include the freedom of religion he was being denied.

He appealed to the Seventh Circuit Court of Appeals, writing out a brief in longhand once again. He detailed his complaints and the course of events in the case. He noted that the warden "feared I was an organizer and had ulterior motives." Before being put in segregation, "I was always surrounded by . . . [a] hundred to 150 inmates (mostly colored and Mexican). . . . He feared that I and my associates would be able to control his prison."

Warden Pate, represented by the attorney general's office, alleged in response that "the 'Black Muslim Movement,' despite its pretext of a religious facade, is a subversive organization proscribed by the laws of the United States and the State of Illinois. Therefore the plaintiff may constitutionally be debarred from overt participation in its activities and its publications may be censored, at least in a prison." He cited and attached a copy of the Chicago Police Department's report and asked the court to "take judicial notice" of it—that is, to accept the statements in it as true, without hearing evidence in court. (This is done with facts in a few official documents and encyclopedias.)

The court of appeals denied Cooper's motion to have a lawyer appointed to assist him and his motion for release to attend the argument on his appeal. The state's attorneys appeared for Pate and Ragen, but the court ruled that it would decide the case solely on the briefs and not hear oral argument. In November 1963, it affirmed the dismissal of Cooper's complaint, holding that courts should avoid interfering in matters of prison discipline, even when a claim of infringement of constitutional rights is made. The court did take judicial notice of the police report as evidence that "the Black Muslim Movement, despite its pretext of a religious facade, is an organization that, outside of prison walls, has for its object the overthrow of the white race, and inside prison walls, has an impressive history of inciting riots and violence." Thus, the court concluded, Cooper's demands were a matter of prison discipline more than religious freedom.

Cooper then wrote to the American Civil Liberties Union in Chicago for help in taking the case to the United States Supreme Court. The ACLU attorneys agreed to represent him. They argued to the Supreme Court that Cooper's right of religious freedom had been violated by denying him literature and religious counsel; that his isolation in prison was a violation of equal protection of the laws and of due process of law; that the court of appeals had no right to say that a movement professing to be a religion was not a religion; and that the court's refusal to appoint a lawyer for Cooper was unconstitutional.

The Illinois attorney general argued that there was no ground for granting Cooper's demands, which were a matter of internal prison routine and order, and that therefore the court's dismissal of his complaint was valid.

By definition, a person loses many freedoms when he is put behind bars. Should he also lose the freedom to exercise his religion as he wishes? Does the Constitution permit this? Does prison discipline require this? Can a court rule that an organization is not a "religion" without hearing evidence?

The Supreme Court filed a unanimous opinion one paragraph long, announced "per curiam" (by the Court as a body). It stated the long-standing rule that a motion to dismiss (such as the one filed by Pate and Ragen) can be granted only if the court assumes that the plaintiff's allegations are all true, and still finds that his complaint does not state a "cause of action" (grounds for a lawsuit). The Supreme Court examined Cooper's complaint and ruled that it "stated a cause of action and it was error to dismiss it."

The case went back to the federal district court for decision on the issues Cooper had raised. The judge then ruled that the Black Muslims were a religious organization at least in part, that Cooper should be allowed to buy the Quran and to see a Black Muslim minister. However, the court said the warden did not have to permit him to have Muslim periodicals and newspapers or Swahili and Arabic language books. The court also held that the prison could not automatically refuse to hold Muslim services, although it could regulate when these services might take place and how many and which prisoners might attend. If no minister were available, or if the services became the excuse for improper behavior, no services need be held, said the judge. As for Cooper's claim that he was being kept in segregation as a religious persecution, the judge disagreed, finding that this treatment was a disciplinary matter.

Both Cooper and the prison officials appealed the parts of the decision that went against them. The court of appeals affirmed all of the lower court's holdings and that case ended.

But the issue of the treatment of people while they are behind bars is very much alive. Prisoners at Attica and elsewhere have forced the general public to demand studies of conditions in prisons and juvenile detention centers. Many experts and laymen are challenging the practice of having segregated units for "incorrigible" prisoners. More and more people are asking whether governments can continue to isolate people in small cells for a term of years as a method of preparing them to return to society as law-abiding citizens.

The four sets of parties demanding protection from the Supreme Court for their free exercise of religion were also facing the broader social questions of war, racism, prisoners' rights, and academic freedom. It is typical of our judicial system that such questions reached the Supreme Court in the form of First Amendment cases to be decided on their particular facts but having much wider implications.

CHAPTER 6

Freedom of Association

When the colonists wanted to overthrow the English rule in America, they recognized that they had to band together. The right to do this, the right of association, is implicit in freedom of speech and press and all the other rights listed in the First Amendment. In some ways, it may be said that without freedom of association, the other rights cannot be exercised. Opponents of new ideas therefore launch their first and strongest attacks against the right of people to unite in groups to discuss such ideas and to carry out joint actions. When freedom of association is under attack, few people will dare to assemble together, and it takes rare courage for an individual, standing alone, to exercise his freedom to speak, write, read, or petition on behalf of dissenting views.

Freedom of association has been subjected to almost continuous attack since Truman's term. For years after Earl Warren became Chief Justice, the Court spent a good part of its energies dealing with cases inherited from two repressive movements of the past. One movement was known as McCarthyism—it was an intense series of cold war attacks on individuals and organizations that would not denounce the Communist Party of the United States or the government of the Soviet Union. Senator Joe McCarthy of Wisconsin led the charge against the Communist Party, its leaders, members, and sympathizers (so-called fellow travelers). Anyone who agreed with the Communists on any issue was fair game.

The other movement was racism or white supremacy—led by southerners who wanted to continue the unequal treatment and segregation of blacks. They openly rejected the Supreme Court's 1954 and 1955 decisions in *Brown* v. *Board of Education* (discussed in chapter 22), ordering desegregation of the public schools. Segregationist forces sprang into action after the *Brown* decision to fight to retain their basic lifestyle. They took the offensive in attacking blacks and civil rights advocates in organizations such as the National Association for the Advancement of Colored People (NAACP), the Congress of Racial Equality (CORE), the Student Nonviolent Coordinating Committee (SNCC), and the Southern Christian Leadership Conference (SCLC).

Struggles over McCarthyism and white supremacy led to endless litigation involving organizations, their leaders, and their individual members, who sometimes were charged simply with membership in the denounced organization, but often were harassed by arrests, administrative proceedings, firings from jobs, and threats or violence because of their beliefs.

When these cases reached the Supreme Court, they posed a real problem for the justices. On the one hand, the federal government was filing lawsuits to outlaw the Communist Party, to jail its leaders, and to harass its members and sympathizers. At the same time, the southern state governments were filing lawsuits to outlaw the NAACP and other civil rights groups, to jail their leaders, and to harass their members and sympathizers.

If the Court said that the Bill of Rights permitted the outlawing of the Communist Party, how could it say the Bill of

Rights forbade the outlawing of the NAACP, CORE, and SCLC? The public might not criticize outlawing the Reds, but many with political power would criticize outlawing the blacks. On the other hand, if the Court said the Bill of Rights protected the blacks, and therefore also protected the Reds, the Court would be saying the Communist Party was an organization like any other, and that the same law should apply to it as to other organizations. The Court faced political attack if it treated both organizations the same, or an enormous inconsistency in logic if it treated the two groups differently.

Yet the Red and the Black cases presented the same legal questions: Could a state, county, city, or federal government agency require an organization to register its existence, demand a list of its officers, members, and contributors, and label its publications as "subversive"? Could government agencies deny members certain rights and privileges, take away old-age benefits, and send them to jail for advocating fundamental changes in the present economic or racial systems? Could it send them to jail for leading peaceful boycotts and teaching political or racial theories?

As you will see, the Court never did face this contradiction and deal with it clearly and decisively. It made few ringing pronouncements of universal truths on the right of association. Nonetheless, over the years of hearing and deciding cases of the Reds and the Blacks, the Warren Court finally did encourage greater respect for the concepts of freedom of expression and association set forth as absolutes in the First Amendment, and did encourage, if not start, a return to reasoning debate on questions of social change. This spirit, so essential for the solution of weighty public problems, seems to be continuing in the present decade.

A. The Communist Party Cases

An outbreak of fear of Communism in this country arose after World War I in 1919–1920, after the Russian people had revolted against the Czar and established the first socialist nation in the world. United States Attorney General Palmer ordered the arrest of ten thousand "radical aliens" across the country in what were later condemned as the "Palmer raids." Those arrested were held for long periods but finally had to be released, many because they were not aliens but citizens, and others because they could not be deported, since the countries of their birth would not readmit them.

During the 1920s and 1930s, many people came in contact with the Communist movement, especially during the Great Depression. Unemployed workers and land-poor farmers were looking for explanations of their poverty. Blacks were attracted by the black Communist Party candidate for vice-president in 1932 and the emphasis on racial equality.

In 1940, just before American entry into World War II, antialien hysteria developed again, and Congress passed the Smith Act, giving the government additional powers to deport, refuse citizenship to, or take away the U.S. citizenship of "radical" aliens. Tacked onto the act was a little-debated clause making it a crime to organize a group advocating overthrow of the government by force and violence. This prohibition applied to both native-born and foreign-born persons in the United States.

While the United States and the Soviet Union were military allies in World War II, the American people looked on the Russians as courageous and loyal comrades-in-arms against the fascists. During this period, the U.S. Supreme Court decided several cases filed by the federal government in the 1930s. The Court held in 1943, in *Schneiderman* v. *United States,* that membership in the Communist Party in itself was not ground for stripping away the citizenship of a foreign-born American who had become naturalized. In 1945, in *Bridges* v. *Wixon,* it reversed the deportation order of a militant union leader for alleged membership in the Communist Party, when the witnesses against him proved totally unreliable.

However, the end of the hot war against fascism was followed quickly by the beginning of the cold war against socialism and communism. President Harry Truman issued Executive Order 9835 in 1947, imposing a loyalty oath on government workers. The U.S. Attorney General compiled a list of "subversive" organizations, and no one who was a member of these groups could be a government employee. The House Un-American Activities Committee subpoenaed Hollywood writers and accused them of subversive activities. Ten were sent to jail for contempt of Congress when they refused to answer HUAC's questions (*Trumbo* v. *United States*). Hundreds of others were blacklisted in Hollywood and on Broadway. The Justice Department used the 1940 Smith Act to indict national leaders of the Communist Party of the United States for conspiracy to organize a group that would later advocate the overthrow of the government by force and violence. After a long trial, the thirteen leaders were convicted and sentenced to five years in jail; even their lawyers were sent to jail for contempt of court in an unprecedented decision (*Sacher* v. *United States*).

The United States Supreme Court heard the Party leaders' appeal in 1951 (*Dennis* v. *United States*). The justices voted six to two to affirm their convictions, but could not agree on the reasons. The majority upheld the constitutionality of the Smith Act against the charge that it violated the First

Amendment right of freedom of association. Justice Black dissented on that precise point. Justice Douglas dissented because there was no evidence that these Communists presented a clear and present danger to the United States government. Following this ruling, the government started prosecuting over a hundred Communist Party leaders around the country.

In 1950, after several years of lobbying by then-Senator Nixon and others, Congress passed the Internal Security Act of 1950, also known as the McCarran Act. The act declared: "There exists a world Communist movement which, in its origins, its development, and its present practice, is a world-wide revolutionary movement whose purpose it is, by treachery, deceit, infiltration into other groups (governmental and otherwise), espionage, sabotage, terrorism, and any other means deemed necessary, to establish a Communist totalitarian dictatorship in the countries throughout the world through the medium of a world-wide Communist organization."

The act then required the United States arm of the Communist movement, and organizations with similar political viewpoints, to register with the government as "subversive" organizations.

If an organization failed to register itself, the act provided that the Subversive Activities Control Board was to hold hearings to determine whether it was a "Communist-action organization" or a "Communist-front organization."

The SACB could then order the organization to register and could subject it to many restrictions. Its members could not apply for, renew, or use a passport; they could not be employed by any labor union or represent any employer before the National Labor Relations Board; they were ineligible for old-age benefits even if they had put money into the Social Security system; any members who were aliens or naturalized were subject to denaturalization and possible deportation; all members were forbidden to hold nonelective offices or any employment with the United States government or in any defense facility. The organization had to label its publications and communications as Communist; it could not get tax exemption; it and its members could not seek or receive any classified information concerning security. Justice Black later commented, the act "makes it extremely difficult for a member of the Communist Party to live in this country and, at the same time, makes it a crime for him to try to get a passport to get out."

If the SACB ordered an organization to register and its officers refused to do so, the organization could be fined $10,000 for each offense. Its officers as individuals could be sentenced to five years in prison for each offense, and fined $10,000. Each day of failure to register was a separate offense.

The untainted administration of justice

Communist Party v. Subversive Activities Control Board (1956)

351 U.S. 115, 76 S. Ct. 663, 100 L. Ed. 1003

Hearings before the Subversive Activities Control Board against the Communist Party began April 23, 1951, and ended July 1, 1952. During these fifteen months, twenty-two government witnesses and three Party witnesses gave 14,000 pages of testimony and introduced 507 exhibits, including many books. The vast bulk of the evidence introduced by the government related to the Party's activities before 1940, when it had stopped its participation in the Communist International, an organization of Communist parties of many countries.

After hearing the evidence, the SACB found the Communist Party to be subversive and ordered it to register. The Party appealed the order in the federal courts.

When Chief Justice Warren was appointed to the Supreme Court in 1953, appeals from the second and third rounds of Smith Act trials of local Communist leaders were pending as well as appeals from SACB registration orders. The first case to reach the Warren Court under these statutes was *Communist Party* v. *Subversive Activities Control Board.*

The Party attacked every section of the McCarran Act and the SACB's method of conducting the hearings in its appeal to the federal court of appeals. Then some interesting events occurred. The government had been calling the same witnesses over and over to testify in cases of alleged Communist Party leaders and members charged either under the Smith Act or before the SACB or called before the House Un-American Activities Committee or in deportation cases. Slowly the defense lawyers were able to establish that these were paid "informer" witnesses whose testimony must be scrutinized very carefully. And finally, under cross-examination, three of these witnesses—Crouch, Johnson, and Matusow—told conflicting stories in various courtrooms at various times, all under oath.

The Communist Party then argued on appeal that these "professional informers heretofore employed by the Department of Justice as witnesses in numerous proceedings, have committed perjury, are completely untrustworthy and should be accorded no credence," and that the case should be sent back to the SACB for a rehearing.

The court of appeals rejected this argument, and the Party

then became a petitioner in the United States Supreme Court. This was the first opportunity for the high Court to decide whether the 1950 McCarran Act was constitutional.

What should the Court have done? Was the charge that key government witnesses had committed perjury before the SACB four years earlier enough to justify reversal of the SACB's orders?

The Supreme Court split six to three. Justice Frankfurter delivered the majority opinion in April 1956. "No doubt a large part of the record consisted of documentary evidence," he granted. "However, not only was the human testimony significant but the documentary evidence was also linked to the activities of the petitioner and to the ultimate finding of the Board by human testimony, and such testimony was in part that of these three witnesses." He listed how much testimony the three had given and concluded that it "cannot be deemed insignificant."

"This is a proceeding under an Act which Congress conceived necessary for 'the security of the United States and to the existence of free American institutions,'" said Justice Frankfurter (quoting the McCarran Act). "The untainted administration of justice is certainly one of the most cherished aspects of our institutions. Its observance is one of our proudest boasts." The majority pointed out that the Court must not only do justice; it must do justice publicly, so that everyone can see that it is being done.

The Court rejected as insufficient the government's contention "that there is ample innocent testimony to support the Board's findings." It held, "If these witnesses in fact committed perjury in testifying in other cases on subject matter substantially like that of their testimony in the present proceedings, their testimony in this proceeding is inevitably discredited and the Board's determination must duly take this fact into account."

(In a similar case that year, Chief Justice Warren spoke even more sharply for the Court about a paid informer for the government who committed perjury: "by his testimony, [he] has poisoned the water in this reservoir, and the reservoir cannot be cleansed without first draining it of all impurity." The Court has a duty "to see that the waters of justice are not polluted." He added, "The government of a strong and free nation does not need convictions based upon such testimony." *Mesarosh* v. *United States.*)

Justice Frankfurter here noted that "the basis for challenging the testimony was not in existence when the proceedings were concluded before the Board." The Court held that the Party "should therefore be given leave to make its allegations before the Board," but it did not tackle the question of the constitutionality of the McCarran Act.

Justices Reed and Minton agreed. Justice Clark considered this decision an evasion of the constitutional issue. "I abhor the use of perjured testimony as much as anyone," he said, "but we must recognize that never before have mere allegations of perjury, so flimsily supported, been considered grounds for reopening a proceeding or granting a new trial. The Communist Party makes no claim that the Government knowingly used false testimony, and it is far too realistic to contend that the Board's action will be any different on remand. The only purpose of this procedural maneuver is to gain additional time before the order to register can become effective. This proceeding has dragged out for many years now, and the function of the Board remains suspended and the congressional purpose frustrated at a most critical time in world history."

When the case went back before the Subversive Activities Control Board, the Board did expunge the entire testimony of the alleged perjurors, but it concluded that the remaining evidence was sufficient to support an order compelling the Communist Party to register.

Abstract argument divorced from action

Yates v. *United States* (1957)
354 U.S. 298, 77 S. Ct. 1064, 1 L. Ed. 2d 1356

For the next act of our drama, we flash back to July 26, 1951, when ten men and five women were arrested in California under the 1940 Smith Act, and taken to the Los Angeles County Jail as federal prisoners. The men joined other convicts on a corridor containing ten cells. Among their cellmates were several youths who had spent most of their lives in juvenile detention homes and prisons. They asked the ten men what they had done. The articulate leaders of the Communist Party could not adequately explain their presence to the other convicts. The young inmates had lived by force and violence all their lives; they could not see how simply reading and discussing books of political ideology could lead to arrest.

The federal district court judge before whom the defendants appeared set bail for them at $50,000 apiece. When they protested that such high bail was unwarranted and that they couldn't afford it, he asked how much they earned. Most of them earned around $40 a week, working for the Communist Party or its newspaper, the *People's World*. The judge said he didn't believe that people would engage in such a hazardous occupation for so little pay, and he refused to lower the bail.

After 4½ months of appeals, bail was finally lowered and the defendants were released from jail.

The fifteen were brought to trial in February 1952 on charges of conspiracy to violate the Smith Act.

A long trial is something like an ocean voyage. The same characters are enclosed in a room together all day for weeks or months. They get to know each other's foibles and mannerisms; a kind of grudging camaraderie even develops. But a courtroom drama is a real-life story and must end in victory for one side and defeat for the other.

All the Smith Act trials were pretty much the same. The United States Attorney introduced witness after witness for the government. They testified to the content of books allegedly read, discussed, and taught by the defendants and other leaders of the Communist Party. Occasionally a witness would testify that he had attended a meeting at which one of the defendants was present, and sometimes one would testify to what a particular defendant had said. When specific testimony was given about certain defendants, some curious discrepancies developed. For example, John Lautner testified as a former leader of the Communist Party. He had already appeared in a number of similar trials around the country. He gave considerable testimony about defendant Al Richmond's attendance at the 1945 Communist Party convention, describing what Richmond had said. On cross-examination, the defense counsel put into evidence Richmond's record in the United States Army, which showed that he had spent the entire year of 1945 in Dorsetshire, England, as a surgical technician in an Army hospital.

When the government completed its case, the defendants put on the stand one of their own number, Oleta O'Conner Yates, a state official in the Communist Party. This extremely articulate witness testified on direct examination for two full weeks, telling the jury in detail how she had come to join the Communist Party and what she understood its program and

Oleta O'Connor Yates, one of the fifteen Communist Party leaders
indicted in the California Smith Act trial.
Credit: The People's World

goals to be. She described the role of American Communists in the Civil War, in organizing unions, and in other historic events; she explained the meaning of such terms as "smash the state," "dictatorship of the proletariat," and "revolution" in Marxist-Leninist doctrine. Toward the end of the direct examination, her attorney, Ben Margolis, asked:

"Have you ever agreed to conspire with anyone at all to advocate the overthrow of the government of the United States by force and violence?"

"No, certainly not," Mrs. Yates replied.

"Has your connection with the Communist Party ever had, from your standpoint, the purpose of advocating the overthrow of the government of the United States by force and violence?"

"No, it has not."

"According to your understanding, has the Communist Party ever had that purpose?"

"No, it has not."

When it came time to cross-examine Mrs. Yates, the prosecutor began with four routine questions and then asked which of the other defendants Mrs. Yates had met with in Communist Party meetings.

This question put Mrs. Yates in a difficult situation. She answered:

"I am quite prepared to discuss anything that I did, but I am not willing to provide names and identities of people other than those that I have indicated, because I believe that in the case of the other defendants their case is already rested and I would only be contributing . . . to the prosecution case against them, and I think that would be becoming a government informer and I cannot do that."

The prosecuting attorney continued, "You are willing to state what you know, are you not, Mrs. Yates?"

"I am willing to state anything you want to know about me and what I have done and what I think and what my intent is," she replied, "but I am not willing to do anything that is going to harm the defense of other people and I am not willing to do anything that is going to open up the door to persecution and harassment of other people."

"I understand, from your testimony, that you state you had no intent to violate the law with which you are charged," said Prosecutor Neukom.

"I did not, indeed."

"Then what have you to fear?"

"I have nothing to fear, nothing to fear, Mr. Neukom."

But after a while, the judge intervened and told Mrs. Yates, "You will answer the questions which the Court directs you to answer; the Court directs you to answer that question."

"I am sorry, Your Honor," said the witness, "I cannot be an informer."

"You are instructed, Madam, to answer that question," the judge repeated.

Mrs. Yates respectfully declined.

"You understand the possible consequences of your refusal to answer, I take it?" the judge asked.

"I am afraid I do, but the possible consequences, grim as they may be, are not as bad as going around hanging your head in shame for the rest of your life."

The U.S. Attorney dropped this line of questioning for a while. But later he returned to it. Each time Mrs. Yates refused to answer a question about someone's relationship with the Communist Party, the judge cited her for contempt of court. There were eleven separate citations, on which the judge sentenced Mrs. Yates to a year in jail.

After listening to testimony from February to August, the jurors finally heard the judge's instructions on the law they should apply to the case. The twelve debated for 4½ days about the verdict, then found all of the defendants guilty.

The judge refused to set bail pending appeal. He said the defendants' guilt was so clear that he considered any appeal to be "frivolous." Another legal battle was required before the defendants could be released while they appealed.

The defense lawyers, physically and financially exhausted, appealed to the State Bar of California for help in the appeal of the case. "We ask you to find top-notch appellate lawyers to participate in this case, which will undoubtedly be decided by the United States Supreme Court and which will have tremendous impact on the constitutional history of this country."

One former member of the Board of Governors of the State Bar, Augustin Donovan, quickly rose to the challenge. This outstanding California lawyer agreed to serve as defense counsel for Richmond and Connelly, the two newspapermen whose convictions involved not only freedom of expression and association, but also freedom of the press. Donovan refused to meet the defendants; he wanted to avoid all personal feelings about them and to conduct the appeal solely on constitutional grounds. He also refused any fee for his work, but asked that money be raised to pay a young lawyer or law student to assist him in the research. These conditions were accepted by the defendants, and Donovan handled the appeal with Ben Margolis, from the trial team, and Robert W. Kenny, a former Superior Court judge who had been defeated by Republican Earl Warren for Attorney General of California in 1948.

The appeal of the *Yates* case reached the United States Supreme Court in October 1956. (A separate appeal of Mrs. Yates's contempt convictions was still pending.) The membership of the Court had changed since the *Dennis* decision upholding both the Smith Act and the convictions of the Communist Party leaders in 1951.

The two dissenters in *Dennis*, Justices Black and Douglas, were both in agreement that the Smith Act convictions violated the First Amendment. Justice Clark had not participated in *Dennis*; he could in *Yates*. Justices Brennan and Whittaker took no part in *Yates*.

How do you think the other justices voted? Would any change their minds? Could they logically acquit the defendants in *Yates* while defendants charged with the same crime had been convicted in *Dennis*?

Justice Harlan wrote the opinion for the majority. Dealing first with the charge that the defendants conspired to organize the Communist Party in violation of the Smith Act, he accepted the defense argument that " 'organize' means to 'establish,' 'found,' or 'bring into existence,' and that in this sense the Communist Party was organized by 1945 at the latest." The indictment brought in 1951 was therefore too late—there was a three-year statute of limitations for prosecutions under the Smith Act, and this meant that the case had to be filed by 1948, three years after organization.

Moving to the question of jury instructions, Justice Harlan found that the trial judge had led the jury to believe that "illegal advocacy was made out simply by showing that what was said dealt with forcible overthrow and that it was uttered with a specific intent to accomplish that purpose." In other words, the judge had considered that "all such advocacy was punishable 'whether it is language of incitement or not.' "

"We are thus faced with the question," said Justice Harlan, "whether the Smith Act prohibits advocacy and teaching of forcible overthrow as an abstract principle, divorced from any effort to instigate action to that end, so long as such advocacy or teaching is engaged in with evil intent. We hold that it does not."

The Court examined Congress's intent in enacting the law, and concluded: "The legislative history of the Smith Act and related bills shows beyond all question that Congress was aware of the distinction . . . and that . . . the statute was aimed at the advocacy and teaching of concrete action for the forcible overthrow of the Government, and not of principles divorced from action."

The justices distinguished the *Dennis* case on the ground that the defendants there were found to be a group "attempting to indoctrinate its members and commit them to a course whereby they will strike when the leaders feel the circumstances permit." Advocacy of violence as a "principle of action," said Justice Harlan for the Court, "is not constitutionally protected when the group is of sufficient size and cohesiveness, is sufficiently oriented towards action, and other circumstances are such as reasonably to justify apprehension that action will occur.

"This is quite a different thing from the view of the District Court here that mere doctrinal justification of forcible overthrow, if engaged in with the intent to accomplish overthrow, is punishable *per se* under the Smith Act. That sort of advocacy, even though uttered with the hope that it may ultimately lead to violent revolution, is too remote from concrete action to be regarded as the kind of indoctrination preparatory to action which was condemned in *Dennis.*"

In other words, the Court did not overrule its decision in the *Dennis* case. The majority said the trial judge in *Yates* had given the jury the wrong statement of the law. He had said they could convict all of the defendants if they simply believed in violent overthrow, even if they did nothing whatever to bring it about. "We must regard the trial court's charge in this respect as furnishing wholly inadequate guidance to the jury on this central point in the case. We cannot allow a conviction to stand on such 'an equivocal direction to the jury on a basic issue.'"

After striking from the record evidence of "organizing," the Court examined the evidence that remained on the advocacy charge to determine whether some defendants were to be acquitted and others might just have their convictions reversed and be sent back for retrial. From the record of the case, it found, "a jury could justifiably conclude" that advocacy of the abstract doctrine of forcible overthrow "was one of the tenets of the Communist Party; and there was no dispute as to petitioners' active identification with Party affairs.

"But when it comes to Party advocacy or teaching in the sense of a call to forcible action at some future time we cannot but regard this record as strikingly deficient. At best this voluminous record shows but a half dozen or so scattered incidents which, even under the loosest standards, could be deemed to show such advocacy. Most of these were not connected with any of the petitioners, or occurred many years before the period covered by the indictment. We are unable to regard this sporadic showing as sufficient to justify viewing the Communist Party as the nexus [connection] between these petitioners and the conspiracy charged."

As to five of the defendants, the record did not show that any "of them has engaged in or been associated with any but what appear to have been wholly lawful activities, or has ever made a single remark or been present when someone else made a remark, which would tend to prove the charges against them." The others, the Court found, might be retried in light of the Supreme Court's present decision.

Justices Black and Douglas concurred in the acquittals and dissented from sending nine Communists back for new trials. (One had died in the interim.) "In my judgment," said Justice Black, "the statutory provisions on which these prosecutions are based abridge freedom of speech, press and assembly in violation of the First Amendment to the United States Constitution."

He elaborated: "The kind of trials conducted here are wholly dissimilar to normal criminal trials. Ordinarily these 'Smith Act' trials are prolonged affairs lasting for months. In part this is attributable to the routine introduction in evidence of massive collections of books, tracts, pamphlets, newspapers, and manifestoes discussing Communism, Socialism, Capitalism, Feudalism and governmental institutions in general, which, it is not too much to say, are turgid, diffuse, abstruse, and just plain dull. Of course, no juror can or is expected to plow his way through this jungle of verbiage. The testimony of witnesses is comparatively insignificant. Guilt or innocence may turn on what Marx or Engels or someone else wrote or advocated as much as a hundred or more years ago. Elaborate, refined distinctions are drawn between 'Communism,' 'Marxism,' 'Leninism,' 'Trotskyism,' and 'Stalinism.' When the propriety of obnoxious or unorthodox views about government is in reality made the crucial issue, as it must be in cases of this kind, prejudice makes conviction inevitable except in the rarest circumstances."

Justice Black disagreed with the notion that even advocacy that incites to action could be prohibited, and he rejected the idea that a constitutionally protected act, such as attending a public meeting, could be used to prove a conspiracy.

Justice Clark, on the other hand, found the evidence in the *Yates* case "showed guilt beyond a reasonable doubt," and saw no reason to acquit or retry any of the defendants. He dissented.

A few weeks later, the Court handed down a decision granting defendants the right to see all reports given by informer witnesses to the FBI (see *Jencks* v. *United States,* discussed in chapter 16). This decision, plus the *Yates* decision, led the government, in effect, to admit defeat. The complaints against the nine remaining defendants were dropped, and the government did not start any new Smith Act prosecutions.

In all, sixteen groups of defendants had been charged with being leaders of the Communist Party. Only 28 individuals served sentences; 107 were eventually acquitted or never tried, and 3 died during the proceedings.

Oleta Yates was sentenced to jail by the district court judge who had originally tried the case, on the eleven counts of contempt of court for refusing to testify about activities of other people, but she fought that sentence all the way to the United States Supreme Court. The Court (in the 1958 case entitled *Yates* v. *United States*) detailed the long history of attempts by the district court judge to jail Mrs. Yates and to deny bail in connection with the Smith Act prosecution and appeals. It held the contempt was a single offense, not eleven, and that the seven months Mrs. Yates had already served (because of denials of bail) during the course of the proceedings was sufficient punishment. She was finally free.

A fateful moment in the history of our country

Communist Party v. Subversive Activities Control Board (1961)

367 U.S. 1, 81 S. Ct. 1357, 6 L. Ed. 2d 625

In 1961, the Communist Party as an organization was again before the United States Supreme Court, battling the 1950 Internal Security Act. By then, the political climate in the country was different. There was widespread recognition that the McCarthy hysteria had hit many liberals and non-Communists, even including officers in the U.S. Army. There was also some recognition that the cold war had been based on lies about so-called atomic secrets and Soviet intentions, and that the period had prevented healthy discussion of the country's real problems.

The Party was again appealing from an order by the Subversive Activities Control Board (SACB) to register as a Communist-action organization. This case had been shuttling back and forth between the courts and the SACB since 1951. The Party and the government raised many questions for the Court to decide: Can Congress declare that a worldwide Communist conspiracy exists and that member organizations must register with the government? Or is such a declaration forbidden by the Constitution as a bill of attainder—that is, a law passed by Congress that names a specific person or group as being guilty of a crime? The Constitution separates the powers among Congress, the President, and the courts, and says that Congress can make it a crime to engage in certain kinds of activity, but Congress cannot declare that a particular person has engaged in such activity. Only a court can make that decision after taking evidence about that person's actions.

If organizations really are engaged in illegal, deceitful, and subversive activities, should they merely be asked to register? Wouldn't it be better to prosecute them for fraud, espionage, sabotage, or other criminal acts? Was the Communist Party a single-minded "organization numbering thousands of adherents, rigidly and ruthlessly disciplined," simply masquerading as a political party? Or was it a political organization with as much variation among its members as between Democratic Party leaders Julian Bond of Georgia and Mayor Richard Daley of Chicago? Did the Communist Party constitute such a clear and present danger to the sovereignty of the United States that its constitutional rights had to be severely abridged?

Justice Frankfurter, again writing for the 5½-to-3½ majority (Justice Brennan dissented in part), delivered one of the longest opinions in the history of the Court; it ran 112 pages. After tracing the McCarran Act and the present case in detail, the opinion held that the SACB had ruled correctly on testimony by certain witnesses and production of certain documents. The opinion then tackled the question of the Party's alleged foreign control and subversive objectives. The Court gave full weight to the SACB's findings, since the SACB had heard the evidence; the majority did not find that the Board had erred in its judgment. And the Court rejected the Party's arguments that the evidence of foreign control was stale (pre-1940, when the Party disaffiliated from the Communist International) and that the Board had an interest in ruling against the Party, since the Board's existence depended on such rulings.

It also quickly upheld the SACB's finding that the Party's objective was overthrow of the government—by force and violence if necessary. The Party had argued that this finding abridged its First Amendment freedom of speech since it had not incited illegal action, even assuming it had preached violent overthrow. Justice Frankfurter replied: "The Subversive Activities Control Act is a regulatory, not a prohibitory statute"—therefore it could not be prohibiting protected speech.

Having accepted these basic points, the Court majority had no trouble upholding the SACB's findings that the Party fulfilled all elements of the definition of a "Communist-action" organization. It rejected the Party's claim that the act was a bill of attainder, while agreeing that the Subversive Activities Control Act had been designed to reach the Communist Party's operations. "But whatever the source from which the legislative experience and instruction derived, the Act applies to a class of activity only, not to the Communist Party as such."

"Of course congressional power in this sphere, as in all spheres, is limited by the First Amendment," Justice Frankfurter declared. "Individual liberties fundamental to American institutions are not to be destroyed under the pretext of preserving those institutions, even from the gravest external dangers." But, he went on, since the act did not "prohibit individuals from organizing" a group whose goal was overthrow of the government but merely prescribed "the conditions under which such organization is permitted," the legislation "must be respected."

All arguments that registration was self-incrimination, that the penalties imposed on registered individuals were unconstitutional, and that registration had the effect of outlawing the Party and restraining people from associating with it, Justice Frankfurter said were "premature." They could be raised only after the Party and its members did register and actually suffered the consequences they anticipated.

Chief Justice Warren, dissenting, pointed out that the Court could have decided the case without reaching the question of the constitutionality of the Act. He found grounds for reversing the SACB order because the SACB found that the Party had subversive objectives although there was no evidence of incitement to action, and it found that the Party maintained secrecy for subversive purposes although there was no evidence about the purposes.

Chief Justice Warren also noted "that the vast bulk of the

evidence introduced by the Government at the hearing before the Board related to the Party's activities prior to its disaffiliation from the Communist International in 1940. In order to link this stale evidence to the Party's current activities, with which the Act is concerned, the Board indulged in a presumption of continuity, whereby it reasoned that since the Party was under Soviet control prior to 1940, and since the Party still adheres to the principles of Soviet Communism, it must be presumed that the Party is still controlled by the Soviet Union. The validity of such a presumption is certainly dubious. However, if the Board is to be permitted to rely upon this presumption, the least to which the Party is entitled is that the record be free from serious procedural errors and that the findings upon which the Board rests its order be supported by some evidence."

Justice Black also dissented: "I do not believe that it can be too often repeated that the freedoms of speech, press, petition and assembly guaranteed by the First Amendment must be accorded to the ideas we hate or sooner or later they will be denied to the ideas we cherish. The first banning of an association because it advocates hated ideas—whether that association be called a political party or not—marks a fateful moment in the history of a free country," he warned, as he had so often in the past. This time he added: "That moment seems to have arrived for this country."

In Justice Black's opinion, "the principle upon which Congress acted in passing the Subversive Activities Control Act is identical to that upon which it acted in making membership in the Communist Party a crime in the Smith Act," and he found that it "really amounts to nothing more than the idea that the Government must act as a paternal guardian to protect American voters from hearing public policies discussed." He harked back to the history of the 1798 Sedition

Act, which he called "one of the greatest blots on our country's record of freedom," and noted that even this long-repudiated act "did not go as far in suppressing the First Amendment freedoms of Americans as do the Smith Act and the Subversive Activities Control Act." The Jeffersonians had been persecuted, but the Federalists had not dared to outlaw their political party explicitly.

"When the practice of outlawing parties and various public groups begins," Justice Black cautioned, "no one can say where it will end. In most countries such a practice once begun ends with a one-party government. There is something of tragic irony in the fact that this Act, expressly designed to protect this Nation from becoming a 'totalitarian dictatorship' with 'a single political party,' has adopted to achieve its laudable purpose the policy of outlawing a party—a policy indispensable to totalitarian dictatorships. I think we should meet and decide this whole question now in the administration of a sound judicial policy that carries out our responsibilities both to Congress and to the American people."

Justice Black then tackled the First Amendment question of "whether Congress has power to outlaw an association, group or party either on the ground that it advocates a policy of violent overthrow of the existing government at some time in the distant future or on the ground that it is ideologically subservient to some foreign country. In my judgment, neither of these factors justifies an invasion of rights protected by the First Amendment.

"Talk about the desirability of revolution has a long and honorable history, not only in other parts of the world, but also in our own country. This kind of talk, like any other, can be used at the wrong time and for the wrong purpose. But, under our system of Government, the remedy for this danger must be the same remedy that is applied to the danger that comes from any other erroneous talk—education and contrary argument. If that remedy is not sufficient, the only meaning of free speech must be that the revolutionary ideas will be allowed to prevail.

"This conclusion is not affected by the fact that those advocating a policy of revolution are in sympathy with a foreign government. If there is one thing certain about the First Amendment it is that this Amendment was designed to guarantee the freest interchange of ideas about all public matters and that, of course, means the interchange of *all* ideas, however such ideas may be viewed in other countries and whatever change in the existing structure of government it may be hoped that these ideas will bring about. Now, when this country is trying to spread the high ideals of democracy all over the world—ideals that are revolutionary in many countries—seems to be a particularly inappropriate time to stifle First Amendment freedoms in this country. The same arguments that are used to justify the outlawry of Communist ideas here could be used to justify an outlawry of the ideas of democracy in other countries."

Justice Black concluded, "I believe with the Framers of the First Amendment that the internal security of a nation like ours does not and cannot be made to depend upon the use of force by Government to make all the beliefs and opinions of the people fit into a common mold on any single subject. Such enforced conformity of thought would tend only to deprive our people of the bold spirit of adventure and progress which has brought this Nation to its present greatness. The creation of public opinion by groups, organizations, societies, clubs, and parties, has been and is a necessary part of our democratic society." Of course, he explained, there is a difference between thought or opinion and *"actions of* violence and treason. The founders drew a distinction in our Constitution which we would be wise to follow. They gave the Government the fullest power to prosecute overt actions in violation of valid laws but withheld any power to punish people for nothing more than advocacy of their views."

Justices Douglas and Brennan, also dissenting, were primarily concerned that the registration provisions violated the Fifth Amendment privilege against self-incrimination. Since Congress had found and declared that the Communist Party was seeking the illegal overthrow of the United States government and was the agent of a hostile foreign power, any person who filled out the registration forms of the McCarran Act would be forced to incriminate himself as a member of the Party under the Smith Act. Douglas reminded the Court that "force and compulsion were outlawed techniques for federal law enforcement. Coerced confessions are taboo because of the long and bitter experience of minorities in trying to maintain their freedom under hostile regimes."

Later in 1961, the Supreme Court upheld the conviction of Junius Scales simply for membership in the Communist Party. By a five-to-four vote, in *Scales* v. *United States,* he was sent to jail for six years, as the Court upheld the constitutionality of the Smith Act provision making it a crime to be a "knowing member" of an organization that advocates the overthrow of the government by force and violence. However, in a similar membership case, *Noto* v. *United States,* the Court said the government had not produced sufficient evidence to prove that the Communist Party advocated violent overthrow. Scales was granted clemency by the President after two years, charges against eight other individual members were dropped, and the provision fell into disuse.

After these decisions, the Communist Party continued to

refuse to register with the Attorney General as a subversive organization, or to file lists of officers and members. The Attorney General then brought charges against individuals alleged to be members, and asked the SACB to order the individuals to register. The Board held hearings around the country, and invariably ordered the individuals to register.

The individuals then appealed the SACB orders, and four years later the Supreme Court had to face the question the majority had ducked as "premature" in 1961: Did the self-incrimination clause make the registration act unconstitutional? The Fifth Amendment explicitly provides that "[N]o person . . . shall be compelled . . . to be a witness against himself," that is, to give testimony that could lead to criminal charges against him, or to conviction. The McCarran Act, however, said a person had to register that he was a Communist Party member but he would be protected, or given "immunity," from prosecution. With this protection, the privilege against self-incrimination ceased, said the government, because the person could not be prosecuted, no matter what he answered. The Court had to decide whether the government was telling the whole story. Did the Act give complete protection and thus wipe out the privilege?

By 1965, the Court was united on this question; it held unanimously, in *Albertson* v. *Subversive Activities Control Board,* that the registration provision of the Act violated the Fifth Amendment. Justice Brennan, for the Court, said that registration compelled Communist Party members to answer questions "in an area permeated with criminal statutes" and that "response to any of the form's questions in context might involve the petitioners in the admission of a crucial element of a crime."

The Court found that the act's "purported immunity provision" was insufficient. The government argued that the

SACB had already ruled that these people were Party members when it ordered them to register, so the act of registering added nothing incriminatory that the government didn't already know. On the contrary, wrote Justice Brennan, the Court does not decide "whether a disclosure would be 'incriminatory' " by finding out how much of the information the government already possessed.

The Court asked a question: If the information was without value, why could a person be sent to jail for ten years for each day he refused to give the information? "The representation that the information demanded is of no utility is belied by the fact that the failure to make the disclosure is so severely sanctioned." To meet the Fifth Amendment requirements, an immunity provision "must provide 'complete protection from all the perils against which the constitutional prohibition was designed to guard.' "

Other sections of the McCarran Act also were attacked. The Supreme Court upheld the right of a Communist to hold elective office in a labor union (*Brown* v. *United States*), and declared that the McCarran Act provision prohibiting this was a bill of attainder (forbidden by Article I, Section 9, of the Constitution). A Party member won the right to work in a defense facility in *United States* v. *Robel.* The passport restrictions were thrown out in *Aptheker* v. *Rusk.*

So, the Supreme Court ultimately held that most of the McCarran Act's provisions could not be applied to individuals, although it has never ruled that the act itself is unconstitutional as to organizations. The act's provision for establishing "detention centers" for "undesirable" people in times of "emergency" was finally repealed by Congress in 1971, removing this threat of repression from the statute books. Congressmen have proposed abolition of the SACB, since Court decisions have abolished its functions.

B. The NAACP Cases

Southern segregationists felt about civil rights organizations the way McCarthyites felt about the Communist Party—these were vicious subversive organizations eating away the very roots of our American way of life; they must be dealt with ruthlessly and destroyed before they destroyed us. While they could not be outlawed directly, by name (that kind of legislation would, of course, be a bill of attainder), surely there were indirect ways of attacking and demolishing them.

Following the Supreme Court's decision in *Brown* v. *Board of Education* (see chapter 22), requiring desegregation of the nation's public schools, segregationist forces in the South took the offensive. Civil rights groups and their leaders were sued for libel (as in *New York Times Company* v. *Sullivan* —see chapter 3), investigated by state un-American activities committees and ordered to register as subversive organizations (as in *Dombrowski* v. *Pfister*—see page 161), and investigated for tax errors. Virginia, Arkansas, Florida, Georgia, Mississippi, South Carolina, and Tennessee amended their old statutes prohibiting lawyers from stirring up lawsuits to get business (called barratry). The new laws would also prohibit lawyers paid by organizations from representing clients without charge, as lawyers of the National Association for the Advancement of Colored People (NAACP) had done in the *Brown* case. The southern establishment realized that implementation of the 1955 *Brown* decision would require suits by Negro plaintiffs against school boards, and they knew the plaintiffs generally could not afford to go to court without NAACP lawyers and funds to pay litigation costs.

Compelled disclosure of membership

NAACP v. *Alabama* (1958)

357 U.S. 449, 78 S. Ct. 1163, 2 L. Ed. 2d 1488

Alabama went further than simply limiting the actions of the NAACP legal staff. In 1956, the Alabama attorney general brought suit to bar the whole organization from operating in the state. He charged that the association had failed to register as a foreign (out-of-state) corporation and that it had engaged in activities injurious to the property and civil rights of the citizens of Alabama.

The NAACP had been formed in 1909 and incorporated in 1911 as a nonprofit corporation with headquarters in New York City. But it had established more than one thousand branches as unincorporated affiliate associations throughout the country. The Alabama branch believed itself to be exempt from the foreign corporation statute. The attorney general, however, sued for an injunction prohibiting the organization from all further activities in the state because it had opened a regional office and several branches without qualifying as a foreign corporation. Other charges against the association were that it had helped Negro students to enter the University of Alabama, and had supported the Negro boycott of buses in Mongomery, Alabama, to end segregated seating (described in chapter 25).

On the day the complaint was filed in the county circuit court, the attorney general also obtained a temporary restraining order from the court, saying the NAACP could not do business in the state or attempt to qualify to do so, until the case had been decided. The NAACP replied that it was exempt and said the restraining order violated the guarantees of free speech and association, which applied to the states under the Fourteenth Amendment. Although the foreign corporation law itself required only routine information (name and address of the organization and of an agent to receive legal notices), the attorney general asked the court to order the NAACP to produce a number of documents, including financial statements and names and addresses of *all* Alabama "members" and "agents." The judge issued the order.

The NAACP completed the qualification forms but refused to produce the documents. The judge held the NAACP in contempt, and prescribed a fine of $10,000, specifying that the fine could be reduced or eliminated if the required documents were produced within five days, but if not it would be raised to $100,000.

After five days the NAACP produced all the documents except the membership lists, arguing that Alabama could not constitutionally force it to reveal its membership. But the circuit court judge confirmed the contempt citation and raised the fine to $100,000.

Under Alabama law, once a court has issued an order to do something and has issued a contempt citation for not doing that thing, the only way the defeated party can test whether the court order was constitutional is to comply with the order. In this case, the only way the NAACP could get an Alabama appellate court to rule on the validity of the trial court order to produce membership lists was to turn over the membership lists. And there was no way to continue to do any business legally in Alabama without turning over the lists.

The NAACP tried to get a stay of the contempt order from the Alabama courts so that it could go on operating in Alabama while the case was on appeal. The motion was denied and the NAACP proceeded to appeal the case up to the United States Supreme Court.

The Alabama attorney general contended that the organization had no standing to appeal the case—the members themselves had to press their claims. He also denied that the state was violating freedom of expression or association by merely enforcing state laws requiring registration. He said any action taken against someone for belonging to the NAACP would come from private individuals, not from the state. In other words, he argued that this case should be turned into a suit by an individual member of the NAACP against an individual private citizen who attacked him because of his NAACP membership (which the private citizen discovered because the state obtained the NAACP list).

Do you think membership in an organization is a form of expression? Is membership protected against action by the state government by the Fourteenth Amendment? Why did Alabama need to get the list of NAACP members? What state interest would this serve? Can a state interfere with freedom of expression when the state has a very strong interest in preventing that expression? For example, if an individual has an interest in keeping it a secret that he is a member of an organization and the state has an interest in finding out about his membership, whose interest should prevail?

Justice Harlan, writing for a unanimous Court, first dealt with the NAACP's standing to appeal the case. To require the members themselves to claim the right to conceal their membership "would result in nullification of the right at the very moment of its assertion," he said. Furthermore, the association had standing to pursue the case in its own interest, since "the Association itself through diminished financial support and membership may be adversely affected if production [of the membership lists] is compelled."

Then Justice Harlan proceeded to the questions of free speech and association. "It is beyond debate that freedom to engage in association for the advancement of beliefs and ideas is an inseparable aspect of the 'liberty' assured by the Due Process Clause of the Fourteenth Amendment," the Court asserted, and "abridgment of such rights, even though unintended, may inevitably follow from varied forms of governmental action." Justice Harlan listed many government regulations that the Court had struck down because they had the effect of curtailing constitutional liberties. "Compelled disclosure of affiliation with groups engaged in advocacy" may constitute just "as effective a restraint on freedom of association," he said.

"This Court has recognized the vital relationship between freedom to associate and privacy in one's associations," said the justices. The NAACP had "made an uncontroverted showing that on past occasions revelation of the identity of its rank-and-file members has exposed these members to economic reprisal, loss of employment, threat of physical coercion, and other manifestations of public hostility. Under these circumstances, we think it apparent that compelled disclosure of petitioner's Alabama membership is likely to affect adversely the ability of petitioner and its members to pursue their collective effort to foster beliefs which they admittedly have the right to advocate, in that it may induce members to withdraw from the Association and dissuade others from joining it because of fear of exposure of their beliefs shown through their associations and of the consequences of this exposure."

The state could not disclaim responsibility for possible reprisals taken by private individuals and companies, when "it is only after the initial exercise of state power represented by the production order that private action takes hold," Justice Harlan noted.

The Court accepted the argument that the state might override the constitutional protection, if it had sufficient justification, and next examined what the justification might be. The two issues in the suit to oust the NAACP from doing business in the state were "whether the character of petitioner and its activities in Alabama had been such as to make petitioner subject to the registration statute, and whether the extent of petitioner's activities without qualifying suggested its permanent ouster from the State." Although the Court could not consider the merits of these issues at this stage in the lawsuit, the justices said: "We are unable to perceive that the disclosure of the names of petitioner's rank-and-file members had a substantial bearing on either of them."

Summing up, the Court held "that the immunity from state scrutiny of membership lists which the Association claims on behalf of its members is here so related to the right of the members to pursue their lawful private interests privately and to associate freely with others in so doing as to come within the protection of the Fourteenth Amendment. And we conclude that Alabama has fallen short of showing a controlling justification for the deterrent effect on the free enjoyment of the right to associate which disclosure of membership lists is likely to have. Accordingly the judgment of civil contempt and the $100,000 fine which resulted from petitioner's refusal to comply with the production order in this respect must fall."

The Court sent part of the suit back to the state court. The Alabama trial court was told to hold a hearing on whether the NAACP should be restrained from conducting business in Alabama in the future, and its decision was "not [to be] inconsistent with this opinion."

When the United States Supreme Court tells a lower court

to do something, the lower court follows that order. The Supreme Court relies solely on the force of its constitutional authority, and the tradition of compliance with its decisions. The Court has no soldiers at its disposal to see that its orders are carried out, but only public disapproval of anyone who refuses to do so.

In this instance, the Supreme Court explicitly said the contempt order against the NAACP "must fall." The Alabama courts openly ignored this ruling, and proceeded to affirm the contempt judgment. Again the NAACP appealed to the U.S. Supreme Court. In the 1959 case entitled *NAACP* v. *Alabama*, the Court reversed the contempt and remanded the case a second time, telling the Alabama courts to get on with the hearing on the merits of the ouster suit.

Protection against harassment, humiliation, or exposure by government

Bates v. *City of Little Rock* (1960)
361 U.S. 516, 80 S. Ct. 412, 4 L. Ed. 2d 480

In Arkansas, another device was invented for discouraging civil rights activity by ferreting out NAACP membership lists. Cities were empowered by state law to levy a license tax on businesses, trades, professions, or vocations. Charitable organizations were exempt from the tax.

In the fall of 1957, Little Rock was facing the test of a school integration order that would pit Governor Faubus against President Eisenhower and arouse international comment. At that moment, the cities of Little Rock and North Little Rock amended their business license ordinances to require every organization in the city limits to furnish its official name, office address, officers and employees, a statement of how its funds were spent, and all dues and contributions received and from whom—in effect, the membership list. The purpose was ostensibly to learn whether the organization was subject to the business license tax. The information would be "subject to the inspection of any interested party at all reasonable business hours." These laws were passed by many cities and became known as "Bennett ordinances" because Arkansas Attorney General Bruce Bennett had been instrumental in devising them.

Daisy Bates was Arkansas president of the NAACP and custodian of records for the Little Rock branch. She had been a key force in helping nine Negro students to attend Little Rock's Central High School for the first time that fall, despite violence by segregationists. Now, faced with the Bennett ordinances, she and Mrs. Williams, president of the North Little Rock NAACP, submitted the requested information, except for the lists of members. "We base this refusal on the anti-NAACP climate in this state," because "public disclosure of the names of our members and contributors might lead to their harassment, economic reprisals, and even bodily harm," Mrs. Williams wrote. She said their members had the constitutional right to participate in the organization's work anonymously.

Mrs. Williams and Mrs. Bates were arrested and tried for refusing to furnish the lists. At the trial, Mrs. Bates testified that enactment of the amended ordinances had already intimidated people: "For the past five years I have been collecting, I guess 150 to 200 members each year—just renewals of the same people. This year, I guess I lost 100 or 150 of those same members," she said. The people told her, "Well, we will wait and see what happens in the Bennett Ordinance."

Mrs. Williams had been known in her community as an

NAACP leader for years. She testified, "We were not able to rest at night or day for quite a while. We had to have our phone number changed because they call that day and night." Harassment was coupled with violence and threats: "They have throwed stones at my home. . . . I received a letter threatening my life and they threaten my life over the telephone. That is the way."

Mrs. Bates and Mrs. Williams were convicted and fined. They appealed to the Arkansas Supreme Court, which upheld the convictions: compulsory disclosure of the lists was not an abridgment of constitutional rights but a "a mere incident to a permissible legal result." The women sought review by the United States Supreme Court.

Each attorney usually has one hour to argue his case to the Court. The justices can interrupt him with questions and they may vote against his client if they aren't satisfied with his answers. In his oral argument, the attorney for Little Rock could not name any activity of the NAACP that might be subject to the city's license tax. North Little Rock did not send an attorney to argue on appeal.

The Court again faced the issue of whether NAACP membership lists could be demanded for a compelling governmental reason or for any reason. The justices had already established that forced disclosure of these lists violated freedom of association, unless there was an overriding necessity. Should they go further here and declare that the right to remain anonymous is absolute?

Justice Stewart, writing for the unanimous Court, asserted that freedom of speech and association was "protected not only against heavy-handed frontal attack, but also from being stifled by more subtle governmental interference," and "compelled disclosure of affiliation with groups engaged in advocacy" can be one kind of subtle interference.

Sticking to its position in the first *NAACP* v. *Alabama* case, the Court said, "Where there is a significant encroachment upon personal liberty, the State may prevail only upon showing a subordinating interest which is compelling." Justice Stewart, for the Court, then examined what the cities' interest had been in demanding the membership lists. He agreed that "no power is more basic to the ultimate purpose and function of government than is the power to tax," and "the proper and efficient exercise of this essential governmental power may sometimes entail the possibility of encroachment upon individual freedom." But "in this record we can find no relevant correlation between the power of the municipalities to impose occupation license taxes and the compulsory disclosure and publication of the membership lists of the local branches of the National Association for the Advancement of Colored People."

"The petitioners cannot be punished for refusing to produce information which the municipalities could not constitutionally require," the Court concluded, and reversed their convictions.

In concurring, Justices Black and Douglas made a flat assertion: "First Amendment rights are beyond abridgment either by legislation that directly restrains their exercise or by suppression or impairment through harassment, humiliation, or exposure by government. One of those rights, freedom of assembly, includes of course freedom of association; and it is entitled to no less protection than any other First Amendment right." Once again, justices used a double negative to state a positive: Freedom of association is a basic First Amendment right that will be enforced.

Manifestly untenable charges

NAACP v. *Alabama* (1964)
377 U.S. 288, 84 S. Ct. 1302, 12 L. Ed. 2d 325

In October 1961, the case of *NAACP* v. *Alabama* came to the Supreme Court for the third time. In 1959, the Supreme Court had for the second time reversed the contempt judgment and sent the rest of the suit back to the state courts, for decision on whether to oust the organization from the state.

A year passed with no progress in the suit in Alabama courts. The state's "temporary" restraining order still barred the NAACP from all activities while the litigation was pending. Obviously the Alabama attorney general had nothing to gain by bringing the case to a decision.

In 1960, the NAACP went to the federal district court for relief. NAACP officers said they could not operate in Alabama until the state court moved, and it refused to move, so the federal court should stop the state from enforcing its restraining order. The district court dismissed the NAACP petition. The NAACP appealed. The federal court of appeals told the district court to hold onto jurisdiction of the case, but to let the Alabama state courts decide the merits of the ouster suit. The NAACP appealed this ruling to the U.S. Supreme Court, which ruled in October 1961 that unless the Alabama courts had heard the ouster case by January 2, 1962, the federal district court was to hear it (*NAACP* v. *Gallion*).

In December 1961, the Circuit Court of Montgomery County finally heard the evidence against the NAACP. The state's complaint, as amended over the five years since the ouster suit was filed, now raised eleven charges against the NAACP:

(1) that it had "employed or otherwise paid money" to

Autherine Lucy and Polly Meyers Hudson to encourage them to enroll as students in the University of Alabama in order to test the legality of the university policy against admitting Negroes;

(2) that it had furnished lawyers for Autherine Lucy in her suit to obtain admission to the university;

(3) that it had "engaged in organizing, supporting and financing an illegal boycott" to compel a bus line in Montgomery, Alabama, not to segregate passengers according to race (see chapter 25);

(4) that it had "falsely charged" state and university officials with acts in violation of state and federal law;

(5) that it had "falsely charged" the attorney general of Alabama and the Alabama courts with "arbitrary, vindictive, and collusive" acts intended to prevent the NAACP from contesting its ouster "before an impartial judicial forum," and had "falsely charged" the state courts with deliberately denying it a hearing on the merits of its ouster;

(6) that it had "falsely charged" the state and its attorney general with filing contempt proceedings against it, knowing the contempt charges to be false;

(7) that it had "willfully violated" the order restraining it from carrying on activities in the state;

(8) that it had attempted to "pressure" the mayor of Philadelphia, the Governor of Pennsylvania, and the Penn State football team into "a boycott of the Alabama football team" when the two teams were to play each other in the Liberty Bowl;

(9) that it had "encouraged, aided, and abetted the unlawful breach of the peace in many cities in Alabama for the purpose of gaining national notoriety and attention to enable it to raise funds under a false claim that it is for the protection of alleged constitutional rights";

(10) that it had "encouraged, aided, and abetted a course of conduct within the State of Alabama, seeking to deny to the citizens of Alabama the constitutional right to voluntarily segregate"; and

(11) that it had "carried on its activities in Alabama without complying with state laws requiring foreign corporations to register and perform other acts in order to do business within the State."

The judge heard the testimony and handed down his decision on December 29, just four days before the Supreme Court's deadline. He found that NAACP activities "have been a usurpation and abuse of its corporate functions and detrimental to the State of Alabama," and he made the five-year-old "temporary" restraining order a permanent order, ousting the organization from the state.

The Alabama Supreme Court affirmed the judgment, relying solely on a technical error in the NAACP's appeal papers. The NAACP then sought review for the fourth time by the U.S. Supreme Court. This time the Court could deal with the merits of the eleven charges in the case because the state court had heard evidence on them.

If the eleven charges were all true, should the Supreme Court affirm the ouster of the NAACP from Alabama? Does a state have the right to prevent a voluntary association from carrying on such activities?

Justice Harlan, writing for a unanimous Court once again, dealt first with the final allegation, concerning registration by foreign corporations. Even if the allegation were true, he said, it did not constitute grounds for the association's ouster from the state. Indeed, Alabama law supplied an entirely different remedy for failure to comply with the state's corporate registration requirements—a fine of $1,000. Alabama had not cited a single prior case "in which a foreign corporation was ousted from Alabama for failing to comply with the registration statute."

Justice Harlan then knocked down the other ten charges. The first two were "manifestly untenable." Since the Supreme Court, in *Lucy* v. *Adams,* upheld the rights of Autherine Lucy and Polly Anne Meyers to enroll at the University of Alabama as early as 1955 (even before the ouster suit was first filed), the NAACP's efforts in their behalf could not be used against it.

The third charge was "scarcely more substantial," he wrote. "Even if we were to indulge the doubtful assumption that an organized refusal to ride on Montgomery's buses in protest against a policy of racial segregation might, without more, in some circumstances violate a valid state law, such a violation could not constitutionally be the basis for a permanent denial of the right to associate for the advocacy of ideas by lawful means."

The fourth, fifth, sixth, and seventh charges furnished "no basis for the restriction of the right of the petitioner's members to associate in Alabama," even if the charges were true. As to the eighth charge, "by no stretch can it be considered germane to the present controversy," said Justice Harlan. The Court also dismissed the ninth charge because the state had appropriate remedies for the alleged breaches of the peace without resorting to so sweeping an action as the ouster of the organization. The tenth charge Justice Harlan said was simply a challenge to "the right of petitioner and its members to express their views, by words and lawful conduct, on a subject of vital constitutional concern. Such a challenge cannot stand."

Justice Harlan stated explicitly the distinction that required the Court to rule for the NAACP: the case involved "not the privilege of a corporation to do business in a State, but rather the freedom of individuals to associate for the collective advocacy of ideas." The state court's decision was reversed.

The NAACP had asked the Supreme Court to formulate a decree for the state courts to enter, not trusting the state courts to act properly even now. Although, Justice Harlan said, "we prefer to follow our usual practice and remand the case" to the state supreme court, he specified that the Alabama court was to enter "a decree, in accordance with state procedures, vacating in all respects the permanent injunction order issued by the Circuit Court of Montgomery County, Alabama, and permitting the Association to take all steps necessary to qualify it to do business in Alabama. Should we unhappily be mistaken in our belief that the Supreme Court of Alabama will promptly implement this decision, leave is given the Association to apply to this Court for further appropriate relief."

Alabama finally conceded the defeat, and the NAACP officially reactivated its Alabama branches in the fall of 1964. By this time, of course, another organization, the Southern Christian Leadership Conference, had built a following in Alabama, and its leader, Reverend Martin Luther King, had become famous. He and his group did not escape the wrath of segregationist forces either. (See *New York Times* v. *Sullivan,* discussed in chapter 3, and the transportation cases discussed in chapter 25.) The vacuum created by the strategy of the southern establishment had been filled by an active new group, and the NAACP had never completely stopped functioning there, despite the court order.

Litigation as a form of political expression

NAACP v. Button (1963)
371 U.S. 415, 83 S. Ct. 328, 9 L. Ed. 2d 405

One of the NAACP's chief activities has been to provide a legal staff to represent Negro people in litigation of their constitutional rights. The NAACP limits the kinds of cases its attorneys undertake. They do not handle ordinary suits to collect money damages for personal injuries (as a result of auto accidents, for example); they do not represent Negroes charged with crimes where there is no question of racial discrimination, and they do not sue to get equal treatment in separate facilities, but only to desegregate such facilities.

NAACP support of a case means that the association pays the costs of suit and the lawyer's salary for the days he spends working on the case. The client pays the lawyer nothing. It is well recognized that the NAACP fees are less than a lawyer would get for handling similar cases in private practice.

A person does not have to be a member of the NAACP to get help from the legal staff. Any Negro may apply for assistance, and his case will be considered. The client in effect retains not a single lawyer but the "firm" of the NAACP legal staff—a firm skilled in representing clients with legal difficulties involving racial discrimination. After assignment to the case, however, the staff lawyer is in complete charge as long as his conduct of the case is consistent with NAACP policy. The client, of course, is free to withdraw at any time.

In 1956, Virginia enacted a series of laws broadening its barratry statutes (prohibiting lawyers from stirring up law business) and related criminal laws to apply to activities like those of the NAACP and its legal staff. This time, the NAACP did not wait to be prosecuted. It brought suit in federal district court against Virginia Attorney General Robert Button and others, to restrain them from applying the acts to the NAACP on the ground that such an application of state law would violate the First Amendment guarantees of free expression and association and equal protection, carried into the Fourteenth Amendment to protect against state action. This constitutional challenge was heard by a three-judge district court, which struck down three of the laws as unconstitutional, but declined to pass on two others until they had been interpreted by the state courts.

The NAACP then went back to the Virginia courts. The Richmond Circuit Court held that the two laws were both constitutional and applicable to the NAACP. The association appealed the ruling to the Virginia Supreme Court, which found one of the laws unconstitutional but upheld the other. This was Chapter 33, making it a crime for a nonlawyer to solicit business for a lawyer (a practice called "running" or "capping"). As newly drawn, the statute defined as a runner or capper any agent for any organization that compensates any attorney in connection with any case in which the *organization* does not have a claim for money.

The state argued that the NAACP violated Chapter 33, by sending letters urging "active steps to fight segregation," distributing petitions for desegregation, and instructing branch officials to obtain clients for possible litigation. The NAACP contended that Chapter 33 was aimed directly at prohibiting its activities; indeed, although running and capping provisions had existed since 1849, until 1956 no attempt had been made to apply them to the NAACP. The association also argued that in all cases the clients had been free to make up their own minds about whether to become plaintiffs in a lawsuit, and the suits were not solicited to make money for the NAACP.

The Virginia Supreme Court held that the NAACP and the

NAACP Legal Defense Fund were "fomenting and soliciting legal business in which they are not parties and have no pecuniary right or liability, and which they channel to the enrichment of certain lawyers employed by them, at no cost to the litigants and over which the litigants have no control."

The NAACP sought review by the United States Supreme Court. It was clear that the association did encourage people to become plaintiffs who otherwise might never have gone to court, and this resulted in more civil rights litigation.

Was it unconstitutional for the association to encourage these litigants? Is it unethical? Statutes and legal canons of ethics had forbidden running and capping for lawyers for centuries. Is civil rights litigation different from litigation concerning property rights or money damages? If so, how? Could the NAACP's suits be classified as a form of expression protected by the First and Fourteenth Amendments?

Justice Brennan wrote the majority opinion for a divided court (5½-to-3½, with Justice White concurring in part and dissenting in part).

The Court quickly ruled that it had jurisdiction to hear the case and the NAACP had standing to sue. Justice Brennan's opinion then turned to the constitutional issues.

Virginia had argued that solicitation of business was not a protected right and that was all that was involved. "To this contention there are two answers," wrote Justice Brennan. "The first is that a State cannot foreclose the exercise of constitutional rights by mere labels. The second is that abstract discussion is not the only species of communication which the Constitution protects; the First Amendment also protects vigorous advocacy"—particularly when it is advocacy "of lawful ends."

The NAACP filed litigation to correct the unequal, unconstitutional treatment of Negroes, the Court noted, not to resolve private differences. "It is thus a form of political expression." Getting right to the root of the problem, the Court explained that "under the conditions of modern government, litigation may well be the sole practicable avenue open to a minority to petition for redress of grievances." Since, at this point, blacks had little economic power and little power in the major political parties, the justices saw that, "for such a group, association for litigation may be the most effective form of political association."

The state argued that it had an overriding interest to ensure high standards of legal professional conduct. However, said Justice Brennan, "regulations which reflect hostility to stirring up litigation have been aimed chiefly at those who urge recourse to the courts for private gain, serving no public interest."

When people "resort to the courts to seek vindication of constitutional rights," that "is a different matter from the oppressive, malicious, or avaricious use of the legal process for purely private gain. Lawsuits attacking racial discrimination, at least in Virginia, are neither very profitable nor very popular." Virginia lawyers could scarcely be accused of competing for these cases. "There has been neither claim nor proof that any assisted Negro litigants have desired, but have been prevented from retaining, the services of other counsel.

"We realize that an NAACP lawyer must derive personal satisfaction from participation in litigation on behalf of Negro rights, else he would hardly be inclined to participate at the risk of financial sacrifice. But this would not seem to be the kind of interest or motive which induces criminal conduct," the Court noted. Statutes against solicitation of business are designed to prevent situations in which lawyers feel they must serve two masters whose interests differ. But the state showed no evidence "of a serious danger here of . . . conflicts of interest" between the lawyer's duty to his client and his duty to the NAACP.

"Because First Amendment freedoms need breathing space to survive, government may regulate in the area only with narrow specificity," the Court ruled. Instead, the Virginia Supreme Court had construed the running and capping statute to give it "so broad and uncertain a meaning" that anyone who referred a client to the NAACP and then "had any connection with any litigation supported with NAACP funds" risked arrest. The Court's opinion concluded that "nothing in this record justifies the breadth and vagueness of the Virginia Supreme Court of Appeals' decree."

Justice Douglas, concurring, cited the finding of a lower court that the Virginia statutes had been enacted "as parts of the general plan of massive resistance to the integration of the schools of the state" under the *Brown* decision. "The fact that the contrivance used is subtle and indirect" does not make it less discriminatory and invalid, said Justice Douglas.

Justice White's partial dissent expressed concern that the majority opinion might invalidate a narrowly drawn statute prohibiting laymen from controlling legal actions to which they were not parties, as well as the broadly sweeping Virginia act.

Justice Harlan, joined by Justices Clark and Stewart, dissented. He found that the NAACP did solicit business for its lawyers; that litigation, while valid, was not a form of speech but rather *action;* and that there was a possibility that clients and the NAACP might disagree on tactics—in which case the lawyer would be caught in a conflict of interest between two duties: his duty to his individual client and his duty to his organizational employer.

Justice Harlan also argued that the NAACP's lack of financial gain or malicious motives in soliciting lawsuits did not make its actions valid. He explained that a number of state courts had prohibited unions from supplying lawyers to members with personal injury lawsuits, even though the motive was to prevent members from being "rooked" by private lawyers. (An appeal from one of these state court decisions reached the U.S. Supreme Court soon after—see *United Mine Workers* v. *Illinois State Bar,* discussed next.)

Justice Harlan believed that the First Amendment permitted the Court to balance the interests of a state against the interests of individuals and groups in order to decide cases like this. Balancing state interests in regulating legal conduct against the possible impairment of NAACP activities, he felt that the organization would not be seriously hampered by the statute. It could continue to refer clients to lawyers, as long as the lawyers were not subject to its control. He did not find the act ambiguous, and if the majority of the Court found parts of the act ambiguous, they should strike only those parts, he said.

The right to hire attorneys

United Mine Workers v. *Illinois State Bar* (1967)
389 U.S. 217, 88 S. Ct. 353, 19 L. Ed. 2d 426

The unions that were finding lawyers to represent their members did not miss the lesson of *NAACP* v. *Button.* Within a year of the decision, the case of the *Brotherhood of Railroad Trainmen* v. *Virginia* came before the United States Supreme Court. The trainmen's union had established a Department of Legal Counsel, which for many years had been referring members to lawyers it considered honest and competent to handle claims of union members injured or killed on the job. The Virginia State Bar sued to enjoin the railroad union from "solicitation of legal business and the unauthorized practice of law" for furnishing these lawyers. The Court vacated the injunction by a six-to-two majority in an opinion by Justice Black. The Court held that the union members had a right to associate, under the First and Fourteenth Amendments, and that this included the right to assist and advise each other about lawyers, among other matters.

Justice Clark dissented. He warned that the Court's decision "will be a green light to other groups who for years have attempted to engage in similar practices." One of these was the United Mine Workers union.

Illinois enacted workmen's compensation statutes in 1911 so that workers injured on the job could get money from their employers to cover medical expenses and wages lost. The union soon found that workers going to private attorneys with their claims were sometimes overcharged, and sometimes the lawyer sold out his own client by agreeing to accept a lower payment from the company than was reasonable. In order to ensure fair treatment of its members, the union established a legal department to handle workers' compensation cases.

The union employed one attorney on an annual salary, with the stipulation that his duty was to the clients he represented, not to the organization. An injured worker would receive a report form from the union, which he could fill out and submit to the union's legal department. The client was entitled to employ an outside attorney, and the union attorney frequently suggested this. If a worker did so, the union attorney immediately turned over his files to the new attorney.

If the client decided to retain the union's attorney, the union's legal department would file the claim for him and the attorney would begin negotiations with the coal company lawyer, usually without further discussion with the client. If the two lawyers reached a settlement, however, the client had the final decision to accept or reject it. The union attorney took the claim before the workmen's compensation board if no settlement was reached. The client was paid the full amount of any settlement or award.

After fifty years, the Illinois State Bar Association sued the union for unauthorized practice of law. The Illinois Circuit Court enjoined the union from carrying on its activities with respect to workmen's compensation cases, and the Illinois Supreme Court affirmed the injunction. The union claimed that its members "had a right, protected by the First and Fourteenth Amendments, to join together and assist one another in the assertion of their legal rights by collectively hiring an attorney to handle their claims." The court disagreed, and distinguished the opinion in *Brotherhood of Railroad Trainmen* v. *Virginia,* because the trainmen's union merely recommended lawyers; it did not hire them. And the ruling in *NAACP* v. *Button* was not applicable because it dealt with litigation as a form of political expression.

Do you see a basic difference between the Supreme Court's decisions in the NAACP case and the railroad workers case? If an organization exercises its right to freedom of association by hiring a lawyer to help its members get equal treatment, what happens when the lawyer helps the members by getting them money in workmen's compensation benefits? Is that a different situation entirely?

In delivering the eight-to-one majority opinion, Justice Black declared, "We do not think our decisions in *Trainmen* and *Button* can be so narrowly limited" as the Illinois Court said. Drawing parallels between the principles of the three cases, Black said that in *Button* "we held that dangers of baseless litigation and conflicting interests between the association and individual litigants were far too speculative to justify the broad remedy invoked by the State." In the *Trainmen* case, the "very distant possibility" that a conflict of interest between the union and a member would divide the loyalty of the attorney "could not justify a complete prohibition of the Trainmen's efforts to aid one another in assuring that each injured member would be justly compensated for his injuries."

The Court concluded: "We hold that the freedom of speech, assembly, and petition guaranteed by the First and Fourteenth Amendments gives petitioner the right to hire attorneys on a salary basis to assist its members in the assertion of their legal rights."

Justice Harlan dissented for the reasons he had raised in *NAACP* v. *Button*.

By the time Earl Warren resigned as Chief Justice in 1969, more and more lawyers and would-be clients had realized that only the wealthy and the very poor could get adequate legal services—the former from private lawyers paid forty to one hundred dollars an hour, the latter from government-sponsored OEO legal service programs. When the executive branch threatened to dismantle this program and to clip its wings and its budget, clients suddenly realized how much law affects the ordinary person's life today. They knew they needed the help of a lawyer to fill out many government forms and to protect themselves against many large institutions (see chapter 28). They lobbied and demonstrated for a continuation of this limited kind of legal service program, while unions, cooperative societies, and even bar associations proposed other forms of group legal services, building on the pioneering work of the mine workers and railroad trainmen.

Thus, the segregationist attacks on the NAACP to prevent integration of the schools led to Supreme Court decisions on other legal questions that helped both whites and Negroes, northerners and southerners, trade unionists and lawyers. Some critics believe these attacks on the NAACP also forced that organization to revitalize its approach and helped in the creation of another viable civil rights association, the Southern Christian Leadership Conference.

C. The Chilling Effect

Irreparable injury

Dombrowski v. *Pfister* (1965)
380 U.S. 479, 85 S. Ct. 1116, 14 L. Ed. 2d 22

Attorney Benjamin Smith surveyed the scene with considerable satisfaction. The conference seemed to be going very much as planned, and he was delighted at the attendance.

For years he had been traveling to lawyers' conferences in the North and Middle West, but he had never been able to invite his colleagues to his home state of Louisiana until now.

Smith had been an assistant district attorney of New Orleans for several years and then had entered private practice to become one of the rare southern white attorneys handling civil rights cases. The minute he won a series of suits desegregating New Orleans motels, he reserved space in one of them for the first integrated conference of lawyers to be held in Louisiana in the twentieth century (and perhaps the first altogether). It was October 1963, and black and white lawyers from Louisiana and across the country were meeting for two days to discuss the best techniques for handling personal injury litigation (mostly automobile accident suits) and civil rights cases in a National Lawyers Guild conference.

The atmosphere was relaxed. Many delegates and their families had already integrated the motel's swimming pool. The president of the State Bar had indicated he might drop by during the conference, and Smith hoped he would.

Suddenly several policemen strode into the conference room and arrested Smith and his partner Bruce Waltzer. They hauled the two lawyers off to jail, where they found one of their clients, Dr. James A. Dombrowski, director of the Southern Conference Educational Fund, which Smith served as treasurer and Waltzer as an attorney. The organization had worked for many years, mostly among southern whites, combatting racism and white supremacy and encouraging whites and blacks to join forces in fighting for better economic and social conditions. In the past few years the Fund had been very active in support of the southern civil rights movement.

The three men were told that the charge against them was failure to register under two Louisiana subversive activities control laws. These acts required members of any group that was labeled a "communist action organization, communist controlled organization, communist front organization, or communist infiltrated organization" by the attorney general, the Subversive Activities Control Board, or any congressional committee, to register with the Louisiana Un-American Activities Committee.

James H. Pfister, chairman of the Louisiana committee, told the press that the Smith, Waltzer, and Dombrowski arrests were made because of "racial agitation."

The three wives came down to the jail with more bad news: Police at gunpoint had ransacked their offices and homes and had taken every single item from the SCEF office—typewriters, filing cabinets, files, membership lists, correspondence, and even a copy of Thoreau's *Journal*.

Although all three had stable ties to the community, several judges said informally that they would refuse to set bail. Finally, late that evening, the men secured their release. Undaunted, they returned to the lawyers' conference. Of course, the legal issues presented by these arrests caught the attention of the conference, and attorneys there immediately began debating what, if anything, should be done.

Some, of course, advised caution: "Wait and see what the prosecutor does next." Many others argued that unless the attorneys filed suit in federal court for a declaration that the laws were unconstitutional, they would never undo the harm they would suffer from a long criminal prosecution, almost certain conviction, and costly appeals. They would lose clients because of the state court convictions, and their right of association with the Southern Conference Educational Fund would be illegally abridged for years. "This is an open and shut case," they said. "You must take the offensive and ask the federal court to step in. Get the court to order the state to stop the criminal prosecution, return the files and other property taken, and pay you damages for false arrest and illegal seizure of records."

The three defendants followed this approach and, within a short time, filed five lawsuits. The most important case, filed in federal court, argued that the Louisiana statutes were unconstitutional on their face—that is, there could be no doubt that these laws violated the First and Fourteenth Amendment guarantees of freedom of expression and association. The specific right to sue for protection of these freedoms is spelled out in the Civil Rights Act of 1871, passed by Congress in the Reconstruction period to protect black

October 5, 1963: Dr. James A. Dombrowski is released on bail after being charged with failure to register as a "subversive."
Credit: Wide World Photos

citizens after the Civil War (see chapters 12, 24, and 25); it can be found today in 42 U.S.C. §1983.

The problems of the two lawyers were not unique: several black southern civil rights lawyers at that point faced contempt citations or close scrutiny of their tax returns following the filing of desegregation suits. And their lawsuit was not unique, but it certainly was not typical. Usually a person charged with a crime in a state court must be tried, be convicted, and appeal through the state procedures before he can get the United States Supreme Court to give a definitive ruling on his claim that the state statute is unconstitutional under the federal Constitution. State courts must consider claims under the federal Constitution, but they have a natural tendency to uphold state statutes and are somewhat less familiar with federal law. In this case, the defendants were trying to bypass the state trial altogether, by starting out in federal court with their federal claim that the state statute was unconstitutional.

The State of Louisiana contended that the usual rule should apply in this case, particularly since the statutes being attacked "concerned the State's 'basic right of self-preservation'" from "sedition or treason or acts designed to substitute a different form of local government by other than lawful means." Federal interference in this area "would be a massive emasculation of the last vestige of the dignity of sovereignty," said the state's attorney.

When someone challenges the constitutionality of a state statute in federal court, the case is heard by three judges, rather than one. Here the judges split two to one, ruling against Dombrowski, Smith, and Waltzer. In such cases, the loser can appeal immediately to the United States Supreme Court, and the three did so.

Although the criminal prosecutions against them had

never been carried forward, the threat of these prosecutions still hung over the men, and SCEF, of course, had been almost paralyzed by the seizure of all its documents, lists, and equipment, and resulting lack of donations.

Do you think the appellants really had to bypass the state criminal trial in order to receive justice? Did they have the right to do this? Or should they have followed the regular procedures? Would that have done them irreparable harm? Do you think the Louisiana laws were clearly unconstitutional?

In April 1965 (a year and a half after the arrests), the United States Supreme Court decided the case, five to two (Justices Black and Stewart took no part in the decision). Justice Brennan wrote the majority opinion. The Court had no trial record before it, because there had been no trial. All it had was the complaint, answer, sworn affidavits by the parties, briefs, and the two opinions by the three-judge federal court.

The appellants, Smith, Waltzer, and Dombrowski, alleged that the arrests, the seizures of their property, and the threats of prosecution had been used merely "to harass" and "discourage them and their supporters from asserting and attempting to vindicate the constitutional rights of Negro citizens of Louisiana." Chairman Pfister and the police had never expected to make the charges stick, they contended.

Brennan's opinion responded that the Supreme Court had to assume that state courts would act constitutionally and in good faith; "the mere possibility" that they would make a wrong decision about a constitutional question "will usually not amount to the irreparable injury necessary to justify a disruption of orderly state proceedings," it said.

"But," the opinion went on, "the allegations in this complaint depict a situation in which . . . a substantial loss or impairment of freedoms of expression will occur if appellants must await the state court's disposition and ultimate review in this Court of any adverse determination. These allegations, if true, clearly show the irreparable injury."

Any "criminal prosecution under a statute regulating expression" has a tendency to "inhibit the full exercise of First Amendment freedoms," the Court explained. "When the statutes also have an overbroad sweep, as is here alleged, the hazard of loss or substantial impairment of those precious rights may be critical." Broad statutes regulating speech, press, and other forms of expression "lend themselves too readily to denial of those rights." When a denial occurs, it cannot be assumed that a person will regain his rights adequately by simply defending himself in a state court criminal prosecution.

If that assumption were made, said the Court, freedom of expression "would have to be hammered out case by case— and tested only by those hardy enough to risk criminal prosecution to determine the proper scope of regulation." It was no answer to say that an improper prosecution probably would not succeed and therefore would not harm the person prosecuted: "The chilling effect upon the exercise of First Amendment rights may derive from the fact of the prosecution, unaffected by the prospects of its success or failure," said Justice Brennan, coining a phrase that has become the most famous of his career. The idea that an action by government can have a "chilling effect" on people engaging in political action was so apt that the phrase quickly became part of the arsenal of the constitutional lawyer.

The Court next disposed of the argument that federal courts should abstain from deciding this case until the state courts interpreted the statutes, since the state courts might hold that the statutes did not apply to SCEF or were unconstitutional as applied to SCEF. "We hold the abstention doctrine is inappropriate for cases such as the present one. . . . The interpretation ultimately put on the statutes by the state courts is irrelevant. For an interpretation rendering the statute inapplicable to SCEF would merely mean that appellants might ultimately prevail in the state courts." It would not stop the state from using the statutes unconstitutionally and in bad faith to harass and inhibit others, as the petitioners alleged. "We believe that those affected by a statute are entitled to be free of the burdens of defending prosecutions, however expeditious, aimed at hammering out the structure of the statute piecemeal, with no likelihood of obviating similar uncertainty for others," said the Court.

It then tackled the question of constitutionality of the statutes on their face, and found they were "unduly vague, uncertain and broad," they denied due process, and they "cast an impermissible burden upon the appellants to show that the organizations were not Communist fronts." In free speech cases, the government must "bear the burden of persuasion to show that the appellants engaged in criminal speech." The Court held the Louisiana statutes were unconstitutional.

Justice Harlan, dissenting, argued that the Supreme Court should have abstained from interfering in the state court's business until the Louisiana courts had actually ruled erroneously. It would be possible to apply the statutes constitutionally to persons engaged in "what might be called 'hardcore' conduct" by reading the statutes narrowly. "For all we know," said Justice Harlan, "appellants' conduct in fact would fall within even the narrowest reading of the

Louisiana Subversive Activities and Communist Control Law, but since appellants were able to reach a federal court before the state instituted criminal proceedings against them, they are now immunized with a federal vaccination from state prosecution."

The *Dombrowski* affirmation that "subversive" registration statutes are unconstitutional added disrepute to this type of legislation and witchhunting, although many such statutes remain on the books.

Ten legislators had served on the Louisiana Un-American Activities Committee in 1963. They had brought about the search for subversive materials, and the arrests. Smith, Dombrowski, and Waltzer sued them for $750,000 to compensate for the damage to their reputations, to their law practice, and to SCEF. Four years after the Supreme Court decision, nine of the legislators issued a public statement retracting all charges against the three. "After carefully reevaluating the available evidence and taking into consideration subsequent court decisions," their statement said, "we find that there exists no basis for the charges that any of these parties have taken any steps that threatened the safety and well-being of the state or the nation, or that they are guilty of any un-American activities." They refused to retract as to the SCEF organization. Thereafter, the damage suit was dropped.

The material seized by the state committee found its way into the hands of Mississippi Senator James Eastland, chairman of the Internal Security Subcommittee of the Senate Judiciary Committee. When Dombrowski sued Eastland and his committee's attorney, the lower federal courts dismissed the case. But the Supreme Court, in 1967, in *Dombrowski* v. *Eastland,* ordered the subcommittee's attorney to pay court costs and held that he should stand trial on the question of involvement in getting the papers from the state committee. The Court agreed that Eastland was protected by Congressional immunity.

The Supreme Court's decision in *Dombrowski* v. *Pfister* had two long-range effects. First, it reminded people that the mere passage of a law by Congress or a state legislature can discourage the exercise of First Amendment freedoms. The same is obviously true when a high school principal makes a rule or a government agency makes a regulation. Second, it helped state, and federal, defendants take the offensive in some cases. Citizens suffering under state procedures, particularly black people battling state-entrenched discrimination and poor people subjected to unlawful welfare procedures, could cut through delays to get relatively rapid constitutional relief in federal courts. Some federal statutes have been attacked successfully under the *Dombrowski* theory that a criminal defendant can get affirmative relief in a civil suit when he was arrested under an unconstitutional law. But this decision has been attacked continuously since it was announced, precisely because it is a very strong weapon for the disadvantaged, the scapegoat in society.

All of the bitterly fought cases on association described here, and many more not mentioned, have helped teach Americans not to give up their organizational ties lightly, that solidarity can bring victory. Lessons learned so slowly and painfully may endure.

Prosecutors at all levels have also learned some lessons. They have stopped bringing suits against organizations and their leaders for strictly organizational activities that might be protected by the First Amendment under Warren Court decisions. They have turned, instead, to prosecutions of individual leaders of "radical" organizations for "straight" crimes, such as murder and assault, leading to the highly publicized, long jury trials of Angela Davis in California, the Panther 21 in New York, and many other so-called political trials in the late 1960s and 1970s. The outcome of these cases has often turned on the jurors' concern to protect freedom of speech and action and to prevent conviction on the basis of racial prejudice, according to interviews after acquittal verdicts.

CHAPTER 7

Right to Privacy

When the Constitution was written, it was quite easy to find a private place; it was possible to live in complete privacy by leaving the civilized areas and taking off for the west. By the turn of the twentieth century, the whole continent had been populated, and millions of people lived in close proximity. Americans began to think about their lost privacy, and to seek methods of insuring some measure of isolation from their fellows.

Lawyers began to talk about the right of privacy as a legal right. They said a person should be able to sue another person, or a government agency, or a newspaper that violated his right. Slowly this concept has been accepted by the courts in cases involving privacy of political beliefs and association and also privacy in family matters.

A. Political Privacy

Legislative bodies have, as their primary function, proposing and enacting statutes. In order to carry out this function, they sometimes establish committees to investigate alleged wrongdoing. But the purpose of such investigation must be to enable them to propose statutes to meet the problem studied, not to punish any wrongdoers uncovered in the process.

Congressman Dies of Texas established the Committee on Un-American Activities in 1938 to attack many people and ideas connected with the New Deal era of Franklin Delano Roosevelt. Under a series of publicity-hungry chairmen, the committee held innumerable hearings that produced a series of tragicomedies on stages in various cities across the country. Witnesses from all walks of life had been called to answer questions about their political beliefs, affiliations, and activities, and about the affiliations of their friends, relatives, and associates. As a result of the publicity, many were fired and some could not get jobs in their line of work for years.

Ten leading writers and directors from Hollywood refused to answer the committee's questions about their affiliation with the Communist Party or a number of other groups. They maintained that under the First Amendment the committee had no right to ask them the questions. The committee asked Congress to cite them for contempt, and Congress did so. They were convicted in federal district court, lost on appeal, and the United States Supreme Court refused to hear the case (*Trumbo* v. *United States*). The "Hollywood Ten" went to jail.

From then on, people subpoenaed before HUAC refused to answer questions on the basis of the Fifth Amendment privilege against self-incrimination, as well as the First Amendment. They also were cited for contempt of Congress and convicted. Soon after Chief Justice Warren's appointment, the Court agreed to hear the appeal of three of these witnesses in *Quinn, Emspak, and Bart* v. *United States*. The

Fifth Amendment guarantees the privilege against self-incrimination in "any criminal case." The Court held in 1955 that this also covers Congressional hearings, and it reversed the contempt convictions.

Still, many witnesses felt this was an insufficient and undignified method of refusing to answer questions about their political beliefs and membership in organizations. Some tried again to convince the Court that the First Amendment made it illegal for a congressional committee even to ask such questions. One of these was a United Auto Workers official named Watkins.

The right to silence

Watkins v. United States (1957)
354 U.S. 178, 77 S. Ct. 1173, 1 L. Ed. 2d 1273

John Watkins started out working in the International Harvester factory in the 1930s. There he joined the Farm Equipment Workers Union. By the 1940s he was working for the union, and in 1953 he became an organizer for the United Auto Workers.

When Watkins joined his first union in the 1930s, millions of people were unemployed. Other millions had jobs, but under terrible working conditions—low pay, long hours, no union contract, and constant threat of firing. Everyone was angry and confused about why there was a Great Depression following the affluent 1920s. The Communist Party and other radical groups discussed this problem and seemed to have some answers. The Party conducted classes on Marxism, and helped organize the unemployed into councils and the employed into unions. Radical ideas and groups attracted hundreds of thousands of people, many of whom joined the industrial unions being organized in steel, auto, and other fields. Then World War II pulled working men into the armed forces. While there was a shortage of workers, militant unions forced employers to grant demands for improved working conditions in collective bargaining contracts.

After the war, when returning veterans swelled the labor supply, many corporations rejected new demands by employees for improved status. The vets were determined not to return to the old grind. Long and bitter strikes resulted. Political attacks were made on militant unions for having "Reds" in their leadership and among the rank-and-file. It was charged that the unions were "Communist-dominated." This paved the way for passage of the Taft-Hartley Act by Congress, in 1947, requiring union leaders to file oaths with the government that they were not members of, or affiliated with, the Communist Party.

This was the first time people who did not work for the government were required to sign loyalty oaths by the government. If the officers of the union refused to sign, the union could not use government facilities, that is, the National Labor Relations Board (NLRB). The NLRB helped unions in several ways. It could order employers to stop unfair labor practices and it could hold elections among workers to choose a bargaining agent when a union representing a majority of the workers was not recognized by the employer or when two unions were competing to represent the workers.

At first, the big CIO unions united to challenge the constitutionality of the oath. When the Supreme Court upheld its constitutionality in 1950, in *American Communications Association* v. *Douds,* it created a crisis in the labor movement. Many unions kicked out their radical leadership so they could still use the services of the NLRB in labor disputes. Some radical unionists publicly denounced the oath but said they were not Communists and signed. A handful of unions refused to comply with the act, kept their radical leaders and organizers, and lost their right to use the NLRB. In those industries, competing unions were organized whose officers took the oath. The new unions could use the services of the NLRB to hold elections to encourage members to leave the unions that refused to sign the non-Communist oath. (See *Jencks* v. *United States,* discussed in chapter 16.)

The House Un-American Activities Committee, in its junkets to different cities, invariably subpoenaed left-wing trade unionists as one of its chief target groups. Often they were called on the eve of contract negotiations or a union election. In hearings in 1952 and 1954, two witnesses mentioned John Watkins as someone associated with or a member of the Communist Party. Watkins was subpoenaed and appeared before the committee in April 1954. He said he had never joined the Party, although he had supported and cooperated with many of its activities from 1942 to 1947. He was quite candid in almost all his replies to the committee, but when asked to tell whether a list of other people had been members of the Party in the past, he replied: "I will answer any questions which this committee puts to me about myself. I will also answer questions about those persons whom I knew to be members of the Communist Party and whom I believe still are. I will not, however, answer any questions with respect to others with whom I associated in the past."

He explained, "I do not believe that such questions are relevant to the work of this committee nor do I believe that this committee has the right to undertake the public exposure of persons because of their past activities."

Watkins was prosecuted for contempt of Congress, waived a jury, and was convicted. After a series of appeals the case reached the United States Supreme Court.

Watkins contended that the committee was engaged in "exposure for exposure's sake," and he marshalled an impressive array of documents and quotations from committee members stating that the committee's main purpose and activity were to shine "the spotlight of publicity" on Communists and former Communists. He argued that the information sought by HUAC was not pertinent to the committee's sphere of inquiry, and that the definition of that sphere was unconstitutionally broad and vague, allowing HUAC to encroach on First Amendment rights. He maintained that he had a right, under the First Amendment, to privacy about his associations, expressions, and beliefs.

The government argued that Congress and its committees should be left alone by the Court, unless they clearly abused their power; that the committee was investigating efforts to overthrow the government by force and violence, and its purpose was to propose safeguarding legislation—a matter of clear public interest; that questions about a person's past "subversive" activities cast light on his present intentions; and that if the questions were pertinent to *any* legislative purpose, Watkins had to answer them.

Do you think Congress has the right to pass legislation in the area of political belief and association? If not, why not? If so, are there any limits on such legislation? Where would you draw the line between Congress's need for information in order to enact effective legislation and the citizen's right to privacy from investigation and protection against persecution for his beliefs and associations? This committee is investigating political beliefs and associations rather than election procedures or gambling practices—does that make a difference in how much power it can exercise to compel an unwilling witness to testify?

The Supreme Court's six-to-one decision was delivered by Chief Justice Warren. (Justices Burton and Whittaker did not participate.) The Court stated at the outset: "The power of the Congress to conduct investigations is inherent in the legislative process," and it traced the history of that power as exercised both in England and by Congress.

"Clearly, an investigation is subject to the command that the Congress shall make no law abridging freedom of speech or press or assembly," the Court continued. "Abuses of the investigative process may imperceptibly lead to abridgment of protected freedoms. The mere summoning of a witness and compelling him to testify, against his will, about his beliefs, expressions or associations is a measure of governmental interference. And when those forced revelations concern matters that are unorthodox, unpopular, or even hateful to the general public, the reaction in the life of the witness may be disastrous. This effect is even more harsh when it is past beliefs, expressions or associations that are disclosed and judged by current standards rather than those contemporary with the matters exposed. Nor does the witness alone suffer the consequences. Those who are identified by witnesses and thereby placed in the same glare of publicity are equally subject to public stigma, scorn and obloquy."

The Court recognized that balancing "the congressional need for particular information with the individual and personal interest in privacy is an arduous and delicate task for any court." An essential factor was the need for Congress to insure that compulsory orders to testify were "used only in furtherance of a legislative purpose. That requires that the instructions to an investigating committee spell out that group's jurisdiction and purpose with sufficient particularity."

When Congress established the House Committee on Un-

American Activities, it was empowered to investigate "(1) the extent, character, and objects of un-American propaganda activities in the United States, (2) the diffusion within the United States of subversive and un-American propaganda that is instigated from foreign countries or of a domestic origin and attacks the principle of the form of government as guaranteed by our Constitution, and (3) all other questions in relation thereto that would aid Congress in any necessary remedial legislation."

"It would be difficult to imagine a less explicit authorizing resolution," Chief Justice Warren declared for the Court. "Who can define the meaning of 'un-American'? What is that single, solitary 'principle of the form of government as guaranteed by our Constitution'?" And the Court concluded, "No one could reasonably deduce from the charter the kind of investigation that the Committee was directed to make."

Watkins was charged under a statute making it a crime to refuse "to answer any question pertinent to the question under inquiry" by Congress or a congressional committee. It is obvious, said the Court, that the person being questioned must know what question is under inquiry in order to decide whether the question asked him is pertinent. Examining the HUAC charter, the opening speech of its chairman at the hearings, and the questions and responses made when Watkins refused to answer, the majority of the Court concluded that the subject of inquiry "was not adequately revealed to petitioner when he had to decide at his peril whether or not to answer. Fundamental fairness demands that no witness be compelled to make such a determination with so little guid· ance."

Watkins "was thus not accorded a fair opportunity to determine whether he was within his rights in refusing to answer, and his conviction is necessarily invalid under the Due

Process Clause of the Fifth Amendment," the Court ruled.

Justice Clark, a former Attorney General of the United States, dissented on the grounds that the Court was unduly hampering congressional investigations. "My experience in the Executive Branch of the Government leads me to believe that the requirements laid down in the opinion for the operation of the committee system of inquiry are both unnecessary and unworkable." He felt that many committees needed and had investigative powers over broad areas. In addition, the committee's subject of inquiry with Watkins was quite clear to Justice Clark: "the extent of infiltration of communism in labor unions." And he denied that the First Amendment provides a "right to silence." Clearly the former prosecuting attorney was unhappy to see the Court close one more door to compulsion of testimony from an unwilling witness.

The *Watkins* decision led many people to believe that the Warren Court would take the next step and uphold the right of a witness, not only to refuse to answer questions about others, as Watkins had done, but also to refuse to answer questions about himself. As a result, two college professors, an organizer of the Southern Conference Educational Fund in Kentucky, and a Los Angeles leader of the National Committee to Abolish HUAC all refused to answer questions by the committee solely on the basis of the First Amendment (in *Barenblatt* v. *United States, Braden* v. *United States,* and *Wilkinson* v. *United States*). The Supreme Court did not take the next step, and those witnesses went to jail and served six-to-twelve-month sentences. Many other witnesses argued that the committee had not followed fair procedures in their cases; their convictions were reversed by the Supreme Court on due process grounds.

Intrusion into the realm of associational privacy

DeGregory v. New Hampshire (1966)
383 U.S. 825, 86 S. Ct. 1148, 16 L. Ed. 2d 292

The House of Representatives was not the only legislative body with an un-American activities committee. The Senate had two similar committees, and many states established committees that engaged in further investigations, accusations, and prosecutions for contempt. In New Hampshire, the state attorney general was given responsibility for investigating alleged subversives and reporting to the legislature. One of the people Attorney General Louis Wyman called for questioning in 1956 was Hugo DeGregory, a bookkeeper who had run for lieutenant governor of Massachusetts on the Communist Party ticket in 1940. Wyman did not realize that he was embarking on a legal struggle with DeGregory that would continue for the next ten years.

DeGregory refused to answer Wyman's questions, was prosecuted and sentenced to jail, appealed through the state courts, and ultimately went to the United States Supreme Court in *DeGregory* v. *Wyman*. The Court dismissed the appeal in a short note (memorandum decision), saying no federal question had been raised. Justices Warren, Black, and Douglas noted their dissent.

By this time (1959), the statute under which DeGregory had been prosecuted had expired, but a new one had been enacted in 1957, and Wyman again subpoenaed DeGregory for questioning. DeGregory steadfastly refused to answer whether he was or had been a Communist. He was sentenced to one year in jail, and appealed all the way to the United States Supreme Court again. The Court's 1961 memorandum decision in *DeGregory* v. *Attorney General of New*

Hampshire affirmed DeGregory's conviction. This time Justice Brennan joined the three dissenters.

Faced with this setback, DeGregory then purged himself of contempt by answering the question: "Are you presently a member of the Communist Party?"

His answer was, "No."

The publicity surrounding the DeGregory and other New Hampshire Red-baiting cases boosted Attorney General Wyman into a seat in Congress. But in 1963, his successor as attorney general called DeGregory to answer further questions about Communist activities and associations. DeGregory then stated: "I am not now a member of the Communist Party and have not been at any time since this [law] has been on the statute books; . . . I have no knowledge of any communistic activities in New Hampshire during this period, or any violations of law during this period of six and one-half years. In fact, I have not even been aware of the existence of any Communist Party in the State of New Hampshire at any time that this authority has been on the statute books." He then refused to answer questions about events before 1957, and contended that he had a First Amendment right to privacy about matters so far in the past. The inquiries were asked for exposure's sake, and not for any legitimate lawmaking function, he said.

The attorney general prosecuted DeGregory for contempt. He was again convicted and sentenced to one year in jail. For the third time he appealed through the state courts and up to the Supreme Court in 1966.

Do you think the Court would make the same decision in 1966 as in 1959 and 1961? Or was it necessarily a different Court because it was a different era? Would one more justice come over to DeGregory's side? Or was the whole question irrelevant and the case moot, since there wasn't even one Communist left in the state of New Hampshire?

Justice Douglas wrote the Court's six-to-three opinion. He noted that DeGregory had refused to answer questions mainly about periods "over 10 years prior to the investigation giving rise to the present contempt," and that DeGregory "had every reason to anticipate that the details of his political associations to which he might testify would be reported in a pamphlet purporting to describe the nature of subversion in New Hampshire." The attorney general's basis for subpoenaing DeGregory was "a 1955 Report on Subversive Activities in New Hampshire," which itself had no information connecting DeGregory with the Party after 1953. The Court held that "the staleness of both the basis for the investigation and its subject matter makes indefensible such exposure of one's associational and political past—exposure which is objectionable and damaging in the extreme to one whose associations and political views do not command majority approval."

The state had failed to show an "overriding and compelling state interest," said the Court, "that would warrant intrusion into the realm of political and associational privacy protected by the First Amendment. The information being sought was historical, not current. Lawmaking at the investigatory stage may properly probe historic events for any light that may be thrown on present conditions and problems. But the First Amendment prevents use of the power to investigate enforced by the contempt power to probe at will and without relation to existing need." The majority summed up: "New Hampshire's interest on this record is too remote and conjectural to override the guarantee of the First Amendment that a person can speak or not, as he chooses, free of all governmental compulsion."

Justice Harlan, joined by Justices Stewart and White, dissented. If the majority rule were followed, he said, to justify an investigation the state would have to produce the very information it was seeking in the investigation. "I cannot say as a constitutional matter that inquiry into the current operations of the local Communist Party could not be advanced by knowledge of its operations a decade ago."

The Court's ruling finally removed the publicity and the jail sentence that had plagued Hugo DeGregory for ten years. His refusal to capitulate in the face of this long-continued persecution had finally brought him victory.

Thousands of other witnesses called before various un-American activities committees refused to answer all questions. They cited grounds ranging from the privilege against self-incrimination in the Fifth Amendment, to denials of due process when the committees failed to follow even their own rules for questioning witnesses, to racial discrimination forbidden in the Fourteenth Amendment.

Of the thousands of public and private employees who lost their jobs or occupational licenses or security clearances due to adverse testimony before such investigating committees, some sued for reinstatement and back pay and were successful. See the *Elfbrandt* case, discussed in chapter 8. Toward the end of the Warren Court era, the House reorganized its Committee on Un-American Activities into the House Internal Security Committee, and some of its most flagrant practices fell into disuse. Several state committees put themselves out of business, as serving no useful function.

The 1970s seemed to usher in the era of sweeping grand jury investigations of political association and activity. Many of the abuses charged against HUAC are now charged against these grand juries. In addition, they function in secret, and witnesses may not be accompanied by their attorneys during questioning. Problems arise concerning forced self-incrimination in return for partial immunity from prosecution. Witnesses who reject immunity and continue in their refusal to answer are cited for contempt.

Whether the procedural protections finally developed to protect congressional committee witnesses will be applied to grand jury witnesses is not yet clear.

B. Family Privacy

The penumbra of the First Amendment

Griswold v. *Connecticut* (1965)
381 U.S. 479, 85 S. Ct. 1678, 14 L. Ed. 2d 510

It was a long-standing joke in Connecticut that people bought contraceptives at drugstores "for medicinal purposes." While it was legal to use a contraceptive to "prevent disease," a Connecticut statute made it a crime to use one "for the purpose of preventing conception"—and it was punishable by $50 or more fine and sixty days to one year in jail.

The law had been on the books since 1879. In 1940 a test case was brought by the state against two doctors and a nurse, charging them as accessories to the crime of using contraceptives by giving contraceptive information to people who might use contraceptives. The Connecticut Supreme Court upheld the statute as valid.

In almost every legislative session during the forties and fifties, bills were introduced amending the statute to allow doctors to prescribe contraceptives for married women when their health required it. None of these bills passed the state senate.

Dr. C. Lee Buxton, an obstetrician and gynecologist, and three of his married patients decided in the late fifties to bring a test case themselves. Their attorney, Catherine Roraback of New Haven, filed an affirmative suit, asking the court to declare the statute unconstitutional because it deprived the plaintiffs of life and liberty without due process of law. The patients explained how their previous pregnancies had caused serious, almost fatal, illness, and said they were prevented from using contraceptives by the threat of prosecution. Dr. Buxton argued that he was prohibited from practicing his profession to the best of his ability.

The Connecticut courts followed the 1940 precedent: The law was valid and the legislature clearly did not intend to change it. The women plaintiffs therefore were forbidden to use contraceptive devices. Their only protection against pregnancy was to refrain from sexual intercourse.

Dr. Buxton and the patients appealed to the United States Supreme Court. In 1961, the Court held that there was no real threat of prosecution against private doctors and their patients, and that until an actual prosecution took place the Court should refrain from deciding the constitutionality of the statute. Justice Frankfurter wrote the opinion for the five-to-four majority in *Poe* v. *Ullman.* Justices Black, Douglas, Harlan, and Stewart each dissented. "A sick wife, a concerned husband, a conscientious doctor seek a dignified, discrete, orderly answer to the critical problem confronting them. We should not turn them away and make them flout the law and get arrested to have their constitutional rights determined," said Justice Douglas in his dissent.

Dr. Buxton saw the route the majority of the court seemed to point out to him. He and Estelle Griswold, the Executive

Director of the Planned Parenthood League of Connecticut, decided to open a League Center in New Haven. The center was to advise only married persons about contraception. It opened November 1, 1961, and was closed on November 10, when Ms. Griswold and Dr. Buxton were arrested as accessories to violating the anticontraceptive statute. They were tried, convicted, and fined $100. They took their case to the U.S. Supreme Court, after a ruling in the Connecticut courts that the statute was constitutional.

Do you think the federal Constitution protects individuals from this kind of prosecution? Since there is no specific statement in the Constitution on this point, is a state free to legislate in this area? Or is there a broader constitutional protection of individual rights that extends to the private married life of a couple?

The Supreme Court split seven to two, with Justice Douglas writing for the majority. "We do not sit as a super-legislature to determine the wisdom, need, and propriety of laws that touch economic problems, business affairs, or social conditions," he noted. "This law, however, operates directly on an intimate relation of husband and wife and their physician's role in one aspect of that relation."

Then Justice Douglas, for the Court, announced that "the First Amendment has a penumbra where privacy is protected from governmental intrusion." This penumbra or partial shadow over congressional action had already been extended by the Court to include: the right to educate children in public, private, or parochial schools as the parents choose; the right to distribute and receive information; the right to teach and academic freedom in general; the right to associate freely with other people; the right to express beliefs by joining an organization. These, said Justice Douglas, illustrate "that specific guarantees in the Bill of Rights have penumbras, formed by emanations from those guarantees that help give them life and substance."

"We have had many controversies over these penumbral rights of 'privacy and repose,'" said Justice Douglas, citing six recent examples. "These cases bear witness that the right of privacy which presses for recognition here is a legitimate one."

Turning to the specifics of the Connecticut prohibition, Justice Douglas asked, "Would we allow the police to search the sacred precincts of marital bedrooms for telltale signs of the use of contraceptives? The very idea is repulsive to the notions of privacy surrounding the marriage relationship.

"We deal with a right of privacy older than the Bill of Rights—older than our political parties, older than our school system. Marriage is a coming together for better or for worse, hopefully enduring, and intimate to the degree of being sacred. It is an association that promotes a way of life, not causes; a harmony in living, not political faiths; a bilateral loyalty, not commercial or social projects. Yet it is an association for as noble a purpose as any involved in our prior decisions." On this reasoning, the Court reversed the Connecticut courts' rulings.

Justice Goldberg, in a long concurring opinion, concluded: "I believe that the right of privacy in the marital relation is fundamental and basic—a personal right 'retained by the people' within the meaning of the Ninth Amendment. Connecticut cannot constitutionally abridge this fundamental right, which is protected by the Fourteenth Amendment from infringement by the States."

Justice Harlan also concurred separately, because he disagreed with the implication of the other opinions that "the

Due Process Clause of the Fourteenth Amendment does not touch this Connecticut statute unless the enactment is found to violate some right assured by the letter or penumbra of the Bill of Rights." He found that the Connecticut statute violated the due process clause simply by infringing on "basic values 'implicit in the concept of ordered liberty.' " (See the further discussion of the Fourteenth Amendment's application in chapter 20.)

Justice White's concurring opinion stressed that the state's infringement of due process might be found valid if it were needed for a legitimate and substantial state interest. The interest here appeared to be "the State's policy against all forms of promiscuous or illicit sexual relationships, be they premarital or extramarital." But since the ban on contraceptives applied sweepingly to people engaged in both legitimate and illicit relationships, Justice White found the statute unconstitutionally broad.

Justices Black and Stewart dissented. They did not approve of the Connecticut statute, but they found no grounds for holding it unconstitutional.

It is interesting that the Court did not use the new-found penumbra protecting privacy in marriage when faced with a test of interracial marriages in the *Loving* case, discussed in chapter 27.

Nonetheless, the right to privacy that the Court found protected by the penumbra of the First Amendment is becoming increasingly important to us as the technology for invading our privacy is perfected, expanded, and made more widely available. For example, many civil libertarians are concerned about the increase in the number of agencies requiring people to identify themselves by giving their Social Security numbers. Will the federal government develop a giant computer system recording information on each person's voter registration status, employment, credit rating, educational qualifications, and other previously private aspects of his life? In the decades ahead, the voters may insist that Congress and state legislatures write legislation to supplement tne undefined right to privacy uncovered by the Court.

CHAPTER 8

Academic Freedom

The business of industry is to produce and distribute goods. The business of education is to distribute old ideas and to produce new ones. Good teachers and professors, at whatever level, always remain students, looking for new answers. As long as man has questions without answers, the academic community must help search for new answers.

In the process of finding answers, academicians are bound to come up with a number of theories that challenge existing doctrine. These must be tested and analyzed. If the media report the theories as "answers," some people get upset. To those who feel comfortable when everything remains the same, new theories are always disturbing. This explains the charges made against public school teachers and college professors from time to time because of their research or for what they teach in the classroom. Often when the incident that started the trouble is analyzed, it turns out that the teacher did not give a "wrong answer" but rather asked a "new question." The teacher tried to get the students to think about a new problem or to think about an old fact in a new way.

Teachers are subject to attack because of their obvious impact on future generations. During any repressive period, attacks on the school system are multiplied. A Red scare against teachers flourished in New York City in 1940 at the same time as the antialien scare. From 1950 until the mid-1960s, many states and school districts passed statutes requiring teachers to sign oaths of loyalty to the United States government. Many teachers were denied tenure when complaints were made about the content of the material they were teaching their students. Others were fired for making comments about actions of their supervisors or school boards.

To protect their jobs, and the right of free inquiry, professors and teachers have banded together in organizations such as the American Association of University Professors to promote the concept of "academic freedom." This phrase, of course, is just another way to say that the First Amendment must apply to teachers and students. The only reason it needs special mention is that teachers and students run into the problem of freedom of inquiry and expression more often in their work than some other workers do. (Other occupations that deal in ideas and expression have developed similar concepts, such as "independence of the bar." Part of this idea is that the First Amendment applies to lawyers.)

The United States Supreme Court was the only branch of the federal government concerned with the maintenance of academic freedom during the so-called McCarthy period. Neither Congress nor the President took steps to ensure this freedom, and, on the contrary, Congress passed loyalty oaths and the President issued executive orders that related to professors and students.

In 1957, the Court expressed its position on academic freedom in *Sweezy* v. *New Hampshire,* the case of a college professor convicted of contempt for refusing to answer questions of the New Hampshire attorney general. Chief Justice Warren wrote: "The essentiality of freedom in the community of American universities is almost self-evident. No one should underestimate the vital role in a democracy that is played by those who guide and train our youth. To impose any strait jacket upon the intellectual leaders in our colleges and universities would imperil the future of our Nation. No field of education is so thoroughly comprehended by man that new discoveries cannot yet be made. Particularly is that true in the social sciences, where few, if any, principles are accepted as absolutes.

"Scholarship cannot flourish in an atmosphere of suspicion and distrust. Teachers and students must always remain free to inquire, to study and to evaluate, to gain new maturity and understanding; otherwise our civilization will stagnate and die."

The Court had an opportunity to apply these principles in the case of an Arizona teacher, Barbara Elfbrandt, and some Iowa public school students named Tinker.

An involved negative oath

Elfbrandt v. Russell (1966)
384 U.S. 11, 86 S. Ct. 1238, 16 L. Ed. 2d 321

Barbara Elfbrandt was a young eighth-grade teacher in Tucson, and a Quaker. In 1961 she faced a moral question: Should she sign the new loyalty oath passed by the Arizona legislature in the waning days of McCarthyism?

The legislative committee that urged the passage of this oath admitted: "The communist trained in fraud and perjury has no qualms in taking any oath; the loyal citizen, conscious of history's oppressions, may well wonder whether the medieval rack and torture wheel are next for the one who declines to take an involved negative oath as evidence that he is a True Believer."

Nonetheless, the Arizona legislature passed the Communist Control Act, requiring every state employee to "swear (or affirm)" his "true faith and allegiance" to the United States and Arizona constitutions and his willingness to "defend them against all enemies whatever." The act also provided that any employee who took the oath and "knowingly and wilfully becomes or remains a member of the Communist Party of the United States or its successors or any of its subordinate organizations or any other organization having for one of its purposes the overthrow by force or violence of the government of the state of Arizona" would be fired from his job and prosecuted for perjury (which was made a felony).

Mrs. Elfbrandt talked about the oath with two other teachers, Gerald Dulgov and Clyde Appleton. None of them thought the oath was constitutional and none thought they should sign it. But there was another problem about not signing: Even if you still could teach, you couldn't get paid for teaching until you had signed. Nonetheless, the three refused to sign and Mrs. Elfbrandt asked her attorney, Edward Morgan, to sue the school and state officials, asking the court to declare the oath unconstitutional and to enjoin the officials from withholding her salary and the salaries "of all others similarly situated." By adding this phrase, the suit became a "class action"; if she won, all other teachers who refused to take the oath would automatically win also, without having to sue.

For five years, while her case was pending, Barbara Elfbrandt continued to teach without pay. The Elfbrandts' landlord, sympathetic to her stand, declared a moratorium on the rent until the case should be won and the money recovered. To support the family, pay the costs of litigation, and spread publicity about the case to teachers and others throughout the country, an Emergency Committee to Defend Liberties

Barbara Elfbrandt, teaching without pay after refusing to sign a loyalty oath, sues the state, claiming the oath is unconstitutional.
Credit: Wide World Photos

of Arizona Public Employees was formed by public school teachers, professors from the University of Arizona, housewives, friends, attorney Morgan, and his secretary. Its members wrote and handed out brochures, spoke to civic groups, prepared dinner parties and other fund-raising events, and got out mailings; soon support began to come in from across the country and as far as Canada, Mexico, Europe, and South America.

The case went first to the county superior court, where attorney Morgan called the oath "an insult to the employees, school teachers, and administrators of the state." He also specified how it infringed the constitutional rights of his client by violating her conscience, abridging her freedom of speech, association, and petition, depriving her of her right to be paid without due process of law, being too vague to be clearly understood by a reasonable person, denying her equal protection of the laws, constituting a bill of attainder, compelling self-incrimination, and violating her right to privacy.

The state's attorneys maintained that the legislature had every right to enact and enforce such a law to ensure "the fitness of its employees" and "to protect our citizens."

The judge upheld the constitutionality of the oath and the Arizona Supreme Court affirmed the lower court's decision. Mrs. Elfbrandt sought review by the United States Supreme Court.

The state of Washington had adopted an oath similar to Arizona's six years before. The Washington law provided that "no subversive person" would be eligible to work for the government. It defined "subversive person" very broadly (for example, any person who "aided" another person in an act attempting to "alter" the "constitutional form" of the federal or state government was subversive). In 1955, two professors at the University of Washington attacked the oath without success. Later, sixty-four employees of the university sued to have that oath and a previous Washington oath declared unconstitutional. In June 1964, the United States Supreme Court decided their case, *Baggett* v. *Bullitt,* in favor of the employees. The Court held that "a law forbidding or requiring conduct in terms so vague that men of common intelligence must necessarily guess at its meaning and differ as to its application violates due process of law." The Washington oath, it held, "is unconstitutionally vague."

Justice White, writing for the seven-to-two majority, pointed out: "The Washington oath goes beyond overthrow or alteration by force or violence. It extends to alteration by 'revolution' which, unless . . . its ordinary meaning [is] distorted, includes any rapid or fundamental change." Would support for "repeal of the Twenty-second Amendment [limiting the President to two terms] or participation by this country in a world government" be considered "subversive activity"? Justice White asserted, "Those with a conscientious regard for what they solemnly swear or affirm, sensitive to the perils posed by the oath's indefinite language, avoid the risk of loss of employment, and perhaps profession, only by restricting their conduct to that which is unquestionably safe. Free speech may not be so inhibited."

A few days later, the *Elfbrandt* case came before the Court. Instead of deciding it, the Court sent the case back to the Arizona Supreme Court to reconsider its previous decision in light of the *Baggett* ruling. This approach was used repeatedly by the Warren Court. It gave state courts an opportunity to follow U.S. Supreme Court holdings, rather than deciding all state constitutional questions in the Supreme Court.

Here, as in many other cases during this period, the state

court was not compliant. On reconsideration, the Arizona Supreme Court again held the loyalty oath constitutional, by a vote of four to one. The dissenting justice said the statute was unclear and unconstitutional. Mrs. Elfbrandt had to seek redress from the United States Supreme Court a second time. The financial resources would not have been available for this long legal battle, but help came from the National Emergency Civil Liberties Committee, an organization in New York formed to aid people defending their civil liberties from McCarthyite attacks. NECLC lent its resources to publicize the case nationally.

The Arizona court had ruled that this oath, unlike the vague and broad Washington oath, was no more than a restatement of the duties of citizenship. Do you agree? Does the law's specific mention of Communist Party membership and overthrow of the government by force and violence save it from being too vague?

Justice Douglas delivered the five-to-four opinion of the majority of the Court. The Court found the statute unclear and unconstitutional. It attacked those who were members of an organization, even if they had no intent to commit illegal acts or to further the organization's illegal purposes. This was an unconstitutional abridgment of freedom of association.

Justice Douglas quoted heavily from the dissenting opinion of the Arizona Supreme Court justice, and explained: "People often label as 'communist' ideas which they oppose; and they often make up our juries." A jury might then convict a teacher for such innocent activities as "going to a Pugwash Conference" (international conferences of scholars to discuss problems of world peace in a nuclear age), or joining "a seminar group predominantly Communist and therefore subject to control by those who are said to believe in the overthrow of the Government by force and violence."

The opinion concluded, "A law which applies to membership without the 'specific intent' to further the illegal aims of the organization infringes unnecessarily on protected freedoms. . . . Such a law cannot stand."

Justice White, who wrote the majority opinion outlawing the Washington oath two years before, now wrote the dissent in favor of the Arizona oath. He was joined by Justices Clark, Harlan, and Stewart. White found no abridgment of freedom of association in the oath, and asserted that a state had a right to require its employees not to be members of the Communist Party. He also accepted the provisions for criminal prosecution of an employee who took the oath and later was found to be associated with a proscribed organization. If the majority of the Court had difficulty with this provision, said Justice White, it should strike down only the portion that was not proper, not the entire statute.

Nevertheless, the entire statute had been struck down by the Court, which meant that similar statutes in other states were also unconstitutional.

It took another year before attorney Morgan was able to wrest the five years' back pay plus accrued interest from the coffers of Arizona. The Elfbrandts were finally able to pay their rent, their court costs, and their attorney's fee. The rest of the money they gave to the indefatigable Emergency Committee, which passed it on to other civil liberties groups in Arizona, to use in pending cases.

Barbara Elfbrandt eventually decided to leave the classroom job she had fought so hard to hold. After winning the right of all Arizona teachers to teach without taking a loyalty oath, she enrolled in the University of Arizona Law School, to learn more about fighting for constitutional rights as a lawyer. To support herself through school she worked part time in the office of her former attorney, doing draft counseling.

Freedom of expression inside the schoolhouse gate

Tinker v. *Des Moines Independent Community School District* (1969)

393 U.S. 503, 89 S. Ct. 733, 21 L. Ed. 2d 731

Once a person makes up his mind about a political question he considers important, he usually wants to tell people what he thinks. He may want to start by telling his friends, but if he opposes a policy of the federal government, ultimately he will want to find an effective way to tell the policymakers. How can one person hope to affect a policy of an institution as enormously powerful as the federal government? How can one person even make himself heard?

These were the problems facing three or four families in Des Moines, Iowa, as the Christmas season approached in 1965. They had decided they were against the war in Vietnam, and they favored a truce. The father in one family, the Tinkers, was a Methodist minister working for the American Friends Service Committee, an organization founded by Quakers to oppose war and help solve social problems in a friendly spirit. The mother in another family, the Eckhardts, was an officer in the Women's International League for Peace and Freedom, founded during World War I by Jane Addams and others to bring together women around the world to work for greater freedom and an end to war. There were five children in the two families who attended grade school, junior high, and senior high.

When they met in December, they tried to think of a

forceful way to make their protest. In addition to all of the usual problems already mentioned, they realized that the students could not have much effect on their congressmen and senators, since they could not even threaten to vote against them. They decided on an extremely simple approach: Each one would make a personal statement by wearing a black armband to mourn the war dead during the holiday season, and by fasting on December 16 and 31.

The principals of the Des Moines schools heard about the plan, and on December 14, they met and adopted a policy that any student wearing an armband to school would be asked to remove it. If the student refused, he would be suspended from school until he did remove it.

Nonetheless, the Tinker children, Christopher Eckhardt, and two other students did wear black armbands to school on December 16 and 17. The silent protest evoked comments and jokes from some students. Others said, "Leave them alone." There was no shouting or boisterous behavior.

The teachers, following the new policy, asked the students to remove their armbands. Five of the students refused. They were promptly suspended, and did not return to classes until January, after the planned protest had ended.

If nothing more had happened, the incident would have ended very quietly with no visible effect on the society at large, or on the lives of the two families. But the parents decided to bring this issue into court—not the issue of the wisdom of the war in Vietnam, but the issue of the right of students to express their view on that war. They sued on behalf of their children to restrain school officials from applying the antiarmband policy again, and for a small amount of money damages to compensate for the schooling their children had missed. The suit, filed in federal court, was based on a section of the Civil Rights Act of 1871 (now 42 U.S.C. §1983). Since its adoption by Congress during Reconstruction, both black and white citizens have filed suits under it to protect their rights against people acting "under color of law," such as government officials.

The federal district court judge said the school principals' policy was constitutional, because it was a reasonable regulation to prevent disturbance of school discipline. The parents appealed to the federal court of appeals. The appellate justices split equally on the question, and when this happens the lower court decision stands. The parents then asked the Supreme Court to hear the case.

For the first time, the Supreme Court agreed to hear a case raising the question of whether students have the right to express political viewpoints on school property during school hours. It may seem strange that the issue had not been settled before, but the struggles of many groups are slow to get into court, and even slower to reach the highest court of the land. Student rights were no exception.

When the Bill of Rights was written in 1789, the authors talked about the rights of the people. Actually, they had in mind only free white adult males. But they *said* "the people," which, of course, includes everyone. They wrote more wisely than they realized, because all people came to feel that they were included in these protections against government action. And one group after another demanded its rights—Negroes, immigrants, Indians, women, poor people, the mentally ill. And now, young people.

Do you think that the students were correct? Does the First Amendment apply in high school and junior high? Does the First Amendment protect the wearing of armbands? Or were the principals correct in saying that this "demonstration" would disrupt teaching, and therefore should be forbidden?

By a seven-to-two vote, the Court held that wearing armbands to school "was closely akin to 'pure speech,' " which "is entitled to comprehensive protection under the First Amendment."

"First Amendment rights, applied in light of the special characteristics of the school environment, are available to teachers and students. It can hardly be argued that either students or teachers shed their constitutional rights to freedom of speech or expression at the schoolhouse gate. This has been the unmistakable holding of this Court for almost 50 years."

The Court's opinion by Justice Fortas noted that "the Court had repeatedly emphasized the need for affirming the comprehensive authority of the States and of school officials, consistent with fundamental constitutional safeguards, to prescribe and control conduct in the schools." Here the students' constitutional rights conflicted with a school regulation.

The regulation was adopted out of "fear of a disturbance," although "no threats or acts of violence" had actually occurred. "Any departure from absolute regimentation may cause trouble," Justice Fortas commented. "Any word spoken, in class, in the lunchroom, or on the campus, that deviates from the views of another person may start an argument or cause a disturbance. But our Constitution says we must take this risk," the Court asserted, "and our history says that it is this sort of hazardous freedom—this kind of openness— that is the basis of our national strength and of the independence and vigor of Americans who grow up and live in this relatively permissive, often disputatious, society."

There was no "evidence that the school authorities had reason to anticipate that the wearing of the armbands would substantially interfere with the work of the school or impinge upon the rights of other students," said the Court. "On the contrary, the action of the school authorities appears to have been based upon an urgent wish to avoid the controversy, which might result from the expression, even by the silent symbol of armbands, of opposition to this Nation's part in the conflagration in Vietnam."

The Court found it "relevant that the school authorities did not purport to prohibit the wearing of all symbols of political or controversial significance. The record shows that students in some of the schools wore buttons relating to national political campaigns, and some even wore the Iron Cross, traditionally a symbol of Nazism. The order prohibiting the wearing of armbands did not extend to these." The Court held that "the prohibition of expression of one particular opinion, at least without evidence that it is necessary to avoid material and substantial interference with schoolwork or discipline, is not constitutionally permissible."

The Court held more broadly: "In our system, state-operated schools may not be enclaves of totalitarianism. School officials do not possess absolute authority over their students. Students in school as well as out of school are 'persons' under our Constitution. They are possessed of fundamental rights which the state must respect, just as they themselves must respect their obligations to the State."

Then the Court stated its test for similar cases: "In the absence of a specific showing of constitutionally valid reasons to regulate their speech, students are entitled to freedom of expression of their views."

Justice Stewart, concurring, specified that he did not think all "First Amendment rights of children" were necessarily "co-extensive with those of adults," but that the areas in which children's rights might be different had to be "precisely delineated." Justice White, also concurring, stressed that the Court was still making a distinction between "speech" and "action."

Justice Black, who usually took an absolute view of First Amendment rights (holding that they simply could not be abridged), here dissented angrily. "The Court's holding in this case ushers in what I deem to be an entirely new era," he wrote, "in which the power to control pupils" in the public schools "is in ultimate effect transferred to the Supreme Court."

Despite his former absolutist stands, Justice Black explained, "I have never believed that any person has a right to give speeches or engage in demonstrations where he pleases and when he pleases." And, he said, "if the time has come when pupils of state-supported schools, kindergartens, grammar schools, or high schools, can defy and flout orders of school officials to keep their minds on their own schoolwork, it is the beginning of a new revolutionary era of permissiveness in this country fostered by the judiciary."

Although Justice Fortas had carefully limited the scope of the majority's ruling, saying "It does not concern aggressive, disruptive action or even group demonstrations," Justice Black warned grimly that the decision "subjects all the public schools in the country to the whims and caprices of their loudest-mouthed, but maybe not their brightest, students."

Reaching what perhaps was the underlying cause of his anger, Justice Black said, "We cannot close our eyes to the fact that some of the country's greatest problems are crimes committed by the youth, too many of school age. School discipline, like parental discipline, is an integral and important part of training our children to be good citizens—to be better citizens." He asserted, "One does not need to be a prophet or the son of a prophet to know that after the Court's holding today some students in Iowa schools and indeed in all schools will be ready, able, and willing to defy their teachers on practically all orders.

"This is the more unfortunate for the schools since groups of students all over the land are already running loose, conducting break-ins, sit-ins, lie-ins, and smash-ins. Many of these student groups, as is all too familiar to all who read the newspapers and watch the television news programs, have already engaged in rioting, property seizures, and destruction. They have picketed schools to force students not to cross their picket lines and have too often violently attacked earnest but frightened students who wanted an education that the pickets did not want them to get. Students engaged in such activities are apparently confident that they know far more about how to operate public school systems than do their parents, teachers, and elected school officials."

Justice Black reminded his audience, "The original idea of schools, which I do not believe is yet abandoned as worthless or out of date, was that children had not yet reached the point of experience and wisdom which enabled them to teach all of their elders." In his view, "taxpayers send children to school . . . to learn, not teach." And in a parting jibe, he stated: "I, for one, am not fully persuaded that school pupils are wise enough, even with this Court's expert help from Washington, to run the 23,390 public school systems in our 50 States."

Justice Harlan wrote a short dissent, saying that the parents had not shown to his satisfaction that the school principals were motivated to pass the regulation by some reason other than legitimate school concerns; therefore the regulation was not invalid.

The *Tinker* case, holding that the First Amendment does not stop at the schoolhouse gate, and the opinion in *Gault* (discussed in chapter 19), saying that many rights accorded to adults in criminal cases must be accorded to young people brought before juvenile courts, are often thought of as constituting a students' Bill of Rights.

The law as stated in these decisions has been publicized slowly around the country among young people. School authorities, juvenile court personnel, and others who work with youth are beginning to change their regulations to satisfy the Court's decisions. Dress codes and standards for student behavior are being revised in many schools. Some concerned parents, teachers, staff members, and students are trying to deal with underlying causes of student unrest by weeding out irrelevant courses and improving instruction. With passage of the eighteen-year-old vote, a class of citizens long ignored has suddenly achieved a measure of political power that will enable it to fight for greater protections in the future.

PART II

JUSTICE

FOURTH AMENDMENT:
The right of the people to be secure in their persons, houses, papers, and effects against unreasonable searches and seizures, shall not be violated, and no Warrants shall issue, but upon probable cause, supported by Oath or affirmation, and particularly describing the place to be searched, and the persons or things to be seized.

FIFTH AMENDMENT:
No person shall be held to answer for a capital, or otherwise infamous crime, unless on a presentment or indictment of a Grand Jury, except in cases arising in the land or naval forces, or in the Militia, when in actual service in time of War or public danger; nor shall any person be subject for the same offense to be twice put in jeopardy of life or limb; nor shall be compelled in any criminal case to be a witness against himself, nor be deprived of life, liberty, or property, without due process of law; nor shall private property be taken for public use, without just compensation.

SIXTH AMENDMENT:
In all criminal prosecutions, the accused shall enjoy the right

to a speedy and public trial, by an impartial jury of the State and district wherein the crime shall have been committed, which district shall have been previously ascertained by law, and to be informed of the nature and cause of the accusation; to be confronted with the witnesses against him; to have compulsory process for obtaining witnesses in his favor, and to have the Assistance of Counsel for his defence.

SEVENTH AMENDMENT:

In suits at common law, where the value in controversy shall exceed twenty dollars, the right of trial by jury shall be preserved, and no fact tried in a jury, shall be otherwise re-examined in any Court of the United States, than according to the rules of the common law.

EIGHTH AMENDMENT:

Excessive bail shall not be required, nor excessive fines imposed, nor cruel and unusual punishments inflicted.

FOURTEENTH AMENDMENT, Section 1:

. . nor shall any State deprive any person of life, liberty, or property, without due process of law. . . .

CHAPTER 9

Fairness at Every Step

"The forces of law and order are pitted against the criminal element and organized crime"—that is how some commentators characterize the two sides in criminal law cases. But this formulation is too simple. There are two faces of law and order. The acts that society has condemned are one part of our criminal law; they have been spelled out in state and federal statutes (forbidding acts from murder and rape to failure to pay taxes). The fair procedures that must be used to determine whether a person shall be punished for a crime are also a part of our criminal law; they are spelled out in federal and state constitutions and court decisions. Under this definition, a call for "law and order" is both an appeal to citizens to obey the penal statutes (or to face penalties for their violation), and an appeal to law enforcement officers to obey the constitutional law (or to face penalties for its violation).

Our law enforcement system includes two basic concepts often discussed in Supreme Court decisions. First, each person accused of a crime is entitled to "due process of law" to determine whether he is guilty. Second, the government can use only certain limited means of proving guilt. While this may mean that a guilty person will occasionally be acquitted, conviction of an innocent person would be an even greater danger to society. The founding fathers recognized that the ability of the prosecutor to convict is almost always superior to the ability of the individual defendant to defend himself. They were prepared to take certain risks, not only with freedom of speech and expression, but also by limiting police practices in law enforcement to those that do not tend to entrap both innocent and guilty.

In deciding cases on the basis of these concepts, the Supreme Court has to answer some difficult questions: What protections are included in "due process of law"? When does a person have a right to due process?

Over the years, the Supreme Court studies due process requirements at almost every stage in a criminal case. A case begins when a person is arrested by the police on a warrant (or without a warrant under certain circumstances), when he is given a citation notice ordering him to appear before the police without a formal arrest, or when he is called before a grand jury to testify. Often an arrest is accompanied by a search of the person, his automobile, or his home. Sometimes wiretapping or electronic surveillance is used. The arrested person is taken to a police station where he is booked (his arrest is recorded). He is then either released on his own recognizance (on his promise to appear at later proceedings), or told how much bail he must put up in order to be released, or he is denied release on bail.

Throughout his arrest, booking, and incarceration, police officers of various ranks give him orders, permit or deny him the right to make phone calls (to his attorney, family, or bail bondsman), and ask him questions. The character of this treatment may become an important issue in his trial or appeal. For example, if the police get him to make a confession at this time, before he has hired or consulted his lawyer, he may later claim that the confession was coerced or caused by illegal, third-degree methods. This can lead to exclusion of the confession at trial and result in a not guilty verdict, or if the confession is read at trial it can lead to a conviction that must be reversed on appeal. (See chapters 12, 14, and 18.) If he is released without charges after arrest and incarceration, he may sue the police because of their conduct during the arrest and incarceration, as in *Monroe* v. *Pape*, discussed in chapter 12.

The next step for the defendant is arraignment—appearance before a judge or judicial officer to hear the charge against him and to make a plea (guilty, not guilty, no contest, or no plea). The arraignment is supposed to take place soon after arrest. Then either the defendant appears at a preliminary hearing before a judge or a grand jury determines that the prosecutor has enough evidence to hold the defendant for trial (with or without hearing the defendant testify).

At this step, and at all other steps in the procedure, the defendant does not have to prove his innocence in order to win. If, after the preliminary hearing, the judge rules that the prosecutor has made a showing that a crime was committed and that the defendant may have committed it, the state issues charges against the defendant (called an information). If the grand jurors decide that the prosecutor has put in enough evidence to indicate that the defendant must be tried for the crime, then charges are issued (called an indictment). The defendant then faces trial.

If the prosecutor uses improper methods to obtain an indictment or information (such as secretly wiretapping conversations between the suspect and his attorney, or using police undercover agents to encourage suspects to commit illegal acts so that they can be entrapped), and if the defendant can prove such acts, he may be able to get the charges against him dismissed.

During the pretrial period, the prosecutor and the defense attorney try to find out all they can about the events leading to the charge. The defendant may also try to move the trial to another place where a more favorable jury climate might exist (by a motion for change of venue), or he may challenge the people called for jury duty in his case on the ground that they are not representative of the community and will not be impartial in deciding his case.

Most criminal cases are tried by a judge and a jury. At the trial, either the defendant or the prosecutor may challenge individuals selected for jury duty, if he finds them biased against him. (See chapter 15.) Many questions will arise concerning the facts and legal issues. Each side may argue that testimony of the opposition should not be admitted. Each side may seek to discredit the witnesses for the opposition by proving that they gave contradictory testimony at earlier stages in this case. The fundamental rule is that the prosecution has the burden of proving that a crime was committed and that the defendant committed it. These facts must be proved beyond a reasonable doubt or the jury must acquit. The defendant has no burden of proof. In other words, the defendant can be acquitted without presenting *any* evidence if the jury decides the prosecution did not put in enough proof.

At the conclusion of the prosecution and defense cases, the judge instructs the jury what law is to be applied to the facts in the case; he decides all questions of law, while the jury decides all questions of fact. The losing side may argue on appeal that the judge gave wrong instructions and therefore the case should be retried, but the jury verdict on the facts cannot be challenged on appeal unless the defendant was convicted and he can prove that the verdict was clearly contrary to the weight of the evidence presented or can offer newly discovered evidence casting serious doubt on the verdict.

If the defendant is convicted, the next step is for the judge to sentence him, usually on the basis of his previous criminal record, if any, and the recommendation of a probation officer, in light of the nature of the offense.

At this point the defendant can appeal from the verdict of guilt (claiming it is based on some kind of unfairness). Occasionally he appeals from the sentence (claiming it violates the "cruel and unusual punishment" rule in the Eighth Amendment—see chapter 17). If his appeals to state or federal courts are unsuccessful, the defendant may seek to prove error in his case by means of a petition for a writ of habeas corpus (discussed in chapter 18).

If a defendant is mistreated by prison officials while serving his sentence, he can file a habeas petition challenging such treatment.

After release, an ex-convict can seek to have his civil rights restored and, under certain circumstances, to have his criminal record wiped out or expunged.

At each stage in these proceedings, the defendant is entitled to certain protections, and the police and prosecutor are forbidden to use certain techniques to build a case against him. These due process protections are spelled out in the Fourth, Fifth, Sixth, Seventh, Eighth, and Fourteenth Amendments to the federal Constitution and in similar provisions in most state constitutions.

The Supreme Court frequently faces due process problems under these amendments. The broadest and most common problems involve police behavior: defendants charge that they were searched unreasonably, that their confessions were coerced, that they were not permitted to consult with their attorneys soon enough, or that they were not warned by the police that they had a right not to answer certain questions.

The Supreme Court also has to decide whether *all* persons charged with criminal activity are entitled to these due process protections. Juveniles, people committed to mental hospitals, young men drafted by the Selective Service System, and noncitizens facing deportation all demand the same procedural rights accorded to defendants in criminal cases.

Any study of the operation of our legal system must include full consideration of the Supreme Court and its decisions on due process of law. This focus quickly leads to concentration on decisions of the Court handed down while Earl Warren was Chief Justice because the Court devoted more attention to due process questions in criminal cases in that period than in any previous one, just as it had to civil liberties questions. This early attention to due process led to expansion of due process problems when the Warren Court held that defendants charged with serious offenses who had no funds for legal services had the right to be defended by lawyers paid by the government (see chapter 13). This led indigent defendants charged with less serious crimes to demand free lawyers at trial and on appeal.

What about criminal charges brought by cities, counties, and states? Could these governmental units provide fewer procedural protections to the criminally accused than the federal government provided? In other words, should the Court reverse the convictions of state court defendants who had received the protections required by state constitutions but not those required by the federal Constitution? After the Civil War, the concept of states' rights lost support. Lawyers began to argue that the Fourteenth Amendment requirement of due process of law meant that states must abide by the same protections for individuals spelled out for the federal government in the Fourth, Fifth, Sixth, Seventh, and Eighth Amendments. Differences between federal and state procedures in criminal cases began to disappear. In the early twentieth century, the Supreme Court slowly applied to the states many of the higher standards for fairness and freedom demanded in the federal system. The Warren Court was asked to take the process further (see chapter 20).

What type of restrictions should the Court impose on prosecutors and police officers who ignored its rulings? For example, what should be done when a police department continued certain practices even after the Court had held that such treatment of defendants was unconstitutional and had actually reversed convictions of particular defendants for this reason? Before announcing a strict new standard for law enforcement officers, the justices often described the many cases in which officers had participated in illegal conduct. These acts by particular police officers, police departments, and deputy sheriffs led the Court to make general rules limiting the practices of all law enforcement officers. As a result of some of its new standards, the Warren Court was charged by some with being soft on crime. Others hailed its return to constitutional requirements of due process. Each reader will undoubtedly form his own opinion as he studies the cases in part II.

Most of the people raising fair trial questions that get to the United States Supreme Court are individuals charged with violating the criminal laws. Many described here were charged with felonies, particularly murder and rape. Their cases reached the Court in significant numbers because these men were sentenced to death or life imprisonment, and they could not afford to give up their legal battles until the very last appeal had been made.

The points raised by defendants in capital cases are also

raised by defendants charged with less serious crimes or so-called political crimes. But often they are decided only in the capital cases. The Supreme Court cannot hear every constitutional case that comes before it; it selects the cases in which the legal issue is clearly raised and in which the outcome will make a significant difference to the parties. Judges who might avoid questions of fairness where the penalties are fines or short jail sentences are forced to face these ultimate questions when the defendant faces capital punishment or life imprisonment. The procedural rules the judges announce are then also applied in noncapital cases, and often find their way into civil and administrative cases as well.

Thus, ordinary people who have never committed crimes are indebted to the struggles of criminal defendants and their lawyers for a whole series of clear pronouncements by the Supreme Court concerning the rights of everyone. It is true, as moralists and poets have long said, that, in any society, life for the majority cannot be a great deal better than life for the most despised. We are increasingly discovering this in terms of our environment, particularly in urban areas. The other side of the coin is also true, although it is less often mentioned: The best of us gain a great deal from the struggles of the worst of us.

Most people tend to dislike someone who is charged with a crime. We are inclined to think that someone who was arrested must be guilty. Lawyers who defend criminal defendants have to remind themselves that a person charged with committing a gruesome crime is a human being. He had motivations, relationships, experiences, and a heredity that led to his actions (whether those actions were actually criminal or merely suspicious enough to lead to his arrest). Defense lawyers in criminal cases may not like or even respect their clients, but they understand that justice cannot be achieved for some if it is denied to others. If a guilty defendant can be convicted by police use of unconstitutional practices, is there any way to keep an innocent defendant from being convicted by use of the same practices?

The clients in the civil liberties and civil rights cases reported in parts I and III in this book were most often plaintiffs suing the government. Sometimes they were arrested and charged with criminal acts like the defendants in this part of the book. But the parties struggling for civil liberties and civil rights usually worked in groups for a common social end, such as wiping out discrimination or organizing a union. They were often interesting and sometimes charismatic leaders. The people involved in cases raising due process questions in part II are often loners; they have no broad social viewpoint. They tend to be difficult to know or like; few have defense committees to help them explain their cases or to raise money for lawyers and investigators. Many are poor and uneducated. Some appear to be mentally ill or deficient. Usually criminal defendants do not trust their lawyers; frequently they do not trust anyone. Still you will find in this collection of clients and lawyers a number of remarkable people who fought for an individual's freedom in such a way that the freedom of all Americans was enhanced.

Due process battles take time. The victories for human freedom recounted in this part of the book often were won after several years had been spent in pretrial motions, a jury trial and conviction, a reversal on appeal, a second jury trial and conviction, a second reversal on appeal, sometimes a third jury trial, followed finally by a Supreme Court decision on a procedural point raised in a habeas corpus proceeding.

A person who observes this long process may take pride

that justice is achieved in this country, even when it takes considerable time to reach that conclusion in a particular case. Or he can complain that there is too much delay in the trial courts and too many appeals are permitted. He can demand that something be done to speed up jury trials and to limit the "clowning around" by lawyers for those accused of crime.

The latter view usually gains support when leaders of unpopular movements (like the Black Panthers or war objectors) are charged, tried, and acquitted after long jury trials. Part of the public tends to forget that any legal proceeding may take a long time, whether there is a jury or not. Litigation over increases in phone company rates takes long administrative hearings followed by long trials and appeals in the courts. Bankruptcy proceedings of major railroads or industrial firms cannot be wound up quickly, even when everyone is working as rapidly as he can. Large issues require time for analysis, briefing, presentation, and decision. While some small procedural changes can be very helpful, cries for speeding up justice are not helpful because our goal is not speed, but justice.

Commentators have pointed out that the due process decisions of the Warren Court will not delay jury trials or criminal appeals very much, if at all, once law enforcement agencies have incorporated the new standards and rules into their normal operating procedures and explained them to their employees in manuals and training sessions. Efforts to ignore or minimize adherence to these rules and standards, on the other hand, will cause new delays in the administration of the judicial system. Efforts to abolish twelve-person juries and to accept six or eight jurors instead, to permit less than unanimous verdicts, or otherwise to tinker with the traditional jury system will undoubtedly be made in the 1970s and beyond. (See chapter 20.) You may have an opportunity to vote on these proposals in referendum elections in your state or, indirectly, by selecting legislators who will vote on statutory changes.

CHAPTER 10

Right to Security from Unreasonable Searches

The British subjected colonists to many unreasonable and demeaning searches of their homes before the Revolution. This was a major complaint of the revolutionaries—who conducted a few unreasonable searches themselves of the homes and persons of those loyal to the British crown. Before the ink was dry on the Constitution, they proposed an amendment to guarantee that in the new United States the old English law would be followed: Each man's home is his castle, where his person and papers can be secure "against unreasonable searches and seizures" by government agents.

The right of privacy discussed in chapter 7 is a first cousin to the right to be secure against unreasonable searches and seizures. A man, woman, or child has a right to privacy in his lawful behavior and in his thoughts, just as he has a right to privacy against unreasonable searches and seizures of his home, his place of work, or his person.

In order to conduct a lawful search, a police officer has three basic alternatives. He must obtain a warrant from a judge specifying the person and place to be searched and the material to be seized, or he must get the consent of the individual whose person or place will be searched, or he must be able to prove to a court that he had probable cause to believe that a crime was committed and the person to be searched committed it.

By 1900, it was clear that police officers sometimes did violate the Fourth Amendment. They conducted searches without first obtaining search warrants from the courts, and they conducted general searches when their search warrants limited the area and persons to be searched. In 1914, in *Weeks* v. *United States*, the United States Supreme Court ruled that, in order to enforce the Fourth Amendment in criminal prosecutions in federal court, it would exclude all evidence obtained by a federal officer in violation of the Fourth Amendment. In 1920, the Court extended this rule to exclude not only evidence found in the illegal search but also evidence obtained as a result of information or leads gained from the illegal search, known as "fruits of the search."

The United States Supreme Court has supervisory power over federal officers and the federal court system. Asserting this power in 1956, in *Rea* v. *United States*, the Court enjoined a *federal* officer from giving testimony in a *state* criminal prosecution concerning evidence illegally seized by him. In 1960, in *Elkins* v. *United States*, the Court excluded from a *federal* criminal prosecution evidence illegally seized by a *state* officer.

Eleven years earlier, in 1949, a defendant in a *state* criminal case had asked to make this exclusionary rule apply to *state* criminal prosecutions. At that time, two-thirds of the states opposed the exclusionary rule, feeling that police officers so rarely engaged in illegal searches that a "deterrent remedy" was unnecessary. Taking this into account, the Supreme Court in *Wolf* v. *Colorado* decided that the Fourteenth Amendment did not forbid the admission of evidence obtained by an unreasonable search or seizure in a state court trial. Even then the Court held that a person's right to privacy from arbitrary intrusion by the police was "implicit in the concept of ordered liberty" and as such was enforceable against the states through the due process clause of the Fourteenth Amendment. The Court concluded that other means of protecting the citizen's right to privacy were readily available.

That was the state of the law when the case of *Mapp* v. *Ohio* arose in 1957.

"My home is my castle"

Mapp v. *Ohio* (1961)
367 U.S. 643, 81 S. Ct. 1684, 6 L. Ed. 2d 1081

Dollree Mapp lived with her fifteen-year-old daughter in the top flat of a two-family house in Cleveland. At 1:30 in the afternoon of May 23, 1957, three policemen rang her doorbell. She came to the window and asked, "What do you want?"

"We want to ask you some questions," the officers answered.

"What about?" she asked.

The policemen had received information that a person who was wanted for questioning in connection with a recent bombing was hiding in the house, and they also suspected that a numbers business was going on there, but they did not tell Ms. Mapp this.

She had a lawyer for a civil suit then pending, so she told the officers she was going to phone him to ask whether she should let them in. The lawyer told her the policemen had to have a valid search warrant to enter her house, and she told the officers she wouldn't let them in without one.

The policemen radioed back to headquarters and then took positions watching all doors of the house for about 2½ hours, until four or more additional policemen reached the scene.

Ms. Mapp's attorney also arrived, and one of the officers told him they now had a search warrant, but refused to show it.

The policemen again demanded to enter. Ms. Mapp started downstairs toward the front door, but before she reached it, officers at the back door broke the glass, reached inside, and let themselves into the house. Ms. Mapp demanded to see their warrant. One of the policemen waved a paper in front of her face, without letting her read it. She then grabbed the paper and stuffed it down the bosom of her dress. At this, the officers grabbed her and, after a struggle, got the paper back. They handcuffed her to one of the policemen and took her upstairs. While she was forced to sit on her bed, the rest of the police officers thoroughly searched the rooms of her apartment and the basement of the house, going through dresser drawers, suitcases, photograph albums, closets, personal papers, etc. Ms. Mapp's attorney tried to see her but the police officers would not let him in the house.

The search turned up four pamphlets, two photographs, and a pencil doodle that the officers claimed were pornographic. They charged Ms. Mapp under an Ohio statute prohibiting possession of lewd or lascivious books and pictures. According to the police officers, the materials had been found in Ms. Mapp's dressers and a suitcase beside her bed. According to her, one of the articles was found in the suitcase, but the rest were in the basement, and they all belonged to a recent boarder who had left for New York and had not yet returned. Ohio law made it a crime to have the materials in her possession even if they were someone else's property, however.

Ms. Mapp was tried, found guilty, and sentenced to from one to seven years in prison. She appealed to the Ohio Supreme Court on the ground that the Ohio obscenity statute violated freedom of the press guarantees in the First and Fourteenth Amendments. Her attorney did not press for a new rule excluding illegally seized materials in state cases.

The Ohio Supreme Court found that Ms. Mapp's conviction was based primarily on illegally seized evidence. But after weighing the various factors, the court decided that since the evidence was not taken "from defendant's person by the use of brutal or offensive physical force against defendant," it was admissible at the trial under Ohio law.

On the question of constitutionality of the obscenity statute, a majority of the Ohio Supreme Court found that it *was* unconstitutional, in that it would punish anyone who simply "looks at a book and finds it lewd." But Ohio law required more than just a majority decision of its Supreme Court to declare a statute unconstitutional; if more than one justice dissented, the statute remained valid. In the *Mapp* case, three of the seven justices dissented. Ms. Mapp's conviction was therefore upheld.

She appealed to the United States Supreme Court, raising the First, Fourth, Fifth, and Fourteenth Amendment questions again. The state argued that the obscenity law was valid and that illegally seized evidence was admissible in state court cases under the 1949 Supreme Court decision in *Wolf* v. *Colorado*.

Do you think that a person should be prosecuted for possession of illegal material if the material belongs to someone else? If police officers had asked for a warrant to search the Mapp house, would a court have issued one? If not, should this prevent them from searching the house? If police officers often conduct illegal searches, how can this practice be stopped? If material was seized in an illegal search, should it be admitted into evidence at the trial? Is there a difference between state and federal trials that justifies a difference in rules on excluding such evidence?

The Supreme Court split six-to-one-to-three, the one being Justice Stewart, who voted for the same result as the majority but on different grounds. Justice Clark wrote the majority opinion.

The majority decided that the key question was the issue of illegally seized evidence, and that the Court would not deal with other issues in the case. Justice Clark, for the Court, traced the history of Supreme Court decisions in federal and state cases. He found that the factual grounds for the difference in rules had changed. Now more than half the states that had considered the exclusionary rule since the 1949 *Wolf* decision had adopted it. Why? In the words of the California Supreme Court, "because other remedies have completely failed to secure compliance with the constitutional provisions." Justice Clark added: "The experience of California that such other remedies have been worthless and futile is buttressed by the experience of other States."

In light of these changed circumstances, the justices now reexamined the *Wolf* ruling and decided "to close the only courtroom door remaining open to evidence secured by official lawlessness in flagrant abuse of" the Fourth Amendment. "We hold that all evidence obtained by searches and seizures in violation of the Constitution is, by that same authority, inadmissible in a state court."

This new holding "is not only the logical dictate of prior cases, but it also makes very good sense," said Justice Clark. "There is no war between the Constitution and common sense." Under the old rule, a federal prosecutor, forbidden to use illegally seized evidence, could and did pass it on to "a State's attorney across the street" to use. "Prosecution on the basis of that evidence was then had in a state court in utter disregard of the enforceable Fourth Amendment. If the fruits of an unconstitutional search had been inadmissible in both state and federal courts, this inducement to evasion would have been sooner eliminated."

The Court felt the *Mapp* rule would encourage "federal-state cooperation in the solution of crime under constitutional standards," and that even if the exclusionary rule appeared to benefit a guilty person in a particular case, in the long run it would make law enforcement more effective. Illegal "short-cut methods" by police officers cannot be tolerated. "Nothing can destroy a government more quickly than its failure to observe its own laws, or worse, its disregard of the charter of its own existence," said Justice Clark. Quoting the late Justice Brandeis, he asserted, " 'If the government becomes a lawbreaker, it breeds contempt for law; it invites every man to become a law unto himself; it invites anarchy.' Nor can it lightly be assumed that, as a practical matter, adoption of the exclusionary rule fetters law enforcement. . . . The federal courts themselves have operated under the exclusionary rule of *Weeks* for almost half a century; yet it has not been suggested either that the Federal Bureau of Investigation has thereby been rendered ineffective, or that the administration of criminal justice in the federal courts has thereby been disrupted."

Justice Black concurred. He did not base his decision on the Fourth Amendment, but rather on the Fifth Amendment prohibition against self-incrimination. The illegally seized evidence was akin to information coerced from a person and then used against him in a trial. This was forbidden by the Fifth Amendment.

Justice Douglas, also concurring, felt the *Mapp* case was a particularly appropriate one in which to put teeth back into the prohibition against unreasonable searches and seizures "because the facts it presents show—as would few other cases—the casual arrogance of those who have the untrammelled power to invade one's home and to seize one's person."

Justice Stewart disagreed, but felt the case should be reversed because Ohio's obscenity law infringed free thought and expression. Justices Harlan, Frankfurter, and Whittaker dissented, finding that the *Wolf* decision was proper and that the Supreme Court should not dictate to the states what rules of evidence to follow.

The *Mapp* decision had broad implications for appeals then pending and for prisoners serving long sentences that they claimed were based on illegally seized evidence. A flood of litigation was filed to determine whether *Mapp* was to be applied to past criminal cases, and even to civil cases. The Supreme Court held in 1965, in *Linkletter* v. *Walker,* that it did not apply to past cases. The Court went on to impose some restrictions on electronic eavesdropping (in *Alderman* v. *United States* and *Katz* v. *United States*) and to require municipal fire, health, and housing inspectors to obtain warrants before they could enter buildings against the wishes of the occupants (in *Camara* v. *Municipal Court* and *See* v. *Seattle*).

In a number of other decisions, the Supreme Court clarified the search and seizure rules. According to *Chapman* v. *United States,* whenever practicable, officers must obtain a search warrant before they may make a search. Officers may make a search incident to an arrest, but only for the purposes of self-protection and preventing the destruction of evidence. Therefore, the Court ruled in *Chimel* v. *California* and *Stoner* v. *California,* an officer can search only the person and the area within his immediate control, and can search only for weapons and destroyable evidence. Any search that goes beyond that is illegal unless a warrant has been issued.

The rules on officers breaking into homes, by force or by using pass keys, are based on the same reasoning, set forth in *Ker* v. *California.* If the policemen have no warrant, they must have probable cause to make an arrest, a reasonable belief that the person is there, and a reasonable belief that the person is armed and dangerous or that he may destroy the evidence if they announce their presence first.

To justify a search on the basis of consent, the Court held in *Bumper* v. *North Carolina,* that the consent must be given freely and voluntarily.

The courts are more lenient in upholding searches based on warrants than warrantless searches, because a warrant is based on a magistrate's decision rather than on the officer's decision, unless it can be shown that the magistrate is acting merely as a rubber stamp for the police. In *Aguilar* v. *Texas,* the Court specified that the officer's affidavit supporting the warrant cannot be based on suspicion. It must show the officer's personal observations or explain why information received from other persons is considered reliable. The warrant itself must be specific in describing what may be seized, the Court held in *Stanford* v. *Texas.*

Standards for police in conducting raids and arrests seem to fluctuate with the daily headlines. When police officials of the FBI, CIA, or local sheriff's department make a few mistakes and break into the wrong houses searching for suspects, local citizens and judges tend to demand more care in issuing search and arrest warrants. When an individual or group commits acts of violence against people and property and remains at large for a period of time, public clamor for stern law enforcement increases. The citizen may finally respond by making his own standards for police conduct and urging these on police agencies, in season and out. Warren Court decisions may serve as a useful basis for such standards.

Dollree Mapp, the woman unwilling to let policemen invade her home at will, faded from view, although her name lives on in this decision. She illustrates what happens in many Supreme Court cases: The citizen must fight for his or her rights at the outset and at every step of the way, but by the time the United States Supreme Court decides the case, the role of the client has diminished to a fraction of its initial importance, while the law has become the central character in the play.

CHAPTER 11

Burden of Proof

Apparently it is sometimes necessary to labor the obvious. Owing to the tenacity of a Louisville, Kentucky, citizen, we now have a Supreme Court opinion to illustrate the rule that a person cannot be arrested and convicted if there is no evidence of his guilt.

The case of Sam Thompson, which follows, also stands for the proposition that a citizen who claims he is being treated unfairly by the authorities can get the ear of the highest court in the land, and this may be the only court that will ever hear his case on appeal.

What is due process of law, after all? It is a combination of procedures that, if followed in the spirit of justice and to the letter of the law, is more likely to result in justice being done than if the procedures were not followed. One of the fundamental features of due process is that a person cannot be convicted in a criminal case unless there is evidence of guilt. That evidence must be provided by the prosecution and must be evidence beyond a reasonable doubt. In some states, defense lawyers tell the jury the standard is "guilt beyond a reasonable doubt and to a moral certainty."

The corollary of this rule of law is equally important. A defendant in a criminal case does not have to prove his innocence. He does not have to prove that the crime was not committed. If it was committed, he does not have to prove who did it. Unless the prosecution proves that the defendant is guilty of committing the crime, the defendant must be acquitted, even if he says nothing and produces no witnesses to prove his innocence.

Very slowly, over the centuries, all societies have learned that for some crimes the guilty person may not be discovered. Society has also learned the pain of convicting and punishing a person who later is proved innocent. Respect for the requirements of due process of law has developed out of this experience.

A police officer, trained to anticipate trouble and to guard against it, and, in this country, wearing a deadly weapon at all times while on duty, must seek to prevent criminal activity, while at the same time being careful not to infringe on the rights of citizens. The unadorned story of Sam Thompson's stop at a small cafe ironically named the Liberty End teaches much about the problems of police officers and ordinary citizens in this era.

Is it a crime to pat your foot?

Thompson v. *City of Louisville* (1960)
362 U.S. 199, 80 S. Ct. 624, 4 L. Ed. 2d 654

Sam Thompson stopped in at the Liberty End Cafe in his home town of Louisville a little after six in the evening on Saturday, January 24, 1959. There were a dozen or two customers in the place; some were eating and drinking beer, and the juke box was playing.

About half an hour after Mr. Thompson arrived, Officers Barnett and Lacefield of the Louisville police came in on a "routine check." Thompson was in the middle of the floor, by himself, doing a little dance or shuffle in time to the music.

One policeman went over to the cafe manager and asked how long Thompson had been in the place.

"A little over half an hour."

"Did you sell him anything to eat?"

"No."

"Any beer?"

"No."

The policeman then went over to Mr. Thompson and asked, "What is your reason for being here?"

"I'm waiting on a bus," he answered.

"You're under arrest," said the officer, and he took Mr. Thompson outside.

Thompson began arguing with the two policemen, asking what they were arresting him for, and "so then we placed a disorderly conduct charge on him," Officer Lacefield said.

Mr. Thompson was charged with loitering in the cafe under a city ordinance that made it unlawful for "any person . . . , without visible means of support, or who cannot give a satisfactory account of himself, . . . to sleep, lie, loaf, or trespass in or about any premises, building, or other structure in the City of Louisville, without first having obtained the consent of the owner or controller of said premises, structure, or building."

The prosecution said that in loitering cases guilt or innocence cannot be determined by "the same tangible modes of proof that disclose most offenses," since "they arise more from a course of conduct or a manner of life than from an isolated act." The prosecutor maintained that "many major crimes have been nipped in the bud" by the kind of vigilance used in this arrest for loitering.

Thompson's case came up for trial in the police court before Judge Taustine on February 3. The city attorney presented evidence of the events at and outside the cafe. When he concluded, Mr. Thompson moved that the charges be dismissed. The evidence did not support them, he said, and showed, in fact, that the policy of the police department was unconstitutional. The department had bluntly said that the question was not what the defendant had done but what kind of man the police officers thought he was. In fact, his arrest and prosecution were simply police reprisals against him because of an incident that had occurred ten days before. At that time, Mr. Thompson had been arrested on other charges he claimed were baseless, and he had hired a lawyer and demanded a trial to defend himself against them. The police were angry about that. At the earlier trial, the prosecutor had tried to introduce into evidence a list of fifty-four previous misdemeanor arrests, compiled from private police department records. Thompson's attorney, in cross-examination, brought out that there was a confusion between two Sam Thompsons, and the list was rejected as evidence in that case.

Judge Taustine denied Mr. Thompson's motion to dismiss the loitering and disorderly conduct charges, and the defendant presented his case. He said he had bought a dish of macaroni and a glass of beer at the cafe—from an employee, not the manager. He had told the police his address when they arrested him. He had had money with him at the time. He owned a little property in Louisville. He had worked at least one day a week for the same family in town for thirty years and had other occasional work. He lived within his meager income. He was a frequent customer at the Liberty End Cafe, known by the manager, and had never been asked to leave. The manager on that Saturday evening had seen him "standing there in the middle of the floor and patting his foot," and did not object, nor did the other customers find his behavior boisterous or offensive. He had even had a bus schedule with him, showing that a bus going to his home stopped half a block from the cafe at about 7:30.

Thompson's lawyer permitted himself to characterize the case against his client by saying: "The year is now 1960. It is not 1600; nor, if we may be permitted to say so, is it 1984." The lawyer went on to discuss the charge that the defendant was "without visible means of support." For a person to prove to a policeman that he has visible means of support when the officer doesn't even question him about it might require "the wearing of a sandwich sign carrying a current personal balance sheet and operating statement, duly certified. It is hard to see how anything less would serve."

At the end of his presentation, Mr. Thompson again moved that the charges be dismissed, saying that to convict him on the evidence presented would deprive him of liberty and property without due process of law in violation of the Fourteenth Amendment. Judge Taustine denied the motion and ruled, "Let the judgment be a $10 fine on each charge."

Sam Thompson decided he had had enough. He asked the judge to stay (postpone) the judgments until he could appeal. Since police court fines of less than $20 per charge are not appealable under Kentucky law, he intended to ask the United States Supreme Court to review the case and decide his due process claims under the Fourteenth Amendment. Judge Taustine granted a twenty-four-hour stay.

This wasn't enough time, so Thompson went to the state circuit court for a longer stay. The circuit court granted his request. The city of Louisville appealed this decision to the Kentucky Court of Appeals, but the appeals court ruled that Thompson's claims were substantial and not frivolous, and again granted the stay.

At last Mr. Thompson was able to petition the United

States Supreme Court to review the case, with the Kentucky Civil Liberties Union assuming the burden of the expense. The Court looked over the papers, found that "although the fines here are small, the due process questions presented are substantial," and agreed to hear his petition for certiorari.

Between Thompson's arrest on January 24, 1959, and January 11 and 12, 1960, when the United States Supreme Court heard oral argument in his appeal, Thompson had been arrested twelve times by the Louisville Police Department, and he was at that moment in the county jail for failure to make a $500 peace bond, a method used in some areas of the country for requiring citizens to either post money or be incarcerated because otherwise they would disturb the peace. A judgment requiring a peace bond is not appealable under Kentucky law, so that Thompson would have had to go straight to the United States Supreme Court to challenge that action, just as he had had to go directly to the highest court to challenge his original arrest.

Can the police arrest a person for a style of life rather than for an act? If so, who is to determine what styles of life warrant arrest and what styles of life are protected from arrest? Are arrests to prevent crime constitutional in our system? What was the evidence against Thompson? Was he proved guilty beyond a reasonable doubt? Was there something wrong with Kentucky procedures if Thompson had no method of getting his conviction reviewed by a higher Kentucky court? Should the United States Supreme Court have to concern itself with cases in which the fines are as small as in this one?

The Supreme Court's unanimous decision was delivered by Justice Black. "The ultimate question presented to us is whether the charges against petitioner were so totally devoid of evidentiary support as to render his conviction unconstitutional under the Due Process Clause of the Fourteenth Amendment. Decision of this question turns not on the sufficiency of the evidence, but on whether this conviction rests upon any evidence at all," he said.

On the loitering charge, the Court noted that Thompson accounted for his presence in the cafe by saying he was waiting for a bus. "The city concedes that there is no law making it an offense for a person in such a cafe to 'dance,' 'shuffle' or 'pat' his feet in time to music. The undisputed testimony of the manager, who did not know whether petitioner had bought macaroni and beer or not but who did see the patting, shuffling or dancing, was that petitioner was welcome there. The manager testified that he did not at any time during petitioner's stay in the cafe object to anything petitioner was doing and that he never saw petitioner do anything that would cause any objection. Surely this is implied consent, which the city admitted in oral argument satisfies the ordinance.

"The arresting officer admitted that there was nothing in any way 'vulgar' about what he called petitioner's 'ordinary dance,' whatever relevance, if any, vulgarity might have to a charge of loitering. There simply is no semblance of evidence from which any person could reasonably infer that petitioner could not give a satisfactory account of himself or that he was loitering or loafing there (in the ordinary sense of the words) without 'the consent of the owner or controller' of the cafe."

As to the second charge, "the only evidence of 'disorderly conduct' was the single statement of the policeman that after petitioner was arrested and taken out of the cafe he was very argumentative. There is no testimony that petitioner raised his voice, used offensive language, resisted the officers or engaged in any conduct of any kind likely in any way to adversely affect the good order and tranquillity of the City of Louisville."

"Thus, we find no evidence whatever in the record to support these convictions," the Court concluded, and it held that it is "a violation of due process to convict and punish a man without evidence of his guilt."

The *Thompson* case has been frequently cited by frustrated lawyers handling other cases in which they felt there was simply no basis for an arrest. Few cases have reached the highest court in which the facts were so clear; seldom has the Court written such a clear opinion.

CHAPTER 12

Rights after Arrest

The Bill of Rights contains specific guarantees to protect a person from injustice after he is arrested. The Sixth Amendment provides "in all criminal prosecutions, the accused shall enjoy the right . . . to be informed of the nature and cause of the accusation [against him]," and he "shall enjoy the right to a speedy and public trial." Meanwhile, "excessive bail shall not be required" for his release before trial, under the Eighth Amendment.

These specific rights fit into the general framework of the Fifth Amendment protection that "no person shall . . . be deprived of life, liberty, or property, *without due process of law."*

In spelling out the conditions under which law enforcement officers may make arrests, question suspects, seek confessions, and so forth, Congress and state legislatures have passed many statutes over the years and the Supreme Court has had many occasions to consider their constitutionality.

Chronologically, the first question is, What is to be done after the person has been arrested? In federal arrests, Congress has declared that the arresting marshall or deputy shall take the defendant before the nearest United States commissioner for arraignment—a hearing to determine whether he shall be held on the charge and, if so, to determine the question of bail pending trial.

The requirement of prompt arraignment was discussed at length in a famous 1943 decision, *McNabb* v. *United States.* Justice Frankfurter, who sat on the Court from 1939 until 1962, wrote in the *McNabb* opinion that the purpose of prompt arraignment was plain: "A democratic society, in which respect for the dignity of all men is central, naturally guards against the misuse of the law enforcement process. Zeal in tracking down crime is not in itself an assurance of soberness of judgment. Disinterestedness in law enforcement does not alone prevent disregard of cherished liberties."

The Court recognized that a suspect was at the mercy of his detainers. "Experience has therefore counseled that safeguards must be provided against the dangers of the overzealous as well as the despotic. The awful instruments of the criminal law cannot be entrusted to a single functionary. The complicated process of criminal justice is therefore divided into different parts, responsibility for which is separately vested in the various participants upon whom the criminal law relies for its vindication."

Then Justice Frankfurter got down to the real problem— concern about use of the third degree: "Legislation . . . requiring that the police must with reasonable promptness show legal cause for detaining arrested persons, constitutes an important safeguard—not only in assuring protection for the innocent but also in securing conviction of the guilty by methods that commend themselves to a progressive and self-confident society. For this procedural requirement checks resort to those reprehensible practices known as the 'third degree' which, though universally rejected as indefensible, still find their way into use. It aims to avoid all the evil implications of secret interrogation of persons accused of crime. . . . It outlaws easy but self-defeating ways in which brutality is substituted for brains as an instrument of crime detection."

The purpose of granting bail pending trial is similar to the purpose of requiring prompt arraignment. A defendant kept in jail before his trial is at a distinct disadvantage. Aside from the central fact that he prefers freedom to imprisonment, he is prevented from carrying out necessary activities. He cannot work to support his family and to earn money for his legal costs; he cannot help his lawyer investigate the facts for his defense; and he cannot contact character witnesses to support him in seeking a better sentence.

The defendant who is released can do all these, and in addition can show that he is trustworthy enough to come to court under his own steam when required. He can appear in court in his own clothing rather than prison garb, and this may affect both his demeanor and the response of the judge and jury. There is some evidence that defendants released before trial tend to get more favorable verdicts and lighter sentences than those kept in jail between arrest and trial.

Both federal and state laws require that the question of release be decided by a judge or commissioner, not by the arresting officers. The defendant seeking his release tries to convince the judge that he will not be a threat to society if released and will appear in court each time he is required.

During the 1960s, many jurisdictions changed their policies on release pending trial. It had been assumed for centuries that defendants in criminal cases would not appear for pretrial proceedings or for trial unless they were kept in custody or released on bail. The practice was to set bail at, for example, $10,000, and the defendant would have to pay a bail bondsman a percentage of that amount for a bail bond, often 10 percent. The bondsman then notified the defendant when he was required to appear in court. The defendant did not get any part of his 10 percent back, even if he made all his court dates. If he defaulted, the bonding company paid the court the $10,000 and went after the defendant, if he could be found, to get reimbursed.

If a defendant had unmortgaged property worth $10,000, he could put the property up as his bond, instead of using a bondsman. If he defaulted, the court would take over his property, but if he made all his court dates, he would get back his property free and clear. Or, if he had it, he could put up $10,000 cash, all of which would be returned to him at the end of the case if he always appeared when summoned.

A few people, respected citizens in the community with stable jobs, family ties in the area, and permanent addresses, were released on their promise to appear, which is called release on own recognizance (sometimes referred to as ROR or OR).

Of course, thousands of defendants had to stay in jail pending trial because they could not put up the whole amount of the bond or pay a bondsman his percentage fee. An experimental project studying the bail system in New York City in the 1960s had a profound effect on this procedure. It showed that ordinary defendants showed up as often when released on their own promise as when released on bail, and that thousands of dollars in jail costs could be saved by releasing them before trial.

The federal government now has a policy of encouraging release on own recognizance. Many states follow that policy also. Local volunteers and funded groups help defendants fill out questionnaires that indicate whether they are likely to appear for court dates if released on their own recognizance. Some states now release on lower bail when defendants also sign promises to appear.

The guarantee of speedy and public trial is a third specific effort made by the framers of the Constitution to be sure that the presumption of innocence remains with every defendant until the trial has been completed and he has been found guilty. The longer a person remains incarcerated before trial, the harder it is for him to face trial with an affirmative spirit, even if he is innocent. Also, of course, the time spent in jail prior to trial is wasted: If the defendant is acquitted, society admits that the time was spent unfairly; if the defendant is convicted, the time he has already spent in jail is not counted toward his sentence.

The Warren Court heard many cases in which a defendant claimed that his rights under one of these three provisions (to know the charge, to have a speedy, public trial, and not to have excessive bail imposed) had been violated. The Court had to reverse rulings setting very high bail in cases such as *Yates* (discussed in chapter 6) and to reverse decisions allowing the trial to be held years after the arrest (for example, in (*Klopfer* v. *North Carolina* the trial was still pending three years after arrest). The most notable case concerning rights on arrest is *Mallory* v. *United States.*

Preventing the third degree

Mallory v. *United States* (1957)
354 U.S. 449, 77 S. Ct. 1356, 1 L. Ed. 2d 1479

This controversial case began in the spring of 1954, around six in the evening, when a Washington, D.C., woman went down to the basement of her apartment to do a wash. She couldn't get a hose disconnected and went to the janitor's basement apartment to get help. The janitor wasn't there but his nineteen-year-old half-brother, Andrew Mallory, was. Mallory fixed the hose and went back to the basement apartment, where he lived with the janitor, his wife, and their three sons (two of them older than Andrew).

A short while later, the woman was attacked and raped by a black man wearing a mask. Since the woman had not heard anyone come down the basement stairs, she probably assumed he must have been there already. She said the rapist resembled Mallory and his two grown nephews.

Mallory and one of the nephews disappeared from the apartment and did not come back that night. Police officers arrested him around two o'clock the next afternoon, and he was taken to the station, along with his nephews. The policemen told him that his half-brother, the janitor, thought he was the rapist. Mallory denied it strenuously. Several of the officers questioned him in a group for thirty or forty-five minutes. He maintained he was innocent. After the interrogation, he was allowed to see his nephews and half-brother. The policemen then asked the three suspects to take lie detector tests. They agreed, but the officer who operated the machine was not available for another two hours.

At 8:00 P.M. this officer began questioning Mallory alone in a small room. The interrogation went on for almost an hour and a half before Mallory began to "break." He first said he "could have" done it or he "might have" done it, and finally that he *had* done it. The lie detector operator took him back to the group of officers, and Mallory repeated the confession to them. It was then 10:00 P.M., and the officers tried to arrange for an arraignment hearing. Since the crime had taken place in the District of Columbia, which is governed by federal law, arraignment had to be held before a United States commissioner. But all the commissioners had gone home for the day. The police officers then called in the deputy coroner, who examined Mallory for signs of physical or psychological coercion and found none.

Next he was taken before the victim and just about "every man in the Sex Squad," where he was questioned by three policemen and repeated his confession. Around midnight, he dictated the confession to a typist.

The next morning he was arraigned before a United States commissioner. Trial of the case was delayed for a year, however, because it was recognized that Mallory was of limited intelligence and that it would be unconstitutional to bring him to trial if he did not have the capacity to understand the situation. Finally he was tried before a jury, and the confession was introduced into evidence. The jury found him guilty, and the judge sentenced him to death.

Mallory's lawyer appealed, charging that the confession should not have been admitted into evidence because it was obtained illegally. The Federal Rules of Criminal Procedure require the police to "take the arrested person without unnecessary delay before the nearest available commissioner" for arraignment. At the arraignment, Mallory would have been told he had a right to remain silent, a right to counsel, and a right to a preliminary examination, and that any statement he made could be used against him. The police instead had held and questioned Mallory, delaying his arraignment unnecessarily until it was too late to find a commissioner. The confession he gave during this illegal detention period should not be allowed as evidence, his lawyer argued.

The assistant attorney general pointed out the deputy coroner's testimony that the confession was not coerced; therefore it was valid and admissible, he contended.

The court of appeals agreed with the assistant attorney

general. Mallory's lawyer sought review by the United States Supreme Court.

Do you think the delay before Mallory was arraigned is significant? Can delay be a form of coercion? Why is it important to make sure that a confession is not coerced? How can a defendant prove to a jury that police officers coerced him into making a confession? Do you think Mallory would have confessed, if he had been told of his rights beforehand? If he would not have confessed, is this a reason for telling him or for not telling him?

The Supreme Court's unanimous opinion was delivered by Justice Frankfurter, who had written the 1943 decision in the similar case of *McNabb*. He explained that the present federal rule "is part of the procedure devised by Congress for safeguarding individual rights without hampering effective and intelligent law enforcement." The Court found that "the scheme for initiating a federal prosecution is plainly defined. The police may not arrest upon mere suspicion but only on 'probable cause.' The next step in the proceeding is to arraign the arrested person before a judicial officer as quickly as possible so that he may be advised of his rights and so that the issue of probable cause may be promptly determined. The arrested person may, of course, be 'booked' by the police. But he is not to be taken to police headquarters in order to carry out a process of inquiry that lends itself, even if not so designed, to eliciting damaging statements to support the arrest and ultimately his guilt."

Justice Frankfurter recognized that "circumstances may justify a brief delay between arrest and arraignment, as for instance, where the story volunteered by the accused is susceptible of quick verification through third parties. But the delay must not be of a nature to give opportunity for the extraction of a confession."

In Mallory's case, the Court found that delay and interrogation had taken place although "arraignment could easily have been made in the same building in which the police headquarters were housed." The justices said, "We cannot sanction this extended delay, resulting in confession, without subordinating the general rule of prompt arraignment to the discretion of arresting officers in finding exceptional circumstances for its disregard."

The Court reversed Mallory's conviction, and remanded the case to the federal district court for a retrial without using the confession as evidence. However, the prosecuting attorney felt that he didn't have enough evidence without the confession, and the charge against Mallory was dismissed.

The news media hit upon this turn of events with the force of a hurricane. Editorials charged that the Court was coddling criminals, hamstringing the police, and unleashing confessed rapists to terrorize the women of Washington. Pressure mounted on Congress to do something to nullify the decision.

Several bills were introduced to change the federal rules. Attention centered on one, which specified that no statement could be held inadmissible in evidence "solely because of delay" in bringing the suspect to arraignment. The bill also required police to advise the suspect that he had a right to remain silent and that any statements he made could be used against him. (Efforts to add that he had the right to know the charge against him and the right to counsel were unsuccessful.) In the heavy debate on the bill, Mallory was described as "a confessed rapist, a criminal of long standing and much experience." Passage of the bill was urged to "protect society against confessed dope peddlers, thieves, rapists, murderers, and other crooks and criminals who prey upon their fellow citizens," and to "correct the peril to fair and effective law enforcement which has been created by this decision."

Opposing the bill, Congressman Celler of New York pointed out that "efficiency is not the sole test of our institutions. Efficiency in law enforcement is sometimes hindered by such basic values and practices of our society as the concept that a man is innocent until proved guilty, that he cannot be made to be a witness against himself, that people are to be secure against unreasonable searches and seizures." The *Mallory* decision, he said, "denied the police the major advantage of delayed arraignment—a prisoner who doesn't know his constitutional rights," and he pointed out that this would not be the "hardened or wealthy criminals," but the poor and ignorant.

Congressman O'Hara of Illinois felt that the bill's proponents "prefer to take the chance of innocence being unjustly condemned than to take the chance of one guilty person going free." He reminded the representatives that when an innocent person is convicted, that means the guilty person is still at large.

The bill passed the House. The Senate amended it to say "reasonable delay" would not be ground for ruling statements inadmissible. Senate and House conferees could not agree on the wording, and the bill failed. Similar measures were introduced without success year after year, while courts followed the *Mallory* decision.

Many police departments throughout the country changed their practices to conform to the letter of the *Mallory* decision; others did not. The spirit of providing due process of law to every arrestee continued to be lacking in many jurisdictions. Police behavior in making arrests was criticized in reports by criminologists, the American Civil Liberties Union, and other citizens' groups. It began to be attacked also in lawsuits based on an act passed by Congress in 1871, during the Reconstruction era after the Civil War. A state of affairs had existed at that time in some states "rendering life and property insecure and the carrying of the mails and the collection of the revenue dangerous," according to President Grant. In debate on the Civil Rights Act known as the Ku Klux Klan Act, Congressman Beatty of Ohio summarized the situation: "Men were murdered, houses were burned, women were outraged, men were scourged, and officers of the law shot down; and the State made no successful effort to bring the guilty to punishment or afford protection or redress to the outraged and innocent. The State, from lack of power or inclination, practically denied the equal protection of the law to these persons."

Senator Pratt of Indiana said Congress had heard reports "that of the hundreds of outrages committed upon loyal people through the agency of this Ku Klux organization not one has been punished. This defect in the administration of the laws does not extend to other cases. Vigorously enough are the laws enforced against Union people. They only fail in efficiency when a man of known Union sentiments, white or black, invokes their aid. Then Justice closes the door of her temples."

Because, as Congressman Porter of Virginia put it, "the outrages committed upon loyal men are under the forms of law," the remedy created in the act was not directed specifically against the Klan or its members, but against anyone representing a state in some capacity who was unable or unwilling to enforce a state law. "Every person who, under color of any statute," deprives any citizen of the United States of his constitutional rights is liable to the party injured and can be sued for money damages or for a court order to stop the harassment. This language, now in 42 U.S.C. §1983, is from the 1871 Act.

Suing the police for false arrest

Monroe v. Pape (1961)
365 U.S. 167, 81 S. Ct. 473, 5 L. Ed. 2d 492

Early one morning almost ninety years later, thirteen Chicago policemen, led by Deputy Chief of Detectives Pape, broke through two doors into the apartment of Mr. and Mrs. James Monroe. It was October 29, 1958. The couple and their six children were awakened from their beds at gunpoint. They were herded into the living room and made to stand naked while the police ransacked every room. They dumped out drawers, threw clothing from the closets, and ripped mattress covers. Detective Pape struck Mr. Monroe several times with his flashlight, calling him "nigger" and "black boy." Mr. Monroe was then taken to the police station and held on what were called "open charges" while he was questioned about a two-day-old murder. He was not advised of his rights or allowed to call his family. There were magistrates available before whom he could have been taken, as required by the *Mallory* decision, but this procedure was not followed. Monroe was finally let go after ten hours without being charged with any offense.

The police had no search warrant or arrest warrant. They were acting "under color" of the laws of the city of Chicago. The Monroes filed suit in federal district court against the city and the individual police officers, asking for damages under the old Ku Klux Klan Act. They stated their complaint under oath. The defendants—the individual police officers and the city of Chicago—did not deny the charges, but rather asked the court to dismiss the complaint. They argued that the Monroes could not sue them in federal court under this statute, but must first go to the state courts. Otherwise, the federal act would be a flagrant invasion of states' rights.

The federal district court dismissed the complaint, and the court of appeals affirmed this decision. When the Monroes asked the Supreme Court to hear the case, it agreed.

Do you think police officers are liable to pay money damages to citizens whose rights they violate when they are on duty? If Monroe was deprived of his constitutional rights, should the courts hold the city of Chicago responsible for the acts of its police employees? Can the federal courts step in and demand payment from those who claim they are acting "under color" of a state law or city ordinance? Can a law passed in 1871 against southern supporters of slavery be applied in 1961 to a northern city and its police department?

The Supreme Court was nearly unanimous in its decision, Justice Frankfurter dissenting. Justice Douglas, in the majority opinion, looked back to the adoption of the Ku Klux Klan Act. The Reconstruction law, he said, had several purposes: first, to override state laws calling openly for racial discrimination; second, to provide a remedy where state law was inadequate; and third, "to provide a federal remedy where the state remedy, though adequate in theory, was not available in practice."

Therefore, said the Court in 1961, state and federal laws can provide alternate routes to recovery for the same wrongful conduct. And the injured party need not first ask for and be refused the state remedy before trying for the federal remedy.

The Supreme Court had in previous cases considered

whether the words "under color of law" were meant to give relief to persons deprived of their constitutional rights by an official's *misuse* of his powers as well as by official enforcement of *unconstitutional laws*. In *United States* v. *Classic,* in 1941, the Court had ruled that "misuse of power, possessed by virtue of state law and made possible only because the wrongdoer is clothed with the authority of state law, is action taken 'under color of' state law."

Since this decision by the Court, Congress had considered several bills using the same words—"under color of law." Justice Douglas noted, "If the results of our construction of 'under color of law' were as horrendous as now claimed, . . . if they were such an unwarranted invasion of States' rights as pretended, surely the voice of opposition would have been heard in those [Congressional] Committee reports." The new uses of these words and the lack of criticism reinforced the argument that this decision was correct.

The Court held that the act "should be read against the background of tort liability that makes a man responsible for the natural consequences of his actions." The plaintiffs did not need to prove that the defendants specifically intended to violate their civil rights, since the statute was not directed solely against "willful" violations (as many criminal statutes are).

As to whether the city of Chicago was liable for the wrongdoings of its police, the Court held that Congress had not intended the word "person" in the original act to include municipalities. Therefore the lower courts were right in dismissing the charges against the city, but were wrong to dismiss the complaint against the officials.

Justice Harlan, joined by Justice Stewart, wrote a concurring opinion. He examined the legislative history of the Ku Klux Klan Act to see if the Supreme Court had misconstrued the meaning of its wording in past decisions. He found no indication that would justify a change in the Court's holdings.

Justice Frankfurter, in a long opinion, dissented from the decision upholding the suit against the police officers, while he agreed that the city was not liable. He concluded that this act was intended to cover only instances in which a state law or custom sanctioned the unlawful conduct of a government employee.

The Court reversed the lower courts and sent the case back to the federal district court for trial. A jury decided for the plaintiffs, voting damages of $13,000. The trial judge cut this amount to $11,000 for Mr. and Mrs. Monroe jointly; nothing was awarded to their six children.

The case had dragged on for four years; a team of lawyers had spent hundreds of hours working on it; court costs had been high. But the ruling in *Monroe* v. *Pape* opened the way for success in other lawsuits filed in Chicago and in other cities around the country where plaintiffs claimed improper conduct by members of the police or sheriff's departments or by prison officials.

In 1965 a constable in Whitmore, South Carolina, had to pay $3,500 in actual damages and $500 in punitive damages for hitting a citizen on the head with a blackjack and then arresting the citizen to conceal the unlawful attack. A deputy sheriff in Mississippi at about the same time was charged with beating a black citizen in jail; he settled the case by paying $1,500. In Ruleville, Mississippi, in 1966, a police officer paid a black citizen $500 to settle a case in which the officer shot and wounded the citizen during arrest and departed without attempting to render aid. The court ruled that even though the citizen had pleaded guilty to the arrest charges he could recover damages for the officer's misconduct. A Colorado teacher who hosted a meeting of pacifists was threatened and then arrested along with his guests by the county sheriff. He and one of the guests sued and recovered a total of $22,500 in damages. A fourteen-year-old black youth was awarded $85,000 damages against a trusty at LeFlore County Farm in Mississippi because the trusty shot the youth in the face for not responding to an order. The youth was blinded for life and suffered possible brain damage. The estate of an elderly black man was awarded $1,021,500 damages against the White Knights of the Ku Klux Klan of Mississippi who conspired to abduct him to a deserted place, where they injured, mutilated, and then murdered him. In 1969 a Tennessee university student recovered $10,000 plus $30,-000 in punitive damages from sheriff's deputies who knocked him down while he was visiting a friend in a hospital, and then arrested him without cause. Suits filed in many northern, southern, and western cities also resulted in awards of damages or settlements.

Recoveries against police officers are often reported in the press and on television. So are reports by human relations departments and university study teams seeking methods to improve police-community relations by educating citizens and police officers about their rights and responsibilities. This side of the problem vies for coverage with government reports on the increasing crime rate and demands that law and order be used against antiwar and civil rights demonstrators.

In the election year of 1968, congressmen and presidential candidates again demanded passage of a law overruling the *Mallory* decision of 1957. They also demanded an end to the *Miranda* rule on warnings the police must give to arrested persons (discussed in chapter 14). In the debates, few congressmen talked about the law of due process required by the Fifth Amendment and the order that follows from respect for citizens' rights. The result was passage of the Crime

Control and Safe Streets Act. This statute established the Law Enforcement Assistance Administration (LEAA) to channel large grants to local police and sheriffs' departments for new crowd-control equipment, for computerized methods of checking criminal records, for police training institutes, and for similar programs.

On the *Mallory* rule, the Crime Control Act provides that delay of up to six hours in bringing an accused to arraignment is not a ground for ruling his confession inadmissible, and "reasonable" delay of more than six hours, because of distance from an arraigning officer, is not a ground for inadmissibility either.

It is interesting that under this rule, the outcome in the *Mallory* case would have been the same, since Mallory was held for more than six hours in the same building with arraigning commissioners. Under the 1968 law, however, the defendant seeking to exclude from evidence a confession extracted from him *within* six hours of his arrest must prove to the satisfaction of the jury that he was coerced into giving it. Since coercion is generally denied by the police, the defendant's task is difficult.

New cases of police misconduct continue to find their way into the courts, and often, as in confession situations, the stories of the police officers and the citizen claiming injury conflict. Juries must then determine which side to believe.

CHAPTER 13

Right to Counsel

Food, clothing, shelter, and medical care are necessities of life for human beings. But when the founding fathers wrote the Constitution, they were not thinking about government responsibility to guarantee any of these necessities to Americans. Neither were the more liberal men who wrote the Bill of Rights as amendments to the Constitution. Medical care is a special kind of necessity that requires the assistance of experts. Neither the Constitution nor the Bill of Rights guarantees the right to medical assistance.

But the Bill of Rights does guarantee every person the right to one kind of expert assistance. This document, written largely by lawyers, does recognize that the assistance of a lawyer is necessary under certain circumstances. The Sixth Amendment therefore guarantees the right of a defendant in a criminal case to the assistance of counsel. (In the twentieth century, a document based in part on the American Bill of Rights includes not only the right of all citizens to assistance of counsel, but also the right to food, clothing, shelter, medical care, and to share in the wealth of the country—the United Nations Universal Declaration of Human Rights.)

Defining the limits of the constitutional right to the assistance of a legal expert has occupied the courts since 1789, and efforts to expand this right have led to several questions:

(1) In what kind of case does the right to assistance of counsel exist; (2) when does the right begin in a case; (3) what does the assistance of counsel include; (4) can there be two standards for legal assistance—one for the well-to-do and another for the poor; and (5) when does the right to assistance come to an end?

To answer these questions, it is necessary to consider how a lawyer can assist a client in a criminal case, why a lawyer is needed to give assistance, and the history of Supreme Court opinions on the right to counsel.

Justice Douglas, in *Johnson* v. *Avery,* a 1969 opinion, gives a telling description of the reasons people need lawyers in both civil and criminal cases today:

"The increasing complexities of our governmental apparatus at both the local and the federal levels have made it difficult for a person to process a claim or even to make a complaint. Social Security is a virtual maze; the hierarchy that governs urban housing is often so intricate that it takes an expert to know what agency has jurisdiction over a particular complaint; the office to call or official to see for noise abatement, for a broken sewer line, or a fallen tree is a mystery to many in our metropolitan areas. A person who has a claim assertable in far away Washington, D.C., is even more helpless."

In criminal cases, the need for the assistance of counsel is even more clear. Here a misstep may result in an unwarranted conviction, a fine or sentence, and possibly even a death sentence.

The judicial system in the United States was designed by lawyers who assumed lawyers would participate to assist clients throughout the proceedings. As Justice Black pointed out: "From the very beginning, our state and national constitutions and laws have laid great emphasis on procedural and substantive safeguards designed to assure fair trials before impartial tribunals in which every defendant is equal before the law. This noble ideal cannot be realized if the poor man charged with crime has to face his accusers without a lawyer to assist him."

The case that brought to national attention the need for effective counsel at all stages in the defense of a criminal charge was *Powell* v. *Alabama,* in 1932. This was the first litigation to reach the Supreme Court arising out of the widely known *Scottsboro* case. During the depression, nine young black men were charged with raping two young white women in Alabama. The trial judge appointed local white lawyers for the defendants. These counsel did their court-appointed task quickly and ineffectively while a mob in a lynching mood flooded the courtroom and the town. When news of the trial, convictions, and death sentences spread beyond the small town of Scottsboro, a defense committee was organized in New York, and tremendous public pressure mounted to secure justice for these young black citizens.

Although the case raised many legal issues, the one that had to be settled first was the right of the defendants to the assistance of effective counsel. After several appeals, the case reached the United States Supreme Court, which ordered the defendants retried, saying: "Even the intelligent and educated layman has small and sometimes no skill in the science of law. If charged with crime, he is incapable, generally, of determining for himself whether the indictment is good or bad. He is unfamiliar with the rules of evidence. Left without the aid of counsel, he may be put on trial without a proper charge, and convicted upon incompetent evidence, or evidence irrelevant to the issue or otherwise inadmissible. He lacks both the skill and knowledge adequately to prepare his defense, even though he has a perfect one. He requires the guiding hand of counsel at every step in the proceedings against him. Without it, though he be not guilty, he faces the danger of conviction because he does not know how to establish his innocence."

On retrial, counsel chosen by the defendants were diligent in their efforts but still not able to win acquittals from the all-white juries in Alabama. The cases were appealed and retried again. On the fourth retrial, Haywood Patterson was convicted but sentenced to seventy-five years rather than death. After that, pleas and prison sentences were negotiated for all the remaining Scottsboro defendants.

In 1938, the United States Supreme Court held in *Johnson* v. *Zerbst* that the Sixth Amendment guarantee of the assistance of counsel includes the right of an indigent defendant, being tried in the federal courts, to be furnished counsel paid by the federal government. In 1942, in *Betts* v. *Brady,* the Supreme Court had to decide whether states had the same responsibility. A man named Smith Betts had been indicted for robbery. He had no money to hire a lawyer, so he asked the state court judge to appoint counsel. The judge refused on the ground that the county practice was to appoint a lawyer for indigents only when the charge was murder or rape. Betts was convicted by the judge and sent to prison for eight years. On review, the Supreme Court held that the denial of counsel in this case was not a denial of due process under the Fourteenth Amendment.

The Court said that "the totality of facts in a given case" must be considered in deciding whether due process was denied. In the *Betts* case the Court enunciated the so-called special circumstances rule: Unless a defendant could show "special circumstances" necessitating the assistance of counsel for a fair trial, a court would uphold his conviction although he had been denied assistance of counsel.

Lawyers are necessities not luxuries

Gideon v. *Wainwright* (1963)
372 U.S. 335, 83 S. Ct. 792, 9 L. Ed. 2d 799

When Clarence Gideon was arrested for breaking and entering a poolroom, his acquaintances were ready to write him off as just another loser. But Gideon knew he was innocent and he was a stubborn man. He believed that with the help of a lawyer he could win an acquittal. Not having any money, he asked the judge to appoint an attorney for him.

The judge denied his request saying, "Mr. Gideon, I am sorry, but I cannot appoint Counsel to represent you in this case. Under the laws of the State of Florida, the only time the Court can appoint Counsel to represent a Defendant is when that person is charged with a capital offense."

Gideon replied, "The United States Supreme Court says I am entitled to be represented by Counsel."

The judge followed the Florida rule and denied the request for counsel. At the trial, Gideon did the best he could, cross-examining the prosecution witnesses, presenting his own witnesses, and arguing his case to the jury. But he obviously did not know and understand the law the way the prosecuting attorney did. The jury found him guilty, and the judge sentenced him to five years in the state prison.

From prison Gideon filed a habeas corpus petition (see chapter 18) in the Florida Supreme Court. He claimed that the trial judge had denied him his constitutional rights by refusing to appoint counsel for him. The court denied the petition and Gideon asked the United States Supreme Court to review his case. Because the question of right to counsel in state courts had been a continuing source of trouble since the *Betts* decision, the Court agreed to hear the case and review the problem. It appointed a lawyer to represent Gideon before it—Washington attorney Abe Fortas.

Gideon's position was simple: The Sixth Amendment provides that "in *all* criminal prosecutions the accused shall enjoy the right . . . to have the Assistance of Counsel for his defence." This rule, applied originally to federal courts, had been extended to state courts by the due process clause of the Fourteenth Amendment. The state's attorney argued that the *Betts* rule of "special circumstances" was correct and should be followed.

In your opinion, should a person charged with any felony have the right to a lawyer? Is this necessary in order to permit a fair trial, or is it too expensive for what it is worth? Does the Constitution require that a poor man have as good a lawyer as a rich man? Should the taxpayer have to pay to find a lawyer for a poor man, or is this a form of coddling the poor? Does society benefit when a poor person is provided with a lawyer to help him defend himself in a criminal case?

Of the justices who had been on the Supreme Court when *Betts* was decided, only Justices Black and Douglas remained. By 1963 the Court was unanimous and Justice Black, who had dissented in *Betts,* wrote the majority opinion. The *Betts* holding was a departure from previous decisions, he pointed out, citing *Scottsboro* and later cases. Justice Black also made his continuing argument that the first ten amendments were incorporated in the Fourteenth Amendment and that the Sixth Amendment was only one of many protections available to citizens against their state governments after the Reconstruction amendments were adopted (see chapter 20).

On the question of the right to counsel as a fundamental right essential to a fair trial, Justice Black wrote pointedly: "In returning to these old precedents, sounder we believe than the new, we but restore Constitutional principles established to achieve a fair system of justice. Not only these precedents but also reason and reflection require us to recognize that in our adversary system of criminal justice, any person haled into court, who is too poor to hire a lawyer, cannot be assured a fair trial unless counsel is provided for him. This seems to us to be an obvious truth. Governments, both state and federal, quite properly spend vast sums of money to establish machinery to try defendants accused of crime. Lawyers to prosecute are everywhere deemed essential to protect the public's interest in an orderly society. Similarly, there are few defendants charged with crime, few indeed, who fail to hire the best lawyers they can get to prepare and present their defenses. That government hires lawyers to prosecute and defendants who have the money hire lawyers to defend are the strongest indications of the widespread belief that lawyers in criminal courts are necessities, not luxuries." Therefore, in *Betts*, the Court had gone against both established legal precedent and established practice in our adversary system of criminal justice.

Justice Black noted: "Florida, supported by two other States, has asked that *Betts* v. *Brady* be left intact. Twenty-two States, as friends of the Court, argue that *Betts* was 'an anachronism when handed down' and that it should now be overruled. We agree."

Justice Clark, in a concurring opinion, specifically disagreed with the distinction made in the Florida law—that counsel were to be appointed in murder and rape cases (which carried a possible death penalty), but not in other criminal prosecutions. "The Fourteenth Amendment requires due process of law for the deprival of 'liberty' just as for deprival of 'life,'" he said. "How can the Fourteenth Amendment tolerate a procedure which it condemns in capital cases on the ground that deprival of liberty may be less onerous than deprival of life—a value judgment not universally accepted—or that only the latter deprival is irrevocable? I can find no acceptable rationalization for such a result, and I therefore concur in the judgment of the Court." In August 1963, Clarence Gideon was retried—with the assistance of counsel—in the Florida Bay County Court. He was acquitted of the charges by the jury.

The same day the Supreme Court handed down the *Gideon* decision, the Court also decided whether indigents have the right to court-appointed lawyers in appealing their convictions. The justices showed, in *Douglas* v. *California,* their sharp disagreement about how much equality between rich and poor is required to satisfy the goal of "equal justice under law."

Right to an advocate on appeal

Douglas v. *California* (1963)

372 U.S. 353, 83 S. Ct. 814, 9 L. Ed. 2d 811

Bennie Will Meyes and William Douglas were arrested in California and charged with thirteen felonies, including robbery and assault charges. Since they had no money to hire a lawyer, they were classed as indigents. The court appointed a public defender for them—a lawyer working full-time for the government defending indigents in criminal prosecutions. The lawyer asked the court to delay the trial because he was not sufficiently prepared; this was a complicated case, and he had been trying a different case every day for weeks. He said that the interests of the defendants were not the same, and asked that another lawyer be appointed so that each man would be represented separately. The court refused both requests. The defendants decided their rights were in danger, so they dismissed the public defender and asked the court for a delay and for individual lawyers. The court again refused. Meyes and Douglas were tried together before a jury, which convicted them of all thirteen felonies and gave them prison terms.

The two appealed to the district court of appeal, writing their own papers and again requesting that lawyers be assigned to help them, since they were still indigents. California had established a procedure for this situation. The appellate court was to examine the transcript record of the trial to see whether it would be helpful to the appealing party or to the appellate court to have a lawyer appointed to handle the appeal. The court decided that "no good whatever could be served by appointment of counsel for them." Meyes and Douglas wrote their own appeal briefs without a lawyer. The court noted that "the briefs filed by Meyes conform to the rules in all respects, are well written, present all possible points clearly and ably with abundant citation of pertinent authorities, and were no doubt prepared by one well versed in criminal law and procedure and in brief writing. There was no prejudicial error in not appointing counsel for defendants on the appeal." The court affirmed the defendants' convictions.

The California Supreme Court refused to hear the case, but the United States Supreme Court agreed to review it. The Court restricted itself to one issue: Under the Constitution, can an indigent be denied a lawyer for his appeal in a criminal case?

Do you think appellate court judges can deny a request for counsel if they think the indigent's appeal is not worthy? Does the California procedure provide equal protection to poor defendants? Could a defendant ever have a "good case" that would not show in the record without a lawyer pointing out the errors? Without a preliminary "screening" like the California procedure, would the courts be forced to supply free lawyers for numerous appeals that were without merit or frivolous?

The Supreme Court voted six to three, with Justice Douglas writing the majority opinion. The Court had previously held that "a State may not grant appellate review in such a way as to discriminate against some convicted defendants on account of their poverty." Examining the circumstances here, the Court found that "in spite of California's forward treatment of indigents, under its present practice the type of an appeal a person is afforded in the District Court of Appeal hinges upon whether or not he can pay for the assistance of counsel." Justice Douglas elaborated: "Only the barren record speaks for the indigent" when the appellate court prejudges the merits of his case. "Unless the printed pages show that an injustice has been committed, the indigent is forced to go without a champion on appeal." Any "hidden merit" in his appeal would remain hidden.

Justice Douglas limited the Court's opinion to "the first appeal, granted as a matter of right to rich and poor alike . . . , from a criminal conviction." He stated the rule: "When an indigent is forced to run this gantlet of a preliminary showing of merit, the right to appeal does not comport with fair procedure." While "absolute equality" is not required, "lines can be and are drawn and we often sustain them. . . . But where the merits of the one and only appeal an indigent has as of right are decided without benefit of counsel, we think an unconstitutional line has been drawn between rich and poor."

The California rule discriminated "not between 'possibly

good and obviously bad cases,' but between cases where the rich man can require the court to listen to argument of counsel before deciding on the merits, but a poor man cannot." This means that the rich man "enjoys the benefit of counsel's examination into the record, research of the law, and marshalling of arguments on his behalf, while the indigent, already burdened by a preliminary determination that his case is without merit, is forced to shift for himself." This violates the equal protection clause of the Fourteenth Amendment.

The Court vacated (canceled) the previous decision in the case and sent it back for a new appeal, in which the defendants would have court-appointed counsel to assist them.

Justice Clark dissented. He cited statistics to indicate that the vast majority of indigent appeals were "frivolous"—or at least that the Supreme Court itself turned down 96 percent of the petitions it received from indigents. California's screening procedure was sensible, Justice Clark felt, and "in my view neither the Equal Protection Clause nor the Due Process Clause requires more."

He went on: "With this new fetish for indigency the Court piles an intolerable burden on the State's judicial machinery. Indeed, if the Court is correct it may be that we should first clean up our own house. We have afforded indigent litigants much less protection than has California." He pointed out that the Supreme Court itself did not appoint attorneys for indigents petitioning it for review or an appellate hearing. (The Court did, however, appoint attorneys for all the cases it agreed to hear, and it was *not* the court that heard "first appeals.")

Justice Clark concluded: "There is an old adage which my good Mother used to quote to me, i.e., 'People who live in glass houses had best not throw stones.' I dissent."

Justice Harlan, joined by Justice Stewart, also dissented.

"To approach the present problem in terms of the Equal Protection Clause is, I submit, but to substitute resounding phrases for analysis," Justice Harlan said. "The States, of course, are prohibited by the Equal Protection Clause from discriminating between 'rich' and 'poor' *as such* in the formulation and application of their laws. But it is a far different thing to suggest that this provision prevents the State from adopting a law of general applicability that may affect the poor more harshly than it does the rich." He noted that any law with financial implications—such as those imposing sales taxes, tuition at state universities, fines for criminal penalties, and minimum bail standards—is easier on the "well-to-do" than on the indigent.

"Laws such as these do not deny equal protection to the less fortunate for one essential reason: the Equal Protection Clause does not impose on the States 'an affirmative duty to lift the handicaps flowing from differences in economic circumstances,' " said Justice Harlan, quoting himself in a previous dissenting opinion. "To so construe it would be to read into the Constitution a philosophy of leveling that would be foreign to many of our basic concepts of the proper relations between government and society. The State may have a moral obligation to eliminate the evils of poverty, but it is not required by the Equal Protection Clause to give to some whatever others can afford."

The Supreme Court, then, has settled quite clearly that an accused in a criminal case who does not have the funds to hire an attorney to assist him in his defense can have a court-appointed lawyer in either a federal or state proceeding for a capital crime or any other felony and for both trial and first appeal.

In chapter 14, we see the Court deciding how soon in the criminal process an accused is entitled to the assistance of counsel. The Court has yet to decide clearly how far the right to counsel extends after trial and appeal. Is a prisoner entitled to have a lawyer represent him at a hearing on whether he can be released on parole? Is an ex-convict entitled to a lawyer at a hearing on whether he violated parole and should be returned to prison?

In addition to the assistance of counsel, the assistance of a skilled investigator can be a crucial factor in the acquittal or conviction of a defendant. How much professional assistance must society provide for a defendant who cannot pay the costs, in order to comply with the constitutional guarantees of due process and equality in the eyes of the law? The Court has not yet decided this question.

Nor has the Court said the final word on the right to the assistance of effective counsel. It condemned the ineffective counsel in the *Scottsboro* case, but the justices have not determined the level of effectiveness necessary to satisfy due process.

Once a defendant has won the right to counsel, he may have to struggle with another problem: Who makes the decisions about how the case is to be handled? Trial lawyers who specialize in criminal law, especially in "political" cases, have become aware that the Sixth Amendment does not give the accused the right to counsel as such. On the contrary, the amendment specifically provides: "In all criminal prosecutions, the accused shall enjoy the right . . . to have the *Assistance* of Counsel for his defence." This indicates that counsel is to assist the accused, not take over the defense or make decisions about the defense alone. Since the accused will ultimately pay the price for any defense decision, since he is the one who will be imprisoned or fined, he will want to participate in making important decisions.

CHAPTER 14

Privilege against Self-Incrimination

One provision of the Fifth Amendment is that "no person . . . shall be compelled in any criminal case to be a witness against himself." This means that a person can refuse to answer a question in a federal criminal proceeding if the answer might lead to his being charged with a crime or would lead to evidence from which he could be charged with a crime. An innocent person who could prove his innocence in a trial cannot be required to answer a question that would cause him to be charged with crime and forced to go through a trial in order to prove his innocence. The privilege, then, extends not only to the guilty but also to the innocent, and not only to a person who had nothing whatever to do with a criminal event but also to a person who was involved in some way and who could not answer questions truthfully without exposing himself to possible criminal proceedings.

The privilege not to be compelled to be a witness against yourself is a very old one. Thirteenth-century biblical commentators found a form of it in the Bible. One of them wrote: "The principle that no man is to be declared guilty on his own admission is a divine decree." We can thank a seventeenth-century Englishman, John Lilburn, for stating the privilege clearly and, ultimately, successfully. Lilburn was against the Church of England and against the Stuart family then heading both church and state. He obtained some tracts from Holland advocating the Leveller religious views, and distributed them in London. He was arrested for this heretical and antigovernment act, and brought before the Court of Star Chamber in 1637. There he was asked to take an oath and answer questions about how he came into possession of these religious booklets and about anything else the court wanted to ask. The Star Chamber was not a regular criminal court but a special agency set up to try "political crimes." It did not follow the due process rules being developed in the common law courts of England, and it was known for its injustice.

John Lilburn refused to take the Star Chamber oath, stating that "no man's conscience ought to be racked by oaths imposed, to answer to questions concerning himself in matters criminal, or pretended to be so." For this behavior, Lilburn was sent to the Tower of London. While there, he wrote tracts himself, including one entitled "Jonah's Cry Out of the Whale's Belly." When he was further punished by being whipped through the streets of London, he used this opportunity to pass out his leaflets to onlookers!

It was a tumultuous period in the political and religious history of England. By 1641 Lilburn had won his freedom from the Tower, and before he could be thrown back in, he convinced Parliament to pay him three thousand pounds in reparations, along with a declaration that his punishment had been "illegal and most unjust, against the liberty of the subject, and law of the land, and Magna Carta." Soon after, Parliament abolished the inquisitorial Star Chamber Court.

The privilege against self-incrimination, then, was established in a struggle that Americans would call a First Amendment fight—a man's insistence on the liberty to exercise his religion and to freely publish his views. This struggle produced a due process right. The privilege was formulated and first used by a First Amendment man, not by a person charged with violating the property or person of another.

The privilege is closely related to the right to counsel, discussed in chapter 13; the burden of proof, discussed in chapter 11; and the problem of coerced confessions, discussed in chapter 12.

The right to counsel is inextricably linked to the privilege because, even now, relatively few Americans know how to use the privilege without the advice of an attorney. Even those who know they have a privilege do not know its boundaries.

Of course, the burden of proof in every criminal case is on the government. The privilege is really a corollary of this burden. The government must prove its case against the defendant. The defendant need not prove his innocence, and the government cannot extract its proof from him.

As a result, the privilege is closely related to the question of confessions and coerced confessions. It forbids requiring a person to confess even if no physical or psychological coercion is used.

Perhaps it is significant that the privilege against self-incrimination became widely known by many Americans during the 1950s, when legislative committees were conducting hearings in two major areas—political belief and activity, and organized crime. These committees, established by the Senate and House of Representatives in Washington and similar committees of state legislatures, were like the Star Chamber; they were not regular courts bound by due process protections. Numerous witnesses were called before these bodies and asked questions. Their answers often could have caused the witnesses to be charged with crimes. Witnesses therefore refused to answer questions on a number of grounds. As we saw in chapter 7, many witnesses who were asked about their political beliefs and affiliations refused to answer on the basis of the First Amendment, claiming that the questioner had no right to investigate beliefs and associations—had no right to put the question—and therefore the witness did not have to answer. However, when the United States Supreme Court rejected the First Amendment as a basis for refusal to answer (and witnesses went to jail for such refusal), other witnesses decided to claim not only the First Amendment, but also the Fifth Amendment privilege against self-incrimination. Alleged racketeers and leaders in the business of crime, called before other legislative committees, also were claiming the privilege in refusing to answer questions that could have led to criminal prosecutions.

Into this situation strode Senator Joe McCarthy with his committee hearings. He excoriated witnesses who refused to answer questions about their political beliefs by calling them "Fifth Amendment Communists." Many citizens rejected the value of the privilege until some of them found it necessary to exercise this very privilege to protect themselves.

When McCarthyism lost its flamboyant advocate, people began to reexamine some of the dogmas expounded during the witch hunts, and to test them against the basic tenets of a democratic society. By 1967, Justice Fortas could write: "The privilege against self-incrimination is, of course, related to the question of the safeguards necessary to assure that admissions or confessions are reasonably trustworthy, that they are not the mere fruits of fear or coercion, but are reliable expressions of the truth. The roots of the privilege are, however, far deeper. They tap the basic stream of religious and political principle because the privilege reflects the limits of the individual's attornment [homage and service] to the state and—in a philosophical sense—insists upon the equality of the individual and the state. In other words, the privilege has a broader and deeper thrust than the rule which prevents the use of confessions which are the product of coercion because coercion is thought to carry with it the danger of unreliability. One of its purposes is to prevent the state, whether by force or by psychological domination, from overcoming the mind and will of the person under investigation and depriving him of the freedom to decide whether to assist the state in securing his conviction."

It is important to understand that the privilege against self-incrimination is not all-encompassing. If a witness refuses to answer a question that would perhaps incriminate another person, this refusal is not protected by the privilege. In other words, a witness is not his brother's keeper under the law, and he can be required to answer a question that may cause another person to be charged with a crime, even if this person turns out ultimately to be innocent.

Also, it is very easy to waive the privilege without meaning to. When a witness goes into a hearing, he is asked a series of questions. He may be asked his name, address, and occupation, and then be questioned about his participation in a particular event. If the person is using an assumed name in order to avoid arrest for a crime, he could claim the privilege even as to answering, "What is your name?" If such a witness answers that question, he has then waived the privilege as to all other answers that would connect him with the crime. If a witness is asked what he did on May 1, and he answers that question, he cannot later refuse to answer questions about who was with him, what he saw, etc., on May 1.

This is why witnesses need the advice of counsel before they appear to answer questions put by any kind of investigating body. The Supreme Court had held that the privilege is not limited to "any criminal case," as stated in the Fifth Amendment. It clearly attaches to a witness before any investigating agency, whether the case is called a "criminal case," a "legislative investigation," a "grand jury hearing," or by any other title.

The Supreme Court has also ruled that when a witness is called before a state agency and a federal agency at the same time and questioned about the same event, he can exercise the privilege before either agency even if the answer may lead to criminal charges before only one agency. As the Court put it in *Murphy* v. *Waterfront Commission,* a witness cannot be "whipsawed" by being forced to answer in one jurisdiction questions that could incriminate him in another.

In the 1960s a series of defendants charged with violent crimes raised further questions about the privilege against self-incrimination. The Supreme Court established further guidelines about using the privilege, which clarify the right for all citizens.

This confession cannot be used

Escobedo v. *Illinois* (1964)
378 U.S. 478, 84 S. Ct. 1758, 12 L. Ed. 2d 977

On the night of January 19, 1960, Manuel Valtierra was shot and killed. At 2:30 A.M., police officers arrested his brother-in-law, Danny Escobedo, and questioned him. Escobedo was twenty-two years old, one of seven children who lived with his mother on the South Side of Chicago; his father was dead.

Escobedo gave no statement to the policemen, and they held him in jail. His lawyer, Warren Wolfson, set to work to get him released. Wolfson secured a state court writ of habeas corpus (see chapter 18), and Escobedo was let out of jail the next day.

Later that month, while police officers were questioning Benedict DiGerlando, he accused Escobedo of firing the shots that had killed Valtierra. On the evening of January 30, policemen arrested both Escobedo and his sister, Valtierra's widow. On the way to headquarters, one of the officers told Escobedo that DiGerlando accused him of the shooting. The police said they had the story and that Escobedo "might as well admit to this crime," but he answered, "I am sorry but I would like to have advice from my lawyer."

Escobedo had no previous record. He was nervous and agitated at headquarters. The officers took him upstairs to the Homicide Bureau for interrogation. He was handcuffed in a standing position, hands behind his back. He asked repeatedly to see his lawyer, but the police officers told him, "Your lawyer doesn't want to see you."

On the contrary, Attorney Wolfson had arrived shortly after Escobedo and had been trying desperately to see him. He was refused permission. "I had a conversation with every police officer I could find. I was told at Homicide that I couldn't see him and I would have to get a writ of habeas corpus." He waited a couple of hours and renewed his requests. "I quoted to Captain Flynn the Section of the Criminal Code which allows an attorney the right to see his client," but Wolfson was allowed "no opportunity to talk to my client that night."

Officer Montejano *was* allowed to see Escobedo. Montejano had grown up in Escobedo's neighborhood and knew his family. He talked to Escobedo alone for about fifteen minutes speaking in Spanish. Escobedo later said Montejano told him "that my sister and I could go home if I pinned it on Benedict DiGerlando." According to Escobedo, Montejano said he and his sister "would go home and be held only as witnesses, if anything." Montejano later denied he had said any such thing.

In the questioning that followed, with several police officers present, Escobedo said that DiGerlando was lying.

"Would you care to tell DiGerlando that?" asked one of the policemen.

"Yes, I will," Escobedo answered.

They brought DiGerlando in, and Escobedo accused him of lying. Then he said, "I didn't shoot Manuel, you did it."

He thus admitted, for the first time, that he had some knowledge of the crime. After that he said other things implicating himself in the murder plot.

The police then called in an assistant state's attorney to take a statement from Escobedo. He asked what the Supreme Court later characterized as "carefully framed questions apparently designed to assure the admissibility into evidence of the resulting answers." Neither the state's attorney nor anyone else advised Escobedo that he had a right to remain silent or that his statements would be used against him.

Escobedo tried, both before and during his trial, to keep the incriminating statements out of the record, but to no avail. He was tried for murder, convicted, and sentenced to twenty years in prison.

On appeal, he and his lawyers argued that his statement should not have been admitted into evidence because he had been denied counsel and because Officer Montejano had promised that the statement would not be used against him. Further Montejano had promised that Escobedo would get "immunity" from arrest and trial if he made the statement, even if he said he was guilty. The state's attorney argued that

This time Danny Escobedo is allowed to consult with his attorney promptly; in an earlier case, he was denied this right by police officers until he had implicated himself in a murder.
Credit: Wide World Photos

the denial of counsel was not a ground for holding the statement inadmissible in evidence and that the statement had been made voluntarily.

The Illinois Supreme Court, in February 1963, reversed the conviction and held that the statement was inadmissible, saying that "it seems manifest to us, from the undisputed evidence and the circumstances surrounding defendant at the time of his statement and shortly prior thereto, that the defendant understood he would be permitted to go home if he gave the statement and would be granted an immunity from prosecution."

The state's attorney asked for a rehearing, stressing Montejano's denial that he had offered immunity to Escobedo. Although courts usually refuse to rehear a case they have just decided, the Illinois Supreme Court granted rehearing and changed its mind. This time, the court agreed with the state prosecutor: Montejano had not offered immunity to Escobedo and Escobedo was not injured by the denial of counsel.

Escobedo asked for review by the United States Supreme Court, which agreed to decide whether the denial of counsel at the interrogation made the statement inadmissible at trial.

When a person is arrested, do you think he has the right to counsel from then on, or only after he is formally charged with a crime? Can the police department do effective investigations of crime if suspects can see their lawyers before they are questioned by the police officers?

The Supreme Court split five to four. Justice Goldberg, writing for the majority, said: "Petitioner, a layman, was undoubtedly unaware that under Illinois law an admission of 'mere' complicity in the murder plot was legally as damaging as an admission of firing of the fatal shots. . . . The 'guiding hand of counsel' was essential to advise petitioner of his rights in this delicate situation." Justice Goldberg noted that the interrogation was a most critical stage, affecting the whole trial, and that rights could be lost forever if not protected then and there.

Answering the Illinois attorney, Justice Goldberg said, "It is argued that if the right to counsel is afforded prior to indictment, the number of confessions obtained by the police will diminish significantly, because most confessions are obtained during the period between arrest and indictment, and 'any lawyer worth his salt will tell the suspect in no uncertain terms to make no statement to police under any circumstances.' "

"This argument, of course, cuts two ways. The fact that many confessions are obtained during this period points up its critical nature as a 'stage when legal aid and advice' are surely needed. . . . There is necessarily a direct relationship between the importance of a stage to the police in their quest for a confession and the criticalness of that stage to the accused in his need for legal advice. Our Constitution, unlike some others, strikes the balance in favor of the right of the accused to be advised by his lawyer of his privilege against self-incrimination."

Justice Goldberg went on, "We have learned the lesson of history, ancient and modern, that a system of criminal law enforcement which comes to depend on the 'confession' will, in the long run, be less reliable and more subject to abuses than a system which depends on extrinsic evidence independently secured through skillful investigation. . . .

"We have also learned the companion lesson of history that no system of criminal justice can, or should, survive if it comes to depend for its continued effectiveness on the citizens' abdication through unawareness of their constitutional rights. No system worth preserving should have to *fear* that if an accused is permitted to consult with a lawyer, he will become aware of, and exercise, these rights."

The Court majority announced a new rule to be followed throughout the country in all criminal cases: "Where, as here, the investigation is no longer a general inquiry into an unsolved crime but has begun to focus on a particular suspect, the suspect has been taken into police custody, the police carry out a process of interrogations that lends itself to eliciting incriminating statements, the suspect has requested and been denied an opportunity to consult with his lawyer, and the police have not effectively warned him of his absolute constitutional right to remain silent, the accused has been denied 'the Assistance of Counsel' in violation of the Sixth Amendment to the Constitution as 'made obligatory upon the States by the Fourteenth Amendment,' . . . and . . . no statement elicited by the police during the interrogation may be used against him at a criminal trial." The five justices emphasized, "Nothing we have said today affects the powers of the police to investigate 'an unsolved crime,' . . . by gathering information from witnesses and by other 'proper investigative efforts.' "

Justice Harlan, dissenting, thought that "the rule announced today is most ill-conceived and that it seriously and unjustifiably fetters perfectly legitimate methods of criminal law enforcement." Justice Stewart, in a separate dissent, felt that the right to counsel arose after investigation ended, when the suspect had been charged with crime by formal indictment or information.

Justice White wrote the principal dissent, joined in by Justices Clark and Stewart. He stressed that the key issue was not the right to counsel but coerced confessions. He felt that

Escobedo had made a voluntary statement, and therefore it was admissible in evidence. The *Escobedo* rule, he said, "reflects a deep-seated distrust of law enforcement officers everywhere, unsupported by relevant data or current material based upon our own experience. Obviously law enforcement officers can make mistakes and exceed their authority, as today's decision shows that even judges can do, but I have somewhat more faith than the Court evidently has in the ability and desire of prosecutors and of the power of the appellate courts to discern and correct such violations of the law."

Justice White concluded that law enforcement "will be crippled and its task made a great deal more difficult" by the *Escobedo* ruling. Many apparently agreed with the minority opinion, and the decision caused a furor, particularly in law enforcement circles, that made Escobedo's name famous. Other citizens hailed the decision as a major step away from inquisitorial police practices.

Danny Escobedo was deeply affected by his fame. He lost a dozen jobs after his release in the original case, and in 1967, he accused the Chicago police of harassing him with a series of arrests on various charges, all of which either ended in dismissals or were dropped before trial. He blamed the constant arrests for his present unemployment.

In 1968, Escobedo was arrested for possession and sale of heroin. This time the case did go to trial, and he was convicted. He was sentenced to fifteen years in federal prison at Leavenworth, Kansas.

The *Escobedo* rule was not reversed by the Court or Congress and it did bring about a change in the interrogation procedures in many police departments around the country. While a suspect who had no lawyer still could be questioned by police officers without the advice of counsel, the *Escobedo* rule encouraged police departments to pursue independent investigations and not to rely on confessions made by the suspect before talking with his attorney.

The rule was obeyed, but not with enthusiasm. Law enforcement institutions applied it when required, but they certainly did not seek to enlarge its application. As a result, cases continued to arise in which defendants alleged they had not been told that they could see their lawyers promptly on request and had not been warned that any statement they made might help imprison them.

In 1966, the Supreme Court agreed to hear a series of cases in which defendants convicted in federal and state courts alleged that the *Escobedo* rule had been violated.

"I must warn you that you have the right . . ."

Miranda v. *Arizona* (1966)
384 U.S. 436, 86 S. Ct. 1602, 16 L. Ed. 2d 694

On March 13, 1963, Ernesto Miranda was arrested by the Phoenix police at his home. He was taken to the station and put into a lineup for identification by a woman who had been robbed. Not only did this woman pick out Miranda, but an eighteen-year-old girl who had recently been raped also identified him as her assailant.

Miranda was then taken to an interrogation room and questioned about both crimes by Police Officers Young and Cooley. They did not tell him he had a right to an attorney. Officer Cooley said, "We told him anything he said would be used against him, he wasn't required by law to tell us anything"; Officer Young said they had not given him these warnings.

After two hours, the officers obtained a written confession from Miranda, at the top of which was typed a paragraph stating that the confession was made voluntarily, without threats or promises of immunity, and "with full knowledge of my legal rights, understanding any statement I make may be used against me."

Miranda did not ask for an attorney while being questioned. This was not surprising. Relatively few Americans know, the first time they are arrested, that they have a right to talk to a lawyer. In addition, Miranda was only twenty-three, he had dropped out of school in the ninth grade, and he showed signs of mental incapacity. A psychiatric sanity examination was ordered for him, which revealed that he had a considerable preoccupation with sex. The psychiatrist asked Miranda to explain the meanings of some proverbs. He interpreted "a rolling stone gathers no moss" to mean "if you don't have sex with a woman, she can't get pregnant." He thought "people in glass houses shouldn't throw stones" meant "a person with one woman shouldn't go to another woman." In a nonsexual interpretation, he said "a stitch in time saves nine" meant that "if you try to shut something in, you keep it from going out." The psychiatrist concluded that Miranda had "an emotional illness. I would classify him as a schizophrenic reaction, chronic undifferentiated type." He was adjudged sane by legal standards, however.

Miranda was charged with both the robbery and the kidnapping-rape. The charges were tried separately by juries, but with the same judge. At the rape trial, Miranda's attorney objected when the prosecution introduced the confession into evidence, stating that "the Supreme Court of the United States says a man is entitled to an attorney at the time of his arrest." The defense attorney also found the confession unbelievable because it used words such as "cooperation," "penis," and "vagina," which were inconsistent with his client's vocabulary.

The judge admitted the confession into evidence over the lawyer's objections. The jurors found Miranda guilty in both trials, and the judge sentenced him to between forty and fifty-five years in prison on the two convictions.

Miranda's lawyer appealed the convictions to the Arizona Supreme Court, which treated the two as companion cases. In April 1965, the court held that the confession was admissible because, under the *Escobedo* rule, "the suspect must have requested and been denied the opportunity to consult with his lawyer," and Miranda had not asked for counsel.

Miranda asked the United States Supreme Court to review the case. The Court agreed to hear this case along with three others raising questions about the scope and application of the *Escobedo* rule. As Chief Justice Warren noted, *Escobedo* "has been the subject of judicial interpretation and spirited legal debate since it was decided two years ago. Both state and federal courts, in assessing its implications, have arrived at varying conclusions." The Court agreed now to explore some of the problems raised and "to give concrete constitutional guidelines for law enforcement agencies and courts to follow."

In your opinion, does a suspect have to ask for counsel or do police officers have a duty to tell him that he has a right to counsel? Should a citizen be responsible for knowing and demanding his rights when he is accused of a crime or are law enforcement officials responsible for telling the citizen what his rights are? If police officers do not honor the citizen's right to counsel and privilege against self-incrimination, what can be done to correct this? Should a defendant with a poor education be treated by policemen in the same manner as a well-educated middle-class suspect? Why or why not? What about a defendant who is mentally ill?

The Supreme Court again split five to four. The Chief Justice wrote for the majority: "We have undertaken a thorough re-examination of the *Escobedo* decision and the principles it announced, and we reaffirm it. That case was but an explication of basic rights that are enshrined in our Constitution—that 'No person . . . shall be compelled in any criminal case to be a witness against himself,' and that 'the accused shall . . . have the Assistance of Counsel'—rights which were put in jeopardy in that case through official overbearing. These precious rights were fixed in our Constitution only after centuries of persecution and struggle. And in the words of Chief Justice Marshall, they were secured 'for ages to come, and . . . designed to approach immortality as nearly as human institutions can approach it.' "

Chief Justice Warren detailed past findings that police had used physical brutality to extort confessions, some as late as 1961 and 1965. "The use of physical brutality and violence is not, unfortunately, relegated to the past or to any part of the country," he said. "The examples given above are undoubtedly the exception now, but they are sufficiently widespread to be the object of concern."

The Chief Justice noted that "the modern practice of in-custody interrogation is psychologically rather than physically oriented," and he quoted extensively from police manuals and texts describing interrogation tactics officers were taught to use to obtain statements from suspects. These included interrogation "without relent"; minimizing the crime or blaming the victim as if the officers were on the suspect's side; accusing him of several other crimes the police know he did not commit (even having him identified falsely in a lineup by several "victims"); having two officers do the questioning—the first in a very harsh and hostile tone, the second in a very sympathetic tone as if he were the suspect's best friend; and telling the suspect that he can remain silent but that this will surely be taken as a sign of guilt.

The advice in police manuals was summarized by Chief Justice Warren: "To obtain a confession, the interrogator must 'patiently maneuver himself or his quarry into a position from which the desired objective may be attained.' When normal procedures fail to produce the needed result, the police may resort to deceptive stratagems such as giving false legal advice. It is important to keep the subject off balance, for example, by trading on his insecurity about himself or his surroundings. The police then persuade, trick, or cajole him out of exercising his constitutional rights."

To show that a confession obtained under these conditions is far from voluntary, the Chief Justice quoted an example from a recent law review article:

"Suppose a well-to-do testatrix says she intends to will her property to Elizabeth. John and James want her to bequeath it to them instead. They capture the testatrix, put her in a carefully designed room, out of touch with everyone but themselves and their convenient 'witnesses,' keep her secluded there for hours while they make insistent demands, weary her with contradictions of her assertions that she wants to leave her money to Elizabeth, and finally induce her to execute the will in their favor. Assume that John and James are deeply and correctly convinced that Elizabeth is unworthy and will make base use of the property if she gets her hands on it, whereas John and James have the noblest and most righteous intentions. Would any judge of probate accept the will so procured as the 'voluntary' act of the testatrix?"

The Court concluded: "It is obvious that such an interrogation environment is created for no purpose other than to subjugate the individual to the will of his examiner. This atmosphere carries its own badge of intimidation. To be sure, this is not physical intimidation, but it is equally destructive of human dignity. The current practice of incommunicado interrogation is at odds with one of our Nation's most cherished principles—that the individual may not be compelled to incriminate himself. Unless adequate protective devices are employed to dispel the compulsion inherent in custodial surroundings, no statement obtained from the defendant can truly be the product of his free choice."

In an unusual move, the Court set forth the precise measures police officers must follow in questioning a suspect who is in custody: "He must be warned prior to any questioning that he has the right to remain silent, that anything he says can be used against him in a court of law, that he has the right to the presence of an attorney, and that if he cannot afford an attorney one will be appointed for him prior to any questioning if he so desires. Opportunity to exercise these rights must be afforded to him throughout the interrogation. After such warnings have been given, and such opportunity afforded him, the individual may knowingly and intelligently waive these rights and agree to answer questions or make a statement. But unless and until such warnings and waiver are demonstrated by the prosecution at trial, no evidence obtained as a result of interrogation can be used against him."

Answering the expected criticisms, the majority of the Court said: "In announcing these principles, we are not unmindful of the burdens which law enforcement officials must bear, often under trying circumstances. We also fully recognize the obligation of all citizens to aid in enforcing the criminal laws. This Court, while protecting individual rights, has always given ample latitude to law enforcement agencies in the legitimate exercise of their duties. The limits we have placed on the interrogation process should not constitute an undue interference with a proper system of law enforcement. As we have noted, our decision does not in any way preclude police from carrying out their traditional investigatory functions." Chief Justice Warren also took pains to show that in each of the four cases being considered, the police had evidence other than the confessions, with which to prove the defendant's guilt; society's need for protection did not, therefore, outweigh the need for the privilege against self-incrimination.

Justice Clark dissented as to three of the cases and concurred as to one. He thought the Court might be going "too far too fast."

Justice Harlan, joined by Justices Stewart and White, dissented in all four cases. He felt the majority was pursuing " 'voluntariness' in a utopian sense, or to view it from a different angle, voluntariness with a vengeance." He found in the majority opinion "no adequate basis for extending the Fifth Amendment's privilege against self-incrimination to the police station." The Fifth Amendment "has never been thought to forbid *all* pressure to incriminate one's self in the situations covered by it," said Justice Harlan. "Until today, the role of the Constitution has been only to sift out *undue* pressure, not to assure spontaneous confessions."

Justice White wrote a separate dissent, joined by Justices Harlan and Stewart. "The obvious underpinning of the Court's decision is a deep-seated distrust of all confessions," he felt. "I see nothing wrong or immoral, and certainly nothing unconstitutional, in the police's asking a suspect whom they have reasonable cause to arrest whether or not he killed his wife or in confronting him with the evidence on which the arrest was based, at least where he has been plainly advised that he may remain completely silent. . . . Moreover, it is by no means certain that the process of confessing is injurious to the accused. To the contrary it may provide psychological relief and enhance the prospects for rehabilitation.

"This is not to say that the value of respect for the inviolability of the accused's individual personality should be accorded no weight or that all confessions should be indiscriminately admitted. This Court has long read the Constitution to proscribe compelled confessions, a salutary rule from which there should be no retreat."

As to the new rule's effect, Justice White warned: "There is, in my view, every reason to believe that a good many criminal defendants who otherwise would have been convicted on what this Court has previously thought to be the most satisfactory kind of evidence will now under this new version of the Fifth Amendment, either not be tried at all or will be acquitted if the State's evidence, minus the confession, is put to the test of litigation.

"I have no desire whatsoever to share the responsibility for any such impact on the present criminal process."

A week after it was handed down, the Supreme Court held that the *Miranda* rule would be applied only to trials begun after the date of the decision, not to cases already tried (even if the proper warnings had not been given to the defendants in those cases).

Many police chiefs copied the Court's holding, labeled it "the *Miranda* warning," and directed all officers to give it to all suspects. A study by the Los Angeles County District Attorney's office in August 1966 revealed that a slightly *higher* percentage of defendants made statements or confessions after being given the constitutional warnings than before the *Miranda* rule was handed down. The report added that the rule was causing some problems in prosecutions of cases that had begun before the *Miranda* decision, but it was expected to create no significant difficulties in future prosecutions. *Miranda* spawned studies in other major cities and innumerable articles by law professors and law enforcement officials.

Today, the *Miranda* warning is commonly given to men and women being questioned by the police while in custody in most jurisdictions in the United States. Whether it is understood by every person to whom it is given is, of course, another matter. Police enforcement officials have not stopped their efforts to have it overruled. In 1968, Congress passed Title II of the Omnibus Crime Control and Safe Streets Act, which sought to soften the application of the *Miranda* and *Mallory* decisions (see chapter 12). The statute lists all the protections required by the Supreme Court in those two cases, but says, "The presence or absence of any of the above-mentioned factors to be taken into consideration by the judge *need not be conclusive* on the issue of voluntariness of the confession." In other words, a police department may be able to get a conviction by methods the Court has condemned.

As long as *Mallory* and *Miranda* remain in the law books, unreversed, as long as this act sits on the books, unrepealed, and as long as citizens and police officers have different attitudes toward crime control and due process of law, cases will find their way to the United States Supreme Court in which the police departments or the criminal defendants allege that they have been wronged under the Constitution.

What happens to a defendant in a criminal trial who exercises the privilege against self-incrimination to the utmost by not even taking the stand? This means he answers no questions concerning himself or the alleged crime or his participation in it. It is clear that a defendant has the right to refuse to take the stand. It is clear that the jurors will notice that he has not taken the stand and answered questions. But may the prosecutor or judge comment on such a refusal? This issue came before the court in *Griffin* v. *California*.

Does silence indicate guilt?

Griffin v. *California* (1965)
380 U.S. 609, 85 S. Ct. 1229, 14 L. Ed. 2d 106

Eddie Dean Griffin was accused of beating up a woman friend and leaving her in an alley to die. He was charged with first degree murder and tried before a jury. The prosecutor presented evidence that Griffin had been seen with the woman named Essie Mae in the alley the night she died and that he had left the alley alone, "cool as a cucumber."

Griffin did not take the stand at the trial. His lawyer relied on the ancient rule that in criminal cases the defendant does not have to prove his innocence; it is the government that must prove his guilt beyond a reasonable doubt. The jurors therefore were not faced with a choice between two conflicting stories. They had only the prosecutor's version, and they had to decide whether it proved guilt beyond a reasonable doubt.

The prosecutor, in closing argument to the jury, made much of the fact that Griffin had not testified. "The defendant certainly knows whether Essie Mae had this beat up appearance at the time he left her apartment and went down the alley with her," he said. "He would know how she got down the alley. He would know how the blood got on the bottom of the concrete steps. . . . He would know whether he beat her or mistreated her. . . . These things he has not seen fit to take the stand and deny or explain. And in the whole world, if anybody would know, this defendant would know. Essie Mae is dead, she can't tell you her side of the story. The defendant won't."

The judge instructed the jurors that they could take into consideration Griffin's failure to testify about evidence that he might be expected to deny or explain, and that his silence tended to indicate the truth of that evidence. The judge cautioned the jurors that the silence did not create a presumption of guilt and did not tend to indicate the truth of any other evidence.

The jurors found Griffin guilty, and decided on a death sentence. On appeal, Griffin's lawyer challenged the California statute allowing judges and attorneys to comment on a defendant's failure to explain or deny evidence against him. This violated the Fifth Amendment privilege against self-incrimination, he said. What good is the privilege if a defendant can be convicted for exercising it?

The state's attorney responded that it was only natural to comment on a fact that the jury had already witnessed in the course of the trial. In fact, the judge's comments would tend to keep the jury from drawing improper inferences from the defendant's silence.

The California Supreme Court rejected Griffin's appeal, and he then sought review by the United States Supreme Court. The Court had recently held, in *Malloy* v. *Hogan,* that the Fifth Amendment privilege was applicable to state court proceedings under the Fourteenth Amendment. Forty-four states had laws or rules that judges and lawyers were not to comment on a defendant's failure to testify. California was one of six states allowing such comments in one form or another. The Supreme Court agreed to decide whether the California law was constitutional.

Do you think an innocent person would ever refuse to testify? Is the defendant's privilege limited when a judge comments on his failure to deny or explain evidence against him? The jury already knows that the defendant has not testified; does the judge's comment give this fact added significance?

The Supreme Court's six-to-two decision was presented by Justice Douglas (Chief Justice Warren did not participate in the decision). The California statute, Justice Douglas said, "is in substance a rule of evidence that allows the State the privilege of tendering to the jury for its consideration the failure of the accused to testify." As if this failure were itself a piece of testimony, "the prosecutor's comment and the court's acquiescence are the equivalent of an offer of evidence and its acceptance."

Explaining why a defendant might not testify, Justice Douglas quoted a Supreme Court opinion from 1893, *Wilson* v. *United States:* "It is not every one who can safely venture on the witness stand, though entirely innocent of the charge against him. Excessive timidity, nervousness when facing others and attempting to explain transactions of a suspicious character, and offenses charged against him, will often confuse and embarrass him to such a degree as to increase rather than remove prejudices against him. It is not every one, however honest, who would therefore willingly be placed on the witness stand."

The Court, speaking through Justice Douglas, held that comment on the failure to testify "is a penalty imposed by courts for exercising a constitutional privilege. It cuts down on the privilege by making its assertion costly."

True, the jury was well aware that the defendant had not taken the stand, Justice Douglas granted. But "what the jury may infer, given no help from the court, is one thing. What it may infer when the court solemnizes the silence of the accused into evidence against him is quite another."

The Court held that "the Fifth Amendment, in its direct application to the Federal Government and in its bearing on the States by reason of the Fourteenth Amendment, forbids either comment by the prosecution on the accused's silence or instructions by the court that such silence is evidence of guilt." Griffin's conviction was reversed.

Justice Harlan wrote a concurring opinion in order to argue again that provisions of the Bill of Rights should not be "incorporated" in the Fourteenth Amendment, as discussed in chapter 20.

Justice Stewart, speaking also for Justice White, dissented. "We must determine whether the petitioner has been 'compelled . . . to be a witness against himself.' Compulsion is the focus of the inquiry," he said. After examining how comments might affect the jury, Justice Stewart concluded: "I think the California comment rule is not a coercive device which impairs the right against self-incrimination, but rather a means of articulating and bringing into the light of rational discussion a fact inescapably impressed on the jury's consciousness."

Later, the Court limited application of the rule in *Griffin* to trials held after that decision was handed down. Judges and lawyers are not prohibited from commenting on the defendant's silence in all state as well as federal criminal trials. The burden of proving guilt beyond a reasonable doubt has always been placed on the prosecutor. The *Griffin* decision made it clear that he cannot get any help from inferences to be drawn from the defendant's failure to testify.

CHAPTER 15

Right to Trial by Impartial Jury

The right not to be searched or arrested without reasonable cause, the right to prompt arraignment and release on reasonable bail or own recognizance, the right to assistance of counsel and to a warning of other rights, the privilege against self-incrimination—all of these are critical rights in the pretrial period of a criminal case. But the decision about the defendant's innocence or guilt determines his fate; all the pretrial rights in the Constitution will not protect a defendant who is tried by a prejudiced judge or jury.

The United States Constitution (in Article III, section 2, paragraph 3) guarantees that "the trial of all Crimes, except in Cases of Impeachment, shall be by Jury." The Sixth Amendment guarantees: "In all criminal prosecutions, the accused shall enjoy the right to a speedy and public trial, by an impartial jury of the State and district wherein the crime shall have been committed." This right to jury trial has always stood at the top of the list of procedural protections for the innocent. It also permits ordinary citizens, acting as jurors, to consider community standards of morality and to temper justice with mercy when the testimony indicates the defendant is guilty of a crime or implicated in it.

Justice White noted in 1968 (in *Duncan* v. *Louisiana*) that "the First Continental Congress, in the resolve of October

14, 1774, objected to trials before judges dependent upon the Crown alone for their salaries . . . [and] declared: 'That the respective colonies are entitled to the common law of England, and more especially to the great and inestimable privilege of being tried by their peers of the vicinage.' " Similar sentiments were expressed in the Declaration of Independence, leading to the article and amendment of the Constitution.

In 1965, Chief Justice Warren explained that the jury trial clause in Article III "was clearly intended to protect the accused from oppression by the Government . . . [and] it is not surprising that some of the framers apparently believed that the Constitution designated trial by jury the exclusive method of determining guilt. . . . [In 1834] Mr. Justice Story, while sitting on circuit, indicated his view that the Constitution made trial by jury the only permissible method of trial. Similar views were expressed by other federal judges."

Chief Justice Warren was writing a unanimous opinion in *Singer* v. *United States,* the case of a federal criminal defendant who wanted to waive (give up his right to) a jury trial, over government objection. The Court forbade waiver unless the prosecution agreed, quoting a 1930 opinion in *Patton* v. *United States:* "Not only must the right of the accused to a trial by a constitutional jury be jealously preserved, but the maintenance of the jury as a fact-finding body in criminal cases is of such importance and has such a place in our traditions, that, before any waiver can become effective, the consent of government counsel and the sanction of the court must be had, in addition to the express and intelligent consent of the defendant. And the duty of the trial court in that regard is not to be discharged as a mere matter of rote, but with sound and advised discretion, with an eye to avoid unreasonable or undue departures from that mode of trial or from any of the essential elements thereof, and with a caution increasing in degree as the offenses dealt with increase in gravity."

In a short, well-reasoned defense of the jury system, Justice Clark made an additional argument in 1966 that "jury service is the only remaining governmental function in which the citizen takes a *direct* part. It is, therefore, the sole means of keeping the administration of justice attuned to community standards. Daniel Webster tells us that justice is the great interest of man on earth. Let us not cut its jugular vein!"

Justice Clark recognized that "many distinguished and learned judges and lawyers have suggested that the jury be dispensed with in civil cases. They argue that the jury is arbitrary." He replied: "In many cases this is true. But judges are also arbitrary at times; and along with it they often get calloused from the daily routine of hearing other people's troubles. I submit that history is against those who depend on this fault—700 years of jury verdicts without a change in procedure is heavy weight to overcome."

The Sixth Amendment has led to two major lines of cases: those in which the defendant challenges the jurors' fairness because of pretrial publicity, and those in which the defendant challenges the fairness of the method of selecting the jurors.

(The Sixth Amendment guarantee is also at issue in cases in which a defendant charges that the police or prison officials have punished him without trial and before conviction by beating or mistreating him at the time of arrest or while he was awaiting trial. Defendants in such cases sometimes sue the police department or sheriff's office for damages for physical injuries resulting from such attacks, and these suits were discussed in chapter 12.)

A. Pretrial Publicity

In a country like the United States, where freedom of expression is guaranteed in the First Amendment, and where papers traditionally compete for readers on the basis of news coverage, the people called for jury duty can be influenced to believe a defendant guilty or innocent long before they receive a summons to serve. Some civil libertarians believe the press should be forbidden to publish information on pending criminal cases, as the British press is. Others believe that this impairs freedom of the press and that, especially in hard-fought cases and in political trials, lack of coverage may harm the defendant more than widespread coverage helps the prosecution. Despite the supposed presumption of innocence, most people feel that a defendant wouldn't be on trial if he weren't guilty of *something.* Therefore, in a typical case, the jurors seem to expect the defendant to prove his innocence. Without an opportunity to explain his side of the case, the defendant doesn't stand much of a chance.

Within limits imposed by the guarantees of freedom of press and of a public trial in the district, a trial judge has considerable control over his courtroom. He can clear the audience whenever this becomes necessary in order to conduct the trial in an orderly fashion. He can cite any lawyer, witness, party, spectator, or reporter for contempt of court for behavior in his presence or outside his presence. He can postpone the trial in order to ensure fairness. He can grant a change of venue so that the trial will not take place where the incident occurred if the defendant has in effect been tried and convicted by the media.

Are there limits to the power of the trial judge? Can a

judge assert this power effectively in every situation? These questions were brought before the Supreme Court in modern garb in a much publicized murder case. The Warren Court, following the policy started earlier in the twentieth century, was prepared to analyze the requirements of due process in state court proceedings.

Trial by newspaper

Sheppard v. *Maxwell* (1966)
384 U.S. 333, 86 S. Ct. 1507, 16 L. Ed. 2d 60

Every so often a murder case becomes a sensation—usually because of the victim, the suspect, or the manner of death. When young, pregnant Marilyn Sheppard was bludgeoned to death in her bedroom in Bay Village, Ohio (a suburb of Cleveland), newsmen quickly perked up their ears. She and her thirty-year-old husband, Dr. Sam Sheppard, an osteopathic surgeon, were socially prominent in Cleveland. His father and two brothers, Richard and Steve, all doctors, practiced with him at Bay View Hospital, which the Sheppard family operated.

Dr. Sheppard said he had been awakened in the early morning hours by his wife's cry. He rushed to her bedroom and saw a "white form" near her bed. In a series of struggles with it he was twice knocked unconscious. When he regained consciousness the second time, he found that his wife was dead and he called a neighbor, who sent for the police and the doctor's brother Richard. When Dr. Richard Sheppard arrived, he looked at his brother's injuries and took him to the Bay View Hospital for treatment.

Dr. Gerber, the coroner, soon arrived with Cleveland police and officials. They searched the house and grounds thoroughly, took photographs, and began interrogating people. The Ahearns, who had spent the previous evening with the Sheppards, said things had been quiet and ordinary. The Sheppards had not quarreled and had been quite affectionate with each other. Nevertheless, the coroner quickly concluded that Dr. Sheppard was the killer. "Well, it is evident the doctor did this," he told his men, "so let's go get the confession out of him."

Coroner Gerber went to the hospital and questioned Sheppard that same day (July 4), although the doctor was under sedation. Later that afternoon the chief of the Cleveland police and two of his men also interrogated Sheppard at length.

On July 7, Mrs. Sheppard's funeral was held, and the *Cleveland Press* printed a story on page one in which the county prosecutor accused the Sheppard family of refusing "to permit the immediate questioning of the victim's husband." From then on, the newspapers repeatedly charged that Sam Sheppard was balking at questioning, uncooperative with the police, and encircled by a "protective ring" of family and friends in high places. The Sheppard family retained a leading Cleveland criminal lawyer, William J. Corrigan, when it became clear that Sam was a suspect. This seemed to inflame the newspapers and the prosecutor even more.

On July 9, at the coroner's request, Sheppard went back to his home and reenacted the course of events in the presence of Dr. Gerber, several policemen, and a group of newsmen apparently invited by the coroner.

The papers in the next few days made much of Sheppard's refusal to take a lie detector test, and then played up "a possible 'other woman' angle." Sheppard at first denied that he had had extramarital relations, but was later confronted with a statement by a former laboratory technician confessing to an affair. When he admitted this, the newspapers gave the story extended coverage.

The *Cleveland Press* ran page one editorials and stories demanding a coroner's inquest. On July 22, Coroner Gerber began a three-day inquest in a school gymnasium with an audience of over 200 people. In addition to wide press coverage, the hearing was broadcast live. Sheppard was questioned for 5½ hours about the night of the murder, his married life, and his love affair.

When the inquest was over, the *Cleveland Press* ran an editorial: "Now proved under oath to be a liar, still free to go about his business, shielded by his family, protected by a smart lawyer who has made monkeys of the police and authorities, carrying a gun part of the time, left free to do whatever he pleases as he pleases, Sam Sheppard still hasn't been taken to Headquarters."

On July 30, the front-page editorial was titled "Why Isn't Sam Sheppard In Jail?" At 10:00 P.M. that night Sheppard was arrested for murder. In the next months the papers gave the case constant coverage, revealing "new evidence," speculation, gossip, and interviews with various participants. Toward the end of September the names and addresses of the seventy-five prospective jurors in the case were published in all three Cleveland papers.

Jury selection began October 18. The courtroom was of moderate size. There were four rows of spectator seats. Within the area normally reserved for the participants (parties in the case, their attorneys, the jury, the judge, court officials, and the witness stand), a long temporary table had been set up from one side of the room to the other. The judge assigned twenty newsmen seats at this table. The first three rows of spectator seats were also assigned to radio, television, newspaper, and magazine reporters. The remaining row of spectator seats was assigned to family members.

That entire floor of the courthouse was given over to the news media, and one room on another floor—the room next to the jury room—was converted to a broadcasting facility for one radio station. Television cameramen and photographers were not allowed to take pictures while court was in session but did extensive photographing during recesses, in the corridors, and at the courthouse steps.

The trial lasted nine weeks. News coverage was extensive. Pictures of and stories about the jurors appeared over forty times in the Cleveland papers. This kind of publicity on jurors was unprecedented and made them celebrities.

Photographs of exhibits and of rooms in the Sheppard house were published, and the transcript of testimony was printed verbatim. In addition, the media reported numerous pieces of "evidence" or "testimony" that were "to be revealed" in the trial; they never materialized. Particularly damaging to Sheppard were reports that his wife had said he was "a regular Dr. Jekyll and Mr. Hyde," reports that a "bombshell witness" would testify that the doctor had sudden outbursts of violence, and a radio and television broadcast by Walter Winchell telling of a woman arrested for robbery in New York who accused Sheppard of fathering her child.

The jurors were not sequestered during the trial, but returned to their homes each night. At the beginning of the trial the judge advised them: "I would suggest to you and caution you that you do not read any newspapers during the progress of this trial, that you do not listen to radio comments nor watch or listen to television comments, insofar as this case is concerned. . . . I am sure that we shall all feel very much better if we do not indulge in any newspaper reading

The Cleveland Press

The Newspaper That Serves Its Readers

NO. 24028   CLEVELAND, FRIDAY, JULY 30, 1954   Phone CHerry 1-1111

City

44 Pages—7 Cents

Why Isn't Sam Sheppard in Jail?

(AN EDITORIAL)

Maybe somebody in this town can remember parallel for it. The Press can't.

And not even the oldest police veterans can, either.

Everybody's agreed that Sam Sheppard is the most unusual murder suspect ever seen around these parts.

Except for some superficial questioning during Coroner Sam Gerber's inquest he has been scot-free of any official grilling into the circumstances of his wife's murder.

From the morning of July 4, when he reported his wife's killing, to this moment, 26 days later, Sam Sheppard has not set foot in a police station.

He has been surrounded by an iron curtain of protection that makes Malenkov's Russian concealment amateurish.

The Suspect

His family, his Bay Village friends—which include its officials—his lawyers, his hospital staff, have combined to make law enforcement in this county look silly.

The longer they can stall bringing Sam Sheppard to the police station the surer it is he'll never get there.

The longer they can string this whole affair out the surer it is that the public's attention sooner or later will be diverted to something else, and then the heat will be off, the public interest gone, and the goose will hang high.

This man is a suspect in his wife's murder. Nobody yet has found a solitary trace of the presence of anybody else in his Lake Rd. house the night or morning his wife was brutally beaten to death in her bedroom.

And yet no murder suspect in the history of this county has been treated so tenderly, with such infinite solicitude for his emotions, with such fear of upsetting the young man.

Gentlemen of Bay Village, Cuyahoga County, and Cleveland, charged jointly with law enforcement—

This is murder. This is no parlor game. This is no time to permit anybody—no matter who he is—to outwit, stall, fake, or improvise devices to keep away from the police or from the questioning anybody in his right mind knows a murder suspect should be subjected to—in a police station.

The officials throw up their hands in horror at the thought of bringing Sam Sheppard to a police station for grilling. Why? Why is he any different than anybody else in any other murder case?

Why should the police officials be afraid of Bill Corrigan? Or anybody else, for that matter, when they are at their sworn business of solving a murder.

Certainly Corrigan will act to protect Sam Sheppard's rights. He should.

But the people of Cuyahoga County expect you, the law enforcement officials, to protect the people's rights.

A murder has been committed. You know who the chief suspect is.

You have the obligation to question him—question him thoroughly and searchingly—from beginning to end, and not at his hospital, not at his home, not in some secluded spot out in the country.

But at Police Headquarters—just as you do everyother person suspected in a murder case.

What the people of Cuyahoga County cannot understand, and The Press cannot understand, is why you are showing Sam Sheppard so much more consideration as a murder suspect than any other person who has ever before been suspected in a murder case.

Why?

Headline calls for Sam Sheppard's arrest. This is a sample of the pervasive publicity that accompanied the case throughout Sheppard's trial.

or listening to any comments whatever about the matter while the case is in progress. After it is all over, you can read it all to your heart's content."

Defense Attorney Corrigan, faced with this level of publicity, moved repeatedly for a change of venue (moving the trial to another area less permeated with prejudicial publicity), for continuance (delay of the trial until the excitement died down), and for mistrial (a declaration that the trial had been tainted so that this jury could not decide the case). The judge denied all these motions.

Each time a piece of damaging publicity appeared, Corrigan asked the judge to poll the jurors on whether they had seen or heard it. Often the judge refused. "It is getting to the point where if we do it every morning, we are suspecting the jury. I have confidence in this jury," he said. "We can't stop people, in any event, listening to it. It is a matter of free speech, and the court can't control everybody."

After the Winchell broadcast, the judge did agree to poll the jurors. Two of them *had* heard the charge that Sheppard had fathered the accused robber's child. The judge then asked them: "Would that have any effect upon your judgment?"

"No," they answered.

He then told the jury generally to "pay no attention whatever to that type of scavenging. . . . Let's confine ourselves to this courtroom, if you please."

Corrigan was not reassured; he moved for a mistrial. The judge said, "I don't justify [these stories] at all. I think it is outrageous," but he denied Corrigan's motion.

At the end of the evidence and arguments, the jury deliberated for five days. They returned a verdict of guilty of murder in the second degree (without premeditation). Sheppard was sentenced to life imprisonment.

His attorneys moved for a new trial. This was denied. They appealed both the conviction and the denial of a new trial. The state court of appeals affirmed both. Sheppard appealed to the Ohio Supreme Court, which upheld the lower court's rulings. Next he sought review by the United States Supreme Court. This was denied.

By then Sheppard had spent two years in prison. He had exhausted the appeal procedure, but a man with a life sentence does not easily give up seeking his freedom. Sheppard petitioned the Ohio Supreme Court for a writ of habeas corpus (see chapter 18); it was denied.

In 1963, he applied for a habeas corpus writ in the federal district court. The federal judge examined the record of pretrial and trial publicity (five large scrapbooks of newspaper clippings), and concluded, in July 1964, that Sheppard had not received a fair trial and therefore his conviction was unconstitutional.

The state appealed this decision to the federal court of appeals. The three appellate judges split two to one, the majority upholding Sheppard's conviction. Sheppard then asked the United States Supreme Court to review the decision. This time the Court agreed.

It is clear that the Sheppard trial had received vast publicity, much of it adverse to the accused. But isn't this part of freedom of the press? Is there such a thing as "objective reporting"? Can a court order the press to limit itself to objective reporting of "facts" and not to speculate or second-guess the prosecution or defense? Should the rules for reporting trials be different from those for reporting public events, such as political campaigns or community protests? Does the prosecutor or the defense attorney have a duty to curb prejudicial publicity and ensure a fair trial?

The Supreme Court's decision was handed down in June 1966, after Sheppard had served eleven years in prison. Justice Clark, writing for the eight-to-one majority, said: "A responsible press has always been regarded as the handmaiden of effective judicial administration, especially in the criminal field. Its function in this regard is documented by an impressive record of service over several centuries. The press does not simply publish information about trials but guards against the miscarriage of justice by subjecting the police, prosecutors, and judicial processes to extensive public scrutiny and criticism. This Court has, therefore, been unwilling to place any direct limitations on the freedom traditionally exercised by the news media." In fact, he said, "we have consistently required that the press have a free hand, even though we sometimes deplored its sensationalism."

Trials, however, "are not like elections, to be won through the use of the meeting hall, the radio, and the newspaper." They require "that the jury's verdict be based on evidence received in open court, not from outside sources."

The justices therefore found that "the arrangements made by the judge with the news media caused Sheppard to be deprived of that 'judicial serenity and calm to which [he] was entitled.' . . . The fact is that bedlam reigned at the courthouse during the trial and newsmen took over practically the entire courtroom, hounding most of the participants in the trial, especially Sheppard."

"Much of the material printed or broadcast during the trial was never heard from the witness stand. . . . As the trial progressed, the newspapers summarized and interpreted the evidence, devoting particular attention to the material that incriminated Sheppard, and often drew unwarranted inferences from testimony. . . . Nor is there doubt that this deluge of publicity reached at least some of the jury."

The Supreme Court placed great responsibility on the trial judge. "The carnival atmosphere at trial could easily have been avoided since the courtroom and courthouse premises are subject to the control of the court." The justices listed the precautions and protections the judge should have taken: "Bearing in mind the massive pretrial publicity, the judge should have adopted stricter rules governing the use of the courtroom by newsmen, as Sheppard's counsel requested. The number of reporters in the courtroom itself could have been limited at the first sign that their presence would disrupt the trial. They certainly should not have been placed inside the bar. Furthermore, the judge should have more closely regulated the conduct of newsmen in the courtroom. For instance, the judge belatedly asked them not to handle and photograph trial exhibits lying on the counsel table during recesses.

"Secondly, the court should have insulated the witnesses. All of the newspapers and radio stations apparently interviewed prospective witnesses at will, and in many instances disclosed their testimony."

"Thirdly, the court should have made some effort to control the release of leads, information, and gossip to the press by police officers, witnesses, and the counsel for both sides."

Not all the blame fell on the judge, however. The Court found that "the prosecution repeatedly made evidence available to the news media which was never offered in the trial. Much of the 'evidence' disseminated in this fashion was clearly inadmissible. The exclusion of such evidence in court is rendered meaningless when news media make it available to the public." The judge could have ordered the lawyers, parties, witnesses, and court officials not to make any prejudicial or speculative statements out of court. He could have asked city and county officials to restrain their staff members similarly. He could have rebuked reporters for publishing stories about matters not actually presented in court. If the pretrial publicity had already poisoned the atmosphere, he could have granted a continuance or a change of venue. The jury could have been sequestered during the trial to protect them from outside sources of "information." If those measures were not effective in providing a fair trial, a new trial could have been ordered.

"Had the judge, the other officers of the court, and the police placed the interest of justice first, the news media would have soon learned to be content with the task of reporting the case as it unfolded in the courtroom—not pieced together from extrajudicial statements," said the Court. The press is free to report what actually takes place in the courtroom. But "information affecting the fairness of a criminal trial is not only subject to regulation, but is highly censurable and worthy of disciplinary measures."

The Supreme Court concluded: "Since the state trial judge did not fulfill his duty to protect Sheppard from the inherently prejudicial publicity which saturated the community and to control disruptive influences in the courtroom, we must reverse the denial of the habeas petition." (Justice Black dissented without an opinion.)

The state chose not to retry Dr. Sheppard, and he was released from prison.

Since this decision, and others raising similar questions of pretrial publicity leading to prejudiced jurors, some judges have issued so-called gag rules—forbidding lawyers to discuss their cases in the media prior to and during trial. There are differences of opinion about the wisdom, constitutionality, and workability of these rules. Some people are most concerned about due process of law and others most concerned about freedom of expression. This debate, long in the making, will undoubtedly continue and grow more intense as television and radio reporting techniques become less obtrusive. Those who now argue that trial coverage disrupts courtroom procedures may not be able to demonstrate this in the future. However, it is clear that broadcasting a trial affects witnesses. The ordinary witness, who is not accustomed to testifying, tends to be self-conscious and ill at ease on the stand. Imagine how these feelings are compounded when his audience is not only the twelve jurors, but also millions of television and radio listeners!

B. Fairness in Jury Selection

The method of selecting jurors to hear the evidence in a case has changed over the centuries. In the Middle Ages, both parties wanted to have their case tried by citizens of the community who knew them and knew all the facts so that the jurors could judge the events on the basis of their own experience with the parties and witnesses. The jurors themselves were often witnesses to the disputed events.

Today the reverse is true. Citizens who know any of the parties or witnesses or the judge are disqualified from serving as jurors. Citizens with too much experience in the area under consideration in the trial may also be dismissed because they may not be able to separate their prior knowledge from the facts put in evidence in the particular case. Jurors are supposed to judge the case impartially solely on the basis of the evidence presented in court.

A defendant in a criminal case may challenge the method by which names are placed on the list of prospective jurors. The Sixth Amendment guarantee of "trial by an impartial jury" has been interpreted with the Fourteenth Amendment equal protection clause in three ways: narrowly to permit a conviction to be overturned if the defendant can prove discrimination in jury selection based on race, national origin, color, sex, age, economic status, or membership in any other group; more broadly to require trial by jurors representing a cross section of the community; or broadly to require trial by a jury of the defendant's peers. The "peer group" requirement would result, for example, in a defendant from a black ghetto being tried by a majority of citizens from a similar background. In cities with large ghetto populations, a defendant tried in a city court with a citywide jury list occasionally today is tried by a jury of his peers. The "cross-section" requirement would result, for example, in a defendant from a poor white neighborhood being tried by citizens from rich, poor, black, and white neighborhoods in the same city, without regard to the percentage on the jury from each group being the same as the percentage in the city population. The "no discrimination" requirement would require a minority group defendant to prove deliberate or long-standing discrimination against placing members of a minority group on jury lists. The "no discrimination" requirement is the one most commonly accepted by courts; the "peer group" is the one most commonly sought by defendants. (See chapter 24.)

A defendant may also challenge a particular juror called for duty in his case; the prosecution may do the same. Each side may challenge any number of prospective jurors "for cause." If the trial judge agrees that the prospective juror has shown prejudice, the judge will excuse him for cause. Each side can also excuse a certain number of prospective jurors with peremptory challenges—that is, without stating any reason. If the attorney senses from something in the juror's manner or background that he may be prejudiced against the attorney's client, but the juror has not shown any overt bias, the attorney can use a peremptory challenge, and no grounds need be given for excusing the juror.

In order to make wise use of their challenges, trial lawyers like to question prospective jurors about their attitudes on issues that will come up during the trial. They ask about prejudices the jurors may have against certain classes of people—youth, men who wear beards or long hair, women who wear miniskirts, blacks, other people of color, people who drink alcoholic beverages, and so forth. From the answers, the lawyers decide which jurors to accept, which ones to remove by using peremptory challenges, and which ones show such bias that the judge will grant a challenge for cause.

This questioning of jurors on *voir dire* is a significant part of the system of jury trials. It permits counsel to get acquainted with the jurors, to get a feel for their reactions to the defendant, to the lawyers, and to the issues they will face if they remain on the jury. (In the federal courts and some state courts, the trial judge does all of the questioning, although he must ask the relevant questions requested by attorneys for both sides.)

The Supreme Court had to face a new issue concerning the questioning of prospective jurors: When the defendant is charged with a capital crime, is it proper to question jurors about their attitudes on the death penalty and to excuse those who are opposed to it? Or is it proper to include such jurors?

"Could you convict in a death penalty case?"

Witherspoon v. *Illinois* (1968)
391 U.S. 510, 88 S. Ct. 1770, 20 L. Ed. 2d 776

William Witherspoon was charged with murdering a police officer. He had no money for a lawyer, so the court appointed a team of three defense attorneys, one the chairman of the Chicago Bar Association Committee for the Defense of the Indigent.

As the selection of jurors began, the judge said, "Let's get these conscientious objectors out of the way, without wasting any time on them." His brusque reference to "conscientious objectors" meant jurors who had "conscientious scruples against capital punishment." Under Illinois law, such a juror could be excused "for cause" from serving in a death penalty case, solely because of those scruples.

The jurors were asked whether they believed in the death penalty or had religious or conscientious scruples against inflicting a death sentence. Half of the ninety-five prospective jurors said they opposed capital punishment, and the judge excused them for cause. Only five of these said that they would not vote to impose a death sentence under any circumstances, however.

Witherspoon's lawyers did not object to this exclusion of the anti–death-penalty jurors. There did not appear to be any chance of winning on that ground as the law existed at that time.

Witherspoon was convicted and the jury sentenced him to death rather than life imprisonment. Another court-appointed attorney raised fifteen points of alleged error in his appellate brief, but did not question the jury selection. The Illinois Supreme Court affirmed Witherspoon's conviction.

He then sought a writ of habeas corpus (see chapter 18) in the trial court, and, when this was denied, in federal court. This was refused, and the United States Supreme Court denied a hearing.

In February 1965, Witherspoon again petitioned the trial judge for relief, raising for the first time the contention that excluding the jurors who opposed capital punishment had denied him a fair trial and was unconstitutional. He relied on recent studies of jury attitudes toward capital punishment. He argued that when the jurors who opposed the death penalty were challenged and removed, the jury no longer was impartial about the death penalty but rather slanted in favor of it. Jurors who accepted the death penalty also tended to look more favorably on the prosecution's case, according to sociological studies discussed in law review articles. Such jurors were not impartial even about the guilt or innocence of the defendant, but rather tended to be prosecution-minded, Witherspoon argued. This was not the impartial jury required by the Sixth Amendment and the due process clause of the Fourteenth Amendment.

The state's attorney contended that a juror *opposed* to the death penalty was not an impartial juror in a death-penalty case, and should rightly be excluded. He pointed out that since the jury's vote on sentencing had to be unanimous in Illinois, allowing anti–capital-punishment jurors to serve would probably mean the end of death sentences in the state. He also denied that jurors who accepted capital punishment would be prosecution-minded.

The trial judge rejected Witherspoon's arguments and he appealed to the Illinois Supreme Court for the third time. That court concluded that Witherspoon's belated claims of a biased jury were without merit. The condemned man again asked the United States Supreme Court to review his case, based on his new argument. This time the justices agreed.

Do you think a jury that excludes men and women opposed to the death penalty is an impartial jury for a capital case? Is a jury that includes these people impartial for such a case? Do all people have prejudices about some things? If so, what does the idea of impartiality really mean? Why should a defendant in a criminal case be entitled to a jury selected from a cross-section of the community?

The Supreme Court's six-to-three decision was handed down in June 1968. Justice Stewart, writing for the majority, first examined Witherspoon's argument that jurors who accept capital punishment are partial to the prosecution on the issue of guilt or innocence. The defense attorney cited a study of 1,248 jurors in New York and Chicago and two small surveys of college students, which supported his argument.

"The data adduced by the petitioner, however, are too tentative and fragmentary," said Justice Stewart, "to establish that jurors not opposed to the death penalty tend to favor the prosecution in the determination of guilt. We simply cannot conclude . . . that the exclusion of jurors opposed to capital punishment results in an unrepresentative jury on the issue of guilt or substantially increases the risk of conviction."

"It does not follow, however, that the petitioner is entitled to no relief," Justice Stewart went on. "It has not been shown that this jury was biased with respect to the petitioner's guilt. But it is self-evident that, in its role as arbiter of the punishment to be imposed, this jury fell woefully short of that impartiality to which the petitioner was entitled under the Sixth and Fourteenth Amendments."

In the area of sentencing, "a jury that must choose between life imprisonment and capital punishment can do little more—and must do nothing less—than express the conscience of the community on the ultimate question of life or death," said Justice Stewart. He noted that "a prospective juror cannot be expected to say in advance of trial whether he would in fact vote for the extreme penalty in the case before him. The most that can be demanded of a venireman in this regard is that he be willing to *consider* all of the penalties provided by state law, and that he not be irrevocably committed, before the trial has begun, to vote against the penalty of death regardless of the facts and circumstances that might emerge in the course of the proceedings." According to public opinion polls, "in 1966, approximately 42% of the American public favored capital punishment for convicted murderers, while 47% opposed it and 11% were undecided." If less than half of the population "believe in the death penalty, a jury composed exclusively of such people cannot speak for the community," said Justice Stewart. "Culled of all who harbor doubts about the wisdom of capital punishment—of all who would be reluctant to pronounce the extreme penalty—such a jury can speak only for a distinct and dwindling minority.

"If the State had excluded only those prospective jurors who stated in advance of trial that they would not even consider returning a verdict of death, it could argue that the resulting jury was simply 'neutral' with respect to penalty. But when it swept from the jury all who expressed conscientious or religious scruples against capital punishment and all who opposed it in principle, the State crossed the line of neutrality. In its quest for a jury capable of imposing the death penalty, the State produced a jury uncommonly willing to condemn a man to die."

"Whatever else might be said of capital punishment, it is at least clear that its imposition by a hanging jury cannot be squared with the Constitution. The State of Illinois has stacked the deck against the petitioner. To execute this death sentence would deprive him of his life without due process of law."

The Court made it clear that the decision would apply retroactively.

Justice Douglas wrote a separate opinion to express his view that the jury should represent a fair cross-section of the defendant's community. "The conscience of the community is subject to many variables, one of which is the attitude toward the death sentence," he said. "I see no constitutional basis for excluding those who are so opposed to capital punishment that they would never inflict it on a defendant. Exclusion of them means the selection of jurors who are either protagonists of the death penalty or neutral concerning it. That results in a systematic exclusion of qualified groups, and the deprivation to the accused of a cross-section of the community for decision on both his guilt and his punishment."

Justice Douglas also disagreed with the majority's ruling that there was insufficient evidence to show that the jury was prosecution-minded on the question of guilt. "We do not require a showing of specific prejudice when a defendant has been deprived of his right to a jury representing a cross-section of the community. . . . We can as easily assume that the absence of those opposed to capital punishment would rob the jury of certain peculiar qualities of human nature as would the exclusion of women from juries. . . . I feel that we must proceed on the assumption that in many, if not most, cases of class exclusion on the basis of beliefs or attitudes some prejudice does result," said Justice Douglas.

Justice Black, joined by Justices Harlan and White, dissented. "If this Court is to hold capital punishment unconstitutional, I think it should do so forthrightly, not by making it impossible for States to get juries that will enforce the death penalty," he admonished.

"As I see the issue in this case, it is a question of plain bias. A person who has conscientious or religious scruples against capital punishment will seldom if ever vote to impose the death penalty. This is just human nature, and no amount of semantic camouflage can cover it up. In the same manner, I would not dream of foisting on a criminal defendant a juror . . . who claims, for example, that he adheres literally to the Biblical admonition of 'an eye for an eye.' "

Justice White wrote a separate dissent as well, stressing that the Court's decision was infringing on the legislative power to decide criminal sentencing procedures and, in his view, did not have an overriding constitutional basis.

In 1968, when the decision was handed down, there were 435 persons on death row in the United States. Many were able to contest their sentences on the basis of the *Witherspoon* decision, because jurors opposed to capital punishment had been excluded from the juries that sentenced these convicts. The Court's opinion had made it clear that the death sentence imposed by such a jury was invalid, but the verdict of guilty was not invalidated. (The future of capital punishment is discussed in chapter 17.)

The Court emphasized in *Witherspoon* the need for impartial juries to try criminal cases. The Court had long required proper selection of persons to be called for jury duty and had rejected many devices to achieve all-white, middle-class juries (described in chapter 24). Changes in jury selection were, according to some commentators, the key factor leading to acquittals in a series of so-called political trials in the early 1970s. Leading members of the Black Panther Party, the peace movement, the Communist Party, and the Yippies were tried before jurors selected from a fairly wide cross section of the community. These jurors had been questioned extensively by defense counsel, both to exclude those with strong bias against the defendants and to educate those who remained concerning their hidden prejudices.

Complaints were raised that this process of questioning jurors took too much time and slowed down the administration of justice. The reply was quick: Justice can seldom be administered in a hurry. Disputes over "trial court delay" versus "full use of the adversary system" are shaping up all over the country. The voters and taxpayers will ultimately have to settle this dispute, as they must all other basic issues.

CHAPTER 16

Right to Confront Witnesses

Most legal problems never get to trial. One party sues another and the parties go through pretrial procedures until they know quite a bit about the opponent's case and what he can prove. Then, before the case actually reaches a judge or jury, the parties decide to settle it. This provides certainty of the outcome and takes less time and less money in attorney's fees. The lesser settlement in the hand is preferred to the possibly better settlement in the bush.

As a result, the cases that do go to trial are hard-fought. In criminal cases, the district attorney has refused to dismiss the charges or accept a plea to a lesser charge, or the defendant has refused to plead guilty to the offense charged or to a lesser offense. Each is counting on vindication from a jury or judge.

The subject matter of a trial is evidence—occasionally exhibits, photographs, or maps, but primarily the words of witnesses. Each party fights hard to put into evidence testimony that will help convince the judge or jury he is right and to keep out of evidence testimony that will hurt him. The defense seeks to shake the testimony of government witnesses about his actions and statements. He often tries to prove that their testimony is not an accurate description of events or is deliberately false. It is fairly easy to show that a witness does not remember every detail or that he is not saying exactly the same things he said earlier about an event. But it is difficult to get a witness to change his story on a significant point, and witnesses seldom break on the stand in real life, however often they may do it on television.

In many criminal cases, the prosecution uses witnesses who live on the fringes of law-abiding society or who have criminal records. Many law-abiding people don't want to get involved in criminal trials, even as prosecution witnesses— trials take time away from ordinary activities and are distasteful because they remind us of the otherwise forgotten world of violence, imprisonment, even executions.

People who live by hustling may not have tight time schedules; they are more likely to be where a criminal incident takes place; they have something to gain by cooperating with the police and district attorney on a case today, since they may be involved in another case tomorrow, or they may be on probation or parole. The defense needs to find out as much as it can about such a witness and about statements he has made from his first visit to the district attorney's office until his testimony in court. If there is a discrepancy between his testimony and earlier statements, the defense may be able to impeach him—prove he is lying about a critical point. This can spell the difference between conviction of the defendant and acquittal.

When a person is charged with a criminal act against a person or property—such as murder or robbery—the victim is clear and the nature of the act is precise. But when the charge is political—conspiracy to commit an act that was never carried out or membership in an allegedly subversive organization, for example—there is no victim and the nature of the act is unclear. The district attorney must prove what was in the defendant's mind when he attended a meeting or discussed political beliefs or affiliations.

In such political cases, the government has frequently used

paid informer witnesses: people who joined political organizations for the sole purpose of informing on other members or people who became informers after joining. The testimony of political informers is notoriously suspect, and Chief Justice Warren used the strongest language to condemn its use in the *Mesarosh* case, discussed at page 116.

No matter what the charge, when a defendant wants to convince the jury not to believe a witness, he has three lines of attack: other witnesses contradicted the witness; the witness contradicted himself on the stand; or the witness had made contradictory statements at an earlier time.

There are two questions about earlier contradictory statements: (1) How will the defense get the prosecution to make these statements available to the defense; and (2) if an earlier statement was not made under oath, is it admissible since the defendant and his attorney were not present to confront and cross-examine the witness, or must the witness appear at trial in person to tell his story?

Both these aspects of the right to confront witnesses were raised sharply before the Supreme Court during Warren's term, resulting in landmark decisions, legislation, and deeper public understanding of due process.

The right to see FBI files

Jencks v. *United States* (1957)
353 U.S. 657, 77 S. Ct. 1007, 1 L. Ed. 2d 1103

Clinton Jencks was a union organizer for the Mine, Mill, and Smelter Workers in New Mexico. The union members were Anglo and Mexican-American workers; they were known for their militance and progressive policies. (The union even made a feature film—*Salt of the Earth*—telling the story of their hard-fought strike and the changes it brought in the lives of the men and women, the Chicanos and Anglos, the strikers and bosses.)

Jencks started as business agent for locals around Silver City in 1946, and later edited the newspaper, the *Union Worker.* When several of the locals merged to form Amalgamated Local 890, the members elected Jencks president.

In 1947, Congress passed the Taft-Hartley Act. Section 9(h) of the act required all union officers to sign an oath that they were not Communists, or "affiliated with" the Communist Party, in order to continue using the services of the National Labor Relations Board. (See *Watkins* v. *United States,* described in chapter 7.) Most unions opposed the oath; they resented government interference with their affairs, and noted that the law did not require employers to sign oaths that they were not members of or affiliated with pro-fascist organizations, or in monopolistic groups that would limit production and competition. They feared this political test for union leaders would frighten their members, discourage all political action, and destroy the militance of their organizations. Large national unions brought test suits challenging the constitutionality of the oath. The Supreme Court upheld it in *American Communications Association* v. *Douds,* in 1950, saying that it did not violate the First Amendment because it did not punish or forbid association with the Communist Party, but merely specified requirements for the use of the services of a government agency, the NLRB. It was proper for the act to regulate labor relations, because they affect the flow of commerce, the Court said. (Three justices did not participate in the decision, and Justice Black dissented on First Amendment grounds.)

After the *Douds* decision, most unions complied with the act, but a few, Mine-Mill among them, refused and instructed their officers not to sign.

It was fine to take a moral position against a government oath imposed on a private institution, but the penalties were heavy. Seeing that Mine-Mill's NLRB fangs had been pulled, employers refused to bargain with or even recognize the union they had been dealing with for decades. Rival unions demanded NLRB elections at plants traditionally represented by the Mine-Mill union; workers who didn't want the hassle split off from the union. Since Mine-Mill was denied NLRB services, the ballot would list only the rival union; workers would be asked to vote either for that one or for no union. Mine-Mill was put in the position of urging workers to vote "no union" so that it could keep its jurisdiction. Staunch trade unionists could not bring themselves to do this unless they fully understood the reasons. This took tremendous educational efforts. Often Mine-Mill could not mount the campaign and lost the elections to the raiding union.

The CIO began taking steps to expel unions whose officers had not signed the Taft-Hartley oath and who openly opposed the Cold War abroad and Senator Joe McCarthy at home. If expelled, a union could no longer count on support from other unions in a strike.

Faced with all these adversities, the Mine-Mill union reconsidered its stand in 1949, and its officers took the non-Communist oath. One officer announced at the time that he had been a member of the Communist Party but was now formally resigning in order to take the oath. The CIO nevertheless expelled the Mine-Mill union in 1950, and rival CIO unions continued to raid.

In 1953, Clinton Jencks was indicted by the federal government for falsely swearing that he was not a member of or affiliated with the Communist Party in 1950. He was brought to trial before a jury in January 1954. The United

States attorney presented a series of witnesses who testified that they were former members of the Communist Party and had met Jencks at some Party meeting, between 1946 and 1948. Only two witnesses, Reverend J. W. Ford and Harvey Matusow, testified about seeing or talking with Jencks at Communist Party gatherings later than 1948. Both of these witnesses were paid FBI informers.

The government said the Communist Party had dictated a policy to the Mine-Mill officials: resign from the Party publicly in order to take the oath, but maintain a secret membership. There were no Party cards, no membership lists, no minutes of meetings to prove membership, so the government said it had to establish its case against Jencks by circumstantial evidence (for example, that he had recommended the *People's World,* an allegedly Communist newspaper, to union members). Matusow even told of a plot by Jencks and Communist labor leaders in Mexico to bring about an international strike that would tie up copper supplies for U.S. troops in the Korean War.

Jencks told his attorney, Nathan Witt, that the testimony given by Ford and Matusow was sheer fabrication. Witt demanded that the reports made by Ford and Matusow to the FBI be brought into court, to check whether their written statements made at the time of the alleged meetings with Jencks corresponded to their testimony in court.

The U.S. attorney objected that the FBI reports were confidential and could not be shown unless Witt could establish beforehand ("lay a foundation") that the statements in them were inconsistent with the testimony in court. The judge denied Witt's motion to see the prior statements.

Witt also objected to several of the judge's instructions to the jury, but he was overruled. The jury returned a verdict of guilty, and Jencks was sentenced to five years in prison.

UNITED STATES OF AMERICA)
)
)
)   No. 54013
vs.   )
)   Criminal
)
)
CLINTON E. JENCKS   )
)

HARVEY M. MATUSOW, being duly sworn, deposes and says:

1. I make this affidavit in support of the motion by the defendant for a new trial, and to do what I can to remedy the harm I have done to Clinton E. Jencks and to the administration of justice.

2. I appeared as a witness for the Government against the defendant in the course of the trial in this Court in January, 1954, on an indictment charging Mr. Jencks with having filed a false non-Communist affidavit with the National Labor Relations Board on April 28, 1950. My testimony appears in the typewritten transcript of the record from p. 579 to p. 703.

3. The matters I testified to were either false or not entirely true, and were known by me to be either false or not entirely true, at the time I so testified, in that:

A. I testified that in July and August, 1950, I visited the San Cristobal Valley Ranch in Northern New Mexico, and met the defendant there. While there, I had three conversations with him. I also testified about a lecture given by the defendant at the Ranch.

I testified that the first conversation took place in the presence of one Marcus. I testified that in the course of this conversation, I stated that I had left New York permanently and was thinking of living either in New Mexico or California, in which

A facsimile of Harvey Matusow's recantation of his testimony that had helped convict Clinton Jencks.

He appealed to the federal court of appeals. While the appeal was pending, Harvey Matusow came forth and publicly recanted the testimony he had given in this case (and in other cases). He said he had deliberately lied about the conversations he had related on the witness stand, which were the only direct evidence that Jencks was a Communist in 1950 (when he took the oath) or afterward.

Jencks immediately moved for a new trial on the basis of this newly discovered evidence. After a lengthy hearing, the federal district court denied the motion.

Jencks appealed this ruling as well, but the court of appeals affirmed both the denial of the motion and Jencks's conviction. He then sought review by the United States Supreme Court.

How could the government prove that a defendant took the non-Communist oath falsely if the defendant did not admit doing so? If the government had to rely on paid informer witnesses, should the defendant be entitled to special protection against perjury by such witnesses because of their inherent unreliability? If no special protection is provided for, what traditional protections should a defendant have? Does the constitutional right to confront and cross-examine one's accuser extend to confronting the accuser with his own prior testimony, in order to determine whether there are any inconsistencies? How else can a defendant catch an informer witness in an inconsistency, assuming that he makes no inconsistent statements on the witness stand?

Justice Brennan wrote the majority opinion in the Court's seven-to-one decision (Justice Whittaker did not participate). The majority of the Court did not deal with Jencks's arguments about the judge's instructions and other claimed errors in the trial, nor with the question of denial of a new trial, but only with the question of withholding the FBI reports. "We hold that the petitioner was not required to lay a preliminary foundation of inconsistency, because a sufficient foundation was established by the testimony of Matusow and Ford that their reports were of the events and activities related in their testimony," Justice Brennan wrote for the Court.

"The crucial nature of the testimony of Ford and Matusow to the Government's case is conspicuously apparent. The impeachment of that testimony was singularly important to the petitioner. The value of the reports for impeachment purposes was highlighted by the admissions of both witnesses that they could not remember what reports were oral and what written, and by Matusow's admission: 'I don't recall what I put in my reports two or three years ago, written or oral, I don't know what they were.'

"Every experienced trial judge and trial lawyer knows the value for impeaching purposes of statements of the witness recording the events before time dulls treacherous memory." The accused was demanding specific documents of statements taken from an actual witness about relevant matters, "and did not propose any broad or blind fishing expedition among documents possessed by the Government on the chance that something impeaching might turn up." His request should have been granted, the Court ruled.

Jencks's lawyers had asked merely that the documents be shown to the judge to determine whether parts should be admitted in evidence. The Supreme Court went even further: "We now hold that the petitioner was entitled to an order directing the Government to produce for inspection all reports of Matusow and Ford in its possession, written and, when orally made, as recorded by the F.B.I., touching the events and activities as to which they testified at the trial. We hold, further, that the petitioner is entitled to inspect the reports to decide whether to use them in his defense. Because only the defense is adequately equipped to determine the effective use for purposes of discrediting the Government's witness and thereby furthering the accused's defense, the defense must initially be entitled to see them to determine what use may be made of them. Justice requires no less."

"The practice of producing government documents to the trial judge for his determination of relevancy and materiality, without hearing the accused, is disapproved. Relevancy and materiality for the purposes of production and inspection, with a view to use on cross-examination, are established when the reports are shown to relate to the testimony of the witness."

The government had a choice, Justice Brennan explained: it could prosecute a person for crime and allow him access to all "relevant statements or reports in its possession of government witnesses touching the subject matter of their testimony at the trial," or it could keep its information confidential and not undertake the prosecution. It was up to the government to decide which was more important for the public good.

The lower court's decision in *Jencks* was reversed and a new trial ordered.

Justices Burton and Harlan, concurring, felt the documents could not be withheld, but should have been shown to the *judge* to decide whether they contained matter of "evidentiary value." These two justices also believed that the judge's instructions to the jury in the *Jencks* trial were erroneous and that this error should have been ruled on by the Court for future trials.

Justice Clark dissented. "Unless the Congress changes the rule announced by the Court today," he said, "those intelligence agencies of our Government engaged in law enforcement may as well close up shop, for the Court has opened their files to the criminal and thus afforded him a Roman holiday for rummaging through confidential information as well as vital national secrets. This may well be a reasonable rule in state prosecutions where none of the problems of foreign relations, espionage, sabotage, subversive activities, counterfeiting, internal security, national defense, and the like exist, but any person conversant with federal government activities and problems will quickly recognize that it opens up a veritable Pandora's box of troubles. And all in the name of justice."

The government did not retry Jencks. Rather than allow his attorneys to see the FBI files, it dropped the charges against him. In light of the *Jencks* and *Yates* decisions (see page 117), the Justice Department also dropped the prosecutions of almost one hundred Communists around the country for alleged violation of the Smith Act.

Suits against other leaders of the Mine-Mill union were pursued late into the 1950s, however, and congressional committee investigations were added to harass this organization. Union spokesmen claimed that the big mining and metals companies encouraged the government attacks. Eventually, however, the Mine-Mill union merged with the steelworkers' union and rejoined the CIO.

Congress took heed of Justice Clark's dissent in *Jencks* and quickly enacted what became known as the Jencks Act—a federal law stating that a defendant is to be shown reports of earlier statements by government witnesses only if the entire document relates to the witness's testimony; otherwise, the document is to be shown to the trial judge, who will pick out the relevant portions and show only those to the defendant.

The FBI and some state investigating agencies thereafter modified their practices and seldom made written records of their interviews with prospective witnesses. This led defense counsel to seek information on the existence of tapes made by prosecution agents without the knowledge of the defendant, and tapes of conversations between clients and their attorneys. Courts ordered the prosecution to divulge such material, sometimes affecting the outcome of a case.

The principals in the *Jencks* case went their separate ways. Harvey Matusow testified for the defense in trials of some Communist leaders, recanting his earlier testimony. He wrote a book, *False Witness*, describing his transformation from liberal youth leader to anti-Communist witness with ambitions to become famous and rich. He charged that a government lawyer encouraged him to embellish his testimony in the prosecutions of Communists. For these recantations the federal government charged him with perjury and won his conviction. Ironically, he, not Clinton Jencks, ended up serving a five-year sentence. Jencks eventually left the Mine-Mill union to get a doctorate in economics and become a college professor.

Some years after the political confrontation issues raised in *Jencks,* the Supreme Court was asked to rule that a defendant in a state court criminal trial was entitled to confront and cross-examine his accuser exactly as he would be entitled to do in a federal criminal trial, such as the *Jencks* case. Once again the Court had to decide the scope of due process available under the Fourteenth Amendment to defendants in state criminal cases and whether the protections available in the federal courts under the Bill of Rights apply equally in the states.

Cross-examining the witness at trial

Pointer v. *Texas* (1965)
380 U.S. 400, 85 S. Ct. 1065, 13 L. Ed. 2d 923

Bob Pointer and a man named Dillard were arrested in Texas and charged with robbing Kenneth Phillips of $375 at gunpoint. The police brought them before a judge for a hearing at which the prosecuting attorney presented evidence and the judge decided whether the defendants should be formally charged with the crime and allowed bail. (In Texas, this hearing is called the examining trial; in other jurisdictions, a similar hearing is called a preliminary examination.)

Pointer and Dillard were not represented by a lawyer at the hearing. The district attorney presented several witnesses, the chief one being the victim, Phillips. Dillard tried to cross-examine Phillips, and Pointer tried to cross-examine some of the other witnesses. Phillips described in detail how Pointer had held a gun on him and taken the money.

Pointer was indicted. Before the case came to trial, Phillips moved to California, and the prosecution did not bring him back to testify at the trial. Instead, the district attorney introduced the transcript of Phillips's testimony at the first hearing. Pointer's lawyer immediately objected, because this method of putting in Phillips's testimony prevented the defendant from confronting Phillips at the trial, and prevented his lawyer from cross-examining Phillips. The judge overruled the objection. The defense attorney repeated his objection several times, but the judge overruled him again and again, apparently reasoning that Pointer had had ample opportunity to confront and cross-examine Phillips when the victim had testified at the earlier hearing.

Pointer was convicted, and he appealed to the Texas Court of Criminal Appeals. His lawyer argued that he had been denied counsel at the *examining* trial and denied a chance to have his counsel cross-examine the witness against him at the *trial*, both in violation of the Sixth Amendment. The Texas appellate court disagreed, and affirmed Pointer's conviction. He then asked for review by the United States Supreme Court.

Why is it important to give a defendant a chance to confront and cross-examine the witnesses against him in a trial before a jury? If he has already confronted and cross-examined at a preliminary stage, does he have a right to repeat the process at trial? Does it matter that the defendant didn't have a lawyer's assistance when he cross-examined witnesses at the preliminary? Do you think Pointer had had his chance to cross-examine Phillips and had just let it go by?

The Supreme Court's decision was unanimous, although Justices Harlan and Stewart did not agree with the majority's reasoning. Justice Black, writing for the seven, noted: "There are few subjects, perhaps, upon which this Court and other courts have been more nearly unanimous than in their expressions of belief that the right of confrontation and cross-examination is an essential and fundamental requirement for the kind of fair trial which is this country's constitutional goal."

Examining the facts, the Court found that "the Sixth Amendment's guarantee of confrontation and cross-examination was unquestionably denied petitioner in this case." This would not have been true "had Phillips' statement been taken at a full-fledged hearing at which petitioner had been represented by counsel who had been given a complete and adequate opportunity to cross-examine."

The Court concluded: "Because the transcript of Phillips'

statement offered against petitioner at his trial had not been taken at a time and under circumstances affording petitioner through counsel an adequate opportunity to cross-examine Phillips, its introduction in a federal court in a criminal case against Pointer would have amounted to denial of the privilege of confrontation guaranteed by the Sixth Amendment."

The Court majority quoted one of its recent opinions, which noted that some past decisions by the Supreme Court were being reexamined by the Warren Court, namely, decisions that accorded the Fourteenth Amendment "a less central role in the preservation of basic liberties" than the authors of that amendment had intended.

The seven justices then held that "petitioner was entitled to be tried in accordance with the protection of the confrontation guarantee of the Sixth Amendment, and that that guarantee, like the right against compelled self-incrimination, is 'to be enforced against the States under the Fourteenth Amendment according to the same standards that protect those personal rights against federal encroachment.' " (This rule is discussed in chapter 20.)

The case was reversed and remanded for retrial without use of the transcript as evidence.

CHAPTER 17

Prohibition against Cruel and Unusual Punishment

The American colonists suffered from the British practice of inventing unusual punishments for political acts and crimes by the Sons of Liberty and their friends. When the Revolutionary War was over and the victors were writing their Bill of Rights, they forbade the infliction of "cruel and unusual punishments " in the Eighth Amendment, copying the language from the English Bill of Rights of 1689.

Some of the punishments the framers had in mind are now obsolete, while modern penal technology has devised punishments never imagined by those early revolutionaries. One of the continuing questions in American constitutional law is whether the courts should stick to the concepts accepted by the framers of the Constitution and Bill of Rights, or whether they should apply the broad language in those documents to the changing problems and standards of the current period. This question arose concerning the phrase "cruel and unusual punishment" almost two centuries after its enactment, in a drug addiction case, *Robinson* v. *California.* The justices sitting in the mid-twentieth century were ready to hear and decide such a case.

Is drug addiction a crime or a disease?

Robinson v. California (1962)
370 U.S. 660, 82 S. Ct. 1417, 8 L. Ed. 2d 758

Lawrence Robinson was accosted one evening by Officer Brown of the Los Angeles Police Department, although he was not engaged in any illegal or irregular conduct. The officer noticed some discoloration on the inside of Robinson's arm, numerous apparent needle marks, and a scab below his elbow. He arrested Robinson and took him to jail.

The following morning, Officer Lindquist, a ten-year veteran of the Los Angeles Police Narcotics Division, examined Robinson and concluded that the marks and discoloration resulted from injecting unsterile hypodermic needles into his veins. According to Lindquist, the scabs were somewhere between three and ten days old, and the defendant was not under the influence of narcotics or suffering withdrawal symptoms. Robinson was charged with violating a California statute making it a crime to be "addicted to the use of narcotics." Lindquist and Brown both said that, under questioning, Robinson admitted he had been using narcotics for three or four months, three to four times a week, and admitted that he had last used narcotics eight days before his arrest.

At the trial, Robinson told the jury he had never said any of those things to the police officers. He also denied that he had ever used narcotics or been addicted to them, and he said the marks on his arms were from shots for an allergy he had contracted while in the service. His testimony was corroborated by two witnesses.

The trial judge instructed the jury that it was a misdemeanor "either to use narcotics or to be addicted to the use of narcotics." The statute distinguished between the two, but he told the jurors they could vote to convict without deciding whether the defendant was guilty of use or of being addicted. All the prosecution had to prove was "either that the defendant did use a narcotic in Los Angeles County, or that while in the City of Los Angeles he was addicted to the use of narcotics." The jury believed the police officers and found Robinson guilty. The statute specified a sentence of ninety days to one year in jail, without possibility of suspended sentence.

Robinson appealed the case, saying the statute violated the Fourteenth Amendment. The appellate court expressed some doubt as to the constitutionality of "the crime of being a narcotic addict," but it affirmed the decision. Robinson sought habeas corpus relief (see chapter 18) from the higher state appellate courts, but without success. He then appealed to the United States Supreme Court, arguing that it was cruel and unusual punishment to make addiction a criminal offense, and that the states are forbidden to mete out such punishment under the due process clause of the Fourteenth Amendment.

Do you think a ninety-day sentence can ever be called cruel and unusual punishment? Should the condition of being an addict be considered a crime? Will jail help an addict? Will jailing an addict protect society, and does this justify the statute? Is an addict by definition unable to stop taking narcotics, or are there different levels of addiction, some minor enough for the addict to overcome by will power?

The Supreme Court's six-to-two opinion was delivered by Justice Stewart. (Justice Frankfurter took no part in the decision.) The Court made it clear at the outset that the state's power to regulate drug traffic was not in question and that the state had a wide variety of ways to do this. It could make it a crime to manufacture, prescribe, sell, purchase, or possess drugs without authorization; it could carry on public health education activities; it could try to eliminate the economic and social conditions that tend to lead to addiction; and it could set up a compulsory *treatment* program for addicts. In fact, California had such a program under another statute, but the procedures were not used in Robinson's case.

The statute in question here did not punish a person for the use, purchase, sale, or possession of drugs, nor did it make any effort to require or provide medical treatment, Justice Stewart noted. The statute made addiction a punishable crime. This meant a person could "be continuously guilty of this offense, whether or not he has ever used or possessed any narcotics within the state." And since it was impossible to know from the verdict whether the jury convicted Robinson for actually *using* narcotics or merely being *addicted* to them, the conviction must be reversed.

No state today would attempt to make it a crime "to be mentally ill, or a leper, or to be afflicted with venereal disease," the Court declared. Back in 1925, a Supreme Court opinion had recognized that addiction to narcotics was an illness; and it was one that could be contracted involuntarily or innocently. "We hold that a state law which imprisons a person thus afflicted as a criminal, even though he has never touched any narcotic drug within the State or been guilty of any irregular behavior there, inflicts a cruel and unusual punishment in violation of the Fourteenth Amendment."

It was true that punishment of ninety days in jail was not, in the abstract, cruel and unusual, the Court conceded. "But the question cannot be considered in the abstract. Even one day in prison would be a cruel and unusual punishment for the 'crime' of having a common cold."

Justice Douglas concurred separately in a memorable

opinion, saying, "I wish to make more explicit why I think it is 'cruel and unusual' punishment in the sense of the Eighth Amendment to treat as a criminal a person who is a drug addict." He provided the legal community with a valuable summary of medical, legal, and legislative wisdom on the subject at that point.

In sixteenth-century England, he noted, "one prescription for insanity was to beat the subject 'until he had regained his reason.' " In America the insane had been whipped, imprisoned in dungeons, burned at the stake, pilloried, and hanged. "Today we have our differences over the legal definition of insanity," Justice Douglas said, but "it is in end effect treated as a disease. While afflicted people may be confined for treatment or for the protection of society, they are not branded as criminals."

Drug addiction, on the other hand, was labeled a crime in the California statute, as if addicts "could, if they would, forsake their evil ways." Justice Douglas noted that addiction could start with an innocent puff of a cigarette or a prescription. Some babies of addicted mothers are even born addicted, and treatment of these infants has given some evidence that addicts have a physical need for the drug for a longer time than is generally assumed—perhaps a reason why so many addicts return to drugs even after being "cured."

"Some say the addict has a disease," Justice Douglas continued. "Others say addiction is not a disease but a 'symptom of a mental or psychiatric disorder.' " A 1960 legal journal had described the extreme symptoms of addiction in these terms: "To be a confirmed drug addict is to be one of the walking dead. . . . The teeth have rotted out; the appetite is lost and the stomach and intestines don't function properly. The gall bladder becomes inflamed; eyes and skin turn a flaming red; the partition separating the nostrils is eaten away—breathing is difficult. Oxygen in the blood decreases; bronchitis and tuberculosis develop. Good traits of character disappear and bad ones emerge. Sex organs become affected. Veins collapse and livid purplish scars remain. Boils and abscesses plague the skin; gnawing pain racks the body. Nerves snap; vicious twitching develops. Imaginary and fantastic fears blight the mind and sometimes complete insanity results. Often times, too, death comes—much too early in life."

Justice Douglas pointed out that although some states punish addiction, most do not. In Great Britain, "addicts are patients not criminals," entrusted to the care of doctors who are given "almost complete professional autonomy in reaching decisions about the treatment of addicts." Addiction has not disappeared in Britain but it has decreased, and there is now little "addict-crime."

These facts do not, of course, "establish the unconstitutionality of California's penal law," said Justice Douglas. "But we do know that there is 'a hard core' of 'chronic and incurable drug addicts who, in reality, have lost their power of self-control.'" Community alarm and punitive measures are justified when they relate to acts violating the law, but "I do not see how under our system *being an addict* can be punished as a crime. If addicts can be punished for their addiction, then the insane can also be punished for their insanity. Each has a disease and must be treated as a sick person."

If it was unlawful "to exact capital punishment for a petty crime," it was also unlawful "to punish a person by fine or imprisonment for being sick." A drug addict may "be confined for treatment or for the protection of society," Justice Douglas felt. "Cruel and unusual punishment results not from confinement, but from convicting the addict of a crime." It is unjustifiable to stigmatize an addict as a criminal, when he can be confined for treatment by means of a civil procedure, which would protect society from him just as well. In fact, the Council on Mental Health had reported that criminal sentences interfered with treatment and rehabilitation of addicts, and it recommended that these sentences be abolished.

"We would forget the teachings of the Eighth Amendment if we allowed sickness to be made a crime," Justice Douglas concluded. "This age of enlightenment cannot tolerate such barbarous action."

Justice Harlan concurred on different grounds. He was "not prepared to hold on the present state of medical knowledge" that it was unconstitutional for a State to treat addiction as "something other than an illness" or to subject addicts to criminal law. But in this case the trial judge's instructions permitted the jury to convict Robinson if he were merely present in California while addicted to narcotics, without committing any criminal act. This was unconstitutional.

Justice Clark dissented. California's criminal provision, he asserted, applied to the incipient narcotic addict who still had self-control. The state's civil confinement statute dealt with addicts who had lost the power of self-control. Robinson obviously fell into the first category. "I submit that California's program relative to narcotics addicts—including both the 'criminal' and 'civil' provisions—is inherently one of treatment and lies well within the power of a State," Justice Clark concluded.

Justice White also dissented, finding that Robinson had been convicted not for having an illness or condition, "but rather . . . for the regular, repeated or habitual use of narcotics immediately prior to his arrest." He could find no "indications in this record that California would apply [the criminal statute] to the case of a helpless addict" rather than one who still had "the power to control his acts."

Increasingly, alcoholism has come to be considered a medical, rather than a legal, problem. Under our law, crimes require some kind of intent or willfulness on the part of the defendant, whereas illness is an involuntary act, and it cannot be "cured" by incarceration. According to many medical studies, the common drunk is suffering from the disease of alcoholism rather than from the crime of being drunk and disorderly. Arrests for drunkenness have therefore been called cruel and unusual punishment.

Prisoners and their lawyers are arguing that solitary confinement is also cruel and unusual punishment.

The main issue, however, has been the death penalty. In eighteenth-century England and America, the death penalty was accepted by most people as just and reasonable punishment for a great many crimes. Hanging pickpockets was thought to be a deterrent, even after it was discovered that many pockets were picked in the crowds observing the hanging of pickpockets. Slowly nations and states have changed their views, having studied the causes of crime and the methods of rehabilitation. Now an increasing number of governments have rejected capital punishment in favor of imprisonment for life or for a term of years. During the Warren Court era, New York and Vermont abolished capital punishment for almost all crimes, while West Virginia, Iowa, Oregon, Michigan, Alaska, and Hawaii joined Maine and Minnesota in completely abolishing it. Local and national committees urged abolition, joining many death row defendants in arguing that, at this stage in our nation's development, it is cruel and unusual punishment. Supreme Courts in California and Mississippi, among others, have adopted this view.

The Burger Court touched on this problem in *McGautha* v. *California* in 1971, finding no requirement in the due process clause of the Fourteenth Amendment that juries be given instructions as to when the death penalty should be imposed. In 1972, the Court finally decided the issue itself, holding in four cases (*Furman* v. *Georgia*) that the death penalty was cruel and unusual punishment in violation of the Eighth and Fourteenth Amendments. The vote was five to four; the decisions were announced in a short per curiam (unsigned) opinion. Each of the five justices in the majority wrote a separate opinion in support of the decisions; each of the four minority justices wrote a separate dissenting opinion.

The nine opinions discuss a great deal of English and colonial American history, as well as past and current attitudes on penology. But the precise ruling of the Court remains to be tested. Clearly the majority justices oppose capital punishment in part because it has been executed so selectively. Proponents of the death penalty therefore argue that it is still constitutional when it is mandatory, when every person convicted of a certain crime must be executed. Opponents reject such arguments and oppose legislation to make the death penalty mandatory for any crimes.

This issue will remain with us for some time. Certainly the opinion in *Robinson* v. *California* helped open the way for this debate.

CHAPTER 18

Right to Use Habeas Corpus

Habeas corpus is the strongest procedure for challenging the imprisonment of a person by any government agency. The prisoner files a petition to the court, alleging that he was taken into custody unlawfully—that is, that somewhere in the course of his arrest, detention, trial, appeal, and imprisonment, he was not accorded due process of law. He, or someone acting on his behalf, may petition for the writ at any point that he is in custody and claims the government acted unlawfully to put him there.

The government must come into court immediately to prove that the prisoner's allegations are untrue, that it has not violated his rights. If the government cannot prove this, the judge issues the writ ordering the jailer to free the prisoner. The fact that a habeas corpus petition requires immediate action does not mean that the petitioner always wins. On the contrary, few habeas corpus petitions are successful. However, the prisoner does get consideration of his claim and, if it is denied, he may file any number of petitions charging violations of his rights.

The writ is the ultimate weapon an accused can use to ensure that he is not imprisoned unjustly, and it has always been known as the Great Writ. "Although in form the Great Writ is simply a mode of procedure," Justice Brennan wrote in 1963, "its history is inextricably intertwined with the growth of fundamental rights of personal liberty. For its function has been to provide a prompt and efficacious remedy for whatever society deems to be intolerable restraints. Its root principle is that in a civilized society, government must always be accountable to the judiciary for a man's imprisonment: if the imprisonment cannot be shown to conform with the fundamental requirements of law, the individual is entitled to his immediate release."

Use of the writ was guaranteed in the Magna Carta after the struggle by the nobles against the king in thirteenth-century England. It came to the American colonies as part of the common law. When the Constitution was framed, the right to use the writ in federal courts was explicitly recognized in Article I, Section 9. This is part of the original document, not an amendment like the guarantees in the Bill of Rights.

One of the legal issues involved in the Civil War was the extent to which the states must follow federal law. The defeat of the Southern armies on the battlefield was the military basis for promulgation of the Thirteenth, Fourteenth, and Fifteenth Amendments by Congress, and their adoption by the several states (see chapter 21). In this spirit of reconstructing the South within the U.S. Constitution, Congress enacted the Judiciary Act of February 5, 1867, permitting *federal* courts to hear petitions for writs of habeas corpus from prisoners held under *state* law. This legislation was intended to give freed slaves an effective weapon against state authorities who might resist Reconstruction.

At first the Supreme Court interpreted the 1867 Judiciary Act as intended by Congress, holding (in *Ex parte McCardle*) that "this legislation is of the most comprehensive character. It brings within the *habeas corpus* jurisdiction of every court and of every judge every possible case of privation of liberty contrary to the National Constitution, treaties, or laws. It is impossible to widen this jurisdiction."

But soon the Court began to ignore the profound constitutional change marked by the defeat of the southern states in the Civil War and began to pervert the intent of Congress by narrowing application of the 1867 act. The Court assented to southern charges that the federal judiciary was encroaching on states' rights. The justices took refuge in the doctrine of abstention, which permits a federal court to duck a state court issue in a case when no state court has issued a final ruling on it. On this basis the Supreme Court ruled that habeas corpus was an inappropriate remedy when the prisoner had not completed his appeal proceedings or exhausted his other state court remedies. A shocking, but logical, consequence of this judicial hamstringing of the Great Writ occurred in the 1915 case *Frank* v. *Mangum.* Frank, a Jew charged with murder, argued he had been denied a fair trial in Atlanta, Georgia, because the courtroom had been dominated by a mob. But the Supreme Court (seven to two) ruled that a federal district court was powerless to hear Frank's contentions because the Georgia state courts had already heard them and decided against him.

Justice Oliver Wendell Holmes, who wrote an angry dissent in *Frank,* was able to write for the majority eight years later in *Moore* v. *Dempsey,* the case of five blacks sentenced to death in an Arkansas court also dominated by a mob. The Court held that the state court's hearing of the issues was not absolutely conclusive and did not prevent federal review by writ of habeas corpus. Various preconditions and restrictions continued to be applied to the Great Writ, however, by some courts in some cases, so that controversy about its use continued through the twentieth century.

The federal statute as codified in 1948 provided: "An application for a writ of habeas corpus in behalf of a person in custody pursuant to the judgment of a State court shall not be granted unless it appears that the applicant has exhausted the remedies available in the courts of the State, or that there is either an absence of available State corrective process or the existence of circumstances rendering such process ineffective to protect the rights of the prisoner.

"An applicant shall not be deemed to have exhausted the remedies available in the courts of the State, within the meaning of this section, if he has the right under the law of the State to raise, by any available procedure, the question presented."

The ultimate weapon for personal liberty

Fay v. *Noia* (1963)
372 U.S. 391, 83 S. Ct. 822, 9 L. Ed. 2d 837

Charles Noia, Santo Caminito, and Frank Bonino were arrested in New York in 1941 for the murder of Murray Hameroff, who was shot and killed during an attempted holdup. The suspects were taken into custody on a Sunday night, separated, and questioned by five or six police officers at a time until about 2:00 A.M. Each spent the night in an unheated cell containing only a wooden bench—no bed or blankets—making sleep difficult or impossible.

They were questioned all the next day. The police kept them incommunicado from each other and from their families, friends, and attorneys, who tried to find out what was happening to them.

On Monday afternoon, two women and a man—all detectives pretending to be witnesses—were brought before each suspect separately and "identified" each as one of the participants in the robbery and shooting.

That night, Caminito and Noia were allowed to see each

other. According to Caminito, Noia said, "Let's give them the same story they gave us. . . . It won't mean anything. . . . We can see a lawyer this way. We will tell the lawyer what happened, and they cannot do us nothing. We did not do it. You don't have to worry. You can prove where you were, and I can prove also."

"No," Caminito said, "it is not right."

But Noia said, "How long can I stand this?"

Caminito had never been arrested before. Noia apparently had a criminal record for previous robberies. They compared what the detectives had told each of them had happened and decided to confess to that story. They were officially "arrested" after confessing, and were arraigned before a magistrate the next day, more than forty hours after being taken into custody.

At the trial, the prosecutor's evidence consisted solely of the three confessions. The defense attorneys objected to their admission into evidence contending that the confessions had been coerced and that convictions based on them would be unconstitutional. The judge said it was up to the jury to decide from the evidence whether the confessions were voluntary.

The jurors returned a verdict of guilty and recommended life imprisonment for all three defendants, rather than the death penalty. The judge accepted the recommendations in sentencing the defendants, but said to Noia on that occasion: "I have thought seriously about rejecting the recommendation of the jury in your case, Noia, because I feel that if the jury knew who you were and what you were and your background as a robber, they would not have made a recommendation. But you have got a good lawyer, that is my wife. The last thing she told me this morning is to give you a chance."

Caminito and Bonino appealed, but Noia did not. He later

testified that he had not wanted to saddle his family with another heavy financial burden that he could not pay himself. His trial lawyer said Noia also feared that if the appeal were successful and he was then retried, he risked another conviction that might result in a death sentence.

The state court appeals by Caminito and Bonino (in 1942 and 1943) were unsuccessful. In 1947, Bonino sought reargument in the New York Court of Appeals (a procedure that can be undertaken at any time in that state). Caminito did the same in 1948 and 1954. Their motions for reargument were denied and the United States Supreme Court refused to review the decisions.

In 1955, Caminito applied for a writ of habeas corpus in the federal district court. His application was denied. He appealed the denial to the federal court of appeals. The three-judge appellate court in 1955 granted his writ and denounced the third-degree tactics used by the police in obtaining his confession: "All decent Americans soundly condemn satanic practices, like those described above, when employed in totalitarian regimes. It should shock us when American police resort to them, for they do not comport with the barest minimum of civilized principles of justice. It has no significance that in this case we must assume there was no physical brutality. For psychological torture may be far more cruel, far more symptomatic of sadism. Many a man who can endure beatings will yield to fatigue. To keep a man awake beyond the point of exhaustion, while constantly pummelling him with questions, is to degrade him, to strip him of human dignity, to deprive him of the will to resist, to make him a pitiable creature mastered by the single desire—at all costs to be free of torment. Any member of this or any other court, to escape such anguish, would admit to almost any crime."

Seeing Caminito's success, Bonino again moved for reargument of his appeal. This time his motion was granted and his conviction was set aside. A new trial was ordered on the ground that his confession was unconstitutionally coerced. It was now fifteen years since the crime, however, and the prosecution's only evidence had been the illegal confessions. The current district attorney decided not to retry Caminito and Bonino.

Noia couldn't ask for reargument because he had never appealed. The time limit for appealing had long past. He therefore applied to the trial court that had sentenced him, asking for a review. The court in 1956 set aside his conviction, but the state appealed this decision, and the appellate court reversed, reinstating Noia's conviction. Noia appealed the reversal, but without success. His failure to appeal originally, said the New York Court of Appeals, foreclosed him from using a procedure for review at a later date, even if he was raising a constitutional issue.

Noia then petitioned for a writ of habeas corpus in federal district court as Caminito had done. The federal judge denied the petition, saying habeas corpus would not be granted unless "the applicant has exhausted the remedies available in the courts of the State." Noia appealed the denial to the federal court of appeals. The state argued that Noia had failed to exhaust his state remedies by appealing the original verdict and that this failure constituted an "adequate state ground" for his imprisonment that would remain valid even if a constitutional ground for his release were found. The federal court of appeals answered that "exceptional circumstances were present" in this case—an "undisputed violation of a significant constitutional right," which had caused Noia's codefendants to be free from prison while he was kept in, although the circumstances of their cases were identical.

Noia's failure to appeal, which would have been "reasonable enough to prevent federal judicial intervention in most cases, is in this particular case unreasonable and inadequate," the court of appeals concluded. It reversed the district court, set aside Noia's conviction, and ordered him discharged from prison unless the state retried him.

The state asked the U.S. Supreme Court to review the case.

Do you think Noia lost his chance to raise issues about his case when he decided not to appeal in 1942? If he were granted a writ of habeas corpus, would that open the door to every convict in the country to reopen his case with a petition for habeas corpus? Should federal courts be required to hear thousands of petitions by prisoners in state institutions? What is the purpose of the Great Writ? What limitations can be put on use of the writ without impairing its purpose?

Justice Brennan delivered the Supreme Court's six-to-three decision in 1963. He traced the history of habeas corpus briefly, and noted that "today habeas corpus in the federal courts provides a mode for the redress of denials of due process of law."

"Of course standards of due process have evolved over the centuries. But the nature and purpose of habeas corpus have remained remarkably constant," he noted. To illustrate that the writ had been used against restraints imposed by courts as well as rulers, he described *Bushell's Case* from seventeenth-century England, in which the judge imprisoned a jury for contempt because it brought back a not-guilty verdict. Bushell, one of the jurors, sought and won release from custody by writ of habeas corpus.

The Supreme Court also rejected the argument that the

writ applied only to questions of jurisdiction—whether the court that had acted was the proper court to take that action. Quoting opinions and legal treatises from early England on, Justice Brennan showed that the writ was considered to apply to both jurisdictional problems and broad due process questions.

The majority justices recognized that the Supreme Court had not "always followed an unwavering line in its conclusions as to the availability of the Great Writ. Our development of the law of federal habeas corpus has been attended, seemingly, with some backing and filling." But the justices found that the trend was to permit habeas review by federal courts of both federal and state cases in increasingly wide areas.

Turning to the facts before it, the Supreme Court held: "Under the conditions of modern society, Noia's imprisonment, under a conviction procured by a confession held . . . to have been coerced, and which the State here concedes was obtained in violation of the Fourteenth Amendment, is no less intolerable than was Bushell's under the conditions of a very different society; and habeas corpus is no less the appropriate remedy."

But, the state had argued, the court in Bushell's case was not operating under a state-federal structure, as the Court in Noia's case was. This structure required restraint by the federal courts when dealing with state convictions.

Justice Brennan reviewed the cases since 1867, noting that "the Court's practice in this area has been far from uniform, and even greater divergency has characterized the practice of the lower federal courts." But he found that on the whole the Supreme Court had "fashioned a doctrine of abstention, whereby full play would be allowed the States in the administration of their criminal justice" while preserving federal questions for final ruling by federal courts if necessary. The Court had frequently denied habeas petitions, telling the petitioner to finish his business in the state courts, but also alerting him to renew his federal petition later if his federal claims were not decided to his satisfaction.

Answering the argument that there were adequate state grounds for sustaining Noia's conviction even if there was a constitutional ground for overturning it, the Court said, "The adequate state-ground rule is a function of the limitations of *appellate* review," not of extraordinary remedies such as habeas corpus. "Habeas lies to enforce the right of personal liberty; when that right is denied and a person confined, the federal court has the power to release him. Indeed, it has no other power; it cannot revise the state court judgment; it can act only on the body of the petitioner." The Court also noted that there was no "substantive state law" independently upholding Noia's conviction. "In Noia's case the only relevant substantive law is federal—the Fourteenth Amendment."

The Court held that Noia had not failed to exhaust state remedies, because there were no longer any state remedies available to him. It also held that a prisoner who had lost on appeal to the highest state court did not need to seek Supreme Court review before petitioning for federal habeas corpus relief. However, the Court explicitly recognized that a "federal habeas judge may in his discretion deny relief to an applicant who has deliberately by-passed the orderly procedure of the state courts and in so doing has forfeited his state court remedies."

Looking at the present case, the Court found, "Under no reasonable view can the state's version of Noia's reason for not appealing support an inference of deliberate by-passing of the state court system. For Noia to have appealed in 1942 would have been to run a substantial risk of electrocution. His was the grisly choice whether to sit content with life imprisonment or to travel the uncertain avenue of appeal which, if successful, might well have led to a retrial and death sentence."

Justice Brennan concluded: "Our decision today swings open no prison gates. Today as always few indeed is the number of state prisoners who eventually win their freedom by means of federal habeas corpus. Those few who are ultimately successful are persons whom society has grievously wronged and for whom belated liberation is little enough compensation. Surely no fair-minded person will contend that those who have been deprived of their liberty without due process of law ought nevertheless to languish in prison. Noia, no less than his codefendants Caminito and Bonino, is conceded to have been the victim of unconstitutional state action. Noia's case stands on its own; but surely no just and humane legal system can tolerate a result whereby a Caminito and a Bonino are at liberty because their confessions were found to have been coerced yet a Noia, whose confession was also coerced, remains in jail for life. For such anomalies, such affronts to the conscience of a civilized society, habeas corpus is predestined by its historical role in the struggle for personal liberty to be the ultimate remedy. If the States withhold effective remedy, the federal courts have the power and the duty to provide it."

Justices Harlan, Clark, and Stewart dissented. Writing for the three, Justice Harlan said: "The federal courts have no *power*, statutory or constitutional, to release the respondent Noia from state detention. This is because his custody by New York does not violate any federal right, since it is pursuant to a conviction whose validity rests upon an adequate and independent state ground which the federal courts are required to respect." Justice Harlan disagreed point by point with the majority's findings, and concluded: "I recognize that Noia's predicament may well be thought one that strongly calls for correction. But the proper course to that end lies with the New York Governor's powers of executive clemency, not with the federal courts."

Justice Clark wrote a separate dissent to stress what he felt the effects of the majority's decision would be: "First, there can be no question but that a rash of new applications from state prisoners will pour into the federal courts, and 98% of them will be frivolous, if history is any guide. . . . Second, the effective administration of criminal justice in state courts receives a staggering blow. Habeas corpus is in effect substituted for appeal, seriously disturbing the orderly disposition of state prosecutions and jeopardizing the finality of state convictions." This "victory for the 'struggle for personal liberty' " would be a defeat, he felt, for "the struggle for law and order," and he was "reminded of the exclamation of Pyrrhus: 'One more such victory . . . , and we are utterly undone.' "

Justice Clark warned that congressional legislation to "repair the judicial loopholes in federal habeas corpus for state prisoners" might now be necessary.

Justices on both sides of this issue were correct. Thousands of prisoners in state courts did file petitions for release on habeas corpus in the federal district courts, but only a handful were ordered released by the district courts, or by courts of appeals or the Supreme Court. Few even were given hearings on their petitions, the courts finding their written arguments without merit. Success came, if at all, only after years of writing petitions and waiting for decisions. (See the *Sheppard* case, discussed in chapter 15.)

The workload facing federal courts increased, but the

prison doors were certainly not swung open for hordes of state prisoners. Many federal courts hired attorneys to screen habeas petitions, providing summaries of the facts and issues for the judges, to save them time in deciding whether to grant hearings.

Thousands of prisoners spent hours poring over lawbooks, trying to find grounds for their release under the U.S. Constitution, statutes, and court opinions. For most, this was their first effort to obtain a goal through the use of law and the legal system rather than by using "street" tactics, including the use of physical force or weapons. Can this be considered part of the rehabilitation of a prisoner? If so, is it worth the added cost to society—the cost of increasing the number of habeas clerks working for the federal courts?

These questions remain to be answered by penologists and, ultimately, by voters whose taxes pay for such clerks. Certainly the release of even one prisoner on a writ of habeas corpus because of the denial of due process in his case has a profound effect on all the prisoners, police officers, prosecutors, trial judges, lawyers, and others familiar with the case.

CHAPTER 19

Rights of Young People

Decisions about due process answer two main questions: What procedural rights are people entitled to when they go to court, and what people are covered by these procedural protections? Chapters 10 through 18 discuss the content of due process; this chapter discusses some of the coverage of due process.

Traditionally, the people with power in a society find a way to convince the government that they are entitled to fair treatment when they sue or are sued. In 1215 in England, the feudal lords threatened King John that they would refuse to give him military and economic support unless he guaranteed them the right to habeas corpus in case his officials should imprison them. Since then, other groups of citizens have successfully demanded that they be covered by due process protections.

By the time the United States Constitution and Bill of Rights were written, it was generally accepted in this country that people were entitled to fair treatment in court. But "people" did not include slaves, American Indians on reservations, noncitizens (aliens), nonvoters (youth), or noncivilians (soldiers). Women were included only as to certain rights. Since 1787, individuals from these powerless groups have been demanding the same procedural rights in litigation as "the rich, the wise, and the good" who Alexander Hamilton thought should rule the new American nation.

After the Civil War, Congress decreed that former slaves must be accorded the same procedural (and substantive) rights as everyone else. While the courts were slow to follow this declaration of national policy, the Warren Court went further in that direction than any previous Supreme Court. The woman suffrage amendment (the nineteenth) marked a serious beginning to changing the laws so that women would be treated in an equal manner in the courts, although we still have many statutes based on the old axiom that man and wife are one, and the one is the man.

Political power has been a major factor in determining what kinds of standards are applied to a group. For example, when aliens' rights are being determined, the decisions are made by administrative agencies rather than courts; the aliens do not go before a judge or jury when questions of fact are raised about their deportation. The facts are determined first by an administrative hearing, and the courts act only as reviewing bodies, not as fact finders. Today, aliens enjoy some of the procedural rights of citizens, but the long struggle to achieve due process in their cases has brought only some reforms, not equal treatment.

Similarly, people without money to pay legal fees have been disadvantaged in civil suits over rent, credit, consumer fraud, and so forth, and in criminal cases. Major efforts to redress this grievance were made for the first time with the so-called war on poverty inaugurated in 1964 (see chapter 28). This led to the establishment of legal service programs that opened law offices in ghettos, barrios, and low-income neighborhoods in many urban and rural communities, while the public, through the Office of Economic Opportunity and local contributions, paid the costs. For the first time, poor people have been able to make meaningful use of procedural protections because they could retain lawyers to alert them to their rights in litigation, both as plaintiffs and as defendants. Of course, legal services lawyers, who represent a massive number of poor clients, don't have time to do the kind of advance planning that wealthy clients and corporations expect as a matter of course from their attorneys; but some progress has certainly been made in evening the scales of justice.

How have young people been treated by American courts? Have they been held entitled to the same kinds of due process protections as adults? There are two major areas in which youths face the legal system: in juvenile courts and in the Selective Service System. In both areas the Warren Court handed down landmark decisions.

A. Juvenile Courts

When a young person breaks the law, he usually is brought before the juvenile court, not a regular trial court. Juvenile courts were developed in this country toward the end of the nineteenth century by reformers who were appalled that children were being treated like adult criminals. Youths who were arrested, tried, and imprisoned with hardened, mature offenders were simply being pushed further along the road to crime, they felt.

The social reformers sought a separate juvenile court that would handle the problems of young people in a totally different way, whether they were charged with violating the law or had been abandoned by their parents and needed foster homes. The youthful offender should be considered basically good but in need of guidance, treatment, correction, and care. He should be taken into custody, not arrested by the police. A petition should be filed on his behalf asking the court to take care of him, rather than an indictment charging him with committing a crime. A hearing should be held at which the judge should try to find out what the youth had done, what his background was, how he felt, and what might be done to help him. This should take the place of a criminal trial, and should not be an "adversary" proceeding, with prosecution and defense arguing back and forth. Rather, all concerned should be seeking information about how best to save the youth from a "dissolute life." In the end, the judge might decide that the petitioner required detention by the state—but this was to be in a separate youth facility, often labeled a detention home, youth authority, or industrial school. This was to be different from a conviction in an adult criminal court and imprisonment in a jail or prison.

This concept of juvenile proceedings caught on rapidly, until every state had adopted a juvenile court system. Whether the system worked at all the way the reformers had planned became a subject of controversy. Did the social work jargon used by juvenile courts mask unfair procedures?

After the Warren Court had taken a hard look at procedures in adult criminal trials and had established new due process standards there, the standards followed in juvenile courts were bound to come up for scrutiny.

Six-year sentence for a two-month charge

In re Gault (1967)
387 U.S. 1, 87 S. Ct. 1428, 18 L. Ed. 2d 527

Fifteen-year-old Gerald Gault and his buddy Ronald Lewis were picked up by the County Sheriff in Phoenix, Arizona, on June 8, 1964. Police had received a complaint from a neighbor, Mrs. Cook, that the boys had called her on the phone and made lewd or indecent remarks ("Are your cherries ripe?" "Do you have big bombers?" and similar adolescent questions).

The boys were taken to the Children's Detention Home. Nobody left word for Gerald's family that he had been taken into custody. When Mrs. Gault got home from work that evening, she sent her older son Louis to look for Gerald at the Lewis's trailer home. There Louis learned where the boys had been taken. He and his mother went to the detention home, saw Gerald, and were told by Probation Officer Flagg why he was there. Flagg said Gerald would be kept overnight and brought to a hearing in juvenile court at 3:00 the next day.

The hearing was held in Judge McGhee's chambers. Mrs. Gault and Louis were there; Mr. Gault was at work out of town. Probation Officers Flagg and Henderson and Gerald were the only others present. No record of the hearing was made and those attending later disagreed about what had been said. Mrs. Gault said Gerald had testified that he only dialed the number and that Ronald had done the talking. The judge and Officer Flagg said Gerald admitted making lewd remarks.

At the end of the hearing, Mrs. Gault asked whether Gerald would be sent to Fort Grant, the state industrial school. The judge said, "No, I will think it over." Gerald was taken back to the detention home. Three or four days later, he was released, without explanation. Officer Flagg sent Mrs. Gault a note saying merely: "Judge McGhee has set Monday June 15, 1964, at 11:00 A.M. as the date and time for further hearings on Gerald's delinquency."

Gerald, his parents, his brother, Ronald Lewis and his father, and Officers Flagg and Henderson appeared this time before the judge. For the second time no record of the testimony was made; for the second time the participants disagreed later about what was said. According to the Gaults, Gerald repeated that he had dialed the number. The judge said Gerald admitted making some of the "less serious" lewd statements. Flagg this time said Gerald didn't admit any statements and that at the detention home each of the boys had put the blame on the other.

Mrs. Gault asked that Mrs. Cook be brought in "so she could see which boy had done the talking, the dirty talking over the phone." The judge said that wasn't necessary.

At the end of the hearing, however, the judge committed Gerald to Fort Grant for delinquency "for the period of his minority, unless sooner discharged by due process of law." Since Gerald was fifteen and would be a minor until twenty-one, this was a possible six-year sentence!

The Gaults suddenly saw that they needed expert help. They went to the Arizona Civil Liberties Union for a lawyer. Under Arizona law, there is no appeal from a juvenile court decision, so Attorney Amelie Lewis filed a petition for a writ of habeas corpus (see chapter 18) in the state court.

Attorney Lewis contended that Gerald had been denied eight basic features of due process of law: He had not been advised of his right to counsel or his right to remain silent; his parents had not been notified of his arrest; no formal notice of the two hearings or the charges had been given to the Gaults; there had been no opportunity to examine or cross-examine key witnesses such as Mrs. Cook; there was no record made of the proceedings so that illegal conduct by the judge could be proved; unsworn and hearsay testimony was permitted; the judge's ruling removed Gerald from his parents' custody without a finding that they were unsuitable to care for him; and with such a severe penalty at stake the lack of an appeal procedure was fundamentally unfair.

The district attorney's answer rested on the concept of the juvenile court as a substitute parental guardian of wayward youth—the *parens patriae* view. It would interfere with the juvenile court's informal and compassionate workings to pin the court personnel down to constitutional due process.

The hearing on the habeas corpus petition was held on August 17, 1964. The Gaults' lawyer cross-examined Judge McGhee vigorously on why he had ruled as he had. The judge revealed that he had taken several factors into consideration. Gerald was on "probation" at the time as the result of a previous brush with the law (he had been with a boy accused of stealing a woman's wallet). The judge recollected an incident two years before when Gerald had been accused of taking another boy's baseball glove and then, as the judge recalled, "lied to the Police Department about it" (although the judge admitted that no charges had been brought against Gerald "because of lack of material foundation"). The judge insisted that Gerald had admitted making the phone call to Mrs. Cook and even admitted making other "silly, or funny calls" in the past.

The judge had concluded that Gerald was "habitually involved in immoral matters," which was a loose definition of delinquency under the Arizona Juvenile Code. The specific charge of using "vulgar, abusive or obscene language" in the presence of a woman, however, was only a misdemeanor under the Arizona Criminal Code, and carried a penalty (for an adult offender) of $5 to $50 fine or imprisonment up to two months.

The superior court dismissed the petition for habeas corpus, and the Gaults appealed to the Arizona Supreme Court. The supreme court upheld the superior court's decision. It agreed that due process was required in cases like Gerald's, but the standards in juvenile court could be different from those in an adult proceeding. The court found that the Gaults knew of the charges against Gerald and the hearings to be held, so they had received adequate notice. It found that the parents and the probation officer were charged with the duty of looking after the child's interests in a juvenile proceeding, and that the judge could decide whether the child also had the right to a lawyer's assistance. The court found that the juvenile court's "necessary flexibility for individualized treatment" required that the judge have discretion to allow or ignore the child's privilege against self-incrimination. Confession might be good for the child, and the judge should be free to encourage it. And the court ruled that there was no constitutional right to appeal, and no need for a transcript since an appeal was not available.

The Gaults appealed this decision to the United States Supreme Court, contending that the Arizona Juvenile Code, on its face and as applied in Gerald's case, was unconstitutional because it did not afford juveniles due process of law as required by the Fourteenth Amendment.

Do you think a young person should be treated the same as an adult when charged with a crime? Is it more important to give a juvenile the constitutional protections of due process of law or the social protections of an informal and "fatherly" court process? Can a juvenile court provide both?

The United States Supreme Court handed down an eight-to-one decision in 1967, with Justice Fortas writing the majority opinion. The Court held, at the outset, that "neither the Fourteenth Amendment nor the Bill of Rights is for adults alone," and the Court would now try to set forth "the precise impact of the due process requirement" on juvenile proceedings that can result in commitment of the child to a state institution.

Justice Fortas examined the *parens patriae* theory, and found that it denied procedural rights to children on the rationale "that a child, unlike an adult, has a right 'not to liberty but to custody.' "

"Accordingly, the highest motives and most enlightened impulses led to a peculiar system for juveniles, unknown to our law in any comparable context. The constitutional and theoretical basis for this peculiar system is—to say the least —debatable. And in practice . . . the results have not been entirely satisfactory. . . . The absence of procedural rules based upon constitutional principle has not always produced fair, efficient, and effective procedures. Departures from established principles of due process have frequently resulted not in enlightened procedure, but in arbitrariness."

Justice Fortas noted, "It is claimed that juveniles obtain benefits from the special procedures applicable to them which more than offset the disadvantages of denial of the substance of normal due process." Examining the supposed benefits, Justice Fortas cited a study by the Stanford Research Institute showing that a very high percentage of youths coming before the juvenile courts were two-time offenders or more. This refuted the claim "that the juvenile system, functioning free of constitutional inhibitions as it has largely done, is effective to reduce crime or rehabilitate offenders." Other so-called benefits of the juvenile court system were no less dubious. Calling a child "delinquent," Justice Fortas noted, "has come to involve only slightly less stigma" than calling an adult "criminal." Supposed confidentiality of juvenile court records was often "more rhetoric than reality." Informal "fatherly" juvenile court proceedings might conclude with stern disciplining, leading the child to feel "that he has been deceived or enticed."

The Supreme Court looked at the reality of the juvenile court process and found that a child charged with misconduct was confined in an institution "for a greater or lesser time. His world becomes 'a building with whitewashed walls, regimented routine and institutional hours. . . .' Instead of mother and father and sisters and brothers and friends and classmates, his world is peopled by guards, custodians, state employees, and 'delinquents' confined with him for anything from waywardness to rape and homicide."

The theoretical concept of juvenile court assumed that the judge would take the time and effort "to establish precisely what the juvenile did and why he did it—was it a prank of adolescence or a brutal act threatening serious consequences to himself or society unless corrected? Under traditional notions, one would assume that in a case like that of Gerald Gault, where the juvenile appears to have a home, a working mother and father, and an older brother, the Juvenile Judge would have made a careful inquiry and judgment as to the possibility that the boy could be disciplined and dealt with at home, despite his previous transgressions." But in fact the judge paid little or no attention to these aspects of the case.

The severe penalty imposed on Gerald was possible only because he was fifteen years old instead of eighteen. If he had been eighteen he would have come under the jurisdiction of the adult criminal court; he would have been subject to no more than a small fine or two months in jail; he would have received all the legal rights and protections of the Constitution. Because he was under eighteen, Gerald was deprived of many key rights and sentenced to six years' confinement. "Under our Constitution, the condition of being a boy does not justify a kangaroo court," the Supreme Court held.

It then considered the specific rights the Gaults claimed had been violated and made a series of rulings:

(1) The juvenile and his parents must be notified of the specific charges against the juvenile and of each scheduled court proceeding in time to prepare for it.

(2) In proceedings that may result in commitment of a juvenile to an institution, "the Due Process Clause of the Fourteenth Amendment requires that . . . the child and his parents must be notified of the child's right to be represented by counsel retained by them, or if they are unable to afford counsel, that counsel will be appointed to represent the child."

(3) The privilege against self-incrimination must be accorded to a juvenile in Gerald's situation. The fact that juvenile court proceedings are labeled "civil," rather than "criminal," does not make them exempt from the Fifth Amendment. Proceedings that could lead to commitment to a state institution "must be regarded as 'criminal' for purposes of the privilege against self-incrimination." The Court also viewed with skepticism the theory that a youth should be urged to confess as part of the rehabilitative process, and gave several examples of false confessions by juveniles in serious cases.

(4) The juvenile judge's reliance on hearsay evidence was also disapproved by the Court. "Absent a valid confession adequate to support the determination of the Juvenile Court, confrontation and sworn testimony by witnesses available for cross-examination were essential for a finding of 'delinquency' and an order committing Gerald to a state institution for a maximum of six years."

The Court declined to rule on whether an appeal had to be provided and a transcript of juvenile court proceedings made, but it noted that the lack of an appeal process and a transcript may "throw a burden upon the machinery for habeas corpus, . . . saddle the reviewing process with the burden of attempting to reconstruct a record, and . . . impose upon the Juvenile Judge the unseemly duty of testifying under cross-examination as to the events that transpired in the hearings before him."

Justice White concurred, but felt there was insufficient evidence that Gerald had been deprived of the privilege against self-incrimination.

Justice Harlan concurred in part and dissented in part, and Justice Black answered Justice Harlan's partial dissent in a separate concurring opinion. Their differences, as in other cases, turned on whether "due process" in the Fourteenth Amendment meant the rights specified in the Bill of Rights or general fundamental fairness to be determined by the circumstances of each case (see chapter 20).

Justice Stewart dissented, saying: "I possess neither the specialized experience nor the expert knowledge to predict with any certainty where may lie the brightest hope for progress in dealing with the serious problems of juvenile delinquency. But I am certain that the answer does not lie in the Court's opinion in this case, which serves to convert a juvenile proceeding into a criminal prosecution." He did not feel that a juvenile necessarily had a right to remain silent under the Fifth and Fourteenth Amendments or a right to court-appointed counsel if indigent.

The *Gault* decision brought certain constitutional guarantees into juvenile court proceedings in which a child might be sentenced to an institution. A continuing struggle is being waged to bring all the specific due process rights set forth in the Constitution into all juvenile court proceedings (even those not resulting in confinement). In the 1970 case called *In re Winship* the Court took another major step forward by ruling that when a juvenile is charged with an act that would be a crime if committed by an adult, and he contests the facts alleged against him, the prosecution must prove its case "beyond a reasonable doubt." Before this decision, many courts had required only proof "by a preponderance of the evidence." The *Winship* rule brought juvenile cases in line with adult criminal cases in terms of the burden of proof.

B. Selective Service System

As the United States became more and more deeply committed to war in Southeast Asia during the 1960s, the protests against this policy deepened and widened. Demonstrators held mass marches, picket lines, sit-ins at induction centers and federal buildings, rallies, and teach-ins. Scores, then hundreds, finally thousands were arrested on one charge or another. Young men of draft age began to examine their beliefs more closely, and many decided they could not, in good conscience, serve in the armed forces. They exercised their beliefs in a variety of ways, some of which led to criminal prosecutions. These cases brought the issues around the war into the courts, despite the efforts of government lawyers to keep them out.

Lawyers began to examine the draft law more closely, as draft clients increased and older answers did not fit the new situation. They began to look at the Selective Service System as they would look at any other government agency—the Internal Revenue Service, the Federal Trade Commission, the National Labor Relations Board. They found that the SSS refused to give draftees the same rights that citizens usually have before administrative agencies. For example, draftees did not have the right to be represented by a lawyer in hearings before the agency. They also found that the SSS didn't follow its own rules in some instances and didn't let the public or the draftees see all the interdepartmental memos.

The lawyers and their clients waged a slow and steady battle to bring the SSS into line with constitutional concepts of fair procedures spelled out in the due process clause of the Fifth Amendment. The government lawyers answered that the SSS has a special status because it supplies armed forces needed for national security.

While these arguments reverberated in the courts, they seldom reached the public ear. But protests from citizens rang in the streets. Thousands of young men burned or turned in their draft cards to indicate their opposition to the war and the draft, and others refused induction into the army.

Drafting a man for burning his draft card

Oestereich v. *Selective Service System Local Board No. 11* (1968)
393 U.S. 233, 89 S. Ct. 414, 21 L. Ed. 2d 402

James Oestereich was a student at Andover-Newton Theological School in Massachusetts, and as such had a IV-D exemption (for divinity students) from the draft. At a demonstration on October 16, 1967, he and other young men sent their draft cards to the Justice Department in what he called "an act of collective conscience in support of our dying and suffering brothers who are presently fighting on our behalf in Vietnam." He felt it was "a responsible expression of concerned citizens, acting in light of the first amendment."

On October 26, 1967, the director of the Selective Service System, General Lewis B. Hershey, sent a letter to all SSS

Young men burn their draft cards to protest the Vietnam War, this time in New York City, April 15, 1967.
Credit: Wide World Photos

personnel, directing them to collect information on protest activities by draft-age men and suggesting that protesters be declared delinquent, reclassified, ordered to report for a new physical, or processed for induction.

Although it was simply a letter, many draft boards treated it as a regulation and proceeded to follow it. James Oestereich's board in Cheyenne, Wyoming, sent him a delinquency notice and reclassified him I-A on November 7, 1967. The board informed him that he was delinquent because of his failure to have his draft card in his possession and his failure to notify the board of "his current status."

Oestereich appealed the I-A classification to the Wyoming Appeal Board. He contended that the delinquency regulations and reclassification had been applied to him as a punishment for his opposition to the war, and that this was unconstitutional: he had a right to dissent, and he could not be punished without being given a hearing complete with protections of due process—right to counsel, cross-examination, impartial jury, etc.

The Appeal Board, however, upheld the local draft board, and Oestereich was ordered to report for induction. At that point Oestereich had several alternatives: he could give up his objection, accept the I-A classification, and be inducted into the army; he could be inducted and then try to get discharged by petitioning for a writ of habeas corpus; or he could reject the classification, refuse induction, and await arrest and prosecution by the United States government (he would be charged with a felony, carrying a possible prison sentence of five years and/or a fine of $10,000). If he could find an imaginative lawyer, he had one other choice: he could sue his local draft board in federal court, charging the members with violation of his constitutional rights and seeking a reversal of the delinquency classification, the I-A classification, and the induction order.

A number of young men in other cities throughout the country faced exactly the same alternatives because the same series of events had occurred after they burned or returned their draft cards. By late 1967 draft lawyers were in touch with one another across the country. The American Civil Liberties Union served as a coordinator of information and participated in a series of suits against local boards from Connecticut to Wyoming.

The hardest question in this case was whether Oestereich had the right to sue his draft board at that point. It was fairly clear that the board had acted to punish him because he had exercised his right of expression using his draft card. But the Constitution does not permit every person who has a grievance to file a lawsuit in federal court, and Congress has limited the kinds of cases the federal courts will decide. It is the responsibility of the person filing a federal suit to convince the court to hear the case according to the facts at that point. This is an acute problem for the person filing a draft case because the government says that the national defense will be disrupted if he wins his point, and that any disruption in this critical area is obviously unjustified.

Nevertheless, Oestereich decided to sue his draft board in federal district court. The government moved that the suit be dismissed and the court promptly granted the motion on several grounds. The judge said Oestereich knew he was supposed to keep his draft card with him at all times, and "exemptions and classifications are a privilege, not an inalienable right conferred by the Constitution or statute." The judge also held that he did not have jurisdiction to decide the case because the 1967 amendments to the draft statute (the Military Training and Service Act) prohibited the courts from reviewing draft classifications until after the draftee had refused or submitted to induction. Finally, the judge stated, the induction order "does not constitute penal action," so there was no need for a hearing with constitutional due process.

Oestereich appealed to the Court of Appeals, which affirmed the district court's decision. He then sought and was granted review by the U.S. Supreme Court. The case had moved with remarkable speed. It had begun only twelve days after General Hershey's letter of October 26, 1967, and was filed in the United States Supreme Court by March 1968—within five months. It was argued October 24, 1968, and decided December 16, 1968. While it was pending, judges in the lower courts held all similar cases pending. This affirmative suit, then, held up the induction orders against fifty or seventy-five registrants who also sued, and probably a number of others whose draft boards decided not to take further steps against them while this case was pending.

In his brief before the Supreme Court, the U.S. Solicitor General made an unusual move: he agreed with the other side. He concluded that the use of the delinquency provision to reclassify Oestereich probably violated the statutory exemption of ministerial students, and the language of General Hershey's letter probably made the reclassification unconstitutional in that it imposed punishment without providing the protections of the Fifth and Sixth Amendments. He joined Oestereich in asking the Court to reverse the lower courts. He noted, however, that the Selective Service System disagreed with his position, and he also presented the SSS arguments in his brief.

The SSS contended that the language in the draft statute was absolute—Oestereich had to be inducted or refuse induction before bringing the issue into court. If an exception were allowed for divinity students, why not for draftees claiming conscientious objector status, extreme hardship, or other exemptions? Yet if all these were allowed, the purpose of the statute—to prevent interruption and delay in the draft process—would be thwarted.

The delinquency provisions, the SSS said, were the method devised for enforcing its requirement that draftees keep in touch with the System. Congress had approved this method. And a draftee's "entitlement to a ministerial exemption is conditioned on compliance with his duties as a registrant." The SSS concluded that "the statutory exemption for ministerial students may be waived or abandoned by the student's failure to comply with his duties as a registrant."

Do you think Congress can prevent a registrant from suing his draft board concerning his classification? Is a draft board decision different from the decisions of other administrative agencies, which can be appealed by a civil suit before the person is arrested on a criminal charge of violating the order? Is draft card burning a form of expression protected by the First Amendment? Should ministers and ministerial students be granted exemption from the draft? If Congress says they should, can a selective service board take away the exemption because of something the registrant does?

The Supreme Court split six to three, with Justice Douglas writing the majority opinion. The Court found the provisions of the draft statute concerning both the IV-D exemption and the prohibition against court review of cases before induction "equally unambiguous."

Dealing first with the ministerial exemption, the Court ruled that, "when Congress has granted an exemption and a registrant meets its terms and conditions," a draft board cannot "withhold it from him for activities or conduct not material to the grant or withdrawal of the exemption." If boards had such power, it "would make the Boards freewheeling agencies meting out their brand of justice in a vindictive manner."

"Once a person registers and qualifies for a statutory exemption, we find no legislative authority to deprive him of that exemption because of conduct or activities unrelated to the merits of granting or continuing that exemption. The Solicitor General confesses error on the use by Selective Service of delinquency proceedings for that purpose.

"We deal with conduct of a local Board that is basically lawless. It is no different in constitutional implications from a case where induction of an ordained minister or other clearly exempt person is ordered (a) to retaliate against the person because of his political views or (b) to bear down on him for his religious views or his racial attitudes or (c) to get him out of town so that the amorous interests of a Board member might be better served."

Moving on to the question of court review before induction, the Supreme Court stated: "To hold that a person deprived of his statutory exemption in such a blatantly lawless manner must either be inducted and raise his protest through habeas corpus or defy induction and defend his refusal in a criminal prosecution is to construe the Act with unnecessary harshness." The Court concluded that there was reason to make an exception and grant courts the jurisdiction to review cases like this, where the exemption was "plain and unequivocal and in no way contested" and where the delinquency regulation conflicting with it was "not broad enough" and not authoritative enough to revoke the exemption specified by Congress. The lower court's decision was reversed.

Justice Harlan concurred, but on different grounds. He assumed that Congress had not meant to prohibit review of the claim that the Selective Service Act and Regulations were themselves invalid on their face, but only to prohibit individuals from getting their specific draft classifications reviewed by civil suits.

This Supreme Court opinion marked the end of the unquestioned power of General Hershey, who had been the Director of the Selective Service System since its formation in 1940. Federal judges throughout the country began to look more closely at draft board decisions being challenged by the defendants in criminal prosecutions for draft refusal. Local draft boards also began to understand that the Selective Service System was not an agency standing alone but was part of a governmental system required to provide certain basic rights.

However, the case did not mean that every draft registrant could go to court to test his classification before being ordered inducted. Nor did it mean that most registrants could avoid the problem of becoming defendants in federal criminal cases when they disagreed with their classifications. On the very same day that the Court announced its decision in *Oestereich*, the justices reached an opposite conclusion in *Clark* v. *Gabriel*, the case of another registrant who had tried to get conscientious objector classification and went to court to test the denial of this status by his local board. In an unsigned, short opinion, the Court held that granting or denying conscientious objector status required discretion on the part of the board, and that Congress did not intend to permit the registrant to get a federal court to review a board decision by suing the board. A person challenging the denial of other kinds of status than delinquency would have to refuse induction and test his classification as a defendant in a criminal case.

In two later cases, the Supreme Court did broaden the *Oestereich* decision against the delinquency regulations so that the SSS finally abolished the status of delinquent and all special processing of delinquents.

In 1970, Congress amended the draft law to correct some obvious due process violations, but voted against permitting lawyers to represent registrants in draft board hearings or requiring the SSS to follow the same procedures required of virtually every other administrative agency under the Administrative Procedure Act. The legislative basis for drafting of men into the armed forces ended June 30, 1973, but the Selective Service System was not dismantled and 18-year-olds are still required to register and to keep their local boards informed of their addresses. Prosecution of draft refusers has continued on cases pending in early 1973. And the rights of members of the armed forces continue to be raised in courts martial and habeas corpus cases.

CHAPTER 20

Rights in State and Federal Trials

Should there be a difference between the protections afforded to a person in a state court and those afforded in a federal court? What did the framers of the Constitution intend? Has anything happened since the Constitution was adopted to change the law on this subject?

These questions plagued the Supreme Court from the time Hugo Black was appointed to the bench by President Franklin Roosevelt in 1937 until his death in 1971, because Justice Black stoutly maintained that a citizen was entitled to precisely the same protections when he went to a state court that he could demand when he went to a federal court. Black argued vigorously and without pause that the Fourteenth Amendment due process clause supported this proposition. His approach is called the incorporation theory—that is, that the due process clause of the Fourteenth Amendment incorporates the whole Bill of Rights.

The founding fathers wrote the first ten amendments as limitations on the new federal government they had just established. They were not concerned about violations of rights by the state governments, which had existed in similar fashion during the colonial period and which seemed small enough to be subject to citizen pressure. But by the time of the Civil War, violations of people's rights by state governments had become widespread. Before the Civil War slaves could not even get their grievances before a court; and the rights of freed slaves were explicitly abolished in the *Dred Scott* decision (discussed in chapter 21). Nor could abolitionists expect justice from southern courts. After the defeat of the southern states, northerners coming to the South as agents of the Reconstruction could not expect to be treated the same as native southern whites, and former slaves could certainly not expect the same treatment as former rebels. Congress heard reports of violations of the rights of citizens at the hands of southern state officials and of unfair procedures in southern state courts. (See the hearings on the Ku Klux Klan Act, quoted in chapter 21.)

Congress passed the Fourteenth Amendment and encouraged the states to ratify it. This amendment included two major provisions, one guaranteeing equal protection without regard to race, creed, or color (discussed in part III), the other guaranteeing that no person would be deprived of life, liberty, or property without due process of law in the state courts. This language was, of course, copied from the Fifth Amendment provision for due process protection against violations by the federal government. (A third provision, forbidding the states to make or enforce laws abridging "the privileges or immunities" of citizens, has never been adequately analyzed and enforced.)

The justices of the Supreme Court, many still sitting with *Dred Scott* attitudes, had their first opportunity to interpret the Fourteenth Amendment in 1873 in business law cases unconnected with Negro freedom. In these *Slaughter-House Cases,* the justices ignored the military and congressional history of the previous decade, ruling that a citizen had no more *federal* protection of his citizenship rights than he had had before the Civil War and Reconstruction. Later, in the so-called *Civil Rights Cases* of 1883, the justices held that the Fourteenth Amendment only permitted Congress to protect the civil rights of black citizens and only against state laws and proceedings. Congress could not guarantee civil rights directly and could not protect against individual (not governmental) attacks. While these interpretations prevailed, the amendment proved to be of limited value in securing the rights of blacks, browns, immigrants, and poor people who alleged unfair treatment by state agencies and officials, because many could not be sued under state sovereign immunity laws, and private individuals could not be sued under the *Civil Rights Cases* rule.

In 1925, a leading constitutional lawyer, Walter H. Pollak of New York, reminded the Supreme Court of the history and meaning of the Fourteenth Amendment due process clause in a civil liberties case entitled *Gitlow* v. *New York,* and urged the Court to apply the protections in the first eight amendments to the defendants in criminal cases by incorporating those amendments into the due process clause of the Fourteenth. This pioneer effort merely stated the issue; it received no support from the justices.

By the time Hugo Black joined the Court, the argument had been researched and Justice Black was ready to do battle. He defended two principles: (1) that all of the protections in the Bill of Rights were incorporated into the Fourteenth Amendment—the justices could not agree to incorporate some but not others; and (2) that state courts must accord these protections exactly as federal courts would—there could be no watered-down versions of the Bill of Rights in state proceedings.

Justice Black described the position of his opponents, and his own basic analysis, in a 1947 dissenting opinion, *Adamson* v. *California:*

"This decision reasserts a constitutional theory . . . that this Court is endowed by the Constitution with boundless power under 'natural law' periodically to expand and contract constitutional standards to conform to the Court's conception of what at a particular time constitutes 'civilized decency' and 'fundamental principles of liberty and justice.'"

"I think that decision and the 'natural law' theory of the Constitution upon which it relies, degrade the constitutional safeguards of the Bill of Rights and simultaneously appropriate for this Court a broad power which we are not authorized by the Constitution to exercise."

"My study of the historical events that culminated in the Fourteenth Amendment, and the expressions of those who sponsored and favored, as well as those who opposed its submission and passage, persuades me that one of the chief objects that the provisions of the Amendment's first section, separately, and as a whole, were intended to accomplish was to make the Bill of Rights applicable to the states."

"I further contend that the 'natural law' formula which the Court uses to reach its conclusion in this case should be abandoned as an incongruous excrescence on our Constitution. I believe that formula to be itself a violation of our Constitution, in that it subtly conveys to courts, at the expense of legislatures, ultimate power over public policies in fields where no specific provision of the Constitution limits legislative power. And my belief seems to be in accord with the views expressed by this Court, at least for the first two decades after the Fourteenth Amendment was adopted.

"I cannot consider the Bill of Rights to be an outworn 18th Century 'strait jacket'. . . . Its provisions may be thought outdated abstractions by some. And it is true that they were designed to meet ancient evils. But they are the same kind of human evils that have emerged from century to century wherever excessive power is sought by the few at the expense of the many. In my judgment the people of no nation can lose their liberty so long as a Bill of Rights like ours survives and its basic purposes are conscientiously interpreted, enforced and respected so as to afford continuous protection against old, as well as new, devices and practices which might thwart those purposes. I fear to see the consequences of the Court's practice of substituting its own concepts of decency and fundamental justice for the language of the Bill of Rights as its point of departure in interpreting and enforcing that Bill of Rights. If the choice must be between the selective process of . . . applying some of the Bill of Rights to the States, or the . . . rule applying none of them, I would choose the . . . selective process. But rather than accept either of these choices, I would follow what I believe was the original purpose of the Fourteenth Amendment—to extend to all the people of the nation the complete protection of the Bill of Rights. To hold that this Court can determine what, if any, provisions of the Bill of Rights will be enforced, and if so to what degree, is to frustrate the great design of a written Constitution."

In the 1947 case, Justice Black secured only four of the five votes he needed to establish the incorporation theory as law. Undaunted by his failure to win the war decisively, he engaged in a number of skirmishes—and got the Court to incorporate one piece of one amendment at a time.

In 1965, Justice Harlan noticed that the incorporation theory "has come into the sunlight in recent years, . . . for some reason that I have not yet been able to fathom." He and some other justices continued to vote to apply specific protections to state court defendants whenever he felt the protection was "implicit in the concept of ordered liberty" or "one of the safeguards essential to fair trial," but not because the protection was contained in the Bill of Rights and thus incorporated in the Fourteenth Amendment. Justice Harlan maintained the incorporation theory was "both historically and constitutionally unsound and incompatible with the maintenance of our federal system on even course." He felt that "the powers and responsibilities of the state and Federal Governments are not congruent, and under the Constitution they are not intended to be."

Yet by 1969, when Chief Justice Warren stepped down from the bench, the Court had ruled, one by one, that the following liberties were incorporated in the due process clause of the Fourteenth Amendment: freedom of religion, speech, press, assembly, association, petition, and privacy (First Amendment); prohibition against unreasonable arrests, searches, and seizures, and exclusion of evidence obtained by illegal search (Fourth Amendment); privilege against self-incrimination (and against comment by the prosecution on the accused's silence as evidence of guilt), prohibition against double jeopardy, and the right to compensation for the taking of private lands for public use (Fifth Amendment); right to speedy trial, public trial, jury trial, and impartial jury, right to notice of charges, to confront opposing witnesses, to have compulsory process for obtaining favorable witnesses, to counsel, and to have counsel early in the proceedings (Sixth Amendment); prohibition against cruel and unusual punishment (Eighth Amendment); and right to privacy (Ninth Amendment as construed).

The Supreme Court has held only two provisions of the Bill of Rights not applicable to the states through the Fourteenth Amendment: the guarantee of indictment by grand jury in criminal cases (Fifth Amendment), and the guarantee of jury trial in all civil suits involving more than $20 (Seventh

Amendment). The new name given to this approach is "selective incorporation."

What does this really mean to the person charged with a crime in a state court and subjected to procedures forbidden by the Fourth, Fifth, Sixth, or Eighth Amendments? Fifty years ago, the state supreme court would have affirmed the conviction (if it did not violate any specific provision of the state constitution) because nothing in the general due process provision of the Fourteenth Amendment required reversal. The United States Supreme Court probably would have refused to hear the defendant's appeal because no federal questions were involved. Today, a state prisoner may get his conviction reversed by the state supreme court, because that court must follow recent decisions of the United States Supreme Court, holding that most of the procedural protections in the Bill of Rights *do* apply in state trials and they must be interpreted the same way they are in federal courts. If the state supreme court did not reverse on this ground, there is great likelihood that the U.S. Supreme Court would agree to hear the case and would determine whether the state courts had followed the procedural guarantees in the incorporated amendments.

This does indeed mark a change in constitutional law. It means that "states' rights" to limit the guarantees of procedural fairness have finally been defeated in the courts only one hundred years after they were defeated on the battlefields and in Congress.

However, the Warren Court paid more attention to listing the rights included in the Fourteenth Amendment than to defining the nature of those rights. The general public assumes that "jury trial" still means traditional twelve-person juries that, in criminal cases, must come to unanimous verdicts; if one juror dissents, the defendant must be retried.

From participation in juries and watching television court-room dramas, Americans generally assume that the lawyers, not the judge, conduct the questioning of prospective jurors. These customs—twelve-person juries, unanimous verdicts, and voir dire by lawyers—have never been universally followed in the United States. Now the Burger Court, in a series of nonunanimous decisions (*Williams* v. *Florida, Apodaca* v. *Oregon,* and *Johnson* v. *Louisiana*), has upheld some state statutes and constitutions permitting fewer than twelve-person juries and nonunanimous verdicts in "less serious" criminal cases. Some state supreme courts have approved questioning of jurors by judges only.

Whether this "watering down" or "streamlining" of jury trial practices will be extended depends on state courts and legislatures and the popular feeling about the importance of retaining all the traditional features of jury trials despite their occasional length or cost.

PART III

EQUALITY

THIRTEENTH AMENDMENT:

Section 1. Neither slavery nor involuntary servitude, except as a punishment for crime whereof the party shall have been duly convicted, shall exist within the United States, or any place subject to their jurisdiction.

Section 2. Congress shall have power to enforce this article by appropriate legislation.

FOURTEENTH AMENDMENT:

Section 1. All persons born or naturalized in the United States, and subject to the jurisdiction thereof, are citizens of the United States and of the State wherein they reside. No State shall make or enforce any law which shall abridge the privileges or immunities of citizens of the United States; nor shall any State deprive any person of life, liberty, or property, without due process of law; nor deny to any person within its jurisdiction the equal protection of the laws.

Section 2. Representatives shall be apportioned among the several States according to their respective numbers, counting the whole number of persons in each State, excluding Indians not taxed. But when the right to vote at any election for the choice of electors for President and Vice-President of the United States, Representatives in Congress, the Executive and Judicial officers of a State, or the members of the Legislature thereof, is denied to any of the male inhabitants of such State being twenty-one years of age, and citizens of the United States, or in any way abridged, except for participation in rebellion, or other crime, the basis of representation therein shall be reduced in the proportion which the number of male citizens shall bear to the whole number of male citizens twenty-one years of age in such State.

Section 3. No person shall be a Senator or Representative in Congress, or elector of President and Vice-President, or hold any office, civil or military, under the United States, or under any State, who, having previously taken an oath, as a member of Congress, or as an officer of the United States, or as a member of any State legislature, or as an executive or judicial officer of any State, to support the Constitution of the United States, shall have engaged in insurrection or rebellion against the same, or given aid or comfort to the enemies thereof. But Congress may by a vote of two-thirds of each House, remove such disability.

Section 5. The Congress shall have power to enforce, by appropriate legislation, the provisions of this article.

FIFTEENTH AMENDMENT:

Section 1. The right of citizens of the United States to vote shall not be denied or abridged by the United States or by any State, on account of race, color, or previous condition of servitude.

Section 2. The Congress shall have power to enforce this article by appropriate legislation.

CHAPTER 21

The Second American Revolution

Ron Dellums, black congressman from California, says that today there are many "niggers"—that this untouchable category includes not only black men and women, not only those who are brown, yellow, and red, but also the young and the elderly, the long hairs and the blue collars. He argues that members of these groups have similar problems and can make common cause to stop discrimination and ensure equal protection of the laws.

This analysis of the population of the United States in the 1970s leads to new ways of looking at the law, the Supreme Court, and the rights of the people. This analysis was not apparent to members of any of the three branches of government until very recently, although it has a Populist ring, as if it might have come out of that movement at the turn of the twentieth century. It resembles the "third of a nation" Franklin Roosevelt talked about in the 1930s, the "ill-housed, ill-clothed, and ill-fed."

Politicians were not thinking along these lines in 1953 when the Warren Court began its deliberations. The phrase "black power" had not yet been coined; the civil rights movement was a thing of the future, and there were no notable stirrings among people with Spanish surnames or among students; there were few discussions about the rights of the aged or the poor or of blue-collar workers. The market-place of ideas had been padlocked by Senator Joseph Mc-Carthy and other high government officials, and the day was not far off when southern school teachers would be required to take an oath that they were not members of the National Association for the Advancement of Colored People.

Few commentators expected a massive change in American constitutional law when the Warren Court convened. Yet, within 16 years, a great many people had changed their views on many subjects, and it is clear that the Court had helped perpetuate this change, and was itself changed by new public attitudes. Events thrust questions of race and racism to the fore until many Americans admitted that to be born white is to have a credit card made out in your name. While other kinds of discrimination exist, some of Congress-man Dellums's "niggers" can wash the sweat off their faces, put on ties or nylon stockings, cut their hair—and find that magic credit card back in their pockets. This does not solve all their problems, but it often makes their problems easier to solve. A white skin makes it more likely that a person will be permitted to explain why an accident occurred, and to have his story believed. A high school dropout from a white suburb can use his middle-class English to get out of a confrontation with the police while a black college graduate, whose diction was learned in the ghetto, may get an arrest record.

Lawyers for black clients made this point in an unprecedented number of civil rights cases coming before the Warren Court; their opponents cited numerous precedents in trying to defeat them. The parties exemplifed the conflicting views on civil rights found throughout American history.

The fundamental approach of one group, stated in its simplest form, is: if the work is hard, hot, and dirty, hire someone of color, pay him low wages, make him live off in a corner, and treat him with contempt. If the black, brown, yellow, or red American defends himself against this treatment, whether nonviolently or with force, arrest him and beat him up, or beat him up and then arrest him. If a white person stands up for the person of color in any way, ostracize him; if he persists, nonviolently or with force, treat him as the person of color is treated. If the legislature, Congress, the President, or the courts pass or enforce laws requiring equal treatment for all, regardless of race, creed, color, or previous condition of servitude, ignore them, openly as long as possible, and then surreptitiously.

When a militant black (or his white supporter) comes before the law, see that he is surrounded by white power and treated as an inferior. Make it clear that a black man has no rights that a white man is bound to respect. If a judge or jury happens to acquit a black defendant, go outside the law to teach him his place. (There were 4,736 recorded lynchings in the United States from 1882 to 1962; 3,442 of the victims were black.)

The second approach on race relations has been very different. Quoting from parts of the Bible, the Declaration of Independence, and amendments to the Constitution, its proponents have argued that equality and brotherhood have always prevailed in America (although with difficulty) and the Court must continue this tradition. White men and women risked their fortunes, their reputations, and occasionally their lives, first to petition Congress for abolition of slavery, then to free fugitive slaves and to run the Underground Railroad. Black men and women escaped from slavery, worked as free Negroes at great personal risk of recapture, saved their meager earnings, bought other members of their families from slaveowners, and reunited in the North, many managing to get an education and become outstanding abolitionist orators. Together, these whites and blacks fought and won the Civil War. In the period right after the war, these groups combined to reconstruct the southern states into a more humane, equal, and democratic society. White and black struggled to enforce the new Thirteenth, Fourteenth, and Fifteenth Amendments to the Constitution. White southerners sitting on grand juries did vote to indict white racists who threatened and murdered blacks. Some did join blacks in voting for black candidates for public office, sending two blacks to the United States Senate, twenty-one to the House of Representatives, and many to state offices.

The justices of the Supreme Court in the mid-twentieth century have been faced with these conflicting views and have been required to study documents and customs from colonial times to the present in order to reach sound decisions.

Historians agree that this country was established on a series of compromises among conflicting groups: between large and small states, between farmers and city dwellers, between agricultural interests and industrial interests, between revolutionaries and conservatives. Many people in this country, and many more around the world, expected the country to fall apart because these compromises seemed an insecure basis on which to establish a government. They were proved wrong. The conflicting groups struggled for supremacy and their struggles pushed the country forward on many fronts. Old ways that could not match new ones were quickly discarded; tradition was given short shrift. What counted was success.

But one compromise proved unworkable and refused to be ignored, even for a year. That was the compromise over the question of slave labor.

When Yankee Doodle was ready to try to cast off the yoke of British imperialist rule, he asked his ablest political scientist to explain his reasons. Thomas Jefferson, southerner, statesman, and slaveowner, made a list of charges against King George for his actions in governing the thirteen colonies, and his Declaration of Independence includes these "injuries and usurpations": "He has waged cruel war against human nature itself, violating its most sacred rights of life and liberty in the persons of a distant people who never offended him, captivating and carrying them into slavery in another hemisphere, or to incur miserable death in their transportation hither." Jefferson condemned "this piratical warfare . . . of the Christian King of Great Britain" and his determination to "keep open a market where Men should be bought and sold" while "suppressing every legislative attempt [by the colonies] to prohibit or to restrain this execrable commerce." In addition to this "assemblage of horrors," Jefferson added that the king "is now exciting those very people [African slaves] to rise in arms among us, and to purchase that liberty of which he has deprived them, by murdering the people [slaveowners] . . . thus paying off former crimes committed against the Liberties of one people with crimes which he urges them to commit against the Lives of another."

If the political leaders of the colonies had listed these acts as reasons to seek independence from England, slavery would have been doomed in this country at the end of the eighteenth century. But slavery was still economically feasible in the South; Jefferson picked up few adherents from there, and not enough from the North to win the point. His condemnation of slavery was left out of the Declaration. Instead, at the Constitutional Convention, when independence had been won, a three-part compromise was reached: the system of chattel slavery was permitted to continue, each slave was counted as three-fifths of a man in determining the number of representatives each state could send to Congress (although slaves could not vote and had none of the rights of a man), and the importation of slaves was, in effect, forbidden after 1808. Abolitionists believed that the end of the slave trade would mark the end of slavery, but the breeding of slaves became a big business in the border and southern states, and "the peculiar institution" (as slavery was called) became more entrenched.

If the treatment of black immigrants from Africa had been unique, their status might have been corrected sooner than it was. But each group of people of color living on United States territory suffered bitter economic hardship at the hands of the white invaders who settled and formed the government. Each group suffered cruel social and political mistreatment.

Native Americans had their vast tracts of land confiscated, their tribes decimated, and their Indian culture virtually destroyed. After the Mexican War in 1848, brown inhabitants of the Southwest had their status changed from being citizens of Mexico who spoke Spanish into citizens of the United States in Texas, New Mexico, and Arizona, who were treated as an inferior minority and whose lands were sometimes obtained by Anglos in questionable transactions. Asians suffered severe economic discrimination in the nineteenth century when they were hired at coolie wages to dig and blast their way through the mountains to lay the transcontinental railroad. And in the mid-twentieth century, Japanese-Americans were ordered to leave their prosperous farms and other businesses to be herded into American concentration camps because of fear that some would not be loyal to the United States (while white Americans of German and Italian extraction were not subjected to such treatment, although this country was also at war with Germany and Italy).

Some cases were brought before the Warren Court by members of these minority groups, but the major issues it heard related to the role of blacks in our society. Their treatment in the twentieth century was clearly based on the savage treatment that had been meted out to them from the time they were snatched from their homelands in a conspiracy between a few African blacks and many European and American whites whose purpose was to build their fortunes by supplying cheap labor for southern plantations.

Under the slave system, "Slaves were not considered men. . . . They could own nothing; they could make no contracts; they could hold no property, nor traffic in property; they could not hire out; they could not legally marry nor constitute families; they could not control their children; they could not appeal from their master; they could be punished at will," wrote black scholar W. E. B. DuBois, in *Black Reconstruction* (1935).

The existence of the slave system had a profound effect on the concept of equal justice throughout the United States, to say nothing of the operation of the judicial system. A slaveowner who did not have life and death power over his workers could not maintain slavery. A slaveowner who could not control the sex lives of his slaves could not breed slaves for his own use and for sale. Even with absolute power, the system could not be maintained efficiently. There were problems even when the slaveowner knew, with certainty, that he would never be tried for murder if he killed a slave and alleged self-defense, and that he would never be tried for rape if he forced himself on a slave woman. From the very beginning, slaves demanded justice. They struck back when treated unfairly, using every tactic used by free workers, and then some. They used the slowdown, refusing to work rapidly or efficiently, as disgruntled workers have done throughout history; they took some of their masters' goods to supplement their meager rations. Their ultimate tactics could only result in freedom or death. They could run away, knowing that bloodhound searches and beatings would be their reward for failure. They could stage a revolt, using arms against their masters, and risking almost certain death.

The power of the slavemaster over his slaves, and his wealth, also gave him an unfair advantage when his treatment of *white* employees was challenged. And his power in Congress (through representation based on three-fifths of his slaves) made it possible to extend slavery into some territories, to wage a war against Mexico for more land where slavery could be practiced, and to pass a Fugitive Slave Law applicable throughout the country.

All of this meant that there could be no commitment to civil rights or to equal protection of the laws while slavery continued. These were only minority demands, unlike the commitments to civil liberties and to due process of law which were made at the time the Constitution was adopted in 1789. In fact, the Supreme Court, in the case of Dred Scott, ruled in 1857, that *no* blacks in the United States, whether free or slave, had any rights except "such as those who held power and the Government might choose to grant them." The blacks imported as slaves and all their descendants "had no rights which the white man was bound to respect." This was a step backward, wiping out the rights painfully achieved by blacks who had managed to escape from slavery by buying their freedom or running away without getting caught.

By the end of the Civil War, most people in this country, regardless of their attitude toward slavery, realized that the defeat of the South meant the defeat of that institution. Clearly, one person could no longer buy and sell another person, or force another to work without any payment in money or freedom to leave the job.

But did this mean enforcement of equal rights for all? Were all distinctions between white and black forbidden or could one person still discriminate against another because he had been a slave or because of his race? Could a former slaveowner continue to treat a black worker as inferior to a white worker? Could a white plantation owner keep a docile work force by shifting his tactics? Could he use the courts to arrange to have innocent blacks arrested, convicted, and placed on work gangs to do agricultural work in virtual slavery while he paid the jailers supplying this labor?

The most crucial question was, Who was going to decide the answers to all of these questions? The government, of course; but which branch of the government?

The southern states had seceded from the Union and had set up a separate national government. That government had been defeated in a war. The state governments established under the flag of the Confederacy therefore had to cease operating and governments had to be reestablished under the banner of the United States. It has always been difficult to negotiate settlements of civil wars because the defeated side tries to retain its governmental power by appealing to people with similar interests on the winning side. At the end of the American Civil War, observers recognized that settlement of the southern question would be complicated by the fact that it would have profound effects on the nation as a whole, not simply on the South.

Before the Civil War, the South had provided more than its share of presidents, justices, diplomats, and chairmen of congressional committees. This had been inevitable, given the southern suffrage and representation systems. Blacks could not vote, but each southern state gained additional representation in Congress based on the slave population. Poor whites could not vote in large numbers because most of them could not meet the property and educational qualifications for voting. By keeping the electorate small, white, and relatively well-to-do, the politicians ensured their reelection year after year, and thus gained key congressional positions, which were then, as now, based on seniority.

If the pre-Civil War voting patterns were reestablished, with large numbers of blacks and poor whites disfranchised (denied the vote), the same group of well-to-do whites could select the representatives of their class to sit in Congress and become committee chairmen, adding two-fifths to their representation now that blacks were counted as whole men. With this power, they could prevent the restructuring of the South and could combine with conservative northern whites to discourage progress in civil rights throughout the country. Without this power in Congress, the remaining vestiges of slavery, the "badges and indicia" of oppression, could be killed.

But political power is ultimately based on force of arms, and since the North had just won the war it had the power to decide how the South would be reconstructed into the union. No southerners sat in the House or Senate and the congressional mood was clearly in favor of profound changes in the former slave states.

Congress is only one branch of the federal government, however. The President, Andrew Johnson, took a much more lenient and accommodating view of the former Confederate states, and he could veto any act of Congress. If Congress could muster a two-thirds vote to override his veto, the Supreme Court could still declare the act unconstitutional, and this was likely, since the Court had never overruled its hated *Dred Scott* decision.

The stakes were high, and every imaginable dispute arose among the three branches of government in resolving the questions raised by the federal victory. President Johnson tried to appoint governors over the southern secessionist states; Congress passed a law denying him this power; the President vetoed the bill. Congress passed a law to protect and assist the black freedmen; the President vetoed it. The secessionist southern legislatures passed Black Codes which sought to deny the freedman all rights of citizenship and return him to virtual slavery. Congress passed a law nullifying these codes. The President vetoed it. Sometimes Congress mustered a two-thirds majority to pass bills over a veto; sometimes it drafted a new bill, stronger than the last, and passed it, only to have it vetoed in turn.

The Republican congressmen took their radical reconstruction plans to the voters in 1866, and won a resounding victory. Armed with this mandate, the House brought charges against the President, impeaching him for his obstructionist actions—the first presidential impeachment in our history. Johnson was tried by the Senate and saved from conviction by one vote.

Ultimately, Congress did determine the requirements for readmission of the southern states and the process to be followed in selecting their government leaders. Congress also proposed, and the state legislatures and conventions adopted, three constitutional amendments to provide a firmer basis for ensuring that the rights of black citizens would be protected and that later Congresses could not simply repeal the civil rights statutes.

In 1868 General Ulysses S. Grant was elected President and many Radical Republican congressmen were reelected.

With Congress and the President in general agreement, federal troops remained in the South to enforce the Thirteenth, Fourteenth, and Fifteenth Amendments, and a series of new civil rights statutes were passed. The Freedman's Bureau was continued. (But former slaves were not given forty acres and a mule, as suggested by many practical politicians who knew this would give them a slim chance of becoming economically independent and, in time, politically powerful.)

During this period of reconstructing the South back into the United States, and with all three branches of the federal government supporting their efforts in varying degrees, black people in the South registered, voted, and gained some political power. They used it to try to obtain economic, legal, and social equality.

Former slaveowners and defeated secessionists rankled under the reversal of roles that accompanied federally imposed Reconstruction. They sought to return black freedmen to a condition as near slavery as possible and to keep poor whites from gaining political power. In the economic sphere, landowners developed the sharecropping system to keep black and white agricultural workers in financial bondage.

The chance to reverse the political picture came in 1876, when the presidential election between the Democrat Tilden and the Republican Hayes was contested in the electoral college, and the presidency was thrown into the House of Representatives for decision. After a good deal of political maneuvering, representatives of the southern states agreed to vote for Hayes in exchange for his promise to remove federal troops from the South. The northern white Republicans accepted this southern support in order to retain power in the White House. Northern industrialists, looking for cheap and docile labor in their new southern plants, saw advantages in the compromise. So did their southern counterparts—some of them plantation owners who had begun to invest in new railroad corporations or businesses in southern cities.

This emerging southern power structure, bowing to inevitable northern dominance, was prepared to settle for as little federal interference as possible. Its leaders were more concerned about industrialization than race. They wanted protection for manufacturing and transportation interests against the demands of small farmers, black and white. They would use black voters to maintain their power at one point and support white supremacy demands at another (see chapter 23).

The Tilden-Hayes compromise marked the end of equal protection efforts in the South. After 1876, the federal government would do nothing when white supremacists violated federal law. With the removal of federal troops, the Knights of the Ku Klux Klan and the Knights of the White Camellia unleashed a reign of terror against southern Negroes who asserted their rights under the Reconstruction amendments, and against those few whites who supported their demands. The political gains of Negroes were largely wiped out. Reconstruction was over, and its accomplishments were almost erased from the history books for more than fifty years. (Justices of the Warren Court discussed this bloody period in opinions described in chapters 23 and 24.)

In 1881, the great black statesman Frederick Douglass reported that Negroes were suffering constant indignities and violence, justified by unreasoning prejudice: "In nearly every department of American life they are confronted by this insidious influence. It fills the air. It meets them at the workshop and factory, when they apply for work. It meets them at the church, at the hotel, and the ballot-box, and worst of all, it meets them in the jury-box. Without crime or offense against law or gospel, the colored man is the Jean Valjean of American society. He has escaped from the galleys, and hence all presumptions are against him. The workshop denies him work, and the inn denies him shelter; the ballot-box a fair vote, and the jury-box a fair trial."

Douglass perceived that the slave system had not been killed, but only altered: "The colored man . . . has ceased to be the slave of an individual, but has in some sense become the slave of society. He may not now be bought and sold like a beast in the market, but he is the trammeled victim of a prejudice, well calculated to repress his manly ambition, paralyze his energies, and make him a dejected and spiritless man, if not a sullen enemy to society, fit to prey upon life and property and to make trouble generally."

By the 1890s, the new southern leaders had consolidated their positions. The economic panics (depressions) of the period left most people with little concern for anyone but themselves, and convinced many small white farmers that the only way to protect their marginal incomes was to keep black workers and farmers down. Watching plantation owners, businessmen, and political bosses use the black vote against them, the poor whites worked to disfranchise blacks, thinking this would make it easier for them to gain political power. (See their later problems with malapportionment, discussed in chapter 23.)

In the period after the Tilden-Hayes compromise, the Supreme Court heard suits by black petitioners seeking protection under the civil rights statutes and the Reconstruction amendments. The Court ruled against them, declaring the statutes unconstitutional and finding no basis for them in the Fourteenth Amendment. (At the same time, the Court managed to give protection to corporations under the due process clause of the Fourteenth Amendment.) In 1896, the

Court was asked to declare that any part of the government or private business could treat people differently on the basis of race, without fear of judicial interference. In *Plessy* v. *Ferguson,* a black man challenged the right of the railroads to force him to sit in a segregated coach. The railroad maintained that the coach was "separate but equal" and therefore constitutional. The Court agreed, although, even then, everyone knew that facilities for blacks were not equal to those available for whites. "Separate but equal" quickly became the rule throughout southern society and much of the North; it ended many steps that had been made toward desegregation.

In the face of this doctrine, the increasing suppression of blacks in the South, and the lack of civil rights progress in the North, black citizens began to organize on a national basis at the turn of the century to demand all of the rights guaranteed to every citizen under the Constitution, the Bill of Rights, and the Reconstruction amendments. In 1905 a group led by the young scholar W. E. B. DuBois met at Niagara Falls to discuss how to make their demands felt. This group became known as the Niagara Movement, and in 1909 was asked to join concerned whites in an effort to stop the endless stream of lynchings. In 1910 the National Association for the Advancement of Colored People was organized from these groups, and other blacks organized in professional and social fraternities increasingly as the twentieth century unfolded. Their common goal was to obtain equal protection of the law, which required, among other things, eradication of the separate-but-equal doctrine.

In the depression of the 1930s, the civil rights movement gained a new militance. The country faced the fact that its economic system was not sound, and it was possible to ask whether its social system was any sounder. With FDR in the

White House talking about freedom from fear, the NAACP engaged in two types of litigation: it continued its efforts to reverse criminal convictions in which defendants charged that their rights were denied because of race, and it filed cases demanding equal rights in education, transportation, public accommodations, housing, and employment.

In every aspect of life, blacks faced the unyielding wall of racism guarded by landlords, school administrators, employers, and storekeepers. As Justice Douglas pointed out later, "The true curse of slavery is not what it did to the black man, but what it has done to the white man. . . . While the institution has been outlawed, it has remained in the minds and hearts of many white men. Cases which have come to this Court depict a spectacle of slavery unwilling to die." Federal Judge J. Waties Waring of South Carolina echoed these thoughts, describing the "sadistic insistence of the 'white supremacists' in declaring that their will must be imposed irrespective of rights of other citizens" as the result of "warped" racial thinking.

In every field, blacks faced statutes and court decisions denying them equal protection of the laws. Justice Douglas made a catalog of the economic and political stumbling blocks that had brought black Americans before the Supreme Court between the Reconstruction period and the present: "We have seen contrivances by States designed to thwart Negro voting. Negroes have been excluded over and again from juries solely on account of their race, or have been forced to sit in segregated seats in court rooms. They have been made to attend segregated and inferior schools, or been denied entrance to colleges or graduate schools because of their color. Negroes have been prosecuted for marrying whites. They have been forced to live in segregated residential districts, and residents of white neighborhoods have denied them entrance. Negroes have been forced to use segregated facilities in going about their daily lives, being excluded from railway coaches, public parks, restaurants, public beaches, municipal golf courses, amusement parks, busses, public libraries [citations omitted]."

Until blacks could get jobs at decent rates of pay, they could not afford decent housing, could not help their children go to college or graduate school, and could not afford to use many recreational facilities. Yet suits against employers were hard to bring and even harder to win than suits for other rights. Employers and their lawyers could defeat black workers in the courts even when they were guilty of racial discrimination. They argued that the workers had come to the wrong agency for relief, or that the particular plaintiffs had not proved that they had been personally damaged by the discrimination (see chapter 29).

Until blacks could obtain housing anywhere in a city, desegregation of neighborhood public schools was impossible. This fact was recognized early by realtors, and every housing discrimination case was hard fought in the courts (and often in the streets) (see chapter 26).

Victories in these cases were harder to achieve than in cases seeking better educational opportunities for black children. Education is the first step toward obtaining employment, which is the first step toward saving money to buy a home. But education is run by the government, not by private business; decisions are made by elected officials who can be voted out of office, not by corporate executives; education is run not to make a profit for anyone, but to provide a service. Perhaps for these reasons, education cases proved easier to win than cases on housing and employment that directly affected big business.

The NAACP worked out a very careful strategy for winning education cases, described in chapter 22. It won significant victories in the 1930s and 1940s, and was ready for a major breakthrough when Earl Warren became Chief Justice. A number of black parents represented by the NAACP asked the Court to abolish the "separate but equal" doctrine in *Brown* v. *Board of Education.* The Court heard the case argued twice, and then decided, unanimously, that the doctrine could not be applied in the public schools. Just as the rule in *Plessy* v. *Ferguson* was soon applied to all kinds of facilities beyond railroad coaches, so *Brown* v. *Board of Education* became the basis for desegregating many aspects of life outside the classroom.

While *Brown* was a great judicial victory, black people, like other litigants, soon discovered that filing a case in a federal district court meant years of litigation and no certainty of ultimate success. Legal principles can be written on a sheet of paper and published in books that are easily assessible. But the human beings with a complaint—the indispensable parties to the lawsuit—do not sit quietly in a file in the courthouse while lawyers for both sides investigate facts, write briefs, argue before the judge and jury, and wait for decisions from the appellate courts. Children in the first grade in 1950 finished grade school in 1956; they graduated from high school in 1962. A couple searching for a home in 1964 might have two or three more children, different jobs, and a profound anger by the time a court in 1968 told them they could buy the house they were denied four years before because of racial prejudice.

Even when the Warren Court agreed to hear a case, even when it decided for the black petitioner, its decision was not self-executing. Often the decision would have no discernible effect on the lives of other blacks who had the same problem.

This recognition was probably one of the factors leading

to the action movements that sprang up after the *Brown* decision, first in Montgomery, Alabama, and then throughout the South and North. In the spring of 1961, groups of young black people, often students, began going to restaurants, lunch counters, swimming pools, and other public places, demanding that they be admitted and served. When service was refused, they sat in or sat down. Within a few weeks or months, they were joined by northern whites, mainly youths, and by some white southerners. (Their tactic was a new version of the sit-down strikes of the 1930s when workers sat at their benches until employers recognized their new unions in the automobile, rubber, and other industries.)

The civil rights activists faced criminal charges, civil suits for damages, court injunctions against their organizations, and unseating of their elected representatives. Their lawyers were kept busy arguing that the activists were entitled to every constitutional protection. Civil liberties arguments are described in part I and due process arguments in part II. Arguments for equal protection of the laws are described here.

Civil rights became the most important issue before the Warren Court. The issue arose in many forms, usually in suits in which black citizens claimed that their rights had been denied because of their race. Occasionally members of other racial, religious, and national minority groups brought civil rights cases to the Court in this period. Frequently the petitioners were poor as well as black and they demanded equal protection of the laws in two areas: race and income.

The Warren Court heard these arguments one hundred years after adoption of the Reconstruction amendments. The justices addressed themselves to a myriad of fundamental problems never faced squarely by previous Courts. In their quiet offices, reading old congressional committee reports on KKK activities, studying sociological and historical material supplied by petitioners, the justices came closer to the spirit of the Civil War-Reconstruction period than any of their recent predecessors. Unlike the justices who sat just after that tumultuous period, the justices of the Warren Court looked out their windows at the clamor in the streets, at the rising black militance, at the figure America was playing on the world stage. They reached new decisions, but they did not do it easily. You will see their conflicts in the following chapters, their need to hear difficult cases argued and re-argued, their uncertainty on how to carry out their decisions, especially those that sharply changed existing law by returning to the intentions of the framers of the Reconstruction amendments and statutes.

The Court based its famous *Brown* desegregation decision on psychological grounds as well as legal precedents. The opinion said that the evidence was not clear on school desegregation attitudes when the equal protection clause was adopted, so it turned to nonlegal authorities to prove that segregation injures school children "in a way unlikely ever to be undone." This approach opened the way for endless attacks on the *Brown* decision, on the desegregation order for public schools, and on the Court itself. (A piece of the story is told at the end of chapter 22.)

However, this was not the only basis for the attack on the Court. If it had been, the attack would have ended when the Court outlawed discrimination in housing, this time basing its decision solely on legal grounds. The Court cited a clearly worded statute prohibiting housing discrimination that had been passed in 1866 and never repealed. But the attack did not end then, nor did it change in character when the Court ordered southern registrars to obey old voting rights statutes that left no room for interpretation. Many commentators have therefore concluded that the attack was based on racism and would have occurred regardless of the basis for the school desegregation decision.

The Warren Court did much to reconstruct the Reconstruction, but left much to be done by lower courts. The justices seemed anxious to require lower court judges to re-read old Reconstruction history and statutes, to rethink their attitudes on race and racism and on the meaning of the Reconstruction amendments. This approach always slowed down enforcement of those amendments; sometimes it made enforcement impossible, and the high court ultimately had to step in.

The congressmen of the 1960s, unlike the Radical Republicans of the 1860s, were not pressing for a new wave of equalitarian legislation. They did not follow up on the Court's 1954 civil rights decision until 1957, when they passed the first civil rights act since Reconstruction. The presidents moved even more cautiously, issuing executive orders on housing and employment discrimination only during election campaigns or when popular pressure had reached a peak.

The failure of the other two branches of government to follow the lead of the Court permitted a severe backlash against the Court and its individual members, particularly Chief Justice Earl Warren. Yet the Court persisted, and made significant changes in the law, not for blacks alone, but for all Americans. While the grievances of other minority groups received less attention during this period, the way was opened for successful suits by Spanish-speaking citizens, by native Americans, by Asian-Americans, and by women suffering from discrimination although members of the majority group in the population. The equal protection

September 26, 1963: Chief Justice Warren accepts a leaflet from a
demonstrator advocating his impeachment because of the Court's
human rights decisions.
Credit: Wide World Photos

clause of the Fourteenth Amendment was applied to the federal government (through an interpretation of the Fifth Amendment), and to the poor and the young, as well as to people from other minority groups.

The Supreme Court under Earl Warren did not write any new civil rights legislation. That is not the function of the judicial branch in our system. It did agree to let the civil rights movement into its chambers, and it listened to the grievances poured out. The Court did revitalize the spirit of the second American revolution by enforcing the language of the law written between 1863 and 1876. It sought to catch up on promises made a century before.

The Court's willingness to hear and decide cases on civil rights in this period led to expectations by civil rights advocates that lower federal courts, state courts, and future Supreme Courts would continue this practice. This led, in turn, to the use of different tactics by activists than those used in periods of legislative activity on social questions (such as the Reconstruction period under Thaddeus Stevens) or presidential activity (such as the New Deal period under Franklin Roosevelt). During the Depression, those who believed in social change complained about "government by judiciary" since "the nine old men" rejected virtually all new social legislation. The reverse became true under the Warren Court.

The body of civil rights decisions handed down by the Warren Court set a heavy precedent that the Supreme Court should hear and decide questions of equal protection of the law. And the opinions provide the student and citizen concerned about the rights of the people with a significant, if unique, body of law on which to base their actions and defenses in the coming era.

CHAPTER 22

Equality in Education

When Abraham Lincoln was President, very few school districts in the United States required all children of certain ages to attend school. In many places there were no public schools. In populated areas of the North, South, and Middle West, many white boys attended public schools, but almost no black boys, few white girls, and very, very few black girls attended school with them. The public school system was even less extensive in the southern states than in the northern states.

After the defeat of the slave system, the Radical Republicans in Congress and the new freedmen campaigned hard for "forty acres and a mule" so that each black family could establish itself on a sound economic basis. They felt this was a more direct answer to the pressing problems of the blacks than integration of the public schools. After this economic proposal was defeated, Negroes fought for equal rights to own property and to vote. Most people assumed that the right to equal educational opportunity would be accepted as soon as the other two rights had been secured.

By the turn of the century, trade unions, educators, and civic groups were working hard to convince citizens in each community to establish public schools supported by property taxes and to pass compulsory education laws. Eventually free education was available everywhere in the country. In the

North there were usually neighborhood schools. In the South, where black servants and sharecroppers lived among their white employers and landlords, separate schools were set up for white and black children from the same neighborhood. Black people had a saying: "In the South they tell us, 'I don't care how close you come, but don't try to rise high.' In the North they tell us, 'I don't care how high you go, but don't come close.' " (This maxim was not restricted to housing and education. For example, South Carolina allowed Negro women to ride in the "whites only" cars of trains with the white children they took care of.)

In almost every area of the country with a sizable black population, there were "black" schools and "white" schools, and the black ones could be easily distinguished by their poorer physical facilities, a larger number of students per teacher, and a smaller expenditure of funds per pupil.

Many parents in the United States have looked to education as the key to their children's future. Immigrants expected the schools to teach their children to read, write, and speak the kind of English that would get them good jobs and status. Black parents tried many methods over the years to obtain a good education for their children. With few exceptions, Negroes could not get elected to school boards in sufficient numbers to affect educational policies. Local political, business, and educational leaders ignored their requests or blamed the black parents and children for their educational problems. When they took the issues to court, the judges said the law was fixed by the 1896 Supreme Court decision in *Plessy* v. *Ferguson*, which made "separate but equal treatment" the constitutional norm in all fields of life.

Little progress was made in challenging the separate-but-equal doctrine until the 1930s, when NAACP lawyers mapped a strategy for reconstructing the Reconstruction amendments. As black citizens in the southern states demanded the right to register and vote, to sit on juries, and to go to state universities, NAACP members and lawyers supported these efforts in carefully selected test cases.

Many of these cases were won. In education, the NAACP lawyers realized that the lawyers on the United States Supreme Court could best understand the inequality of separate education as it related to law schools. They took the cases of black students in Missouri and Oklahoma who were denied admission to the state law schools. In *Missouri ex rel. Gaines* v. *Canada* in 1938, and again in 1948 in *Sipuel* v. *Board of Regents,* the NAACP lawyers convinced the United States Supreme Court that a black student attending a segregated law school could not get the same kind of education he could obtain in a white law school. The reasons were in part intangible, such as the camaraderie he could share with large numbers of students who would later be his colleagues and the judges before whom he would argue cases. As the late Professor Edmond Cahn pointed out: "If you wish a judge to overturn a settled and established rule of law, you must convince both his mind and his emotions, which together in indissociable blend constitute his sense of injustice."

The door had been opened a crack. The Court did not overrule *Plessy* v. *Ferguson,* but it admitted that separate sometimes couldn't be equal.

Separate education is inherently unequal

Brown v. *Board of Education of Topeka* (1954)
347 U.S. 483, 74 S. Ct. 686, 98 L. Ed. 873

Following the strategy it had mapped, the NAACP Legal Defense Fund next took up suits against colleges and graduate schools that denied admission to blacks. Success in these suits led, in the early 1950s, to suits against elementary, junior, and senior high schools. Black parents in Kansas, Delaware, South Carolina, and Virginia sued their local school boards, charging that their children were not receiving the same education as white children because of state statutes and customs requiring segregated education in the public schools.

These suits involved a change of tactics. The goal was still equal treatment for blacks and whites, as guaranteed in the equal protection clause of the Fourteenth Amendment. But the parents no longer wanted to present facts and figures proving that separate black schools were unequal to separate white schools. Instead they wanted to prove that even if a separate black school were equal in every way to a separate white school it nonetheless violated the equal protection clause. They were determined to prove that segregated schooling cannot be equal to desegregated schooling, for either blacks or whites, that separation of the races in classrooms diminishes the quality of the learning process.

The black parents who filed these suits could easily have proved that the education of their children was not equal in most respects to that of white children in the same school districts. But they were through with that approach. Instead, they attacked the constitutionality of the "separate but equal" doctrine; they said separate could never be equal. They demanded that their children be assigned to attend public white schools with white children according to geographic districts, and that school boards abolish schools designated by race.

In three of the cases the parents filed suit in federal district courts, asking that the school board practices be declared unconstitutional and ordered stopped. The school board lawyers and state attorneys responded that the segregated schools were substantially equal or could be made equal and that there was no need to change the existing pupil assignments. The federal courts ruled in favor of the defendants, but in some cases ordered them to equalize the separate facilities; the plaintiffs appealed these decisions.

In the Delaware case, filed in a state court, the judge ordered the immediate admission of the Negro pupils to white schools because the all-black schools were inferior; the defendants appealed.

In South Carolina, the federal judges had split two to one. The dissenter, Judge J. Waties Waring, was already known as a man willing to stick his neck out. In 1947, he had ruled that the South Carolina Democratic Party primary had to be open to Negroes; for this his life had been threatened, his home stoned, and an impeachment movement launched against him. Now, at the age of seventy-one, Judge Waring wrote a dissenting opinion that foreshadowed almost every issue, every tactic, every basic problem in the school desegregation cases that were to follow. He admonished his two colleagues: "If a case of this magnitude can be turned aside and a court refuse to hear these basic issues by the mere device of admission that some buildings, blackboards, lighting fixtures and toilet facilities are unequal but that they may be remedied by the spending of a few dollars, then, indeed people in the plight in which these plaintiffs are, have no adequate remedy or forum in which to air their wrongs. . . . No excuse can be made to deny them these rights which are theirs under the Constitution and laws of America by the use of the false doctrine and patter called 'separate but equal' and it is the duty of the Court to meet these issues simply and factually and without fear, sophistry and evasion."

After discussing the history of slavery in the South, and the meaning of the Reconstruction amendments, Judge Waring faced the fundamental question: Are any racial classifications sound? "The whole discussion of race and ancestry has been intermingled with sophistry and prejudice. What possible definition can be found for the so-called white race, Negro race or other races? Who is to decide and what is the test? For years, there was much talk of blood and taint of blood. Science tells us that there are but four kinds of blood: A, B, AB and O and these are found in Europeans, Asiatics, Africans, Americans and others. . . . The law of South Carolina considers a person of one-eighth African ancestry to be a Negro. Why this proportion? Is it based upon any reason, anthropological, historical or ethical?

"And how are the trustees [boards of education] to know who are 'whites' and who are 'Negroes'? If it is dangerous and evil for a white child to be associated with another child, one of whose great-grandparents was of African descent, is it not equally dangerous for one with a one-sixteenth percentage? And if the State has decided that there is danger in contact between the whites and Negroes, isn't it requisite and proper that the State furnish a series of schools, one for each of these percentages? If the idea is perfect racial equality in educational systems, why should children of pure African descent be brought in contact with children of one-half, one-fourth, or one-eighth such ancestry? To ask these questions is sufficient answer to them. The whole thing is unreasonable, unscientific and based upon unadulterated prejudice."

Appeals were filed in the four desegregation cases and the Supreme Court agreed to hear them argued together in December 1952. The following June, instead of handing down a decision, the Court ordered the cases restored to the docket to be reargued the next December. It asked the lawyers to prepare answers to the following historical and legal questions (among others):

1. When Congress proposed the Fourteenth Amendment and the states ratified it, did they expect it to abolish segregation in public schools?

2. If they did not expect it to do so immediately, did they feel that a future Congress might enact laws to abolish segregated education on the basis of the Fourteenth Amendment or that future courts might interpret the amendment to abolish segregated education?

3. If the framers of the amendment did not expect it to abolish segregation in the public schools, is it still within the Court's power to do so on the basis of the amendment's provisions?

The Court invited the United States Attorney General to appear as a friend of the court (amicus curiae).

This delay in deciding the school cases proved critical. Between the asking of these questions and the reargument before the Court, Chief Justice Fred M. Vinson, a conservative New Deal Democrat appointed by President Harry Truman, died, and Chief Justice Earl G. Warren, a liberal Republican appointed by President Dwight D. Eisenhower, took his place. This shift in make-up of the Court, although it involved only one of the nine seats numerically, came to affect the very style of the entire Court for a significant period.

The slow, logical march of school suits brought by the strong civil rights organizations hit the right combination of lawyers serving in the judicial branch to bring about profound changes throughout our society. The law, the Supreme Court, and the rights of the people converged to mark a turning point.

After three days of reargument in December 1953, the Court handed down its decision on May 17, 1954. The Court gave this decision its maximum weight by issuing a unanimous opinion written by the Chief Justice.

Warren, after a lifetime in politics, as prosecutor and governor of the multi-racial state of California, consciously included in his opinion ideas and language that would be acceptable to all of the other justices.

"The plaintiffs contend that segregated public schools are not 'equal' and cannot be made 'equal,' and that hence they are deprived of the equal protection of the laws," he began.

The lawyers for both sides had presented full argument on "the circumstances surrounding the adoption of the Fourteenth Amendment in 1868. It covered exhaustively consideration of the Amendment in Congress, ratification by the states, then existing practices in racial segregation, and the views of proponents and opponents of the Amendment. This discussion and our own investigation convince us that, although these sources cast some light, it is not enough to resolve the problem with which we are faced. At best, they are inconclusive. The most avid proponents of the post-War Amendments undoubtedly intended them to remove all legal distinctions among 'all persons born or naturalized in the United States.' Their opponents, just as certainly, were antagonistic to both the letter and the spirit of the Amendments and wished them to have the most limited effect. What others in Congress and the state legislatures had in mind cannot be determined with any degree of certainty.

"An additional reason for the inconclusive nature of the Amendment's history, with respect to segregated schools, is the status of public education at that time," said the Chief Justice. He noted that "the movement toward free common schools, supported by general taxation," was just beginning to take root in that era, more in the North than in the South.

"As a consequence, it is not surprising that there should be so little in the history of the Fourteenth Amendment relating to its intended effect on public education."

The Chief Justice summarized a tumultous period of history in a few sentences, writing, "In the first cases in this Court construing the Fourteenth Amendment, decided shortly after its adoption, the Court interpreted it as proscribing all state-imposed discrimination against the Negro race. The doctrine of 'separate but equal' did not make its appearance in this Court until 1896 in the case of *Plessy* v. *Ferguson*, . . . involving not education but transportation. American courts have since labored with the doctrine for over half a century." (Chief Justice Warren mentioned in a footnote that the "separate but equal" doctrine adopted by the Supreme Court in *Plessy* was born in a Boston school case brought in the Massachusetts courts in 1850. Despite the doctrine, segregation was eliminated in Boston in 1855. "But," the Chief Justice noted, "elsewhere in the North segregation in public education has persisted in some communities until recent years. It is apparent that such segregation has long been a nationwide problem, not merely one of sectional concern.")

A study of previous school cases indicated that none had directly challenged the "separate but equal" doctrine. "In the instant cases, that question is directly presented. Here, . . . there are findings below that the Negro and white schools involved have been equalized, or are being equalized, with respect to buildings, curricula, qualifications and salaries of teachers, and other 'tangible' factors. Our decision, therefore, cannot turn on merely a comparison of these tangible factors in the Negro and white schools involved in each of the cases. We must look instead to the effect of segregation itself on public education.

"In approaching this problem, we cannot turn the clock back to 1868 when the Amendment was adopted, or even to 1896 when *Plessy* v. *Ferguson* was written. We must consider public education in the light of its full development and its present place in American life throughout the Nation. Only in this way can it be determined if segregation in public schools deprives these plaintiffs of the equal protection of the laws.

"Today, education is perhaps the most important function of state and local governments. Compulsory school attendance laws and the great expenditures for education both demonstrate our recognition of the importance of education to our democratic society. It is required in the performance of our most basic public responsibilities, even service in the armed forces. It is the very foundation of good citizenship. Today it is a principal instrument in awakening the child to cultural values, in preparing him for later professional training, and in helping him to adjust normally to his environment. In these days, it is doubtful that any child may reasonably be expected to succeed in life if he is denied the opportunity of an education. Such an opportunity, where the state has undertaken to provide it, is a right which must be made available to all on equal terms.

"We come then to the question presented: Does segregation of children in public schools solely on the basis of race, even though the physical facilities and other 'tangible' factors may be equal, deprive the children of the minority group of equal educational opportunities? We believe that it does.

"In *Sweatt* v. *Painter, . . .* in finding that a segregated law school for Negroes could not provide them equal educational opportunities, this Court relied in large part on 'those qualities which are incapable of objective measurement but which make for greatness in a law school.' In *McLaurin* v. *Oklahoma State Regents*, . . . the Court, in requiring that a Negro admitted to a white graduate school be treated like all other students, again resorted to intangible considerations: '. . . his ability to study, to engage in discussions and exchange views with other students, and, in general, to learn his profession.'

"Such considerations apply with added force to children in grade and high schools. To separate them from others of similar age and qualifications solely because of their race generates a feeling of inferiority as to their status in the community that may affect their hearts and minds in a way unlikely ever to be undone.

"The effect of this separation on their educational opportunities was well stated by a finding in the Kansas case by a court which nevertheless felt compelled to rule against the Negro plaintiffs: 'Segregation of white and colored children in public schools has a detrimental effect upon the colored children. The impact is greater when it has the sanction of the law; for the policy of separating the races is usually interpreted as denoting the inferiority of the [N]egro group. A sense of inferiority affects the motivation of a child to learn. Segregation with the sanction of law, therefore, has a tendency to [retard] the educational and mental development of [N]egro children and to deprive them of some of the benefits they would receive in a racial[ly] integrated school system.'

"Whatever may have been the extent of psychological knowledge at the time of *Plessy* v. *Ferguson*, this finding is amply supported by modern authority. Any language in *Plessy* v. *Ferguson* contrary to this finding is rejected."

The Court's ruling, enunciated by Chief Justice Warren, was soon to become famous across the country: "We conclude that in the field of public education the doctrine of 'separate but equal' has no place. Separate educational facilities are inherently unequal. Therefore, we hold that the plaintiffs and others similarly situated for whom the actions have been brought are, by reason of the segregation complained of, deprived of the equal protection of the laws guaranteed by the Fourteenth Amendment."

The justices then announced: "Because these are class actions, because of the wide applicability of this decision, and because of the great variety of local conditions, the formulation of decrees in these cases presents problems of considerable complexity. On reargument, the consideration of appropriate relief was necessarily subordinated to the primary question—the constitutionality of segregation in public education. We have now announced that such segregation is a denial of the equal protection of the laws. In order that we may have the full assistance of the parties in formulating decrees, the cases will be restored to the docket, and the parties are requested to present further argument on [two other questions] previously propounded by the Court for the reargument this Term."

With all deliberate speed

Brown v. *Board of Education of Topeka* (1955)
349 U.S. 294, 75 S. Ct. 753, 99 L. Ed. 1083

The Court had listened to more arguments on these cases than on most other issues, and had spent more months pondering how to satisfy its constitutional responsibilities to all of the parties. Still, it had overestimated the capacity of the parties to deal with the multitude of problems raised. The fourth and fifth questions the Court had posed in 1953 were not considered until 1955; they were:

4. If segregated public schools violate the Fourteenth Amendment,

   a. must the Court order that Negro children be immediately admitted to the schools of their choice within their geographic area, or

   b. may the Court permit gradual desegregation?

5. If gradual desegregation is permitted,

   a. should the Supreme Court work out detailed orders?

   b. what should the orders cover?

   c. should the Court appoint a "special master" to hear evidence and recommend orders, or

   d. should the Court send the cases back to the trial courts for specific orders, and, if so, what general directions should the Supreme Court give and what procedures should the lower courts follow?

The Court heard argument on these issues in April 1955. This time *Bolling* v. *Sharpe,* a District of Columbia case that had been heard and decided separately in 1954, was joined with the other four cases for argument and decision. (The District of Columbia is governed by the federal government, so the due process clause of the Fifth Amendment applies to it, rather than the equal protection clause of the Fourteenth Amendment, which applies only to states.)

The NAACP lawyers urged the Court to order that black children should be admitted immediately to the schools of their choice. They cautioned against sending the cases back to local courts for rulings and orders under broad guidelines that might be interpreted in various ways depending on the particular judge's view of segregated schooling.

Attorneys for the schools pressed the Court to issue only broad guidelines and leave the specifics to the local courts. There was wide variety in the circumstances of school districts in different areas, they pointed out, and flexibility was necessary. Certain communities would surely be resistant to change, and a harsh, unbending order from the Court might spark stronger rebellion from segregationists.

On May 31, 1955, the Court acted again through a unanimous opinion by the Chief Justice.

"Because these cases arose under different local conditions and their disposition will involve a variety of local problems, we requested further argument on the question of relief," he said. "In view of the nationwide importance of the decision, we invited the Attorney General of the United States and the Attorneys General of all states requiring or permitting racial discrimination in public education to present their views on that question. The parties, the United States, and the States of Florida, North Carolina, Arkansas, Oklahoma, Maryland, and Texas filed briefs and participated in the oral argument.

"These presentations were informative and helpful to the Court in its consideration of the complexities arising from the transition to a system of public education freed of racial discrimination. The presentations also demonstrated that substantial steps to eliminate racial discrimination in public schools have already been taken, not only in some of the communities in which these cases arose, but in some of the states appearing as amici curiae, and in other states as well. Substantial progress has been made in the District of Columbia and in the communities in Kansas and Delaware involved in this litigation. The defendants in the cases coming to us from South Carolina and Virginia are awaiting the decision of this Court concerning relief.

"Full implementation of these constitutional principles may require solution of varied local school problems. School authorities have the primary responsibility for elucidating, assessing, and solving these problems; courts will have to consider whether the action of school authorities constitutes good faith implementation of the governing constitutional principles. Because of their proximity to local conditions and the possible need for further hearings, the courts which originally heard these cases can best perform this judicial appraisal. Accordingly, we believe it appropriate to remand the cases to those courts.

"In fashioning and effectuating the decrees, the courts will be guided by equitable principles. Traditionally, equity has been characterized by a practical flexibility in shaping its remedies and by a facility for adjusting and reconciling public and private needs. These cases call for the exercise of these traditional attributes of equity power. At stake is the personal interest of the plaintiffs in admission to public schools as soon as practicable on a nondiscriminatory basis. To effectuate this interest may call for elimination of a variety of obstacles in making the transition to school systems operated in accordance with the constitutional principles set forth in our May 17, 1954, decision. Courts of equity may properly take into account the public interest in the elimination of such obstacles in a systematic and effective manner. But it should go without saying that the validity of these constitutional principles cannot be allowed to yield simply because of disagreement with them.

"While giving weight to these public and private considerations, the courts will require that the defendants make a prompt and reasonable start toward full compliance with our May 17, 1954, ruling. Once such a start has been made, the courts may find that additional time is necessary to carry out the ruling in an effective manner. The burden rests upon the defendants to establish that such time is necessary in the public interest and is consistent with good faith compliance at the earliest practicable date. To that end, the courts may consider problems related to administration, arising from the physical condition of the school plant, the school transportation system, personnel, revision of school districts and attendance areas into compact units to achieve a system of determining admission to the public schools on a nonracial basis, and revision of local laws and regulations which may be necessary in solving the foregoing problems. They will also consider the adequacy of any plans the defendants may propose to meet these problems and to effectuate a transition to a racially nondiscriminatory school system. During this period of transition, the courts will retain jurisdiction of these cases."

The Court then sent the cases back to the lower federal and state courts to receive the specific orders required to admit the black children "to public schools on a racially non-discriminatory basis with all deliberate speed."

The 1954 decision wiping out the separate but equal doctrine in public schools is probably the most important decision the United States Supreme Court has made on any subject in the twentieth century. It is certainly the most important government action for equality since the Reconstruction amendments spelled out the rights won by blacks in the Civil War. All sides of the racial controversy saw the decision as a watershed, marking the beginning of a new era. Chief Justice Warren's words had rung a bell that could never be unrung.

Perhaps the most significant aspect of the decision, however, was that it did not reflect a point of view already reached by the majority of Americans. It probably reflected majority opinion in northern states in 1866–68, after half a century of abolitionist persuasion, and certainly reflected the language and purpose of the Thirteenth, Fourteenth, and Fifteenth Amendments. But these were not the sentiments of most white Americans in the 1950s. The Supreme Court justices, who had been wrestling with school segregation problems in a series of cases, had come to see over a period of time what black Americans had long seen: that racial separation meant educational inequality. The *Brown* decision was for them a natural and necessary development in law and social progress.

But for the majority of white Americans the *Brown* decision was a sudden departure from the traditional way of doing things. It opened old wounds in the South where white supremacist attitudes, defeated in the Civil War, had been returned to power in 1876 and seldom disturbed since that time. These were mingled with feelings of Christian concern for the mistreatment of God's black children, unspoken fear of all people of color, and especially fear of permitting black children to mingle with white children. Many in the North hailed the decision without realizing that it also required desegregation of northern schools where children were separated by neighborhood racial patterns.

The questions of racial separation and unequal educational opportunity had not been debated widely in white communities, North or South, at school board meetings, or among parents, pupils, and teachers. The rest of the world, particularly the Third World, was better informed and more concerned about the treatment accorded to American Negroes than were most white Americans. The *Brown* decision did not grow out of a deep conviction held by the people or by the other two branches of government—Congress and the President. The Court was almost alone in feeling that the time had come to integrate the public schools.

This lack of widespread popular support for the principles

of the 1954 decision profoundly affected the 1955 decision and the ultimate impact of the court order to desegregate the public schools.

Many social scientists now claim that the only way to launch such a basic idea successfully is to make a crystal-clear decision, leaving no loopholes, and to enforce it vigorously and unequivocally (with federal troops, if necessary). Failing this, the psychological momentum swings to the opposition, which can rally its forces with a call for continuation of the old practices, without reexamination to see whether they are still valid. The innovators have a harder task; they must begin to educate and slowly build support based on logic.

But the Supreme Court has no large press corps at its command and no great familiarity with publicity techniques, as some other government agencies have. The Court's budget does not even permit publication of millions of copies of its most significant decisions and distribution to all those affected.

Because neither Congress nor the executive branch was pushing the Court to reach the *Brown* decision, neither of these branches was ready or willing to provide effective support for the decision.

Nor did the Court seek federal enforcement actions. The Court operated on the assumption that the lower courts would follow its rulings, since it was the highest court in the land, the ultimate authority on constitutional rights. This is the basic assumption on which the judicial system functions. The Court similarly assumed that state and local officials would respect the law of the land. When the lawmakers and law enforcement officers ignore the law, society is deeply disrupted, and there can be no justice or order.

The Court could have formulated specific orders for each of the five situations before it in 1955. It did not do this. It could have ordered the federal district judges to appoint special "masters" or "referees" to sort out the issues, handle negotiations between sides, recommend specific orders for the judges to issue, and supervise the carrying out of these orders. (Such referees are often appointed in certain kinds of complex cases, such as the bankruptcy of a large corporation with many creditors and debtors or a dispute between two states over water rights in a river.) It did not do this. It wanted the lower courts to rethink their decisions, which it had just reversed, and to write specific orders in light of the new state of the law in the field of education. The justices knew the problems were complex; they wanted the local federal judges to face them and solve them.

The Court also recognized that desegregation was a bitter constitutional pill for many whites in the South. It wished to show that it would not cram the remedy down the unwilling throats of those who believed in separation without allowing for necessary preparations. The optimistic justices saw progress toward desegregation occurring in several states already and anticipated that this would continue and spread steadily.

But the forces that had opposed integration before the *Brown* decision did not use the preparation time granted by the Court as the Court had intended. They did not search for desegregation plans. Instead, they passed statutes and school board resolutions to prevent compliance with the law. They pounced on the Court's failure to order immediate desegregation as the justification for an endless variety of evasive and delaying tactics.

As a result, in the months and years following the *Brown* decision of 1955, the five original cases stayed on the court dockets, and the parents of the black students continued to come before the judges to demand prompt, specific action to carry out desegregation, not to slow it down or make it meaningless. The five cases slowly wound their way back up to the courts of appeals and occasionally to the Supreme Court for further orders, as the students grew older without seeing the inside of an integrated school. And hundreds of new cases were filed.

City after city saw violent confrontations when blacks sought to attend schools from which they had previously been barred. Judges, school superintendents, and principals who tried to obey the *Brown* decision were attacked in the press and hassled unmercifully. Parents who tried to send their children to white schools or who filed desegregation suits lost their credit at local stores during the growing season, couldn't get work, were harassed and occasionally beaten. The governor of Arkansas sent the National Guard to Little Rock to prevent nine Negro students from entering the white high school; the President of the United States had to send in federal troops to restore order and protect the students from mob violence at the school entrance. The governor of Mississippi personally blocked the entrance of the state university to keep James Meredith from registering; contempt proceedings were filed against him for his open defiance of court orders to admit Meredith, but the court processes dragged on and the charges ultimately were dismissed.

Learned lawyers and respected educators in the South concentrated on finding methods to circumvent the *Brown* decision. They were well trained and their hearts were in their work. The strategies and devices they invented became legendary. They passed "interposition" resolutions, contending that the *Brown* decision violated the sovereignty of the states as guaranteed by the Constitution and therefore was an illegal ruling. They drew up "freedom of choice" plans, which relied on black fear and white intimidation to ensure

September 19, 1966: Joan Baez escorts a young student to a desegregated school in Grenada, Mississippi, after some black students were
beaten on their way to school.
Credit: Wide World Photos

that blacks chose segregated black schools. Legislators enacted tuition grants and tax concessions for all-white private schools, while desegregated public schools had their appropriations cut and a few were completely closed. Districts were rezoned to create virtually all-white and all-black sectors. School boards submitted clearly inadequate "integration" plans to federal judges who ruled that they complied in good faith with *Brown*. Other boards refused to submit any plans at all, claiming the members could not reach agreement or that the threat of violence made desegregation impossible.

More and more black parents throughout the old Confederate states found they had to sue for their rights, school board by school board, city by city, county by county, for a "good faith" desegregation plan, for more "speed" and less "deliberation," for a desegregated teaching staff, for proper facilities and equipment, for protection for their children on the way to school, to prevent the closing of the public schools, to prevent the cutoff of funds, to prevent redistricting along racial lines. South Carolina's Judge Waring had spoken only too wisely when he had predicted in 1951 that "hundreds . . . of cases will have to be brought and in each case thousands of dollars will have to be spent for the employment of legal talent and scientific testimony and then the cases will be turned aside, postponed or eliminated." Almost 500 separate suits were filed in Alabama, Arkansas, Delaware, Florida, Georgia, Kansas, Kentucky, Louisiana, Maryland, Mississippi, North Carolina, Oklahoma, South Carolina, Tennessee, Texas, and Virginia. The parents had to sue and sue and appeal and appeal. Many came again and again to the United States Supreme Court. A comparison of the number of education cases heard by the Court and the number it refused to hear indicates that the Court heard as few school cases as it conscientiously could. Over and over it required federal district court judges to mend their ways, after they had shown total unwillingness to do so. School desegregation faltered where it had begun; never started where it might have; was frustrated at every turn by well-educated, hardworking obstructionists of the law and order enunciated by the high court.

Meanwhile, parents in the North began to look at their children's schools and demand change. Black parents, Chicano and Puerto Rican parents, Asian and Native American parents, and white parents who wanted their children to learn in integrated schools saw that their schools were segregated not by law (de jure) but in fact (de facto) as a result of two northern patterns: segregated housing and neighborhood schools. Some communities set up study groups to develop plans for eliminating racial segregation in the education of their children. In other cities parents had to file suit to get action started. They said the broad tenets of the *Brown* decision applied to de facto segregation every bit as much as to de jure segregation. Over 100 suits were filed in California, Colorado, the District of Columbia, Illinois, Indiana, Massachusetts, Michigan, Missouri, New Jersey, New Mexico, New York, Ohio, Pennsylvania, West Virginia, and Wisconsin, demanding action by school boards to provide equal, quality, desegregated education for all children.

Frequently parents mentioned in their complaints a point the Supreme Court had not noted or mentioned in *Brown*. They said that children from the majority (white) group suffer from segregated education, as well as children from the minority (black) group, although in a reverse manner: they are encouraged to develop false feelings of racial superiority which ill equip them to live and work in our multi-racial nation and world.

Resistance in the North was often as strong and as violent as in the South. Plans for busing children from one neighborhood to another were fought vigorously. Some parents organized boycotts when their schools were desegregated; they preferred to keep their children out of school rather than allow them to participate in desegregated education.

Yet in Princeton, New Jersey, in Berkeley, California, in this town and that city, across the country, parents, teachers, and school administrators began sitting down together, defining the problem, deciding how to solve it, and taking orderly steps to achieve the high quality equal education that the Supreme Court required in *Brown* v. *Board of Education.* They looked at the racial composition of student bodies, teachers, and administrative staffs, the choice of textbooks, the "tracking" and counseling systems, extracurricular activities, intelligence and aptitude testing, achievement tests, and grading systems. In many cases, their plans and programs went beyond the scope of desegregation and encompassed experiments in new teaching and learning methods—team teaching, nongraded classrooms, "open" schools, "alternative" schools, learning laboratories, use of community resource personnel.

The road has not been smooth in any community. It requires great ingenuity, effort, patience, perseverance, devotion, and wisdom. But in some areas, parents of all colors are as committed to integrated education as others in the past have been to separate schools.

In 1964, Congress provided some assistance to the parents North and South who were seeking to make the principles of the *Brown* decision a reality. Title IV of the 1964 Civil Rights Act authorized the Attorney General to file school desegregation suits in certain situations, thus taking some of the costly burden of these cases from individual parents. It also provided for grants and loans to assist schools that were desegregating. Even more effective than this was Title VI of the act, which authorized the cutoff of federal funds to any agency (in any field) that operated in a discriminatory manner. Because substantial amounts of federal money were then going to school districts in all parts of the country, this was a serious threat. It turned the tide in several border and middle south states, where resistance to the *Brown* decision had begun to waver; school boards in some cities began good faith efforts at desegregation. Before passage of the act, only 1.17 percent of black children in the old Confederate states went to desegregated schools. By September 1969, the figure had risen to about 25 percent, largely because of the 1964 act.

Relatively few children sit in desegregated classrooms anywhere in the country today. Yet it is clear to everyone that the *Brown* decision brought profound changes to our society. The black students who sat in at lunch counters in the early 1960s felt justified in their cause by the teachings of the Bible and the Court's statements in *Brown*. The Negroes who organized boycotts, voter registration drives, and protest marches were inspired in part by the *Brown* decision. It started new movements toward equal treatment without regard to race in voting rights and political representation, in public accommodations and transportation, in housing, in legal proceedings, and in employment, as well as in education. The chapters that follow trace these developments and refer again and again to *Brown* as the impetus, the precedent, the touchstone for a wide range of significant actions.

It also inspired one of the strongest backlashes the country has ever experienced. Opponents of the *Brown* decision were not content to fight desegregation of the schools; they launched severe attacks on the Court itself. By refusing to follow its rulings, judges, legislators, law enforcement officials, governors, state attorneys, and local administrators undermined the Court's power and prestige. Some went further and also openly castigated the Court and individual justices. The most rabid initiated a campaign to impeach Earl Warren. Although this extreme tactic did not gain significant public support, the anti-Court movement did grow as the Court took forthright stands upholding the constitutional rights of criminal defendants, of the poor, and of more and more dissenting groups in the country.

The relationship between the rights of the people, the law, and the Supreme Court cannot be understood without a careful look at the attack on the Court in this singular period in our history in which the Court played a forward-looking role on civil rights questions.

The strength of Court opponents is shown by a resolution passed in 1958 by the Conference of Chief Justices of State Supreme Courts. In an unprecedented move, these fifty judges, the highest judicial officers in their forty-eight states and two territories, voted thirty-six to eight (with two abstentions and four absent) to urge the United States Supreme Court "to exercise one of the greatest of all judicial powers—the power of judicial self-restraint" in the interest of "the preservation of local self-government." Justice Jesse W. Carter of California made a stirring response: "While I may not agree with the majority of the Supreme Court in all of the cases criticized by the Conference of Chief Justices in said report, I want to state very positively that I entirely disagree with every word of criticism which has been heaped upon the Supreme Court of the United States since Earl Warren became Chief Justice of that Court, and as a judge, a lawyer and citizen I resent and condemn the vicious attacks which have been made upon Chief Justice Warren and his associates. . . . They are all men of unimpeachable honesty, excellent character and unquestioned loyalty. They are men well trained in the law, and the decisions they have written and the positions they have taken have been the result of their honest approach to the problems as they saw them."

Justice Carter then laid bare the state judges' real disagreement with the nine justices: "The criticism of certain decisions of the Supreme Court of the United States by the report . . . is of little value. Running through this report is an obvious resentment against the Supreme Court for its decisions in the desegregation cases. This resentment, of course, is the result of a deep-seated racial prejudice existing in the minds of many very fine people in this country which will take years to erase. It may be that the desegregation cases were ill-timed, but as a student of constitutional law I am unable to see how a different result could be reached under any reasonable interpretation of the provisions of the Fourteenth Amendment to the Constitution of the United States. . . . When we eliminate the criticism of those who are prejudiced against the Court because of its desegregation decisions and those who would deny to persons charged with subversive activities the civil liberties guaranteed by the Bill of Rights, the criticism of the present Court fades into insignificance."

This sharp, official, high level, national attack on one of the branches of the federal government petered out and ended with the retirement of Chief Justice Warren in 1969. The 1970s present us with a different constitutional crisis: a sharp, official, high level attack on the executive branch. The Warren Court issue arose out of judicial decisions on civil rights and liberties. The Nixon-Agnew issue arose out of executive decisions on the uses of political and economic power to affect the integrity of the electoral process. The executive branch did little to diminish the attacks on the Warren Court, while Congress and its members frequently added fuel to the flames. The judicial branch has many opportunities to react to the conflict between the executive and Congress over Watergate.

Active citizens are searching for ways to live through such crises without losing any of their own rights. They also seek methods of exercising their rights effectively—first in making their views known to those in power and then in having their views followed.

CHAPTER 23

Equal
Voting Rights

Voting rights are written into the United States Constitution and the constitutions of each state as the basic guarantee of a democratic form of government. For our system to continue, the integrity of the electoral process must be insured. If a person cannot register, vote, have his vote counted equally, and his elected candidate seated in office, he is being denied his constitutional right to meaningful participation in government. The Watergate break-in and cover up, plus the "dirty tricks" pulled in the 1972 election, have sharply reminded voters that the rules of political campaigning must also receive their close attention.

The televised hearings of the Senate (Ervin) Select Committee on Campaign Practices have illuminated a series of incidents demonstrating the uses and misuses of executive power in the political arena, and suggest that the following description accurately reflects the practices in our political life.

The most effective way for most Americans to express their views on important questions is through voting in elections. In some states, voters not only select candidates for office but also approve or reject specific referendum measures or constitutional amendments. On most issues, however, the voter has only an indirect vote—through selecting government officials. He cannot know how his candidate will vote on every question while he is in office, since candidates do not discuss every issue, and some issues arise after the campaign.

Some Americans have further avenues to make their political views felt. For example, some citizens are also active in political parties or other organizations with political power. When officers of a parent-teacher association or a trade union, or members of the board of directors of a corporation or a civic organization write letters to government officials expressing viewpoints, they have more impact than letters from single individuals who do not represent blocs of voters. When a group paints picket signs and demonstrates in the streets or holds a press conference to demand action, the members are using other media to influence decisions.

In our system, many decisions that have tremendous impact on people's lives are made outside the government. When a power plant is planned, corporate officials decide where it will be built, how many workers it will require, and the nature of the fuel to be used (which will determine the degree of pollution). Some of these decisions are reviewed later by the government; some are unreviewable. A person sitting on the board of directors of the power company has an early and effective opportunity to vote on these questions. A person who does not sit on that board can vote on them only by voting on a ballot proposition concerning power plants, or by voting for candidates pledged to approve or disapprove the licenses required to build such plants.

Corporate shareholders are sometimes given a chance to vote for or against a company policy. But shareholders holding millions of shares exercise the only effective votes. The small shareholder can affect corporate policy more by voting for a political candidate favoring or opposing a certain corporate action than by voting his few shares in a stockholder's meeting.

Government officials and corporate officials are aware that

their decisions are often related. They know that a corporate decision can be vetoed by a government agency and that many government decisions can be overridden by corporations. (For example, when the government says a corporation can build a shopping center on site B, but not on site A, the corporate interests can decide instead to build a shopping center on site C, or nowhere.)

In a country in which the governmental and economic systems are not run by exactly the same people, each governing group must be sure it can influence the other. (In feudal society, the king and his feudal lords ran both governmental and economic systems.) In a capitalist democracy, the financial leaders selected by corporate structures run the economic system and the political leaders selected by party primaries and popular elections run the governmental system.

Since governmental leaders can have a profound impact on economic life, economic leaders must pay close attention to the governmental political system. For example, changes in federal laws can discourage the formation of conglomerates, can raise the minimum wage to be paid certain workers, can abolish tax loopholes for owners of oil wells, can stop price supports on agricultural commodities, or can require installation of expensive antipollution equipment. Such statutes would have profound effects on large business interests. These interests must participate in political action for self-protection.

Ordinary citizens must also pay close attention to the governmental political system. For example, changes in federal law can bring women under the draft, include students and fathers, or abolish the draft entirely; they can raise or lower social security payments and public assistance rates; they can assist women who work outside their homes by allowing full tax deductions for child care expenses or they can refuse to do so. In the broadest sense, federal lawmakers can subsidize more education or more police weaponry, more space exploration or more wilderness land, more housing and rent supplements or more antiballistic missile systems. Ordinary citizens increasingly feel that they must participate in political action for their self-preservation.

When a few million dollars spent at election time can affect the selection of legislators and congressmen who control the expenditure of billions of dollars by the government, small wonder that people with business interests concern themselves with suffrage. Similarly, when the vast majority of Americans cannot vote on policy questions in large corporations, and can affect the course of events only by exercising their right of suffrage, small wonder that they demand fair and easy voter registration laws, fair drawing of district lines to determine legislators and congressmen, and fair procedures for selecting candidates by political parties.

As long as we live in a system in which the power of the purse can be overruled by the power of the ballot, the relatively few people with much economic power will devote considerable attention (and money) to the electoral process. And people with no economic power will seek to take over the political apparatus by means of their greater numbers.

These rules had a long history before the 1972 election. The recent, numerous examples of their application may lead to amending some practices and perhaps to eliminating some abuses.

These political facts also help explain the significance of the cases that come before the Supreme Court concerning voting rights and equal representation in legislative bodies. While many of these cases arose in the South and involve denial of rights to blacks and urban whites, similar problems also exist in the North and involve other groups of citizens.

A key factor of political power in Congress, and in state capitols, is the seniority system. The more often a congressman or senator gets reelected, the more power he has to become a member or chairman of the committees that consider the most important pieces of legislation. For decades, southern congressmen have carried weight in national policymaking far beyond their numbers because they managed to get reelected year after year in "one-party" states. Northern congressmen and senators had less seniority and lost power because the northern vote is not as controlled or predictable.

The southern electorate was kept small and relatively homogeneous by exclusion of blacks and some poor whites through complex voter registration laws, white primaries, poll tax requirements, and fear. Politicians developed enough control in some areas to be able to pick their successors on retirement.

Different pressures were at work on northern politicians. Blacks who migrated to northern cities retained their concern for relatives in the South, and voted for congressmen who would support strong civil rights measures. The self-interest of many northern politicians required them to support voting rights laws, even when they would hurt southern politicians in the same party.

When citizens filed lawsuits to change election districts or to permit additional citizens to register, northern and southern politicians became concerned. If the suits were successful, some congressmen might lose their seats and committee positions. If the suits failed, black citizens and their white supporters would clamor for tougher civil rights laws.

These underlying factors are frequently alluded to in the

cases discussed in this chapter, but they are seldom stated by the judges, since they were not mentioned explicitly by the litigants and the judges assumed everyone understood them without discussion. It is worth remembering that justices on the United States Supreme Court do not spend their pre-Court years in a vacuum. Most of them participated in political life as elected or appointed officials, and many served on corporate boards of directors and the boards of civic organizations. They often can tell which economic and political interests are concerned in a case by seeing which law firms and parties appear on the pleadings.

The Supreme Court has listened to and acted on a series of important cases that touched the election process. Unlike many of the Court's civil rights decisions, which depended basically on interpretation of the Thirteenth, Fourteenth, and Fifteenth Amendments, these voting rights cases often brought the Court back to the Constitution itself and the intentions of its framers.

There was a profound debate at the constitutional convention of 1787 over the representative nature of the new government. Madison wrote in *The Federalist*, "Who are to be the electors of the Federal Representatives? Not the rich more than the poor; not the learned more than the ignorant; not the haughty heirs of distinguished names, more than the humble sons of obscure and unpropitious fortune. The electors are to be the great body of the people of the United States." There were also many statements at the convention "favoring limited monarchy and property qualifications for suffrage and expressions of disapproval for unrestricted democracy."

At the time the Constitution was ratified, most states had a property owning or taxpaying qualification for voters. For example, the New York Constitution of 1777 restricted the vote to men "possessing a freehold [land owned free and clear without a mortgage] of the value of 20 pounds, . . . or [who] have rented a tenement . . . of the yearly value of 40 shillings, and . . . actually paid taxes to this state." For membership in the legislature, most states also required that the candidate own valuable personal property (money or possessions other than land).

Probably all lawmakers are anxious to avoid the major evils that existed in the previous government. That is particularly true when there is a marked change in the government, such as that created by the American Revolution. One of the British evils that many of the new Americans wanted to avoid was the "rotten borough" system, under which "one man could send two members to Parliament to represent the borough of Old Sarum while London's million people sent but four."

Out of the mighty debate in Philadelphia came several contradictory decisions. It was agreed that each existing state, and each state to come into the union, would have equal representation in the Senate in the person of two senators. However, they were not to be elected directly by the people but by the state legislators. (It took another reform movement culminating in a 1913 constitutional amendment to achieve the direct election of senators by the people, eliminating the power of political leaders to select senators without an opportunity for popular vote.)

Representation of the states in the lower house of Congress was to be "apportioned . . . according to their respective Numbers." The representatives were to be elected by popular vote. The constitutional convention left to the states many decisions about who could vote. For years voters had to satisfy property qualifications to register. Many states required each person to pay a tax before he could register or vote—the so-called poll tax. (This was not abolished until adoption of the Twenty-fourth Amendment in 1964, after a campaign lasting decades.)

Sharp conflict produced a compromise in election procedures concerning the black immigrants enslaved and brought forcibly to North America to labor in the new American states. Slaves could not vote, under the Constitution. But each slave was counted as three-fifths of a man in determining the representation of the state in Congress (a representation exercised by the slaveowners and other white colonists). The revolutionary change in American society brought about by the Civil War also had a direct effect on the electoral process. The Fifteenth Amendment made explicit what had been foreshadowed in the Thirteenth and Fourteenth Amendments: every man had a right to vote whether or not he had been a slave, and Congress was given power to enforce this right by appropriate legislation.

Blacks were quick to exercise the franchise and, with some white votes, elected blacks to office at the city, county, state, and national levels. Two Negroes became United States senators, and twenty-one were elected to the House of Representatives, although blacks did not find their way into the judiciary at state or federal levels to any noticeable degree. The end of the Reconstruction period in 1876 was followed by a long and severe backlash, during which the Supreme Court emasculated the Reconstruction amendments and statutes, including those prohibiting discrimination against blacks in the electoral process. White power reasserted itself as quickly as possible, first using every means to control the black vote and later rewriting state constitutions to prevent blacks from qualifying to vote. Changes favoring equal treatment for blacks in various areas of life could not be made if prejudiced white voters elected white legislators who enacted discriminatory state laws, enforced selectively by white lawmen, and administered selectively by white governors and judges.

By the time Earl Warren became Chief Justice in 1953, there had been decades of discontent about the electoral system in many quarters of the country. The Warren Court heard major complaints about denials of equal representation and voting rights. Its decisions have already had profound effects on the political life of the country, and the long-range effects remain to be charted. In this, as in other areas of popular concern, the struggles of black people for greater civil rights sparked campaigns by other groups of Americans with little economic power—a democratic fallout from the civil rights movement.

A. Equal Representation

Article I, Section 4, of the Constitution provides: "The Times, Places and Manner of holding Elections for Senators and Representatives, shall be prescribed in each State by the Legislature thereof; but the Congress may at any time by Law make or alter such Regulations, except as to the Places of chusing Senators."

At first Congress exercised its power to supervise apportionment by simply specifying in the statutes how many representatives each state was to have. From 1842 until the 1920s, it went further and required that the districts be relatively compact (not scattered areas) and relatively equal in voting population.

Major shifts in population occurred in the twentieth century: large numbers of farmers could no longer maintain small farms and moved to the cities to find employment; rapidly growing industries, organized in factory systems, attracted rural workers; and many blacks who could no longer find work in southern agriculture moved to the North to get better jobs and get away from strict Jim Crow living conditions. The rural areas of the country became more sparsely populated while the city populations swelled.

As these changes were occurring, Congress took less interest in its reapportionment power, and after 1929 did not reenact the requirements. In 1946, voters in Illinois asked the Supreme Court to remedy the serious malapportionment of their state congressional districts. Justice Frankfurter, writing for the Court in *Colegrove* v. *Green,* said the federal courts should stay out of "this political thicket." Reapportionment was a "political question" outside the jurisdiction of these courts. Following the *Colegrove* holding, malapportionment grew more severe and widespread in the United States.

In the Warren Court era, voters again asked the Court to pass on issues concerning the size and shape of electoral districts, partly out of desperation because no other branch of government offered relief, and partly out of hope that the Court would reexamine old decisions in this area as it had in others, looking at basic constitutional principles in the light of modern living conditions.

Once again the Court had to work through the problem of separation of powers, which had stood in the way of court action concerning representation. In this area, too, the Court's rulings were greeted by some as shockingly radical departures from "the American way," while others saw them as a reversion to the democratic processes established by the Constitution, applied to an urbanized setting.

Gerrymandering a square into a sea dragon

Gomillion v. *Lightfoot* (1960)
364 U.S. 339, 81 S. Ct. 125, 5 L. Ed. 2d 110

The town of Tuskegee, in Macon County, Alabama, is perhaps best known for Tuskegee Institute—the famous Negro college founded by Booker T. Washington in 1881. The college attracted a large educated black population to the town, but Alabama voting registrars administered complex literacy tests to citizens wishing to register, and Tuskegee Ph.D.'s were ruled illiterate by the registrars year after year.

Nevertheless, all through the 1950s Negroes put pressure on the registrars and more and more did succeed in voting. Blacks constituted about 80 percent of the Macon County population, and when registered blacks numbered about 25 percent of the Tuskegee voting population, segregationists got worried. They could see that blacks could elect some candidates for city office if they cast "single shot" ballots. Using this tactic, if there were three vacancies on a city council, for example, and six candidates, five white and one black, most whites would vote for three out of the five whites, while most blacks would vote only for the one black candidate, not using two of their votes. As a result of the single shot votes, the black candidate would get all of the black votes, which would probably be enough to get elected. However, if black electors also voted for two of the white candidates, the *relative* size of the vote for the black candidate would decrease and he would not be elected (the white candidates would receive black votes but the black candidate presumably would not pick up any white votes). With this in mind, State Senator Sam Engelhardt of Macon County got a bill through the legislature in 1951, prohibiting single shot voting in city elections: when two or more seats of a position were open, voters had to vote for as many candidates as there were places, or else their ballots would not be counted.

In 1957, when blacks were estimated at 35 to 40 percent of the voting population, Senator Engelhardt introduced a new bill redefining the city boundaries of Tuskegee. As enacted, the law changed the town from a perfect square into a twenty-eight-sided intricate shape, described by the *Montgomery Advertiser-Alabama Journal* as resembling "the outline of a sea dragon." While the zigzagging boundary lines were irregular, they certainly were not haphazard. They removed all but four or five black voters from the city limits, while excluding no white voters.

Engelhardt, who was head of the Alabama Citizens Council—a segregationist organization—was still worried, however. He steered a third bill through the Alabama legislature, setting up a commission to abolish Macon County, dividing it up among the five surrounding counties, so as to scatter the potential black voting majority.

Meanwhile Tuskegee blacks, outraged at the gerrymandering of the town, took action on two fronts. They set up a boycott of white businesses (reducing sales of some by more than 50 percent), and Tuskegee Professor Charles Gomillion and other voters filed a suit in federal district court for themselves "and all others similarly situated." They charged that the new boundary statute violated the Fourteenth Amendment equal protection clause and deprived them of the Fifteenth Amendment right to vote.

The defendants, Mayor Lightfoot and other city officials, moved that the judge dismiss the suit, saying the drawing of city boundaries was the exclusive right of the legislature and that the courts had no remedy for the alleged wrong.

The judge dismissed the complaint, and Professor Gomillion and the other plaintiffs appealed to the federal court of

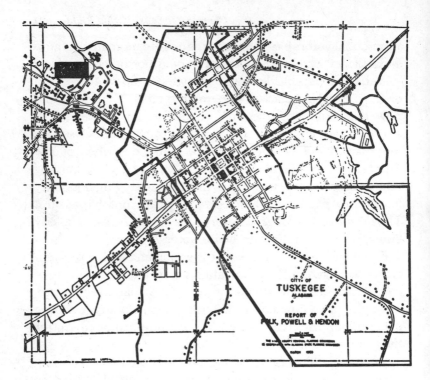

The gerrymander of Tuskegee: the square outline is the former city
boundary, while the odd-shaped darker outline inside it is the new
boundary.

appeals. The three appellate judges split two to one, the majority upholding dismissal of the suit. On petition, the United States Supreme Court agreed to review the case.

Do you think the setting of city boundaries is strictly state business, beyond the jurisdiction of the federal courts? Did adoption of the Fifteenth Amendment mark a change in the relations between the states and the federal government, enlarging the "business" of the federal courts? Do they have the authority to decide complaints by black voters showing that boundary lines were drawn in order to discriminate against them in city elections? Have the excluded voters been deprived of their votes any more than any other citizens who live outside the city limits?

The Supreme Court's unanimous opinion was delivered by Justice Frankfurter in November 1960. The Court examined whether the complaint should have been dismissed, applying the long-standing rule: If we assume that the plaintiffs can prove all of their charges, does their complaint state a case the courts have the power to decide? If not, it was properly dismissed.

If the allegations in this case were true, Justice Frankfurter said, they would "abundantly establish" that the statute "was not an ordinary geographic redistricting measure even within familiar abuses of gerrymandering," but rather "that the legislation is solely concerned with segregating white and colored voters by fencing Negro citizens out of town so as to deprive them of their pre-existing municipal vote."

"The respondents invoke generalities expressing the State's unrestricted power—unlimited, that is, by the United States Constitution—to establish, destroy, or reorganize by contraction or expansion its political subdivisions, to wit, cities, counties, and other local units. We freely recognize the breadth and importance of this aspect of the State's political power. To exalt this power into an absolute is to misconceive the reach and rule of this Court's decisions."

The Court examined its previous decisions and found: "This line of authority conclusively shows that the Court has never acknowledged that the States have power to do as they will with municipal corporations regardless of consequences. Legislative control of municipalities, no less than other state power, lies within the scope of relevant limitations imposed by the United States Constitution."

"The petitioners here complain that affirmative legislative action deprives them of their votes and the consequent advantages that the ballot affords. When a legislature thus singles out a readily isolated segment of a racial minority for special discriminatory treatment, it violates the Fifteenth Amendment. . . . Apart from all else, these considerations lift this controversy out of the so-called 'political' arena and into the conventional sphere of constitutional litigation."

The order dismissing the suit was reversed by the very justice who had refused to look at districting problems in Illinois.

Justice Whittaker concurred on the basis of the equal protection clause of the Fourteenth Amendment rather than the right to vote guarantee of the Fifteenth Amendment.

The decision in effect put the black voters back into the city; they had to wage further battles to get registered. But by the summer of 1964, even before the 1965 Voting Rights Act passed Congress, Negro voters in Tuskegee outnumbered whites. Although many whites feared a black takeover, the moderate Tuskegee Civic Association, headed by Professor Gomillion, put up a slate of two blacks and three moderate whites for the five city council seats. The more militant

Non Partisan Voting League put up four black candidates. When the votes were counted, all the Civic Association candidates had won by comfortable margins.

Interviewed in 1965, Neil Davis, editor of the *Tuskegee News,* felt that Alabama whites had learned little from the Tuskegee experience. It would take large black registrations to bolster the southern whites who were enlightened enough to provide leadership toward integration "if they get the chance. There is one tremendous force working in their favor—the absence of a spirit of revenge on the part of most Negroes," Davis felt.

The Court enters the political thicket

Baker v. Carr (1962)
369 U.S. 186, 82 S. Ct. 691, 7 L. Ed. 2d 663

In small towns and districts held securely by one political party or the other, the old adage to the party regulars used to be "vote early and often." By the middle of the twentieth century, this was no longer necessary to ensure victory for the party in power. By the 1950s, Tennesseeans in Pickett County, with 2,565 voters, elected less than three-fourths of one representative to the state legislature. In Moore County, only 2,340 voters elected two representatives. Gibson County, with only one-fifth more voters than Rutherford County, elected five representatives to its two. The state legislative apportionment system included many examples of similar inequities.

The Tennessee constitution provided the solution to this problem. It specified that representation was to be apportioned "according to the number of qualified voters" in each district and that a census of voters was to be taken every ten years. Under these provisions, the legislature in 1901 passed an act specifying the districts and number of representatives for each. The voting population in 1901 was 487,000. By 1960 it had grown to 2,093,000, and people had made major shifts from rural to urban and suburban areas. During this period, however, the legislators continuously refused to reapportion their districts.

Voters in the underrepresented areas came to feel almost powerless to change the situation. They were convinced that nothing could be done as long as the decision was up to the state legislators. Obviously, each legislator would not want to change the lines of *his* district: in any reapportionment he would lose some voters who had supported him in the past and would have to appeal to different voters to ensure reelection. And almost every legislator would vote against reapportionment of every district now controlled by *his* party. No one wants to cut off the hand that feeds him.

Were there other methods of getting reapportionment? Tennessee had no provision for a popular initiative (legislation proposed by citizens and placed on the ballot at a general election). Citizens could not propose amendments to the state constitution; these could be initiated only by the legislature or by a constitutional convention proposed by the legislature and approved by the voters.

Eventually the most concerned voters filed lawsuits in the state courts, asking the judicial branch to order action by the legislative branch or to correct the inequity by some other means. The state judges rejected these pleas, often citing the *Colegrove* opinion of the United States Supreme Court that these were "political questions" outside the jurisdiction of the courts.

Finally, voters in several underrepresented districts filed suit in federal district court, alleging that the 1901 Apportionment Act was unconstitutional because it deprived them of equal protection of the laws under the Fourteenth

Amendment. They argued that the Tennessee apportionment system cut the value of their votes without "any logical or reasonable formula whatever," and that this was the kind of "invidious discrimination" forbidden by the Constitution. (Significantly, these white voters sued under the same Civil Rights Act provision, 42 U.S.C. §1983, forged in the struggles of blacks after the Civil War. See *Monroe* v. *Pape,* discussed in chapter 12, and *Pierson* v. *Ray,* in chapter 25.)

The defendants, state officers responsible for elections and apportionment, moved that the suit be dismissed because the matter was outside the jurisdiction of the courts.

A three-judge federal district court was convened to hear the case (as in *Dombrowski* v. *Pfister,* discussed at page 161). The judges agreed that "the legislature of Tennessee is guilty of a clear violation of the state constitution and of the rights of the plaintiffs" and that "the evil is a serious one which should be corrected without further delay. But even so," they found, "the remedy in this situation clearly does not lie with the courts." The judges dismissed the suit, and the plaintiffs appealed to the United States Supreme Court.

Do you think the Tennessee voters were being denied equal protection? If so, can a *court* provide a remedy for this problem created by a *legislature?* Can a *federal* court provide a remedy for this problem arising in a *state?* If the *United States Senate* is composed of two senators from each state, without regard to state population, can't a *state legislature* ignore population in establishing state legislative districts?

The Supreme Court heard argument in this case in 1960. Evidently the problem disturbed the justices; they ordered reargument in 1961. They handed down a six-to-two decision in March 1962 (Justice Whittaker did not participate). Justice

Brennan, writing the majority opinion, took up separately the two grounds on which the lower court had dismissed the complaint.

First the Supreme Court held that "the court possessed jurisdiction of the subject matter" and that the voters had stated a cause of action on which they would be entitled to relief. Then the Court ruled that the plaintiffs had a right to raise this question in court because their votes had been debased by the practice.

Justice Brennan documented the bases for these conclusions in a long opinion analyzing the previous cases one by one and as a whole. On the knotty question of justiciability (whether the courts have authority over questions of representation or must bow to the legislature) the Court found that this case turned on the equal protection clause, over which courts have jurisdiction, rather than on any political question on which the legislature or the voters must decide. Justice Brennan explained at length how this issue differed from "political" cases of the past.

Having gone this far, the Supreme Court majority explicitly declined to rule on the merits of the plantiffs' claims. The justices sent the case back to the federal district court for trial, noting "we have no cause at this stage to doubt the District Court will be able to fashion relief if violations of constitutional rights are found." They felt it would be "improper now to consider what remedy would be most appropriate if appellants prevail at the trial."

Justice Douglas, concurring, stressed that the key issue was "the extent to which a state may weigh one person's vote more heavily than it does another's." Justice Clark, concurring, regretted that the majority "refuses to award relief here—although the facts are undisputed—and fails to give the District Court any guidance whatever." He set forth tables and comparisons to illustrate "a few of the horribles" that led him to conclude "that Tennessee's apportionment is a crazy quilt without rational basis." Justice Stewart also wrote a separate concurring opinion.

Justices Frankfurter and Harlan each dissented and joined the other's dissent. Justice Frankfurter thought the majority opinion reversed "a uniform course of decision established by a dozen cases" (in some of which he had written the opinions). He felt that change had to come not from the courts but "through an aroused popular conscience that sears the conscience of the people's representatives." Justice Harlan found no constitutional guarantee of *equal* votes for qualified citizens and thus no grounds for the suit.

The Court's decision in *Baker* v. *Carr* opened the door to suits not only in Tennessee but also in malapportioned states around the nation, in which voters asked the federal district courts to determine whether malapportionment in the state legislature deprived them of equal protection and due process under the Fourteenth Amendment.

The district courts did not hand down uniform decisions, and in several cases the defeated side appealed. Meanwhile, other suits filed in federal court challenged the apportionment of seats in Congress, relying on the *Baker* decision covering state legislative apportionment and the Fourteenth Amendment. In 1964, the United States Supreme Court agreed to hear one of these challenges.

One man, one vote

Wesberry v. *Sanders* (1964)
376 U.S. 1, 84 S. Ct. 526, 11 L. Ed. 2d 481

Georgia was divided into ten congressional districts in a 1931 statute, and each district elected one representative to the U.S. House of Representatives. By 1960, the census showed that Atlanta and the surrounding district contained two to three times as many people as several other districts. Atlanta voters filed suit in federal district court, asking that the 1931 statute be struck down. They said it violated Article I, Section 2, of the Constitution, which provides that "the House of Representatives shall be composed of Members chosen every second Year by the People of the several States," and the Fourteenth Amendment which provides that "representatives shall be apportioned among the several States according to their respective numbers."

The Governor and Secretary of State of Georgia responded that the relevant passage of the Constitution was Article I, Section 4, which they said gave the states the power of apportionment and gave Congress supervisory powers. They contended that the court had no jurisdiction over this issue and asked the court to dismiss the suit.

The court found the Atlanta district "grossly out of balance" with the others, but nevertheless dismissed the suit, ruling that challenges to apportionment of *congressional* districts raised "political questions" beyond the jurisdiction of the courts, and that *Baker* v. *Carr* only covered apportionment of *state* legislatures.

The voters appealed to the U.S. Supreme Court.

If congressmen are elected in an unconstitutional manner, what do you think is the proper way to remedy this situation? Do the *federal* courts have the power to tell *states* how to apportion their *federal* congressional districts? Can federal *courts* review the action (or inaction) of *Congress* in supervising state rules for election of congressmen? If so, how can this be reconciled with the principle of separation of powers among the three branches of government?

Justice Black delivered the Supreme Court's 6½-to-2½ decision. The majority agreed with the Atlanta voters that *Baker* v. *Carr* had paved the way for court action in this suit. The language of Article I, Section 4, of the Constitution did not destroy "the power of courts to protect the constitutional rights of individuals from legislative destruction [by] congressional apportionment laws which debase a citizen's right to vote." The Court held, "The right to vote is too important in our free society to be stripped of judicial protection by such an interpretation of Article I." It was therefore error for the district court to dismiss the complaint.

Turning to the merits of the case, the majority announced a highly significant holding: "Construed in its historical context, the command of Art. I, §2, that Representatives be chosen 'by the People of the several States' means that as nearly as is practicable one man's vote in a congressional election is to be worth as much as another's. . . . To say that a vote is worth more in one district than in another would not only run counter to our fundamental ideas of democratic government, it would cast aside the principle of a House of Representatives elected 'by the People,' a principle tenaciously fought for and established at the Constitutional Convention. The history of the Constitution, particularly that part of it relating to the adoption of Art. I, §2, reveals that those who framed the Constitution meant that, no matter what the mechanics of an election, whether statewide or by districts, it was population which was to be the basis of the House of Representatives."

Justice Black concluded: "No right is more precious in a free country than that of having a voice in the election of those who make the laws under which, as good citizens, we must live. Other rights, even the most basic, are illusory if the right to vote is undermined. Our Constitution leaves no room for classification of people in a way that unnecessarily abridges this right. . . . While it may not be possible to draw congressional districts with mathematical precision, that is no excuse for ignoring our Constitution's plain objective of making equal representation for equal numbers of people the fundamental goal for the House of Representatives."

Justice Harlan dissented angrily, finding Congress was so far from the "one person, one vote" standard that the decision "casts grave doubt on the constitutionality of the composition of the House of Representatives." He said he had counted 398 representatives whose elections could be held invalid under the Court's decision. He considered the decision a "whole-hearted but heavy-footed entrance into the political arena"; the Constitution reserved to the states alone the power to set the time, place, and manner of elections, and reserved to Congress alone the power to supervise the states in their exercise of that power. Therefore, the Court had no business in this case.

Justice Stewart agreed with Justice Harlan except on a slight technical distinction.

Justice Clark concurred and dissented. He thought the courts had the right to determine the issue, particularly under the equal protection clause of the Fourteenth Amendment, but that there was no constitutional basis for a "one person, one vote" rule.

The majority decision led to sweeping charges of malapportionment of congressional districts (as Justice Harlan had predicted). While no one knew which political party would gain most from redistricting, it was clear to all that the major shift would be from rural to urban and suburban power.

Four months later, the Supreme Court rendered a decision in the cases of six states being challenged by voters because their state legislatures were not apportioned according to population. In a third landmark decision, *Reynolds* v. *Sims,* by an eight-to-one vote, the Court ruled that *both* houses of state legislatures must follow the one-person-one-vote principle. The *Wesberry* decision had "clearly established that the fundamental principle of representative government in this country is one of equal representation for equal numbers of people, without regard to race, sex, economic status, or place of residence within a State," said Chief Justice Warren for the Court.

The Chief Justice wrote in plain language: "Legislators represent people, not trees or acres. Legislators are elected by voters, not farms or cities or economic interests. As long as ours is a representative form of government, and our legislatures are those instruments of government elected directly by and directly representative of the people, the right to elect legislators in a free and unimpaired fashion is a bedrock of our political system."

The Court held that "diluting the weight of votes because of place of residence impairs basic constitutional rights under the Fourteenth Amendment just as much as invidious discriminations based upon factors such as race . . . or economic status."

Aroused politicians started a movement to amend the Constitution in order to overturn the Supreme Court decisions. Some wanted only to override *Reynolds* and allow one house of a state legislature to be apportioned on a basis "other than population"; others wanted to forbid the Supreme Court from deciding apportionment cases, to establish a new "Court of the Union," which could review all Supreme Court decisions concerning federal-state relations, and to prohibit federal courts from issuing reapportionment orders in accordance with the Supreme Court's recent holdings.

None of the measures was passed in the 1964 or 1965

sessions of Congress, and the federal courts and state legislatures themselves began redistricting. In the mid-1960s many states and courts applied the one-man-one-vote principle to districting for city and county elections as well as state legislative and congressional districts.

At its 1968 National Convention, the Democratic Party revised its rules for the 1972 convention to reflect the one-man-one-vote principle, rather than the "unit rule," under which all of a state's votes had to be cast for the choice of the majority. The party also took steps to ensure more open participation by members, to meet charges that delegates were always professional politicians and their hand-picked cronies. The 1972 Democratic Convention clearly reflected these changes, both in the many delegations reporting split votes and in the more proportional representation of blacks and other minority groups, women, and people under thirty. (Some Democrats have expressed the hope that the party next will seek proportional representation of a variety of economic groups, including welfare rights activists and blue-collar workers.) The Republican Party is also making reforms in its internal structure and processes.

In 1971 the Twenty-sixth Amendment to the Constitution was adopted, permitting citizens eighteen to twenty-one years old to vote. Its ultimate effect cannot yet be known, but it clearly has opened the way for further profound changes in the nation's political structure.

The movement begun by the black and white communities in these cases was carried forward by the Supreme Court's one-man-one-vote rule and insistence on fairness in fact in the electoral process. It grew in the 1960s, and can continue to produce electoral reform in the 1970s if large numbers of people spend the effort to keep it alive. The Watergate revelations add impetus to this movement.

B. The Right to Vote

After the defeat of the Confederacy, the southern states reentering the union were required to revise their constitutions to reflect the emancipation of the slaves and the new status of blacks as full-fledged citizens. These documents expressed the views imposed on the South by acts of Congress. With the federal government offering some protection, blacks began exercising their citizenship rights, including the right to vote. But after the Tilden-Hayes compromise, when federal troops left the South and the federal government turned its back on charges of racial violence and discrimination, white supremacists launched attacks on several fronts to regain exclusive power.

One of their first goals was to end black suffrage, despite any constitutional guarantees. For example, the Mississippi Constitution written in 1869 gave the right to vote to all adult men who were not insane or mentally deficient and who had not been convicted of certain crimes. They had to meet residence requirements and register to vote. Although there were more blacks than whites eligible to vote in the state after the Civil War, according to population figures, the Reconstruction period was so brief that blacks were never able to exercise majority power. Mississippi Circuit Judge Chrisman, speaking in 1890, described how the blacks had been kept from political control: "It is no secret that there has not been a full vote and a fair count in Mississippi since 1875—that we have been preserving the ascendancy of the white people by revolutionary methods. In plain words, we have been stuffing ballot boxes, committing perjury and here and there in the State carrying the elections by fraud and violence until the whole machinery for elections was about to rot down."

By 1890, leading figures in the white community were prepared to legalize the disenfranchisement of blacks—they were worried that the corrupt practices were getting out of hand. They called a constitutional convention and rewrote the state constitution, adding, in §244, a new requirement that a person registering to vote must demonstrate his ability to read a section of the state constitution or understand one that is read to him or give a reasonable interpretation of it. This requirement gave voting registrars wide power to allow or deny a person the right to vote.

The registrars used their power as the convention delegates had intended. In 1890 over 55 percent of the eligible voters were black; by 1899 less than 10 percent were black, although blacks still constituted about 57 percent of the Mississippi adult population. The Jackson *Clarion-Ledger* explained candidly, "County registrars have kept the Negroes off the books by strict enforcement of the understanding clause in the Constitution."

Judge Loren Miller, writing in *The Petitioners* (1966), noted that "in 1898, the [Supreme] Court indirectly approved Mississippi's 1890 constitution, while noting that it was an instrument that 'swept the field of expedients' to disfranchise Negroes. As we have seen, a veritable tornado of change soon swept through the South. One after another, southern states amended their constitutions to add literacy tests, good-character clauses, reading-and-understanding provisions, and poll tax requirements as prerequisites for registration and voting. Proponents of these provisions said openly that the purpose was to deprive the Negro of the vote. These were fair-on-their-face provisions that could be utilized to deny registration to Negroes but could also be applied in such a manner as to extend the voting privilege to white applicants. Their efficacy may be gauged from the fact that Louisiana amended its constitution in 1898, and that its Negro voter registration dropped from 130,334 in 1896 to 1324 in 1904; 99 out of every 100 Negro voters were lopped off."

Another device used to keep blacks from political power was the white primary. As the southern states became more and more one-party states, policies restricting membership in the Democratic Party to whites effectively disfranchised Negroes from voting in the only election that presented any choice of candidates—the Democratic primary. The party could discriminate, since it was a private organization, its leaders said. In 1924, the Supreme Court, in *Nixon* v. *Herndon,* disagreed. The party was an arm of the state election machinery, the Court declared, and the white-only primary violated the Fourteenth Amendment. In 1944, in the face of southern evasionary tactics, the NAACP again brought suit. Attorney Thurgood Marshall, in *Smith* v. *Allwright,* asked the court to reaffirm its 1924 holding on the basis of the Fifteenth Amendment. The Court agreed.

The white primary was dying, while public education, although separate and grossly unequal, made it possible for more and more blacks to pass the literacy tests. In the ten southern states that had used the white primary device to disfranchise blacks, there were approximately 100,000 registered Negro voters in 1932. By 1947 there were 645,000; and by 1952 more than 1,000,000.

A statewide system to keep the polls white

United States v. Mississippi (1965)
380 U.S. 128, 85 S. Ct. 808, 13 L. Ed. 2d 717

In 1951, a suit filed in federal district court in Mississippi challenged the practice of asking blacks who *could* read to also *interpret* a section of the constitution, which they inevitably failed to do to the registrar's satisfaction. On appeal, the federal Fifth Circuit Court ruled that §244 said the registrant must read *or* understand *or* interpret, and it meant what it said; any one ability would qualify the applicant to vote. The court enjoined registrars from making literate Negroes interpret the constitution.

The legislature quickly proposed a constitutional amendment to §244 to require registrants to read *and* interpret a section. The voters in 1952 rejected the amendment. Two years later the legislators tried again, this time adding that new registrants would have to explain the duties and obligations of citizenship under a constitutional government, but no one already registered would have to reregister. This passed overwhelmingly. About 67 percent of eligible whites and about 5 percent of eligible blacks were then registered to vote in Mississippi.

In May of that year, the Supreme Court had handed down its first opinion in *Brown* v. *Board of Education* (see chapter 22). The *Brown* decision showed that the Court would no longer look the other way when Negroes were denied basic constitutional rights. This gave new impetus to the civil rights movement, North and South. Southern blacks anxious to exercise their citizenship rights were encouraged to find that white northerners supported them. Although they knew that individual acts of terror would continue, they hoped the national attention brought by northern whites might affect the actions of some southern officials.

Here and there, individually and in groups, around the South, Negroes made new attempts to participate in elections. Black teachers working in black schools decided to try to vote; black students reaching their twenty-first birthdays went down to register; mothers who had borne and raised families by sheer grit and determination in the face of poverty and bigotry decided to take on one more battle.

The Student Nonviolent Coordinating Committee, formed in 1960, went from sit-ins to voter registration work. The Congress of Racial Equality, founded in the early 1940s, grew rapidly after 1954 and began to do more voter work. The Mississippi NAACP was spurred into greater activity.

By 1957, Congress began to move on civil rights for the first time since 1875. It passed a civil rights act with emphasis on the right to vote. The United States Attorney General was authorized to file civil suits for injunctions to protect people trying to exercise the franchise. The act also created the United States Civil Rights Commission to investigate violations of all civil rights. Although in the next two years, the Attorney General filed only one suit, the commission issued an extensive report and recommendations on voting problems. This documented the need for stronger voting measures. In 1960, northern congressmen, courting the Negro vote in their districts, proposed and pushed through Congress a second civil rights act. Under its provisions, if the Attorney General could prove to a court that there was a "pattern or practice of discrimination" in voting procedures, a special referee could be appointed to screen individual complaints, and the courts could issue voting certificates to justified complainants.

That same year, Mississippi again amended its constitutional provisions concerning voting. It now provided that an applicant for registration must "be of good moral character," and new statutes provided that the names of applicants had to be published in the newspapers for two weeks so that anyone could challenge their good moral character. Other statutes authorized the destruction of unsuccessful registration records (expressly forbidden by the 1960 Civil Rights

Act), prohibited anyone from assisting an applicant to fill out the form, prohibited registrars from telling applicants why they had failed (since this would "assist" them in filling out the form), and required that all blanks on the form be filled in "properly and responsively."

In August 1962, the United States Justice Department brought suit against the state of Mississippi, three members of the state elections commission (including Governor Ross Barnett and Attorney General Joe Patterson), and the voting registrars of counties throughout the state—Amite, Claiborne, Coahoma, Le Flore, Lowndes, and Pike. The suit charged that since 1890 Mississippi had denied Negroes the right to vote on account of their race, by law, practice, custom, and usage, in violation of the Fourteenth and Fifteenth Amendments and the new civil rights acts. The U.S. Solicitor General gathered numerous proofs of the charges. He showed that the state constitutional provisions were intended to disfranchise blacks and had accomplished this. He showed that statutes were enforced against blacks but not against whites. For example, a Negro in Hinds County (which includes Jackson, the state capitol) was failed because his interpretation of the constitution "missed by one word," while a white man asked to interpret the provision, "There shall be no imprisonment for debt," wrote: "Without due process of time and law," and was passed. In one county, five Negroes were rejected because their names were said to be on the wrong line of the form, while 94 percent of the white applications that were accepted had the same "error."

The attorneys for the United States showed that blacks were given long complex sections of the constitution to interpret and whites short simple sections. They offered proof of numerous instances of intimidation of blacks the minute they tried to register. Negroes were misinformed about the registration requirements, denied credit, not allowed to gin their cotton at the white-owned cotton gins, threatened, beaten, fired from their jobs, and evicted from their homes by white businessmen and landlords.

The Solicitor General asked the court to find that these acts constituted a pattern and practice of discrimination, to declare the Mississippi voter registration requirements unconstitutional, to prohibit the destruction of records, to enjoin further discrimination in registration and voting by blacks, and to order the registrars to register any black citizen, twenty-one or older, who met the residence requirements, could read, had not been convicted of a disqualifying crime, and was not insane.

The attorneys for the state and the individuals charged in the complaint asked the court to dismiss the case. Congress had no constitutional power to attack "the sovereign entity of the state itself," they argued. The three election commissioners were not the right people to sue, they said, because they did not actually enforce the laws being attacked. And there was no evidence that the six county registrars had acted together, so a joint suit against all was improper. Moreover, the defendants argued, the U.S. Constitution gave the states exclusive power to determine voter qualifications.

A three-judge federal court was convened to hear this challenge to the constitutionality of state laws. In the spring and summer of 1963 the defendants filed lengthy lists of questions for the federal government to answer under oath. In the fall of 1963, the government filed voluminous answers.

On March 6, 1964, the district court voted two to one to dismiss the complaint, and the Justice Department appealed to the Supreme Court. In June, two significant institutions turned their attention to voting rights. The Supreme Court agreed to hear the legal issues raised by the federal government against Mississippi state and county officials, while every civil rights organization in the state helped launch the Mississippi Summer Project. Some 600 volunteers were trained to assist Mississippi citizens in attaining equal protection of the laws.

SNCC, CORE, SCLC, and the Mississippi chapter of the NAACP had agreed to cooperate in a Council of Federated Organizations (COFO) to run the Project. The participants decided to concentrate on helping to register black voters and helping to provide meaningful education for black children in "freedom schools." In the course of these activities they focused national attention on Mississippi, arousing a level of publicity previously unknown to the state. Part of the history of that Freedom Summer is told in chapter 24. Its effects are still felt in Mississippi. Some white officials got their first awareness of black power; some black citizens got their first taste of equal treatment by whites. And every volunteer took home with him a continuing concern with affairs in Mississippi.

Some of the Americans affected by the news from Mississippi were members of Congress. They responded to this and other pressures by passing the 1964 Civil Rights Act in June. The act was a comprehensive measure dealing, in part, with voting rights. It prevented registrants from denying applications on the basis of inconsequential errors, or applying different standards and procedures to different applicants. Anyone finishing sixth grade was presumed to be literate and could not be required to take a literacy test unless this presumption was contested. Literacy tests had to be written, not oral. The U.S. Attorney General could sue in federal court to end racial discrimination in voting.

During this tide of events, the United States Supreme Court set about examining the issues of this case.

Do you think Congress has authority to step in and regulate a state's voting process? Can Congress set qualifications and procedures for voter registration? Did the Solicitor General state a lawful claim against the state and the individual election commissioners and registrars named? Were the registrars acting jointly? Were the election commissioners responsible for the practices challenged in the suit?

Justice Black of Alabama delivered the Court's unanimous decision on March 8, 1965. "It is apparent," he began, "that the complaint which the majority of the District Court dismissed charged a long-standing, carefully prepared, and faithfully observed plan to bar Negroes from voting in the State of Mississippi, a plan which the registration statistics included in the complaint would seem to show had been remarkably successful.

"This brings us to a consideration of the specific grounds assigned by the District Court for its dismissal." The district court had held, in effect, that the federal government (or a private citizen) could sue a voting *registrar* who discriminated against blacks, but could not sue to challenge discriminatory state voting *laws*.

The Court found that the federal statutes expressly authorized the Solicitor General to sue on behalf of "citizens of the United States who are otherwise qualifed by law to vote" and are prevented from voting by racial discrimination. "The phrase 'otherwise qualified by law to vote' obviously meant that Negroes must possess the qualifications required of all voters by *valid* state or federal laws. It is difficult to take seriously the argument that Congress intended to dilute its guarantee of the right to vote regardless of race by saying at the same time that a State was free to disqualify its Negro citizens by laws which violated the United States Constitution."

The Court held that Congress had the power to make the state itself defendant in this kind of suit and that Congress had exercised that power in the civil rights acts.

"The District Court held with respect to the three members of the Mississippi Board of Election Commissioners that the complaint failed to show that they had a sufficient interest in administering or enforcing the laws under attack to permit making them parties defendant," Justice Black went on. "We do not agree. Under state laws the Election Commissioners have power, authority, and responsibility to help administer the voter registration laws by formulating rules for the various tests applied to applicants for registration." These officials were therefore proper defendants.

As to the argument for dismissing the joint suit against the six county registrars, the Court ruled, "The complaint charged that the registrars had acted and were continuing to act as part of a state-wide system designed to enforce the registration laws in a way that would inevitably deprive colored people of the right to vote solely because of their color. On such an allegation the joinder of all the registrars as defendants in a single suit is authorized."

The justices concluded: "We have no doubt whatsoever that it was error to dismiss the complaint without a trial. The complaint charged that the State of Mississippi and its officials for the past three quarters of a century have been writing and adopting constitutional provisions, statutes, rules, and regulations, and have been engaging in discriminatory practices, all designed to keep the number of white voters at the highest possible figure and the number of colored voters at the lowest. It alleged that the common purpose running through the State's legal and administrative history during that time has been to adopt whatever expedient seemed necessary to establish white political supremacy in a completely segregated society. . . . The allegations of this complaint were too serious, the right to vote in this country is too precious, and the necessity of settling grievances peacefully in the courts is too important for this complaint to have been dismissed. . . . The case should have been tried. It should now be tried without delay."

The same day, the Supreme Court upheld the decision of a three-judge court in a Louisiana suit (*Louisiana* v. *United States*), ruling that an "understanding" test was applied to deprive Negroes of the right to vote in violation of the Fifteenth Amendment. The Court also upheld the lower court's decree that no newly enacted registration requirements could be applied until all blacks previously excluded were allowed to register under the old, easier requirements, and these requirements must be applied to them as they had been applied to white people in the past.

The civil rights workers who had come to Mississippi in the summer of 1964 brought back many horror stories to widen the eyes of hometown listeners in the North and West. Despite the new federal legislation, most black people were consistently denied their rights, many were intimidated, and some were brutalized when they tried to exercise these rights. The U.S. Civil Rights Commission had documented these charges over and over.

Back in 1959, three members of the commission had recommended a constitutional amendment to remove all voter qualifications except age, residence, and criminal conviction restrictions. The commission as a whole had recommended laws authorizing the President to send federal registrars into states where local officials were discriminating against black applicants. By 1963, the commission was asking Congress to prohibit registrars from denying registration to anyone who met the age, residence, and noncriminal qualifications, had a sixth-grade education, and was not insane. As a last resort, it recommended that Congress apply the provisions of Section 2 of the Fourteenth Amendment. Section 2 provides the strongest remedy in our political medicine chest to cure denial of the Negro's right to vote: it says that if the blacks in a state are disenfranchised because of their race, the number of congressmen representing that state must be reduced in proportion to the number of blacks denied the vote. This provision had never been enforced.

The Civil Rights Commission recommendation fell mostly on deaf ears in Congress. But a group of militant blacks in Mississippi were thinking along the same lines. They established the Mississippi Freedom Democratic Party on April 26, 1964, at Jackson. They organized first on a precinct, and then on a statewide, level that spring. They intended to register voters, to become a force in the Democratic primaries, and, if that failed, to challenge the Democratic delegates and candidates at the Democratic National Convention and in Congress.

The Mississippi Democratic Party not only refused to allow MFDP members to participate but sued the MFDP for use of a name too similar to its own. County registrars refused to register blacks, and got away with it. The MFDP decided to hold its own registration, its own primary, and its own election, to disprove the white-supremacist argument that blacks didn't register and vote because they didn't want to. Of the 435,000 blacks eligible in Mississippi in 1964, only 20,000 were registered at that time. The MFDP launched a campaign to "register" the others on Freedom Registration books.

The previous November, Aaron Henry, the statewide coordinator of COFO, had run in a mock election against Governor Ross Barnett and had amassed 83,000 "votes." But harassment and intimidation of MFDP workers and Negroes who participated in Freedom Party activities were so severe in the summer of 1964 that the Party was able to register only 50,000—still substantially more than were able to register officially.

At the June 2 primary, the MFDP ran Mrs. Fannie Lou Hamer, Mrs. Victoria Gray, Reverend John Cameron, and Mr. James Houston on its own ballots against Senator John Stennis and three Democratic congressmen. The MFDP candidates won the mock election as handily as their opponents won the regular Democratic Party primary. The MFDP then challenged the seating of the regular Democratic Party delegation at the national convention in August at Atlantic City. The MFDP presented briefs to prove that MFDP was in agreement with the national party while the "regular" delegation was opposed to both the national platform and the party's national candidates. Despite some support for the MFDP from northern and western liberals, the "regular" delegates were seated. As a concession, MFDP members were given two seats as "special delegates" to the convention.

The MFDP then took its challenge to Washington. At the opening of Congress in January 1965, New York Representative William F. Ryan led a move not to seat the five Mississippi representatives because they had been elected in an unconstitutional vote that denied the franchise to blacks on account of their race. The move was defeated 276–149. Encouraged by the 149 votes of support, the MFDP pursued a challenge procedure under federal statutes through the spring and summer. Lawyers went to Mississippi to take thousands of pages of testimony from hundreds of witnesses to establish violations of voting rights; the affidavits were published by Congress in three fat volumes. In September 1965, Congress defeated this challenge too, but the proceedings had focused national attention on the denial of Negro voting rights despite the 1957, 1960, and 1964 Civil Rights Acts. The conclusion was inescapable: the federal government had to take much stronger action if blacks were to vote in the deep South.

A month before Congress dealt its final rejection to the MFDP, it passed the Voting Rights Act of 1965, the strongest federal measure ever enacted to enforce the Fifteenth Amendment. The act assumed that a state discriminated if less than half its voting-age residents had voted in the November 1964 election and the state used tests or "devices" to screen voting registrants. Such an assumption is called a legal presumption. This presumption triggered automatic suspension of the tests and devices. And suspension allowed the Attorney General to send in federal voting examiners to register voters. This presumption permitted the federal government to move in before the states could get a court trial on whether the states really were discriminating. The presumption of unfairness was based on 100 years of history and was a powerful weapon providing immediate action. The Attorney General could also seek to suspend tests and devices by suing, if the automatic requirements did not apply. The act finally placed the burden on state officials to prove that they were *not* discriminating, rather than requiring disfranchised voters to prove that their rights had been violated. This made a basic shift in the workload of the two sides.

Southern political leaders were not slow to challenge this frontal attack on their long-established practices.

Sending in federal registrars

South Carolina v. Katzenbach (1966)

383 U.S. 301, 86 S. Ct. 803, 15 L. Ed. 2d 769

The Voting Rights Act became effective on August 6, 1965, and on August 7 the Attorney General applied its provisions to the states of Alabama, Alaska, Georgia, Louisiana, Mississippi, South Carolina, and Virginia, and to certain counties in North Carolina and Arizona. In November more counties in Arizona, Hawaii, and Idaho were added. Voting tests and devices were suspended in these areas.

Alaska, the Arizona counties, and the Idaho county began procedures to establish in court that their low voting rates were not the result of racial discrimination.

In September, South Carolina filed a complaint directly with the United States Supreme Court asking for a declaration that most of the act's provisions were unconstitutional. The state asked for a quick decision before the June 1966 primary.

On October 30, 1965, Attorney General Katzenbach, following procedures in the act, certified the need to send federal examiners to counties in Alabama, Louisiana, Mississippi, and South Carolina. The Civil Service Commission appointed examiners and sent them down. They immediately began registering people to vote (mainly blacks), while some local whites, also following procedures under the act, immediately began challenging the new registrants in an effort to show they were not truly eligible voters.

South Carolina was supported in its suit by Alabama, Georgia, Louisiana, Mississippi, and Virginia, as friends of the court. Twenty-one states supported the U.S. Attorney General in amicus briefs. The southern states contended that this time Congress had surely overreached its powers and was encroaching on powers expressly reserved to the states. They argued more specifically that the presumption of discrimination was a denial of due process and equal protection to the states because federal agents moved in before there was a chance for court review; this presumption assumed guilt, and so it was a bill of attainder (a legislative finding of guilt) forbidden by the Constitution. They also argued that the assignment of federal registrars violated due process and gave the Attorney General powers reserved to the judicial branch of the government. The states complained that the procedures for challenging new registrants were too speedy and that the requirement that suits under the act had to be filed in the District of Columbia was unconstitutional because it was too far away.

Attorney General Katzenbach responded that the Fifteenth Amendment gave Congress the power to enforce the right to vote "by appropriate legislation." He showed that Congress in recent years had tried to stop racial discrimination in voting without sending in federal registrars, but these efforts had failed to accomplish their purpose. The provisions of the Voting Rights Act were thus the next logical step and well within the concept of "appropriate legislation," he argued.

Do you think a law suspending some state voter qualifications and authorizing federal registrars to take over the functions of state registrars is constitutional? In a conflict between

Crowds of black people register to vote when federal registrars are
sent to Birmingham under the 1965 Voting Rights Act.
Credit: Wide World Photos

the rights of citizens and the sovereignty of a state, does the federal government have authority to step in on behalf of the citizens? If so, what gives the government this authority? Is it a denial of equal protection to enact a law that applies to some states and is of no consequence in others?

The Supreme Court's nearly unanimous decision was announced by Chief Justice Warren (Justice Black dissented in part). The opinion began: "The Voting Rights Act was designed by Congress to banish the blight of racial discrimination in voting, which has infected the electoral process in parts of our country for nearly a century. . . . Two points emerge vividly from the voluminous legislative history of the Act contained in the committee hearings and floor debates. First: Congress felt itself confronted by an insidious and pervasive evil which had been perpetuated in certain parts of our country through unremitting and ingenious defiance of the Constitution. Second: Congress concluded that the unsuccessful remedies which it had prescribed in the past would have to be replaced by sterner and more elaborate measures in order to satisfy the clear commands of the Fifteenth Amendment."

The opinion traced the background of the present act from the Civil War through the Civil Rights Acts of 1957, 1960, and 1964. "Despite the earnest efforts of the Justice Department and of many federal judges, these new laws have done little to cure the problem of voting discrimination. According to estimates by the Attorney General during hearings on the Act, registration of voting-age Negroes in Alabama rose only from 14.2% to 19.4% between 1958 and 1964; in Louisiana it barely inched ahead from 31.7% to 31.8% between 1956 and 1965; and in Mississippi it increased only from 4.4% to 6.4% between 1954 and 1964. In each instance, registration of voting-age whites ran roughly 50 percentage points or more ahead of Negro registration."

The justices also remarked on recent events in the civil rights movement: "During the hearings and debates on the Act, Selma, Alabama, was repeatedly referred to as the preeminent example of the ineffectiveness of existing legislation. In Dallas County, of which Selma is the seat, there were four years of litigation by the Justice Department and two findings by the federal courts of widespread voting discrimination. Yet in those four years, Negro registration rose only from 156 to 383, although there are approximately 15,000 Negroes of voting age in the county. Any possibility that these figures were attributable to political apathy was dispelled by the protest demonstrations in Selma in the early months of 1965."

Finally the Court posed the basic question: "Has Congress exercised its powers under the Fifteenth Amendment in an appropriate manner with relation to the States?

"The ground rules for resolving this question are clear. The language and purpose of the Fifteenth Amendment, the prior decisions construing its several provisions, and the general doctrines of constitutional interpretation, all point to one fundamental principle. As against the reserved powers of the States, Congress may use any rational means to effectuate the constitutional prohibition of racial discrimination in voting."

The justices rejected "South Carolina's argument that Congress may appropriately do no more than to forbid violations of the Fifteenth Amendment in general terms—that the task of fashioning specific remedies or of applying them to particular localities must necessarily be left entirely to the courts. Congress is not circumscribed by any such artificial rules."

Characterizing the 1965 act as "inventive," the Court said, "Congress had found that case-by-case litigation was inadequate to combat widespread and persistent discrimination in voting, because of the inordinate amount of time and energy required to overcome the obstructionist tactics invariably encountered in these lawsuits. After enduring nearly a century of systematic resistance to the Fifteenth Amendment, Congress might well decide to shift the advantage of time and inertia from the perpetrators of the evil to its victims."

The Court then examined the act's specific remedies in terms of the conditions they were designed to correct, and found each to be a reasonable and appropriate measure. "We here hold that the portions of the Voting Rights Act properly before us are a valid means for carrying out the commands of the Fifteenth Amendment. Hopefully, millions of nonwhite Americans will now be able to participate for the first time on an equal basis in the government under which they live. We may finally look forward to the day when truly 'the right of citizens of the United States to vote shall not be denied or abridged by the United States or by any State on account of race, color, or previous condition of servitude.' "

Justice Black agreed with the majority except that he found unconstitutional the provision of the act requiring states to submit any new voter qualifications they might enact to the federal courts or the Attorney General for a ruling that the qualification does not abridge voting rights on account of race.

The Court's decision in this case broke the resistance to the 1965 act. Hundreds of thousands of black people in southern states registered and voted for the first time in their lives. The U.S. Civil Rights Commission, for the first time in its eight-year life, had no recommendations to Congress for new legislation, but rather said that federal voter education and encouragement campaigns would be helpful. By 1968, 200,-000 blacks were registered in Mississippi, 3 million were registered in the South as a whole, and 200 blacks held elective positions in the South.

Meanwhile, in June 1966, the Supreme Court ruled on a northern challenge to the constitutionality of the 1965 Voting Rights Act. A few New York voters contested the section providing that citizens who had completed sixth grade in an American-flag school could vote even if they attended schools in which the predominant language was not English. The section was intended to enfranchise Puerto Rican Americans who had gone to Spanish-speaking schools in Puerto Rico and were then denied the right to vote under New York law unless they demonstrated literacy in English. The Court, in *Katzenbach* v. *Morgan,* held that this provision of the 1965 act was a valid and appropriate measure to enforce the equal protection clause of the Fourteenth Amendment.

Once the Warren Court justices embarked on a historical appraisal of questions of fair representation and voting rights, profound changes were bound to take place. Spurred by active black and white citizens determined to exercise their right of suffrage, the Court moved step by step to the rule that each person's vote must have equal weight and to orders forbidding racial discrimination in registering and voting. From complicated arguments using legalistic language, the Court finally spoke plain English. It held that hereafter one man has one vote, and legislators will represent people, not trees or economic interests. It spelled out the gross denials of voting rights to blacks and looked forward to the day when truly the right of citizens to vote would not be denied or abridged on account of race.

The people were quick to pick up on each new Court

decision and to broaden its application. The deep probing of the political process by which the Nixon-Agnew team was elected to the highest national offices in 1972 leads to even broader concerns about the entire electoral system. Will it purify the system to place sharp limitations on campaign spending? Do we need ethical limitations on the spreading of untrue allegations when no legal sanctions are available, and, if so, how can these be formulated and enforced? How can government and business officials be required to admit they frequently have conflicting interests and loyalties? How can those entering government service be required to give up one set of loyalties in order to perform faithfully their duty to make decisions in the interest of the public as a whole?

CHAPTER 24

Equal Justice

Equal justice has never been achieved in the United States judicial system. This is commonly acknowledged, although it is not mentioned very often. We cannot be seriously criticized for this failure—no nation has ever claimed that it has achieved absolutely equal justice. However, we have had a problem for a longer period and in a greater degree than many other countries. People with color and people without money, as groups, have been treated differently by the judicial system from white people and people with money. Courtroom personnel—from judges and clerks to bailiffs—have usually been from white, middle-class, or stable working-class backgrounds. Defendants in criminal cases have usually been black or brown and unemployed or in low-paying jobs.

Despite these hard-to-face facts, a marked change did occur halfway through the history of our country. Almost 100 years after the Constitution went into effect, the Fourteenth Amendment was adopted, for the first time stating the ideal of equal justice for all. The phrase—equal protection of the laws—had more than superficial meaning. It could not be included in our national goals earlier because equal protection is the ideal in a society that has finally destroyed the most basic type of inequity—that is, chattel slavery.

Until slavery was abolished, equal justice could not be attained in the United States; it could not even be stated as an ideal. In the South, slaveholders knew with almost absolute certainty that they would never be charged with the murder or rape of human beings who could be labeled their slaves. And the virus of unequal treatment of black slaves affected the North as well. When the Supreme Court upheld the constitutionality of the Fugitive Slave Law, free Negroes knew they were no longer secure from slave catchers, even if they had the papers to prove their status.

The due process protections contained in the Fifth Amendment of 1789 (discussed in part II of this book) meant in reality that any person who came within a certain class was entitled to fair procedures throughout his trial, and could appeal his conviction if they were denied to him. But these protections were not provided for free blacks, for black slaves (or for juveniles, women, Indians, or "others"). The long campaign to end the slave system included discussions of the denial of all rights to black Americans—not just rights in the courtroom.

The end of slavery and the adoption of the equal protection clause of the Fourteenth Amendment set Americans on the path of universal equal justice under law for the first time. The New Deal of the 1930s and the establishment in 1964 of legal service programs for the poor, the young, and the elderly, smoothed the path a little.

The cases that follow demonstrate how slowly we have proceeded in the century since the Emancipation Proclamation, but they also demonstrate clearly that progress has been made. The cases in chapter 28 describe our parallel efforts to provide equal protection for the poor.

Among the statutes enacted to enforce the Fourteenth Amendment was the Civil Rights Act of 1875, which prohibited racial discrimination in jury selection and levied a fine on state and federal jury commissioners who violated the law. Nevertheless, southern trial juries and grand juries remained all white. The act, passed just before the Tilden-Hayes compromise, was not enforced by federal officials in the South after the removal of federal troops. Negroes indicted by white grand juries and tried by white petit juries could not look to government lawyers to challenge the composition of these juries. They had to find, and pay, defense lawyers to make such challenges, or forget about them.

In the relatively few cases in which challenges were made and appealed, the Supreme Court consistently held that it was improper to exclude blacks from jury service solely on the basis of race; state statutes were invalid if they achieved this effect by defining prospective jurors as white males or by using other all-white categories. But the Court failed to strike at the root of the problem by ordering jury commissioners to use methods of jury selection that would put a cross-section of the community into the jury box. Instead, when a rare Negro defendant challenged his particular all-white jury, the Court insisted that the defendant had the burden of proving that blacks had been excluded because of their race, and sent the case back for retrial by a properly constituted jury. This, in effect, left the courts (northern as well as southern, federal as well as state) free to pursue an almost exclusively white jury system, except when a black defendant somehow got the money or help to mount a series of appeals.

As we have seen (in chapter 15), the jury system is a key factor in achieving justice in all cases. The white jury system became a key factor in destroying justice and reestablishing white supremacy in the southern states when Reconstruction was ended. Not only did it enable white terrorists to escape indictment or conviction for the criminal acts they perpetrated on blacks, but it also could be used to harass and intimidate freedmen who tried to exercise their rights. Blacks were indicted and convicted of crimes they did not commit. They lost civil suits against white opponents when they should have won. As southern blacks lost the right to register and vote at the end of the nineteenth century, whites who opposed the equal protection clause were elected to office and took tight control of the judicial system.

North and South, the courts presented the same white face to black plaintiffs and defendants. In the North, racism took both open and subtle forms. In southern courts, overt acts of racism were common. Courtroom seating, restrooms in the courthouse, waiting rooms for witnesses, and lunchrooms in the building were often segregated—"whites" here, "colored" over there. Cases on the court docket frequently designated the race of the parties; black witnesses were routinely addressed by their first names by white lawyers and judges, while white witnesses were called Mr., Miss, or Mrs.

All these factors combined to encourage both blacks and whites to feel that the blacks were of a lower class, inferior, not to be believed, of no consequence, and guilty. They also made it impossible for a black lawyer to make an equal impression on a judge, jury, opposing counsel, or even his own client. The black lawyer had to present his client's case within the segregated context of the courthouse where his work could not produce the same result a white lawyer could achieve with equal effort. Coming from the "superior" side of the racial fence, the white lawyer had a clear edge over his black colleague.

Under this system, a higher proportion of Negroes than whites were convicted after trial, and there is evidence that their sentences were harsher for the same acts. They were jailed in inferior, segregated facilities, disciplined by guards who considered them incapable of rehabilitation.

Judges everywhere are expected to protect and perpetuate the existing system; they rise to prominence through that system and many are appointed by the leaders of the group in power. This, and the rule of precedent, make our judicial system slow to change, conservative in nature. Breaks in this pattern occurred after the Revolutionary and Civil Wars, but they were short-lived and, after 1876, skin deep. As the prevailing system returned to its white supremacist pattern, what hope could a black person have for equal justice under law?

Each Supreme Court justice since the Civil War has had many opportunities to think about this question, and to decide whether to hear challenges to juries and how to rule on them.

Sitting a century after these events, the Warren Court had several chances to express its views on this question in cases arising in American courts. It had to evaluate equal treatment of defendants before the law under the equal protection and due process clauses of the Fourteenth Amendment and the statutes passed to enforce these provisions. Three cases raising very different issues concerning the legal process are discussed here. All arose in the South, where the most blatant examples could be expected for historical reasons. But serious denials of equal protection were also documented in cases arising in the North and West (see, for example, *Monroe* v. *Pape,* discussed in chapter 12).

A. Jury Selection

As early as 1880, in *Strauder* v. *West Virginia,* the Supreme Court ruled that a state law restricting grand and petit jury service to white males violated the Fourteenth

Amendment and the 1875 Civil Rights Act. It reversed the conviction of a black defendant and held that his motion to remove his case from state court to federal court should have been granted.

The same day, however, the Court ruled in *Virginia* v. *Rives,* that actions by a state *jury commissioner* to exclude Negroes from jury service were not the same as state *laws.* A defendant could not remove his case to federal court on the basis of the jury commissioner's discrimination; he had to prove this discrimination to the state courts. If he failed at trial and on all state appeals, he could then raise the issue in federal court. The Supreme Court also rejected the idea that blacks were entitled to have blacks on their juries; they were entitled only to have blacks *not excluded* from the *panels* of prospective jurors. This was a critical difference, since a jury commissioner could comply with a law and place names of a few blacks on a jury panel, knowing the prosecutor would use peremptory challenges against all blacks (without having to state his reasons), and thus end up with an all-white jury again.

Over the years, the Supreme Court held to these rulings in a long line of cases. The constant flow of litigation raising the issue of racial discrimination in jury selection bears witness to the fact that blacks continued to be excluded from jury service.

In 1954, a Mexican-American defendant asked the Supreme Court to rule that the Texas practice of excluding Chicanos from service as jury commissioners and grand and petit jurors deprived him of equal protection of the laws. In *Hernandez* v. *Texas,* Chief Justice Warren wrote for a unanimous Court, "The exclusion of otherwise eligible persons from jury service solely because of their ancestry or national origin is discrimination prohibited by the Fourteenth

Amendment." The Court was careful to say, however, that it did not accept the "contention that the Fourteenth Amendment requires proportional representation of all the component ethnic groups of the community on every jury."

Exclusion of blacks from the jury

Reece v. *Georgia* (1955)
350 U.S. 85, 76 S. Ct. 167, 100 L. Ed. 77

Amos Reece, a black man of little education, was arrested on October 20, 1953, in Cobb County, Georgia, for the rape of a white woman. He was taken to the county jail and held there. The county grand jury had adjourned the day before, but it was reconvened two days later. Although Reece's arrest was not listed on the reconvening order, the prosecutor presented the case against him, and the grand jury returned an indictment against Reece on October 23.

The next day, two local attorneys were appointed to represent the defendant, who was indigent. Using their courage as well as their legal skill, they immediately started to work on a problem of unfairness in the procedure by which their client had been charged. On October 30, the lawyers moved to quash (wipe out) the indictment on the ground that Negroes had been systematically excluded from serving on the grand jury. To indict a person by means of a grand jury composed in a racially discriminatory manner denied him his Fourteenth Amendment right to equal protection of the law.

In support of their motion to quash, defense counsel showed that there were 55,606 whites and 6,224 blacks in Cobb County, according to the last census. Taking only male citizens twenty-one or older, there were 16,201 whites and 1,710 blacks. By either set of figures, blacks constituted about

10 percent. But of the 534 people on the grand jury list only 6 were Negro—slightly more than 1 percent. And of the six, one was not a county resident, two were over eighty years old and infirm, and the last three were sixty-two years old. Although each of the five residents had lived in the county for thirty years or more, none had ever *served* on a grand jury or known of any other Negro who had served on a grand jury there.

The prosecuting attorney answered that Reece's complaints were too late: objections to the composition of a grand jury had to be made before the grand jury returned an indictment. He cited the 1882 Georgia case that had established this rule, and pointed out that it had been followed consistently ever since. The judge agreed and overruled the motion to quash.

At this point, lawyers in serious felony cases turn their attention to preparing their defense on the facts. Since rape was a capital offense in Georgia, the problems faced by the lawyers were similar to those faced by the lawyers for Dr. Sam Sheppard, discussed in chapter 15. But the fee to be paid the lawyers in this case was set by the court, not paid by the defendant, and it would never cover the cost of a full investigation of the facts, discovery of the prosecution evidence (to the extent discovery was permitted in Georgia at this time), or other pretrial work. It would never cover the number of lawyer hours required to give effective representation to the client in such a case.

In any event, Reece's lawyers did not find a way to stay (postpone) the proceedings, and Amos Reece was tried, convicted, and sentenced to the electric chair, all in the same day. On appeal, the Georgia Supreme Court upheld the judge's ruling on the grand jury challenge, but reversed the case on another ground and sent Reece back for retrial.

Reece's lawyers lost no time, and before the second trial began they filed proceedings to challenge the racial composition of the jury commission that selected the grand jurors, the grand jury that had indicted him, and the trial jury about to be chosen to try him. The prosecution demurred: it did not deny that blacks were not fairly represented on these bodies but contended that this was not a legally acceptable ground for throwing out the indictment. The judge agreed.

Again the defense lawyers needed time to prepare for trial, but again Reece was promptly tried, convicted, and sentenced to death. This time the judgment was affirmed by the Georgia Supreme Court, and Reece asked for review by the United States Supreme Court.

Do you think Reece could have challenged the composition of the grand jury before he was indicted the first time, as Georgia law required? Did Reece's lawyers present enough evidence to prove that blacks were systematically excluded from the grand jury? Do you think a grand jury that was 10 percent black would have examined the prosecutor's evidence in the same light as the all-white grand juries and reached the same conclusions? Why or why not?

Justice Clark, writing for a unanimous Supreme Court, announced: "This Court over the past 50 years has adhered to the view that valid grand jury selection is a constitutionally protected right. The indictment of a defendant by a grand jury from which members of his race have been systematically excluded is a denial of his right to equal protection of the laws. . . . Where no opportunity to challenge the grand jury selection has been afforded a defendant, his right may be asserted by [filing certain motions] . . . before arraignment. . . . Of course, if such a motion is controverted it must be supported by evidence," said the Court.

"We mention these principles since the State contests the merits of Reece's claim of systematic exclusion." Justice Clark then described the facts asserted by Reece's lawyers about the number of black grand jurors who had served in the past eighteen years, and he noted that the prosecution had presented no evidence to contradict these assertions. "This evidence, without more, is sufficient to make a strong showing of systematic exclusion. The sizeable Negro population in the county, the fact that all-white juries had been serving for as long as witnesses could remember, and the selection on the jury list of a relatively few Negroes who would probably be disqualified for actual jury service all point to a discrimination 'ingenious or ingenuous'. . . ."

Then the Court took a new position, holding that "this evidence placed the burden on the State to refute it, and mere assertions of public officials that there has not been discrimination will not suffice."

The justices found that Reece's "motion stated and his evidence supported a prima facie constitutional claim," but they chose to decide the case on another issue: the Georgia rule requiring that objections to the grand jury be made before indictment.

"The right to object to a grand jury presupposes an opportunity to exercise that right," said the Court, and it examined whether Reece had had such an opportunity. "He was indicted by a grand jury that was impaneled and sworn eight days before his arrest. It adjourned the day before his arrest and was reconvened two days later by an order which did not list him as one against whom a case would be presented. . . . We need not decide whether, with the assistance of counsel, he would have had an opportunity to raise his objection during the two days he was in jail before indictment. But it is utterly unrealistic to say that he had such opportunity when counsel was not provided for him until the day after he was indicted." The Court held that this sequence of events denied Reece due process of law, and it reversed his conviction.

In the years that followed, the Court again heard numerous cases challenging grand and petit juries on the basis of racial exclusion. In *Eubanks* v. *Louisiana,* in 1958, it reversed a murder conviction on the ground that the grand jurors had been selected under a system allowing the judges such wide discretion that systematic exclusion of Negroes had resulted. In 1964, *Arnold* v. *North Carolina* was reversed because only one Negro had served on a grand jury in twenty-four years, although the population was 28 percent black; this showed on its face that equal protection had been denied, the Court said.

A woman accused of murdering her husband tried to use the same argument as southern Negroes, in *Hoyt* v. *Florida,* in 1961. She claimed that a state law excluding women from jury service unless they volunteered to serve resulted in systematic and arbitrary exclusion of a class of citizens and denied her equal protection of the law. The Court disagreed, finding that there was no intent to discriminate against women and that excusing women on the basis of their social role and the state's general welfare was not prohibited by the Constitution.

Methods of jury selection were more clearly discriminatory in the South than in the North or West, but similar results were seen by lawyers in all sections: all-white juries were the rule in state and federal courts, regardless of the number or percentage of nonwhites in the population. In the

North and West, this result was often achieved by drawing up jury lists solely from voter lists (knowing that fewer blacks and poor people register to vote than do whites and the well-to-do), or by using literacy tests that gave a passing grade only to people who conformed to middle-class standards. In the South, jurors were often selected from the county tax rolls, since few blacks owned property.

Another simple tactic was for prosecutors to use peremptory challenges against every minority group member called to serve on the jury. Peremptory challenges do not require the statement of a reason, and it was usually possible to get rid of the few minority group members on the jury panel without running out of peremptory challenges. This practice was challenged in *Swain* v. *Alabama,* in 1965, but the majority of the Supreme Court said it did not deny equal protection. (Justices Goldberg and Douglas and Chief Justice Warren dissented.)

In 1968, Congress passed the Jury Selection and Service Act requiring all federal courts to review their systems of jury selection to insure greater fairness in selection, and to provide methods for challenging unfairness.

While juries in the 1950s frequently convicted the defendants in civil liberties cases (see the cases discussed in part I), in the late 1960s and 1970s juries in political and racial cases frequently refused to convict, when the defense attorneys had done a careful job in jury selection. Lawyers began to devote greater attention to questioning prospective jurors in order to take off the jury those with deep prejudices against the groups to which the defendants belonged. Such challenges for cause can be made whenever bias is shown; they are unlimited. (See the *Witherspoon* case, discussed in chapter 15.)

Adoption of the Twenty-sixth Amendment, giving

eighteen-to-twenty-one-year-olds the vote, also gave them the right to sit on juries, and is resulting in further changes in the composition of juries.

B. Court Etiquette

Racial segregation was common in southern courthouses, and some lawyers and clients perpetually battled against it. A black lawyer in Norfolk, Virginia, filed suits against the judges demanding that court personnel, bathrooms, seating arrangements, and all other court facilities and procedures be desegregated. "These desegregation suits didn't change anything but my reputation," he recalls, in *The Relevant Lawyers* (1972). From then on, "I was known as a trouble-maker."

Other lawyers on occasion met with more success, if they were willing to fight the issues all the way to the United States Supreme Court. In 1963, the Court made a key decision that a Virginia black man, Ford T. Johnson, Jr., could not be convicted of contempt of court for sitting in the white spectator section of the traffic court and refusing to move to the Negro section when the judge ordered him to do so. "State-compelled segregation in a court of justice is a manifest violation of the State's duty to deny no one the equal protection of its laws," said the justices unanimously in *Johnson* v. *Virginia.*

"My name is Miss Hamilton"
Hamilton v. *Alabama* (1964)
376 U.S. 650, 84 S. Ct. 982, 11 L. Ed. 2d 979

Mary Hamilton, a twenty-eight-year-old black field secretary for the Congress of Racial Equality (CORE), participated in a demonstration in Gadsden, Alabama, in 1963. White police officers arrested her, along with fellow demonstrators. Believing their arrests to be unlawful, the group petitioned the Circuit Court of Etowah County for release on a writ of habeas corpus (see chapter 18). The hearing on the petition was held on June 25, before Judge Cunningham, a white judge, assisted by white court clerks and bailiffs.

Black attorneys Charles Conley and Norman Amaker represented the petitioners and white Solicitor Rayburn spoke for the state. Mr. Rayburn followed the southern establishment practice of addressing each black witness by his or her first name, despite objections from the opposing counsel.

When Mary Hamilton completed her direct testimony, Solicitor Rayburn began his cross-examination by asking, "What is your name, please?"

"Miss Mary Hamilton."

"Mary, . . . who were you arrested by?"

"My name is Miss Hamilton. Please address me correctly," she said.

"Who were you arrested by, Mary?" the solicitor asked again, deliberately.

"I will not answer a question—" she began, and Attorney Amaker interjected, "The witness's name is Miss Hamilton."

"—your question until I am addressed correctly," she finished.

"Answer the question," Judge Cunningham ordered.

Miss Hamilton would not be intimidated. "I will not answer them unless I am addressed correctly."

"You are in contempt of court," ruled the judge.

"Your Honor—your Honor—" Attorney Conley began, but the judge paid no attention.

"You are in contempt of this court," he went on, "and you are sentenced to five days in jail and a fifty-dollar fine."

Miss Mary Hamilton of the Congress of Racial Equality.
Credit: Wide World Photos

Miss Hamilton was taken to jail then and there, and served the five days. Since she did not intend to pay the fine, and therefore would be subject to another twenty days in jail, she was allowed out on bond to appeal the contempt conviction.

On July 25, she petitioned the Alabama Supreme Court to review the contempt citation on two grounds. Her lawyers contended that the solicitor's manner of addressing black witnesses violated the equal protection clause of the Fourteenth Amendment. Finding no cases on this point, they relied on logic, history, and etiquette. They rejected the state's reliance on Emily Post and Amy Vanderbilt because their books did not discuss the use of first names in a racial situation. They also reminded the court that Miss Hamilton's contempt conviction violated the due process clause because she was summarily sentenced without even being given a trial—an opportunity to present a defense to the charge. (Remember the Red Queen in *Alice in Wonderland*—"sentence first, trial afterward"?)

The Alabama Supreme Court found, however, that "the question was a lawful one and the witness invoked no valid legal exemption to support her refusal to answer it. The record conclusively shows that petitioner's name is Mary Hamilton, not Miss Mary Hamilton. Many witnesses are addressed by various titles, but one's own name is an acceptable appellation at law. . . . In the cross-examination of witnesses, a wide latitude is allowed resting in the sound discretion of the trial court and unless the discretion is grossly abused, the ruling of the court will not be overturned. . . . We hold that the trial court did not abuse its discretion and the record supports the summary punishment inflicted."

The NAACP Legal Defense and Educational Fund then took the case up to the United States Supreme Court for review. The defense lawyers relied on long-standing principles governing the conduct of prosecuting attorneys: as quasi-judicial officers of the court they are under a duty not to prejudice a party's case through overzealous prosecution or to detract from the impartiality of courtroom atmosphere. The defense presented historical and sociological proof that the forms of address used by Solicitor Rayburn were a distinct part of a "racial caste system" that deprived black citizens of equal protection of the laws. They also quoted from novels by Richard Wright, James Baldwin, and Lillian Smith. The attorneys for Alabama contended that the case presented no federal question for review, that the Alabama Supreme Court's decision was clearly correct, and that the United States Supreme Court should refrain from interfering in a valid state decision.

Do you think it really makes any difference whether a person is given a courtesy title? Would the Alabama Supreme Court have reached the same decision if one of the witnesses or attorneys had addressed the *judge* by his first name? Was Miss Hamilton raising a frivolous question? Should she have given up her attack on Solicitor Rayburn's court etiquette instead of bothering the U.S. Supreme Court with her complaint? Can the manner of addressing a witness or a defendant influence the outcome of a trial?

The United States Supreme Court granted review and handed down a summary decision the same day, without even receiving briefs on the merits or hearing oral argument on the case, a procedure followed in very few cases. Five justices joined in an order reversing Miss Hamilton's contempt citation, citing as authority the Court's 1963 decision in *Johnson* v. *Virginia,* desegregating courtroom seating. This implied that the basis of the decision was the equal protection clause.

Justice Black reached the same result but on due process grounds: that Miss Hamilton had been given no notice of the reasons for the contempt charge or chance to defend against it, and that a conviction without evidence to support it violates due process.

Justices Clark, Harlan, and White voted against reviewing the case, without commenting on the merits of the issue.

This short memorandum decision gave civil rights lawyers and activists the weapon they needed to insist that black witnesses be addressed with the same respect accorded to whites. The change did not come automatically or quickly, but the determined efforts of movement people succeeded in eradicating this particular vestige of slavery from almost all United States courtrooms, although racist comments are heard in the halls. More sophisticated putdowns of minority group people continue to flourish in most courtrooms, and more sophisticated arguments are being made against them.

C. Criminal Charges for Racist Activities

Murder of civil rights workers

United States v. *Price* (1966)
383 U.S. 787, 86 S. Ct. 1152, 16 L. Ed. 2d 267

For decades many people in other parts of the country looked down on the South as a backward area full of racist redneck farmers and downtrodden Negroes. Few northerners thought of vacationing in the deep South, although many enjoyed the Mardi Gras in New Orleans and the beautiful Florida winters.

After the *Brown* desegregation decision in 1954, and starting with the Montgomery bus boycott in 1955 (see chapter 25), national attention was slowly directed toward the growing struggle in the South for civil rights. In the early 1960s, newspapers ran headline stories on the latest freedom rides, lunchroom sit-ins, and black student demands. For the first time since the end of Reconstruction, northerners began to look to the South for inspiration in the human rights field and to think seriously about participating in the southern civil rights movement. In 1963, some northern students and a few older activists went South to assist the exciting, innovative civil rights movement. Michael and Rita Schwerner went down from New York with other white and black students and graduates from ghettos and colleges. Michael came from a progressive Jewish family that had always participated in local struggles for civil liberties. He and his wife soon were assisting in the establishment of a Negro community center in Meridian, Mississippi. He became well-known in the area as a white, northern, Jewish, bearded worker for Negro rights. Segregationists apparently referred to him as "Goatee."

By 1964, the Council of Federated Organizations was formed in Mississippi to unite many black organizations and individuals and some stalwart whites. COFO sent out a call for people to come and help register Negro voters in Mississippi, since it seemed possible to make profound changes in the governance of the state only when massive numbers of black voters could go to the polls without fear. That summer almost a thousand civil rights workers went to Mississippi, Georgia, Alabama, and other states under the banners of the Student Nonviolent Coordinating Committee (SNCC), Martin Luther King's Southern Christian Leadership Conference (SCLC), CORE, the NAACP, and other groups.

Every volunteer was repeatedly told that he could be killed in Mississippi that summer. Others had been killed, over the years and recently. "After all," the volunteers were warned, "every section of the country resents 'outsiders' coming in to tell the local people what they should and should not do. And the South remembers John Brown, the Northern white man who thought he had the answers in 1859." All of these spiritual descendants—like Brown opposed to black oppression—faced the hatred he had faced, even though they, unlike him, were specifically committed to nonviolent action.

By summer, white terrorists, often Knights of the Ku Klux Klan, had burned and bombed numerous Mississippi churches used as meeting places of COFO groups. On June 16, 1964, the Mount Zion Church in Neshoba County was burned to the ground, and Michael Schwerner went out to investigate. Andrew Goodman, a twenty-year-old white New York student, who had arrived in Mississippi the day before, and James Chaney, a twenty-one-year-old black plasterer from Meridian, went along. Schwerner apparently urged Goodman and Chaney not to come; he was aware of the community hostility against himself and did not want to inflict it on them. But Chaney felt that his friendships among the Mount Zion congregation would be valuable in the investigation, and Goodman was reluctant to leave Schwerner's side.

The three drove off toward the church in the afternoon on June 21. They were stopped near Philadelphia, Mississippi, on a speeding charge by Deputy Sheriff Cecil Price. He held them in the Philadelphia jail for over six hours, and finally released them around 10:30 P.M., after Chaney posted a $20 bond. Since it was too late to do any investigating that day, the three drove back toward Meridian.

Fearing a mishap, CORE workers had called the FBI to investigate soon after the men were arrested for speeding. When they did not return that night, more calls were made. The next day the FBI began its inquiry. Two days later the station wagon in which the young men had been riding was found burned and abandoned outside Philadelphia. Then days passed with no further news. The families and friends of the three feared they would never be found alive.

A New York attorney for the Schwerner family appealed directly to President Johnson to do something, and public clamor about the disappearance was heard from coast to coast. Johnson ordered four hundred sailors from the Meridian Naval Air Station to help in the search.

On August 4, 1964, FBI agents, apparently acting on a tip, uncovered the bodies of the three under an earth dam that had recently been built on a farm near Philadelphia. They had all been shot.

The FBI pursued its investigation, while civil rights workers demanded arrests. Mississippi Governor Paul Johnson felt called upon to comment, "It is an odd thing that so much hell is being raised over three people missing in Mississippi when ten thousand are missing in New York."

In September, a federal grand jury was convened in Biloxi to hear evidence on violations of federal civil rights statutes in this and other cases. (They could not investigate the murders as such because murder is not a federal crime.) The grand jury voted in October not to indict anyone in the Schwerner-Chaney-Goodman murders (reportedly by a one-vote margin), for lack of evidence.

In November, the FBI secured an eyewitness statement from Horace Doyle Barnette, formerly of Meridian, who had moved to Louisiana a few days after the bodies were discovered.

August 4, 1964: Deputy Sheriff Cecil Price (right) unloads the body of one of the three civil rights workers shot in Mississippi; later he was indicted for the murders (with eighteen others).
Credit: Wide World Photos

On December 4, FBI agents arrested nineteen men in and around Philadelphia and Meridian, including Neshoba County Sheriff Lawrence Rainey, Deputy Sheriff Price, a Philadelphia policeman, a Baptist minister, truckdrivers, salesmen, gas station attendants, and small businessmen, most of them reported to be Ku Klux Klan members. They were charged with violating the 1870 Civil Rights Act provision that made it a crime to "conspire to injure, oppress, threaten or intimidate any citizen in the free exercise or enjoyment of any right or privilege secured to him by the Constitution." The government also said the defendants had acted "under color of law" to deprive the three young men of life and liberty without due process of law, in violation of the Fourteenth Amendment. The federal charges carried a maximum penalty of ten years in prison and/or $5,000 fine. (A murder conviction could carry a death penalty or life imprisonment under Mississippi law.) Two other men were charged with concealing a felony.

The federal government usually waits until a state prosecution for murder has been completed before pressing federal charges. In this instance, state officials took no action. Neshoba Circuit Judge Barnett instructed the county grand jury not to consider state indictments until the Justice Department turned over all its evidence to the local district attorney. The Justice Department agreed to do this only after the trial on the federal charges was over, so as not to reveal the government's entire case to local officials.

The twenty-one law officers and citizens were brought before United States Commissioner Esther Carter for arraignment on December 10. To the consternation of the U.S. attorney, Miss Carter excluded the testimony of an FBI agent as to Barnette's confession, ruling it hearsay, and dismissed the charges against the defendants. The U.S. attorney's arguments, quoting recent Supreme Court holdings to the contrary, did not impress Commissioner Carter.

The government asked for immediate reconvening of the federal grand jury. Meanwhile, it secured a second confession to bolster its case, this one from James Jordan.

On January 15, 1965, the federal grand jury indicted eighteen men on the charges; two previously charged were not now on the list, and one not previously charged had been added—Sam Bowers, alleged to be the Imperial Wizard of the Mississippi White Knights of the Ku Klux Klan.

The government contended that Bowers and the other defendants had developed a plan at a KKK meeting to kill Schwerner; that they had burned the Mount Zion Church to lure him to Neshoba County; that he, Goodman, and Chaney were arrested and detained by Price solely to allow time for the execution group to gather; that after the three were released by Price, he, Rainey, and the Philadelphia patrolman followed and intercepted them again; that the officers turned the civil rights workers over to the lynch group and accompanied them to a lonely country road; and that the group then shot the three, took them to the dam site, and buried them.

The case came before Judge Harold Cox, despite protests from liberal congressmen that Cox's record as a federal judge showed he would not be impartial because he was a confirmed segregationist. On February 25, Judge Cox dismissed the felony charge against all but the three law enforcement officers, saying the others had not acted "under color of law." He noted that murder was not a federal offense unless committed on federal property, and said the government could not use a civil rights statute to prosecute for murder. The United States attorneys appealed these rulings to the U.S. Supreme Court.

If the state refuses to prosecute citizens for violations of state law, do you think it is proper for the federal government to find a way to prosecute them? Can whites be protected by a constitutional provision written to protect blacks? Was killing, under these circumstances, a deprivation of the victims' rights under the federal Constitution? If so, what constitutional rights did it abridge? Were all the defendants acting "under color of law" if only some of them were government officials?

Justice Fortas delivered the Supreme Court's unanimous opinion in March 1966. He dealt with Judge Cox's ruling that the 1870 civil rights statute could not be applied to a murder case, by examining the history of passage of that law. "The Civil War had ended in April 1865. Relations between Negroes and whites were increasingly turbulent. Congress had taken control of the entire governmental process in former Confederate States. . . . For a few years 'radical' Republicans dominated the governments of the Southern States and Negroes played a substantial political role. But countermeasures were swift and violent. The Ku Klux Klan was organized by southern whites in 1866 and a similar organization appeared with the romantic title of the Knights of the White Camellia. In 1868 a wave of murders and assaults was launched including assassinations designed to keep Negroes from the polls. . . . Within the Congress pressures mounted in the period between the end of the war and 1870 for drastic measures."

As soon as ratification of the Thirteenth, Fourteenth, and Fifteenth Amendments was completed, Congress enacted the statute relied on in this case. In that setting, the Court found it "hardly conceivable" that Congress did not intend the statute to apply to Fourteenth Amendment rights. "We are here concerned with allegations which squarely and indisputably involve state action in direct violation of the mandate of the Fourteenth Amendment—that no State shall deprive any person of life or liberty without due process of law."

The Court held that "private persons, jointly engaged with state officials in the prohibited action, are acting 'under color' of law for purposes of the statute. To act 'under color' of law does not require that the accused be an officer of the State. It is enough that he is a willful participant in joint activity with the State or its agents.

"In the present case, according to the indictment, the brutal joint adventure was made possible by state detention and calculated release of the prisoners by an officer of the State. This action, clearly attributable to the State, was part of the monstrous design described by the indictment. State officers participated in every phase of the alleged venture: the release from jail, the interception, assault and murder. It was a joint activity, from start to finish. Those who took advantage of participation by state officers in accomplishment of the foul purpose alleged must suffer the consequences of that participation. In effect, if the allegations are true, they were participants in official lawlessness, acting in willful concert with state officers and hence under color of law."

The Court ruled that it was error to dismiss the indictments, and sent the case back for trial.

The decision is considered a landmark, not for announcing new law, but for reiterating firmly that the old law meant what it said and would be enforced from now on. The decision was unanimous, signaling no chance of a change of heart in the foreseeable future. (The Court emphasized the historic basis for the decision by publishing long excerpts from 1870 speeches by John Pool of North Carolina, a white senator urging Congress to pass the civil rights statute to protect all blacks, and, prophetically, all whites who supported the rights of blacks.)

The same day, the Court handed down its decision in *United States* v. *Guest,* a Georgia case arising under the same 1870 statute. Six white men were charged with conspiring to deprive black citizens of the exercise of rights, including the right to travel interstate without discrimination or harassment. One specific act behind the indictment was the murder of Lemuel Penn, a Negro Army reserve officer, killed while traveling at night on a highway. In this instance, two of the federal defendants had been tried for murder in a Georgia state court and acquitted.

The *Price* case involved rights under the due process clause; the *Guest* case involved rights under the equal protection clause, but the Court made clear that the federal statute covered both, as its language provided.

On September 27, 1966, the *Price* case was again before Judge Cox, and again he dismissed the complaints, this time on the basis of a recent victory for civil rights. The *Rabinowitz* case concerned a young white college student prosecuted for perjury before a grand jury while doing civil rights work in Georgia. The federal Fifth Circuit Court of Appeals ruled that Miss Rabinowitz had a right to have blacks on the grand jury that indicted her. Since the grand jury had not included a fair cross section of the citizens of the community, the court had dismissed the charges against her. Judge Cox now ruled in the *Price* case that the Mississippi federal grand jury had been improperly selected according to the *Rabinowitz* test. "The *Rabinowitz* case is not one I could subscribe to," he said, "but it is the law of the Fifth Circuit."

Before a new, properly selected, grand jury could be called, one side effect of this case began to be felt: the Neshoba County superintendent of schools gave an ultimatum to a small group of community leaders. He told them to stop the Klan from harassing the few Negro students admitted to the public schools under court order, and from threatening him personally, or he would leave town at once. In December, ninety-five leaders swore to put an end to abuse at the school.

In February 1967, a properly selected grand jury was called and returned nineteen indictments for the civil rights murders. Defendant Jordan was severed from the case because he was now living in Florida and would stand trial there.

The eighteen remaining defendants were scheduled to go on trial early in June 1967, but on May 26 Judge Cox postponed the trial because the list of prospective jurors had been released to the defense attorneys ten days before trial, although he had instructed court personnel not to release the list to either side until three days before trial. A whole new list of 250 perspective jurors was drawn up.

Trial of the eighteen finally began on October 9, 1967, more than three years after the murders had occurred. In a community with a large black population, the jury nonetheless wound up all white. The seven women and five men heard about 160 witnesses in nine days of testimony. Defense lawyers made much of the fact that the government's witnesses were mainly paid informers, while they produced numerous alibi and character witnesses on behalf of their clients. The defendants generally expected acquittals, and the U.S. attorney reportedly thought he could get two or three convictions at most.

When the jury did not return quickly with a verdict, some of the defendants began to get edgy. After two days of deliberations, the jury brought in its decisions. It found seven guilty, eight not guilty, and was hopelessly deadlocked as to three. This was the first time a white jury had convicted white men in a civil rights slaying in Mississippi. Deputy Sheriff Price and Imperial Wizard Bowers were among those convicted. Sheriff Rainey was acquitted; he moved to Kentucky.

The judge sentenced Bowers and one other defendant to the maximum ten years; Price and another man to six years; and the remaining three defendants to three years. James Jordan pleaded guilty to the charges in a Florida court and was sentenced to four years in prison.

The state never prosecuted anyone for the three murders.

The Mississippi COFO project in the summer of 1964 had conducted forty-seven Freedom Schools for 2,500 students. Some 750 students, teachers, lawyers, and ministers had come into the state to participate in COFO projects. They had not succeeded in registering many Mississippi Negroes to vote, but they had helped to organize and gain support for the Mississippi Freedom Democratic Party (see chapter 23). In addition to the Schwerner-Chaney-Goodman murders, 4 other COFO workers had been shot and wounded, 52 were beaten or injured in other ways, and 250 were arrested on various charges. But in retrospect it appears that their efforts to influence the thinking of black and white citizens of the state were successful.

In September 1968, the Neshoba County school superintendent shot himself, in despair at the local atmosphere. The white community was apparently deeply shocked by his suicide. In 1969, the United States Supreme Court ordered Philadelphia and thirty other Mississippi school districts to abolish their dual school systems by the end of that semester. Under a new superintendent, 900 white and 500 black students began attending desegregated classes in February

1970 with little commotion. The city's population spurted in the 1960s and new plants opened up, hiring many black workers. A Klan meeting in 1970 drew only three men—and a government source reported that two of the three were secret agents for the FBI.

This report of progress toward ending violence and a reign of terror in Neshoba County argues for strict enforcement of antiracist laws by prosecutors and grand juries, and for public trials of the alleged criminals, regardless of their status in the community.

More subtle forms of discrimination in the judicial process remain to be dealt with in the spirit of the opinions discussed in this chapter. In the criminal courts, observers indicate their belief that a smaller proportion of blacks than whites are released on bail following arrest, that a smaller proportion are acquitted, and that those convicted receive harsher sentences than whites for similar offenses. Extensive studies will be necessary to prove or disprove these observations. In civil cases, juries tend to award lower verdicts to blacks than to whites when they sue for injuries in accidents. The 1970s are already bringing into court many challenges by poor people and by prison inmates alleging practices that deny equal protection in violation of state and federal law (see chapter 28).

The Warren Court only began the herculean task of cleaning this Augean stable.

CHAPTER 25

Equality in Public Accommodations

Jim Crow seemed to be the natural and proper way of life to most southern whites (although the violence in novels by southern writers suggested that a society based on racial segregation was much more tense and complex than appeared on the surface).

To blacks, Jim Crow living was a constant insult and harassment. To be told daily that you must not use the same drinking fountains, schoolrooms, library chairs, bus seats, courtroom seats, taxis, lunch counters, train cars, bathrooms, and hospitals as white people—that's hard to take, especially when the facilities provided for you are inferior and neglected. It is even worse to be excluded completely from restaurants, hotels and motels, apartments and houses, parks, swimming pools, golf courses, law schools, and medical schools, when none are provided for you. Blacks suffered from racism to the point where race became the key question in life. All political, legal, economic, medical, educational, recreational, religious, and survival questions turned on race. And the answer was always: "If you're black, get back, get back, get back."

Rosa Parks was a well-known seamstress and a respected member of the black community in Montgomery, Alabama. In December 1955 she got on a bus on the way home from work and found that all the seats in the back were taken. She took a seat near the front. The bus driver told her to move to the back of the bus. Mrs. Parks was awfully tired—tired from her work and tired of the treatment she had lived with all her life. She acted with the sure instinct of one who had studied all her life how to destroy Jim Crow and survive. She refused to move.

She was arrested for violating the city bus policy requiring segregated seating, but unlike earlier desegregationists (mostly male) she was not physically attacked by her jailers or a white crowd. She was convicted in police court, and fined ten dollars plus costs. On appeal, the circuit court affirmed her conviction.

Mrs. Parks had lost her case, but the story of what she had done spread like wildfire through the well-organized black community of Montgomery. Several black ministers, a leader of the Sleeping Car Porters Union, and a lot of other people asked each other, "If Rosa Parks can take her stand now, why can't we?" The Montgomery bus boycott was born. People walked to work, bicycled, organized car pools. Young Reverend Martin Luther King, Jr., agreed to serve as communications director for the boycott.

The city fought back hard, using its police power to break the boycott, arresting blacks on charges that their car pools were illegal transportation systems, arresting ninety-three boycott leaders on charges of conspiracy to hinder business. But the power of a year-long nonviolent boycott overcame; Montgomery Negroes taught the bus company to treat all customers the same or go out of business, and in 1956 the Supreme Court, in *Gayle* v. *Browder,* affirmed a lower court decision that segregated seating in city buses was illegal.

Thanks to national coverage, Montgomery Negroes also taught their brothers and sisters all over the country that Jim

December 21, 1956: Ralph D. Abernathy, Martin Luther King, Jr.,
and other Montgomery citizens finally sit at the front of the bus they
had boycotted so long.
Credit: Wide World Photos

Crow could be defeated nonviolently. Mrs. Parks's pebble had caused its first ripple; much wider waves were to come.

February 1 had been proclaimed Freedom Day by Abraham Lincoln in 1865. It was an ironic coincidence that that was the day in 1960 when four black freshmen at North Carolina Agricultural and Technical College in Greensboro staged the first sit-in. They had been talking and talking about segregation in nightly bull sessions. Finally one of them announced he was going to "boycott" Woolworth's the next day. The others went along, partly to avoid being called chicken. They walked into the store, sat down at the "whites only" lunch counter, and ordered coffee. The manager said he couldn't serve them. Like Rosa Parks, they just sat there.

It was an idea whose time had come. People sat in everywhere in the South, at lunch counters, parks, swimming pools, churches, led by students whose enthusiasm and dedication often swept the respectable leaders of the black community along before they quite knew what was happening to them. When potential sit-ins were halted at the door, the demonstrators picketed and marched to the seats of power in the towns (see *Edwards* v. *South Carolina,* discussed in chapter 2). In the North and West, progressive supporters of all races boycotted and picketed their local outlets of the chain stores and businesses that were refusing service to Negroes in the South.

Hundreds of students who sat in were arrested—charged with trespass, disturbing the peace, juvenile delinquency, refusal to obey an officer, inciting to riot, a variety of offenses under local ordinances. Almost all were convicted; many went to jail; some appealed and lost; a few kept appealing till they won or could appeal no higher.

Bruce Boynton, a black law student at Howard University

in Washington, D.C., took a Trailways bus from Washington to Montgomery, Alabama, at 8:00 one evening. When the bus made a stop at Richmond, Virginia, at about 10:30, he went into the terminal to get a sandwich and something to drink. The counter had a white section and a colored section. Boynton sat in the white section and refused to move when asked, telling the waitress he was an interstate traveler and had a right to be served without discrimination. He was arrested and convicted; he appealed all the way to the United States Supreme Court, which ruled in December 1960, in *Boynton* v. *Virginia*, that Boynton's statement of his rights was correct. The restaurant was part of the Trailways system supplying service to interstate commerce; the Interstate Commerce Act prohibited "undue or unreasonable" treatment of customers; and segregated eating facilities violated this prohibition.

This decision sparked an idea among activists in the Congress of Racial Equality (CORE). They put together the segregated seating in buses, the segregated lunch counters, the sit-in arrests and convictions, and the *Boynton* decision, and came up with the Freedom Rides.

The first seven Freedom Riders started out from Atlanta to Birmingham in May 1961. The bus they took was attacked, bombed, and burned outside of Anniston, Alabama, by segregationists. No one was killed, but twelve of the seventeen passengers were injured.

The battle was joined. From North, South, East, and West, blacks and whites came to go on Freedom Rides. In Alabama, Louisiana, Mississippi, crowds of hostile whites formed, waited, watched, and sometimes attacked. When the buses arrived at a terminal, the Riders would go in to desegregate the restaurant. Sometimes they were served at the "whites

**End of the run for the first Freedom Ride bus, bombed by segrega-
tionists at Anniston, Alabama, May 15, 1961.**
Credit: Wide World Photos

only" counters, sometimes they were arrested for sitting in, sometimes they were beaten by angry white mobs while police watched motionless at the edge of the crowd.

Southern segregationists denounced the Freedom Riders as outside agitators coming to the South with the sole purpose of provoking trouble. They got what they came for, these southerners felt. Moderate Negro leaders were critical too: the Riders' ultimate aims might be all right, they said, but these extreme tactics were doing the movement more harm than good.

Yet other civil rights groups quickly joined the rides—the Student Nonviolent Coordinating Committee and the Southern Christian Leadership Conference. On May 24, Attorney General Robert Kennedy asked the Riders to show restraint: "A cooling-off period is needed," he said. "It would be wise for those travelling through these two states [Alabama and Mississippi] to delay their trips until the present state of confusion and danger has passed and an atmosphere of reason and normalcy has been restored."

"There should be a cooling-off period all right," Martin Luther King replied. "But it should be a cooling-off period for those who are hot with hatred, hot with violence, but none for people who are seeking their rights."

James Farmer of CORE, writing from a jail cell in Jackson, Mississippi, called for an extension of the strategy to trains and airlines. "The time to act is now," he said.

Prayer pilgrimage or Freedom Ride?

Pierson v. *Ray* (1967)
386 U.S. 547, 87 S. Ct. 1213, 18 L. Ed. 2d 288

In September 1961, fifteen Episcopal ministers, sponsored by the Episcopal Society for Cultural and Racial Unity, set out on a "prayer pilgrimage" by means of a Trailways bus. The twelve white and three black clergymen entered the white waiting room of the Trailways bus terminal in Jackson, Mississippi. Police officers stopped them on their way into the white restaurant. Police Captain J. L. Ray asked them to move on and offered to escort them to their bus. They refused. They were arrested and charged with breach of the peace for failing to obey the officer's orders.

The ministers were defended at trial by CORE attorney Carl Rachlin of New York City. Municipal Judge James L. Spencer (who had heard some 300 Jackson Freedom Rider cases) found them guilty and sentenced each to four months in jail and a $200 fine. Two of the men decided to serve out their sentences; the other thirteen, including Robert L. Pierson, the son-in-law of New York Governor Nelson Rockefeller, posted bonds of $500 each. All appealed their cases.

The appeal consisted of trials de novo (new trials) before the county court. After the prosecution presented its evidence against the first defendant, Attorney Rachlin moved for a directed verdict of not guilty, and the judge granted the motion. The state attorney then dropped the charges against all the others.

In September 1962, four of the ministers, including Reverend Pierson, sued Police Captain Ray, the two officers who had assisted in the arrest, and Judge Spencer for false arrest and imprisonment. They filed the suit in federal district court, under 42 U.S.C. §1983, the same Reconstruction period Civil Rights Act provision used in *Monroe* v. *Pape* (discussed in chapter 12). The ministers asked the court to order the defendants to pay $44,004 in damages ($11,001 to each).

Judge Spencer claimed he was immune from such a suit because of his office. The police officers made the same claim.

They added that they were carrying out the law in good faith at the time. Their defense attorneys introduced evidence to show that the plaintiffs had come to Jackson with the intent of getting arrested, that they were carrying out Freedom Rides, and that their racial views agreed with those published in a Communist Party newspaper.

The plaintiffs denied that they were Freedom Riders and argued that they were engaged in lawful conduct. They presented evidence that the officers were not protecting the peace, which was not seriously threatened, but rather were protecting Mississippi's illegal segregation policies, by arresting them.

The jury returned a verdict for the defendants. The ministers appealed to the Fifth Circuit Court of Appeals. The three appellate judges made three rulings: Judge Spencer *was* immune from suit; the police officers were not immune under the rule of *Monroe* v. *Pape*, even if they acted in good faith with probable cause to arrest under a valid statute (which was later found unconstitutional); it was improper to admit the defense evidence on the plaintiffs' racial views, and this had prejudiced the jury. The court also expressed the view that if the evidence showed that the plaintiffs had intended to get arrested, they had no grounds to sue for false arrest. The appellate court sent the case back for retrial.

Instead, the clergymen asked the United States Supreme Court to review the Fifth Circuit's holdings. In May 1966, the Court agreed to hear the case.

Do you think policemen are liable to pay damages for arrests made under a state law that they think is valid but that actually violates the federal Constitution? Is it the officer's duty to know what laws are valid and which are unconstitutional? Is it a municipal judge's duty to decide that a state law violates the federal Constitution? Can a demonstrator challenge a law by inviting arrest under it, and then sue for damages when he is arrested and convicted?

Chief Justice Warren wrote for eight of the justices: "We find no difficulty in agreeing with the Court of Appeals that Judge Spencer is immune from liability for damages for his role in these convictions. The record is barren of any proof or specific allegation that Judge Spencer played any role in these arrests and convictions other than to adjudge petitioners guilty when their cases came before his court. Few doctrines were more solidly established at common law than the immunity of judges from liability for damages for acts committed within their judicial jurisdiction. . . . We do not believe that this settled principle of law was abolished by §1983, which makes liable 'every person' who under color of law deprives another person of his civil rights."

The Chief Justice then moved on to the police officers' claim that they should not be liable if they made arrests in good faith and with probable cause (good reason) to believe the people arrested had violated a statute that the officers believed to be valid. "Under the prevailing view in this country a peace officer who arrests someone with probable cause is not liable for false arrest simply because the innocence of the suspect is later proved." Referring to a line in Gilbert and Sullivan's comic opera, *The Pirates of Penzance,* the Chief Justice asserted that "a policeman's lot is not so unhappy that he must choose between being charged with dereliction of duty if he does not arrest when he has probable cause, and being mulcted in damages if he does." *Monroe* v. *Pape* did not make a rule so harsh for the police, the Court explained; in fact the defenses of good faith and probable cause were not even raised by police officers in that case (because the facts of the case could hardly support such an argument—see page 251).

The justices held that "good faith and probable cause" *were* defenses to a false arrest suit under the Civil Rights Act, and "that a police officer is not charged with predicting the future course of constitutional law. But the petitioners in this case did not simply argue that they were arrested under a statute later held unconstitutional." They claimed the officers arrested them without probable cause—since no disturbance was actually threatened. The defendant officers claimed there *was* probable cause—people "mumbling in a very ugly mood" at the station. This was a factual dispute to be retried before an unprejudiced jury, said the Supreme Court.

Finally the justices faced the issue of the ministers' intention to get themselves arrested. "We do not agree with the Court of Appeals that they somehow consented to the arrest because of their anticipation that they would be illegally arrested, even assuming that they went to the Jackson bus terminal for the sole purpose of testing their rights to unsegregated public accommodations. The case contains no proof or allegation that they in any way tricked or goaded the officers into arresting them. The petitioners had the right to use the waiting room of the Jackson bus terminal, and their deliberate exercise of that right in a peaceful, orderly, and inoffensive manner does not disqualify them from seeking damages under §1983."

The case was remanded.

Justice Douglas dissented from the Court's holding that the judge was immune from this civil suit. "It is necessary to exempt judges from liability for the consequences of their honest mistakes," he said, "but that is far different from saying that a judge shall be immune from the consequences of any of his judicial actions, and that he shall not be liable for the knowing and intentional deprivation of a person's civil rights."

The *Pierson* decision of 1967 established the right of demonstrators to challenge illegal laws through affirmative civil suits for false arrest even when they got arrested deliberately to make the challenge. Of more practical importance to constitutional clients and their lawyers, it proved that more civil rights clients could collect damages for the violation of their rights, so that they could pay their lawyers reasonable fees for their time and effort. This encouraged clients to ask lawyers to handle civil rights cases—not as a favor, but with the hope of remuneration, and it encouraged lawyers to take the time to handle such cases, with the chance of payment.

Some 350 Freedom Riders had been arrested in the summer of 1961. The national and international publicity they drew created tremendous pressure on the government, particularly the federal government, to close the gap between public pronouncements of equality and the reality faced by blacks in the South. In August, the Justice Department asked the Interstate Commerce Commission to issue new regulations banning racial discrimination and segregation in interstate travel. After holding hearings, the ICC issued rules on September 22 forbidding segregated seating on buses and segregated terminal facilities. The new regulations also required buses, tickets, and terminals to carry notices saying that use of the facilities of interstate commerce was "without regard to race, color, creed, or national origin." This threw the weight of federal power behind the goals of the Freedom Riders and did much to end southern attacks against desegregated travel.

Writing in *The Progressive* in November 1961, James

Farmer summed up the purposes of the Freedom Rides: "We came from all over the country, from both races and of all ages, to test compliance with the law, to exercise the right of all Americans to use all transportation facilities with the dignity of equality, to shake Americans out of their apathy on this issue and expose the real character of segregation to the pitiless scrutiny of a nation's conscience." Farmer recalled with obvious pride: "As I entered the white waiting room in one terminal in the South, a Negro woman passenger from the same bus caught my eye and anxiously beckoned me to follow her into the dingy but safe colored section. Moments later, when she saw me served at the lunch counter in the white section, she joined me for a cup of coffee."

"I do it for my customers"

Bell v. *Maryland* (1964)
378 U.S. 226, 84 S. Ct. 1814, 12 L. Ed. 2d 822

G. Carroll Hooper was president of the Hooper Food Company, and owner of Hooper's Restaurant in Baltimore. Mr. Hooper followed the news and, being a man of forethought, in 1960 he instructed the restaurant hostess what to do if Negroes tried to enter. When fifteen or twenty black students walked in one day, she told them they could not be served. Albert Warfel, the manager, asked the students to leave. Instead they took seats at several tables and insisted that they be served.

Mr. Hooper himself came out to speak with one of the leaders of the group. He later testified: "I set at the table with him and two other people and reasoned and talked to him why my policy was not yet one of integration and told him that I had two hundred employees and half of them were colored. I thought as much of them as I did the white employees. I invited them back in my kitichen if they'd like to go back and talk to them. I wanted to prove to them it wasn't my policy, my personal prejudice. . . . I tried to reason with these leaders, told them that as long as my customers were the [ones] deciding who they want to eat with, I'm at the mercy of my customers. I'm trying to do what they want. If they fail to come in, these people are not paying my expenses, and my bills. They didn't want to go back and talk to my colored employees because every one of them are in sympathy with me and . . . we're in sympathy with what their objectives are, with what they are trying to abolish."

At that point Hooper called in the police and had the demonstrators arrested. They were not charged with their real offense—breaking the rule requiring discrimination in restaurant service. Like most civil rights demonstrators, they were charged with a seemingly neutral crime, unrelated to race or civil rights: trespass. Twelve of them were tried and convicted.

The Maryland Court of Appeals affirmed their convictions on January 9, 1962. But during the intervening years, things had begun to change. Civil rights demonstrations had raised the issue of discrimination in the halls of government, and pressure from the black communities began to be felt. The consciences of white people in this border state were pricked by the charges of racial bias. In June 1962 Baltimore passed an ordinance prohibiting racial discrimination in places of public accommodation, such as restaurants. In March 1963, the Maryland legislature passed a similar statute.

The twelve demonstrators, with the aid of the NAACP Legal Defense Fund, petitioned the United States Supreme Court to review their case. They argued that their arrests and convictions violated the Fourteenth Amendment—state power had been used to enforce unequal treatment. They also argued that their convictions should be struck down because the action they had taken was no longer a crime in Maryland. The state attorneys, defending the arrests, said the Fourteenth Amendment did not apply to private restaurants, and that trespassing was still a crime in Maryland. The Supreme Court agreed in June 1963 to hear the case.

Do you think the students had a constitutional right to be served in a privately owned and operated restaurant? Did the arrests make the government a party to racial discrimination? Were the police officers violating the equal protection clause of the Fourteenth Amendment? Should the enactment of new state and city laws invalidate the convictions under the old law?

Justice Brennan wrote the opinion for the Court's six-to-three majority. Because "a significant change has taken place in the applicable law of Maryland since these convictions were affirmed," the Court decided not to deal with the constitutional issues, but to vacate and reverse the judgments and send the case back to the Maryland Court of Appeals to decide the effect of the new laws on the case. Maryland followed the common law rule that "when the legislature repeals a criminal statute or otherwise removes the State's condemnation from conduct that was formerly deemed criminal, this action requires the dismissal of a pending criminal proceeding charging such conduct." But Maryland law also provided that when a statute was amended or repealed, the former penalty or liability for any act remained in effect unless specifically repealed. The Supreme Court noted that the state public accommodations law was a new, not an amended, statute, that the new law did not repeal the criminal trespass statute, but that the new law went further than abolishing a crime and actually made the former crime into a *right*. The Court noted that the arguments for throwing the convictions out under the new state law "seem quite substantial," but left it for the Maryland court to decide.

Justice Douglas in a concurring opinion, disagreed heartily with this "hands off" policy. "The issue is ripe for decision," he felt, and a majority of the justices (although not a majority of those on the concurring side) wanted to decide the case on the Fourteenth Amendment questions.

"The whole Nation has to face the issue; Congress is conscientiously considering it [the Civil Rights Act of 1964 was then being debated and filibustered]; some municipalities have had to make it their first order of concern; law enforcement officials are deeply implicated, North as well as South; the question is at the root of demonstrations, unrest, riots, and violence in various areas. The issue in other words consumes the public attention. Yet we stand mute, avoiding decision of the basic issue by an obvious pretense. . . . The people should know that when filibusters occupy other forums, when oppressions are great, when the clash of authority between the individual and the State is severe, they can still get justice in the courts. When we default, as we do today, the prestige of law in the life of the Nation is weakened."

Justice Black, joined by Justices Harlan and White, dissented from the majority decision and agreed with Justice Douglas that the Court should have reached the merits of the case. But they went on to express their view that the issue was "whether the Fourteenth Amendment, of itself, forbids a State to enforce its trespass laws to convict a person who comes into a privately owned restaurant, is told that because of his color he will not be served, and over the owner's protest refuses to leave." The three dissenters believed that "the

Amendment does not forbid a State to prosecute for crimes committed against a person or his property, however prejudiced or narrow the victim's views may be. . . . It would betray our whole plan for a tranquil and orderly society to say that a citizen, because of his personal prejudices, habits, attitudes, or beliefs, is cast outside the law's protection and cannot call for the aid of officers sworn to uphold the law and preserve the peace. The worst citizen no less than the best is entitled to equal protection of the laws of his State and of his Nation." In Justice Black's words, "the Fourteenth Amendment of itself does not compel either a black man or a white man running his own private business to trade with anyone else against his will." The three dissenters felt the convictions should have been affirmed.

Justice Douglas answered eloquently: "The issue in this case, according to those who would affirm, is whether a person's 'personal prejudices' may dictate the way in which he uses his property and whether he can enlist the aid of the State to enforce those 'personal prejudices.' With all respect, that is not the real issue.

"The corporation that owns this restaurant did not refuse service to these Negroes because 'it' did not like Negroes. The reason 'it' refused service was because 'it' thought 'it' could make more money by running a segregated restaurant. . . . Were we today to hold that segregated restaurants, whose racial policies were enforced by a State, violated the Equal Protection Clause, all restaurants would be on an equal footing and the reasons given in this and most of the companion cases for refusing service to Negroes would evaporate. Moreover, when corporate restaurateurs are involved, whose 'personal prejudices' are being protected? The stockholders'? The directors'? The officers'? The managers'? The truth is, I think, that the corporate interest is in making money, not in protecting 'personal prejudices.' "

Justice Douglas stressed the importance of the case. "We deal here with public accommodations—with the right of people to eat and travel as they like and to use facilities whose only claim to existence is serving the public." Going back to the constitutional basis of the argument, he wrote: "The Fourteenth Amendment says 'No State shall make or enforce any law which shall abridge the privileges or immunities of citizens of the United States.' The Fourteenth Amendment also makes every person who is born here a citizen; and there is no second or third or fourth class of citizenship." In Justice Douglas's view, "When one citizen because of his race, creed, or color is denied the privilege of being treated as any other citizen in places of public accommodation, we have classes of citizenship, one being more degrading than the other."

Taking on the dissenters, Justice Douglas said: "The problem in this case, and in the other sit-in cases before us, is presented as though it involved the situation of 'a private operator conducting his own business on his own premises and exercising his own judgment' as to whom he will admit to the premises.

"The property involved is not, however, a man's home or his yard or even his fields. Private property is involved, but it is property that is serving the public." Justice Douglas concluded: "Segregation of Negroes in the restaurants and lunch counters of parts of America is a relic of slavery. It is a badge of second-class citizenship. It is a denial of a privilege and immunity of national citizenship and of the equal protection guaranteed by the Fourteenth Amendment against abridgment by the States. When the state police, the state prosecutor, and the state courts unite to convict Negroes for renouncing that relic of slavery, the 'State' violates the Fourteenth Amendment.

History being made at a Woolworth's lunch counter: one of the first sit-ins to desegregate public facilities, this time in Greensboro, North Carolina, February 2, 1960.
Credit: United Press International Photo

"I would reverse these judgments of conviction outright, as these Negroes in asking for service in Hooper's restaurant were only demanding what was their constitutional right."

In an appendix to his opinion, Justice Douglas documented that the owners of the lunch counters and restaurants involved in sit-in cases that had come before the Court were almost all large corporations, not individuals with "personal prejudices." To affirm the convictions of the students sitting in at these establishments, Justice Douglas warned, "would make corporate management the arbiter of one of the deepest conflicts in our society: corporate management could then enlist the aid of state police, state prosecutors, and state courts to force *apartheid* [segregation] on the community they served, if *apartheid* best suited the corporate need; or, if its profits would be better served by lowering the barriers of segregation, it could do so."

Justice Douglas supplied four other appendixes of statistics and evidence to document the corporate nature and structure of these eating places and the profit, rather than personal, motives for segregating them.

Justice Goldberg joined Justice Douglas's concurring opinion in part and wrote his own, joined by Chief Justice Warren and in part by Justice Douglas. He refuted the arguments of the three dissenting justices on the basis of "the intent and purposes" of the Thirteenth and Fourteenth Amendments, and traced the history of the amendments in detail to prove his point. As to Justice Black's pleas for "a tranquil and orderly society," Justice Goldberg replied that the critical question was: "Whose conduct is entitled to the 'law's protection'? Of course every member of this Court agrees that law and order must prevail; the question is whether the weight and protective strength of law and order will be cast in favor of the claims of the proprietors or in favor of the claims of petitioners. In my view the Fourteenth Amendment resolved this issue in favor of the right of petitioners to public accommodations and it follows that in the exercise of that constitutionally granted right they are entitled to the 'law's protection.' "

On remand of the case, the Maryland court of appeal rejected the Supreme Court majority's suggestion that the indictments probably should be voided because of the new statutes; the state court reaffirmed the students' convictions, saying it found no evidence that the Maryland legislature had intended to change any past trespass convictions by enacting its new public accommodations law.

In a later case that year, *Hamm* v. *City of Rock Hill*, the Supreme Court faced this issue squarely and held that a new law authorizing conduct that formerly was prohibited not only stops future arrests for that conduct but also abates (wipes out) punishments for past instances of that conduct. This abatement principle was extremely helpful in civil rights cases; it may have a rebirth of usefulness if and when the draft law expires or is repealed.

While *Bell* and *Hamm* were slowly traveling toward the Supreme Court, clients and their lawyers were racking up a series of victories concerning other public accommodations. Federal courts ordered cities and states to desegregate their parks, playgrounds, tennis courts, swimming pools, bathing beaches, zoos, golf courses, art museums, libraries, and auditoriums. The courts also ordered desegregation of facilities leased from cities, such as airport restaurants and motels. In response, a few cities closed their swimming pools, as some boards of education had closed their schools; in these areas, it was segregated bathing or nothing.

The Supreme Court's decision in *Bell* was handed down in June 1964. In July, the filibuster by congressmen against civil rights legislation (to which Justice Douglas had referred) was broken, and the Civil Rights Act of 1964 was passed.

It was a wide-ranging law, and one of the most bitterly fought parts was Title II, prohibiting discrimination in places of public accommodation. Immediately after its passage, this section of the law was challenged in the courts. The challenge was a natural course for segregationists to take: in 1875 Congress had passed a civil rights act with a very similar public accommodations section. But the Supreme Court in 1883 had ruled, in what were known as the *Civil Rights Cases,* that Congress had exceeded its powers in trying to tell individuals not to discriminate, even if they were engaged in businesses set up to serve the public. White southern businessmen soon asked the 1964 Court to reach the same conclusion.

A businessman's right to discriminate

Heart of Atlanta Motel v. *United States* (1964)
379 U.S. 241, 85 S. Ct. 348, 13 L. Ed. 2d 258

Lester Maddox was the owner of the Pickrick restaurant in Atlanta and an outspoken segregationist. The day after Congress passed the 1964 Civil Rights Act, three black divinity students sought service at the Pickrick. Maddox barred the entrance, brandished a pistol, and vowed he would close the place down rather than integrate it. The owner and operator of the Heart of Atlanta Motel felt pretty much the same way about his business. He and Maddox decided to take affirmative action against the public accommodations title. They filed suit in federal district court asking that Title II be declared unconstitutional. Congress had exceeded its powers to regulate commerce, they contended. Depriving a businessman of the freedom to choose his customers was depriving him of liberty and property without due process of law or just compensation—and it subjected him to involuntary servitude, which was forbidden by the Thirteenth Amendment.

The United States Solicitor General responded that it was frivolous to claim protection for racial discrimination under the very amendment that prohibited slavery and all its disabilities. Defending Congress's power, the solicitor said that the refusal of Maddox and others to serve black people interfered significantly with interstate travel. Reasonable regulations by Congress in this area were not a deprivation of liberty and property without due process and were well within the commerce clause of the Constitution.

The three-judge court upheld the constitutionality of Title II, and granted the Solicitor General's motion for a permanent injunction against continued racial discrimination by the Pickrick and the Heart of Atlanta Motel. The businessmen appealed to the United States Supreme Court, but a technical error delayed Maddox's appeal, and the motel case was heard alone. Both the government and the owner agreed on the facts: the motel was near the downtown area of Atlanta and readily accessible to the major highways in town. It advertised in national magazines, and over 75 percent of the registered guests were from out of the state. It had always refused to rent rooms to Negroes and continued the practice after passage of the 1964 Civil Rights Act. There was no question that the motel would come under the provisions of Title II. The sole question was whether Title II was constitutional.

Do you think congressional power to regulate commerce extends to telling businessmen they cannot practice racial discrimination? If Congress did not have the power to do this in 1883, in the *Civil Rights Cases,* how can it have the power in 1964? What effect do federal laws like the 1964 Civil Rights Act have on hostile businessmen? Can the government legislate morality?

Justice Clark delivered the Court's unanimous opinion in December 1964. According to its committee reports, Congress had based the act "on the commerce power of the Constitution," and the Court found "that Congress possessed ample power in this regard," so the justices did not consider the validity of the Thirteenth and Fourteenth Amendments as bases for Title II.

The Court recognized the problem posed by the 1875 act and the 1883 Supreme Court ruling in the *Civil Rights Cases.* "We think that decision inapposite, and without precedential value in determining the constitutionality of the present Act," they said. "Unlike Title II of the present legislation, the 1875 Act broadly proscribed discrimination in 'inns, public conveyances on land or water, theaters, and other places of public amusement,' without limiting the categories of affected businesses to those impinging upon interstate commerce. In contrast, the applicability of Title II is carefully limited to enterprises having a direct and substantial relation to the interstate flow of goods and people, except where state action is involved.

"Further, the fact that certain kinds of businesses may not in 1875 have been sufficiently involved in interstate commerce to warrant bringing them within the ambit of the commerce power is not necessarily dispositive of the same question today. Our populace had not reached its present mobility, nor were facilities, goods and services circulating as readily in interstate commerce as they are today. Although the principles which we apply today are those first formulated . . . [in an 1824 case], the conditions of transportation and commerce have changed dramatically, and we must apply those principles to the present state of commerce. The sheer increase in volume of interstate traffic alone would give discriminatory practices which inhibit travel a far larger impact upon the Nation's commerce than such practices had on the economy of another day."

Testimony before Congress that year had shown "that our people have become increasingly mobile with millions of people of all races traveling from State to State; that Negroes in particular have been the subject of discrimination in transient accommodations, having to travel great distances to secure the same; that often they have been unable to obtain accommodations and have had to call upon friends to put them up overnight . . . ; and that these conditions had become so acute as to require the listing of available lodging for Negroes in a special guidebook which was itself 'dramatic testimony to the difficulties' Negroes encounter in travel." The problem was nationwide. It placed great hardships on black people who traveled and inhibited any travel at all on the part of "a substantial portion of the Negro community."

Justice Clark did not duck the philosophical question: "In framing Title II of this Act Congress was also dealing with what it considered a moral problem. But that fact does not detract from the overwhelming evidence of the disruptive effect that racial discrimination has had on commercial intercourse. It was this burden which empowered Congress to enact appropriate legislation, and, given this basis for the exercise of its power, Congress was not restricted by the fact that the particular obstruction to interstate commerce with which it was dealing was also deemed a moral and social wrong."

The Court found that Congress both had a rational basis

for enacting Title II and used reasonable means to carry out its goals, so that the motel owner was not being deprived of liberty or property without due process of law.

Justice Black wrote a concurring opinion, apparently to explain that his dissent in *Bell* v. *Maryland* was on the ground that the Fourteenth Amendment *alone* did not give Congress the power to act in the field, but that this 1964 law grounded on the commerce clause was clearly within Congress's power.

Justice Douglas concurred to stress that he would have based Congress's power to legislate in this area on the Fourteenth Amendment as well as the commerce clause of the Constitution. Justice Goldberg, concurring, made substantially the same point.

The Heart of Atlanta Motel lost its case, but Lester Maddox's uncompromising stand on white supremacy drew enough public attention to win him election to the governorship of Georgia in 1967, on a segregationist platform. Southern businessmen of Maddox's extreme persuasion found a variety of tactics to avoid complying with the 1964 law. Some closed their businesses and reopened them as "private clubs" —with nominal membership fees but strict "all-white" membership requirements—since private clubs not operating for profit but only to serve their members were exempted from the Civil Rights Act. Others moved to white suburban areas. A few gave up their businesses, because desegregation was too repugnant to them.

But many southern businessmen simply accepted the new law and followed it, some with a sense of relief that the matter was now finally settled. Most reported that customers accepted desegregation with little fuss. A few customers inevitably said they would take their business elsewhere, but since everyone had to comply in one way or another or go out of business, there was virtually no "elsewhere" to take their business to, and eventually these patrons came back to their customary establishments. Within a decade, southern whites living in large cities became so accustomed to seeing middle-class blacks served in restaurants, cafeterias, motels, and hotels, that they no longer commented on the issue that had caused such violent reactions in the early 1960s.

In many areas, it was the power of the dollar that made changes, even before the courts had their say (as Justice Douglas might have expected). When the black community organized a boycott (or, when boycotts were prohibited by local laws, a "selective buying campaign") against stores that maintained segregated facilities or all-white staffs, it generally didn't take a court order to win desegregation. During these boycotts, black southerners proudly wore old bluejeans and work clothes as a badge of their refusal to patronize racist clothing stores. This practice, adopted by northern students who participated in the southern civil rights movement, may have started the modern trend among young people around the country to sport faded, worn, and patched clothing in preference to new middle-class apparel.

The power of the dollar has cut both ways in the desegregation of public accommodations, however. While the victories in interstate travel were clear cut, most blacks could not afford to patronize the restaurants, hotels, motels, and other facilities that fought longest to continue segregation. Racist hiring and promotion practices excluded them from jobs paying decent wages or in many cases from any jobs at all. The continuously high unemployment rate among young blacks has sharply reduced the significance of the right to an unsegregated cup of coffee.

But the spirit of the sit-ins has taken a deep hold on citizens of southern communities and the idea of equal access to public accommodations has led to demands for equality in the most basic aspects of city life. In the towns of Shaw and Ita Bena, Mississippi, in 1967, black citizens sued their town officials demanding improved streets in the black ghetto, the installation of street lights, the construction of sewerage and water facilities, the collection of garbage—all equal to the facilities and services in the white section. In Humphreys County, Mississippi, citizens filed a similar suit, and also asked for desegregation of the county hospital and all police and fire departments. In California, white citizens with low incomes sued to stop high deposit requirements by the telephone company and the electric power company—both privately owned public utilities.

These isolated demands for equal access to public services, without regard to race or economic condition, were but the tip of an iceberg that may confront legislators, administrators, and judges in the 1970s and beyond. One test of the effective operation of the American judicial system will be its response to these new demands for equal protection.

CHAPTER 26

Equality in Housing

There has been a housing crisis in the United States for decades. It has consisted of two major problems: the inability of people with moderate or low incomes to find decent housing, and the inability of people regardless of income to find decent housing if they are members of a racial or religious minority group. Low incomes and bigotry, in other words, have haunted Americans searching for this necessity of life.

Tenants and home buyers have attacked these twin problems by seeking legislation, executive orders, and judicial decisions, by collective action through tenants' unions, and by individual effort. They have done battle with the federal government when it built and rented low-cost housing on a Jim Crow basis in areas across the country or when "desegregated" government units were built in ghetto areas where, in fact, only minority group citizens would rent. They have complained when low-income areas were razed by private redevelopers and urban renewal agencies to make room for expensive housing units, office or commercial buildings, and parking lots, charging the government with Negro clearance as well as slum clearance. They have gone to court when they were turned away from buying homes by prejudiced developers, realtors, and individual sellers, even though federal funds had helped build or finance the housing. One irate

Negro, turned down by just such developers in Sacramento, California, explained his argument to a county judge in language that became part of the court's opinion: "When one dips one's hand into the Federal Treasury, a little democracy necessarily clings to whatever is withdrawn."

Many supporters of local federal housing projects for low and middle income families were slow to discover that segregationist policies were being practiced by federal housing agencies across the nation, North, South, and West. But by 1965, the pattern had clearly emerged: federal funding and insurance for low-cost high rise apartment houses for blacks in the central cities, and for expensive single-family homes for whites in the suburbs.

In the private housing field, tenants have faced down landlords who refused, openly or deviously, to rent to people because of their race, religion, or national ancestry, or who evicted tenants for having guests of another race. They have confronted realtors who instigated "blockbusting" moves, inducing one white homeowner to sell to a minority group buyer and then scaring others to sell with self-fulfilling rumors that the neighborhood was "going Jewish" or "going black" and that their property would soon lose most of its value.

In response to these tactics, tenants and home buyers sued government agencies, private corporations, and individuals, and finally sought revocation of state licenses of realtors who practiced racism. They lobbied fair housing laws through a few city councils and state legislatures, but that did not end the matter. Realtors and others then got the measures on the ballot, appealing to the latent bigotry in white Protestant Americans to repeal the statutes by referendum.

The response of the United States Supreme Court to these problems during the tenure of Chief Justice Warren is sharply etched in the two landmark cases, *Reitman* v. *Mulkey*, from California, and *Jones* v. *Alfred H. Mayer Company*, from Missouri.

"I won't rent to you"

Reitman v. *Mulkey* (1967)
387 U.S. 369, 87 S. Ct. 1627, 18 L. Ed. 2d 830

Mr. and Mrs. Lincoln Mulkey were looking for an apartment in Santa Ana, California, in 1963. Neil Reitman was the owner and manager of an apartment building with vacancies. But when the Mulkeys asked to rent one of his apartments, Reitman refused. He made no bones about it: the building was occupied by whites only, and the Mulkeys were black. (Other landlords and realtors were more subtle, but achieved the same result; they said that black applicants had poor credit ratings, that the apartment had just been rented, that the vacating tenants had suddenly changed their minds and decided to stay, that the rent had just been raised to an exaggerated figure, that an exorbitant "deposit" or "cleaning fee" or "advance" was required, or that numerous references from past landlords were needed.)

What can a Negro couple do when faced with the frustration and humiliation of a direct refusal like Reitman's? In 1963, the Mulkeys were protected by California law: the Unruh Act, passed in 1959, prohibited discrimination because of race, religion, or national ancestry in all "accommodations, advantages, facilities, privileges, or services in all business establishments of every kind whatsoever." It permitted an aggrieved person to sue for damages against the person who discriminated. The Mulkeys sued Reitman and others connected with the apartment building for $50,000, plus the $250 damages specified in the statute for all cases, and asked for an injunction against Reitman's continued refusal to rent them an apartment.

Discrimination in housing was a hot issue in California that year. Minority group members who had been trying for years to move out of slums and ghettos were exerting pressure on their state legislators. The Unruh Act was not effective enough, they said. Landlords were willing to risk a suit rather than rent to blacks, to people with Spanish surnames, or to other minorities. It was a calculated risk on their part: few of those who suffered discrimination could afford to sue, as the Mulkeys did; even if a suit were filed, it would drag on for more than a year and probably be settled before trial by the landlord paying a small sum of money damages to the tenant, without being forced to rent to him.

In 1963, the legislature passed the Rumford Fair Housing Act, which prohibited racial discrimination in the sale or rental of apartment buildings of more than four units. The act did not apply to all homes and apartments, but it made it easier to get relief by putting the burden of enforcement on the state's Fair Employment Practices Commission, rather than requiring the individual buyer or renter to hire a lawyer and go to court.

It began to look as though a major breakdown of segregated housing patterns might occur, but realtors, already organized, were quick to mobilize, They lambasted the Rumford Act as "forced housing, not fair housing"; they said it would compel a person to betray the friendship of his neighbors by forcing him to sell his house to people who would "cause the neighborhood to deteriorate"; they warned that property values always declined when blacks moved into a white neighborhood; and they expressed concern that the small homeowner and landlord would be harmed the most. The realty interests drew up a proposed amendment to the state constitution, circulated petitions to put it on the ballot as an initiative measure, and secured the necessary number of signatures. The measure, called Proposition 14 on the ballot, prohibited the state government from denying, limiting, or abridging "the right of any person . . . to decline to sell, lease or rent [his] property to such person or persons as he, in his absolute discretion, chooses."

Opponents of the proposition questioned the motives of the realtors and developers. They cited studies showing that realtors consistently sold homes to blacks in white neighborhoods when this produced large commissions, even though critics could call it "blockbusting." For example, when housing was very difficult to obtain in a ghetto, a realtor would sell a home to a black family in a previously all-white neighborhood. The buyer would be willing to pay a premium price because of his great need for housing. Then the same realtor, and others, would visit all the homes in the immediate neighborhood and suggest to the homeowners that they quickly sell their homes before prices went down. This panic selling meant more commissions for the realtors. When black buyers paid higher prices for these houses, this meant higher commissions, as well. The Rumford Act would end such blockbusting by making all housing available without racial discrimination. In time, the population would become more stable, since people would stop moving to get away from "them," and the number of sales—and real estate commissions—would go down.

Literature about the proposition, both pro and con, stressed that it would repeal the Rumford Act and prevent similar laws from being enacted in the future. Amid charges of "forced housing" and "blockbusters," it was clear that the key issue was racial desegregation in housing; although the measure did not mention this in its wording.

Many organizations opposed Proposition 14—unions, the Parent-Teachers Association, the State Bar Association, churches and synagogues—and many "Vote No" meetings were held. But underlying white racist attitudes prevailed: the initiative was passed by California voters in November 1964 nearly two to one (4,526,000 to 2,396,000). The president of the National Association of Real Estate Boards told the *New York Times* on this occasion that private property rights were more basic to human liberty than the civil rights of minority groups. On December 23, 1964, the defendant landlord in the Mulkey suit moved that the complaint be dismissed because the enactment of Proposition 14 (now article I, section 26, of the state constitution) had voided the Unruh Act sections that formed the basis of the charges. The Mulkeys responded that the state proposition violated the federal Fourteenth Amendment and therefore was itself void. The trial judge ruled in favor of the defendants, and Mr. and Mrs. Mulkey appealed to the California Supreme Court.

That court concluded that a state did not have a duty under the Fourteenth Amendment to prohibit racial discrimination, but did have a duty not to promote it. Looking at recent United States Supreme Court decisions touching on the question, the California court found that in enacting Proposition 14 "the state, recognizing that it could not perform a direct act of discrimination, nevertheless has taken affirmative action of a legislative nature designed to make possible private discriminatory practices which previously were legally restricted. . . . Here the state has affirmatively acted to change its existing laws from a situation wherein the discrimination practiced was legally restricted to one wherein it is encouraged." This violated the Fourteenth Amendment, said the court.

Reitman and the other defendants asked the U.S. Supreme Court to review the decision. The Court agreed, feeling that the case raised an important issue concerning the effect of the Fourteenth Amendment on state action to limit civil rights.

Do you think that passage of Proposition 14 put the state in the position of encouraging racial discrimination in housing? Can the law be held unconstitutional because of its *effect* even though its *wording* is "neutral"? If the proposition is unconstitutional, is it unconstitutional to repeal any antidiscrimination law?

The Supreme Court split five to four. Justice White, writing the majority opinion, noted that the California Supreme Court had not just looked at the language of Proposition 14, but had also looked at the law's historical context, immediate objective, and ultimate effect, in order to determine whether it violated the Fourteenth Amendment.

The California Supreme Court had found that the proposition had been enacted against a background of legislative efforts to regulate "private discriminations in residential housing." Its immediate objective, which had been accomplished, was "to authorize private racial discriminations in the housing market, to repeal the Unruh and Rumford Acts and to create a constitutional right to discriminate on racial grounds in the sale and leasing of real property." The ultimate impact of the proposition would be to "encourage and significantly involve the State in private racial discrimination contrary to the Fourteenth Amendment."

The United States Supreme Court had never tried to formulate "an infallible test for determining whether the State . . . has become significantly involved in private discriminations," said Justice White. The facts and circumstances of each case had to be sifted and weighed. Here, the Court accepted the state court decision that the new law "was intended to authorize, and does authorize, racial discrimination in the housing market. The right to discriminate is now one of the basic policies of the State." The Court stepped carefully to uphold the decision of the California Supreme Court rather than announcing its own independent decision under its authority as overseer of state court rulings: "The California Supreme Court believes that the section will significantly encourage and involve the State in private discriminations. We have been presented with no persuasive considerations indicating that these judgments should be overturned."

Justice Douglas wrote a forthright concurring opinion. He said, "This is not a case as simple as the one where a man with a bicycle or a car or a stock certificate or even a log cabin asserts the right to sell it to whomsoever he pleases, excluding all others whether they be Negro, Chinese, Japanese, Russians, Catholics, Baptists, or those with blue eyes. We deal here with a problem in the realm of zoning, similar to [older cases of] . . . restrictive covenants." These were agreements often written into the deeds to property, under which the buyer promised never to sell it to Jews or Negroes or Italians or members of some other minority group. The promise was made by each new buyer and was considered irrevocable, to "run with the land."

"Those covenants are one device whereby a neighborhood is kept 'white' or 'Caucasian' as the dominant interests desire," said Justice Douglas. "Proposition 14 in the setting of our modern housing problem is only another device of the same character.

"Real estate brokers and mortgage lenders are largely

dedicated to the maintenance of segregated communities. Realtors commonly believe it is unethical to sell or rent to a Negro in a predominantly white or all-white neighborhood, and mortgage lenders throw their weight alongside segregated communities, rejecting applications by members of a minority group who try to break the white phalanx . . . unless the neighborhood is in process of conversion into a mixed or a Negro community." Justice Douglas quoted findings by the U.S. Commission on Civil Rights concerning the roles played by realtors, builders, and mortgage lending institutions in perpetuating housing discrimination.

"Proposition 14 is a form of sophisticated discrimination whereby the people of California harness the energies of private groups to do indirectly what they cannot under our decisions allow their government to do," he said. "Zoning is a state and municipal function. . . . When the State leaves that function to private agencies or institutions which are licensees and which practice racial discrimination and zone our cities into white and black belts or white and black ghettoes, it suffers a governmental function to be performed under private auspices in a way the State itself may not act."

Moreover, "since the real estate brokerage business is one that can be and is state-regulated and since it is state-licensed, it must be dedicated, like the telephone companies and the carriers and the hotels and motels to the requirements of service to all without discrimination—a standard that in its modern setting is conditioned by the demands of the Equal Protection Clause of the Fourteenth Amendment," Justice Douglas concluded.

Justices Harlan, Black, Clark, and Stewart dissented. "The Equal Protection Clause of the Fourteenth Amendment, which forbids a State to use its authority to foster discrimination based on such factors as race, . . . does not undertake to control purely personal prejudices and predilections, and individuals acting on their own are left free to discriminate on racial grounds if they are so minded," wrote Justice Harlan for the four of them. He felt that the state was not significantly involved in fostering discrimination by passage of Proposition 14, and that it therefore did not violate the equal protection clause of the Fourteenth Amendment.

The *Mulkey* decision restored California's antidiscrimination laws to full force, and protected existing fair housing laws in other states. The laws have been used successfully to curb racial discrimination by sellers and landlords like Reitman, when the persons discriminated against have filed claims with their state human relations commissions or suits under acts like the Unruh Act.

A number of tenants and home buyers have collected damages from prejudiced landlords and sellers, and many have been able to move into the units from which they had been excluded earlier. Sometimes the defeated realtor has had to pay the fee to the plaintiffs' attorney, as part of the judgment in the case.

Each victory opens another door, but observers are convinced that this type of racism can be eradicated only by massive voluntary acceptance of the concept of equality in housing rights, not by individual lawsuits. A talented young black playwright approached the housing question through another door. She had grown up with the problem in Chicago, where her father had sued to prevent enforcement of a covenant against selling to a Negro buyer, and had won his case, *Hansberry* v. *Lee,* in the Supreme Court in 1940. As the Warren Court faced additional housing litigation, Lorraine Hansberry watched her characters struggle against white landlords and real estate agents in *Raisin in the Sun,* entertaining while educating.

The 1866 law finally is enforced

Jones v. Alfred H. Mayer Company (1968)
392 U.S. 409, 88 S. Ct. 2186, 20 L. Ed. 2d 1189

In the summer of 1965, Joseph Lee Jones and his wife, Barbara Jo, saw an ad in the *St. Louis Post-Dispatch* for a new housing development in the suburbs called Paddock Woods. They went out to take a look and liked what they saw. Paddock Woods was to be a community of about 1,000 in population and was a subdivision of a larger development planned for about 2,700 families (about 10,000 people). When the Joneses inquired about buying a house at lot 7147, they were refused because Paddock Woods had a policy of excluding Negroes. Mr. Jones was black and Mrs. Jones was white.

The Joneses hired a young lawyer, Samuel H. Liberman, to sue the developer, Alfred H. Mayer Company, and its real estate agent, Alfred Realty Company. Missouri did not have a fair housing statute, but when Liberman examined the federal statutes to see what grounds he might have for a lawsuit, he found a law enacted by Congress shortly after adoption of the Thirteenth Amendment forbidding slavery. A statute enacted as a section of the Civil Rights Act of 1866 applied directly to his clients' situation. It provided: "All citizens of the United States shall have the same right, in every State and Territory, as is enjoyed by white citizens thereof to inherit, purchase, lease, sell, hold, and convey real and personal property." The law was appropriate, and still in effect (since Congress had never repealed it), but Attorney Liberman could find no cases in which it had been used successfully to combat housing discrimination, from its adoption in 1866 to the present. Nonetheless, he filed a complaint in federal district court, charging that the Mayer Company had violated this statute. He also contended that the developer of a community this size was in effect acting as the government of the community so that racial discrimination by such a developer violated the equal protection clause of the Fourteenth Amendment.

Mr. and Mrs. Jones asked the court to order the developer to sell them a home in Paddock Woods, to enjoin the developer from selling lot 7147 to someone else while their suit was pending, and to enjoin the developer from further racial discrimination in the sale of Paddock Woods homes.

The Mayer Company asked the district court to dismiss the complaint, arguing that the 1866 act and the Fourteenth Amendment applied only to discrimination by state *governments* or people acting under authority of state law. These laws did not apply to private acts by individuals or companies, the company lawyer said. He cited decisions by the United States Supreme Court interpreting the Civil Rights Act this way, and he contended that the company was not acting as a government.

The district court accepted the defendants' view and dismissed the complaint. Mr. and Mrs. Jones appealed to the court of appeals, which affirmed the district court decision, saying it was bound by the Supreme Court's past holdings. The appellate judges implied that it might be time to overrule those holdings, but they felt this was a task for the Supreme Court, not for lower courts.

The Joneses then asked the Supreme Court to review the case. Friend of the court briefs supporting their arguments were submitted to the Court by a number of civil rights, human relations, and civil liberties groups, religious organizations, trade unions, two cities, one state, and the United States Attorney General. One friend of the court brief supporting the Mayer Company's position was submitted by a Maryland citizens' group.

The Supreme Court heard oral arguments on April 1 and 2, 1968. Ten days later the Civil Rights Act of 1968 was enacted, containing a group of sections on fair housing (Title VIII), the first new federal legislation on this subject since 1866. The 1968 act prohibited discrimination on the basis of race, religion, or national origin in the sale, rental, advertising, financing, or brokerage of housing. It provided for enforcement by government agencies and made available legal remedies by injunction and by award of damages.

The Supreme Court then asked the Joneses and the Mayer Company to submit written memorandums on how the new legislation affected their suit. The company's attorneys argued that the new law covered the situation, that its enactment showed that the 1866 law was inapplicable, and that the suit should now be dismissed. The Joneses' lawyer argued that the new law complemented the 1866 statute but did not replace it, that the new law applied to discrimination taking place *after* its enactment and so would not help Mr. and Mrs. Jones, and that the old law was still valid and applicable to the case.

Do you think the 1866 law applies to private discrimination as well as government discrimination? Why was it originally enacted? Why wasn't it enforced? Does a developer of a large community act as the community's government during the building stages? Did the 1968 Civil Rights Act supersede the old law? Were Mr. and Mrs. Jones the victims of a legal loophole, which left them stranded between the two laws, covered by neither one?

Justice Stewart delivered the Supreme Court's seven-to-two decision. The majority found that enactment of the new Civil Rights Act "had no effect upon §1982 [the old act] and no effect upon this litigation, but it underscored the vast differences between, on the one hand, a general statute [the old act] applicable only to racial discrimination in the rental and sale of property and enforceable only by private parties acting on their own initiative, and, on the other hand, a detailed housing law [the 1968 act], applicable to a broad range of discriminatory practices and enforceable by a complete arsenal of federal authority."

Then Justice Stewart examined whether the 1866 act applied to discrimination by private parties. "On its face," he wrote, "§1982 appears to prohibit *all* discrimination against Negroes in the sale or rental of property—discrimination by private owners as well as discrimination by public authorities. Indeed, even the respondents seem to concede that, if §1982 'means what it says'. . . then it must encompass every racially motivated refusal to sell or rent and cannot be confined to officially sanctioned segregation in housing. Stressing what they consider to be the revolutionary implications of so literal a reading of §1982, the respondents argue that Congress cannot possibly have intended any such result." The developers, looking at the Congress sitting in 1968, could not believe the Congress sitting 102 years earlier had passed such strong civil rights legislation.

This showed an ignorance of the Reconstruction period, which the Court quickly corrected. "Our examination of the relevant history . . . persuades us that Congress meant exactly what it said," the Court announced. The justices recognized that the Reconstruction amendments and the 1866 act were proposed by congressmen known in their time as "Radical Republicans" precisely because they saw the Civil War as an event marking a basic change in American life and law.

Then the Court majority considered "whether Congress

has power under the Constitution to do what §1982 purports to do: to prohibit all racial discrimination, private and public, in the sale and rental of property." Phrasing the question another way, the Court asked: Since the Thirteenth Amendment authorizes Congress to prohibit slavery "by appropriate legislation," does this "include the power to eliminate all racial barriers to the acquisition of real and personal property? We think the answer to that question is plainly yes."

State laws enacted after the Civil War to limit the free exercise of civil rights by black people had been overturned by the Supreme Court in the 1870s under the Thirteenth Amendment, because they were "substitutes for the slave system," Justice Stewart explained. "And when racial discrimination herds men into ghettos and makes their ability to buy property turn on the color of their skin, then it too is a relic of slavery.

"Negro citizens, North and South, who saw in the Thirteenth Amendment a promise of freedom—freedom to 'go and come at pleasure' and to 'buy and sell when they please'—would be left with 'a mere paper guarantee' if Congress were powerless to assure that a dollar in the hands of a Negro will purchase the same thing as a dollar in the hands of a white man. At the very least, the freedom that Congress is empowered to secure under the Thirteenth Amendment includes the freedom to buy whatever a white man can buy, the right to live wherever a white man can live."

Justice Douglas concurred to make a different point. "Enabling a Negro to buy and sell real and personal property is a removal of one of many badges of slavery," he said, and he quoted a pioneering study, *Black Reconstruction,* written in 1935 by the great black scholar Dr. W. E. B. DuBois. Justice Douglas cited a score of recent Supreme Court decisions, in areas from public transportation to marriage, in which

Negroes were seeking to enforce their right to equality. "To-day the black is protected by a host of civil rights laws. But the forces of discrimination are still strong," he declared. He listed a variety of techniques used by segregationists to circumvent court orders and statutes. "This recital is enough to show how prejudices, once part and parcel of slavery, still persist. The men who sat in Congress in 1866 were trying to remove some of the badges or 'customs' of slavery when they enacted §1982. . . . The Congress that passed the so-called Open Housing Act in 1968 did not undercut any of the grounds on which §1982 rests."

Justice Harlan, joined by Justice White, dissented, because he felt that the 1866 act probably did not apply to private actions, and that the 1968 act in effect superseded it, so that the Court was wasting its time on this case.

By the *Jones* decision, the Supreme Court put the nation on notice that private discrimination in housing is illegal. It had taken more than a hundred years for the Court to apply the Reconstruction law the way Congress had intended in 1866. Unlike the *Brown* school desegregation case in 1954, this judical decision came a few years *after* several states and the federal government had taken some steps toward fair housing.

The 1968 Civil Rights Act provided room for action against virtually every type of housing discrimination and segregation. Title VIII states that it is the policy of the United States to provide for fair housing, and prohibits discrimination in the sale or rental of dwellings, in the financing of housing, and in advertising; it prohibits blockbusting and makes it unlawful to deny any person access to any multiple listing service for discriminatory reasons. (The act does not apply to single-family houses sold or rented without the use of a broker and without discriminatory advertising—if the owner owns only three such houses at a time. It does not apply to four-unit dwellings when the owner lives in one, nor to dwellings owned by religious organizations or private clubs for noncommercial purposes when occupancy is limited to members.)

The authority for administering the national fair housing policy is placed on the Secretary of Housing and Urban Development (HUD) and all government agencies are directed to establish affirmative action programs to enforce this policy, not simply to react when complaints are filed. HUD will refer complaints to states and cities with fair housing laws, but if the local agencies do not take action, HUD can process the complaint itself.

Anyone injured by discriminatory housing practices can sue in state or federal courts for an order to stop the practices, for the actual money loss caused by the practices, and for damages up to $1,000 to punish the recalcitrant seller or landlord. The U.S. Attorney General is also authorized to bring a civil suit seeking a court order against the discrimination when he believes Title VIII has been violated. In addition, Title IX prohibits intimidation or attempted injury of any person in a fair housing case because of race, color, religion, or national origin, and carries a criminal penalty of $1,000 and/or one year's imprisonment. If someone is actually physically injured by the defendant, the penalties are $10,000 and/or ten years' imprisonment, and if death results, the penalty is up to life imprisonment.

Civil rights groups, observing the actions of the Court, the Congress, and the President, are now determined to close the gap between legislative promise and accomplishment. They have learned that a law on the books is only as effective as the people's movement that fights for it, both in and out of the courtroom.

CHAPTER 27

Equality in Family Matters

Men and women live together, become parents, raise children, and die, leaving people who were dependent on them. Does government have any interest in how its citizens carry out these activities?

Under the ancient slave system, the slaveowner had absolute power over every aspect of his slaves' lives and even over most aspects of their deaths. In feudal society, the lord retained considerable control over the lives and deaths of his serfs, since he was ruler of the fiefdom, head of its church, and employer of all who lived there. The king sought similar control over his lords, playing the same three roles in their lives as they played in the lives of their serfs.

Marriages in that era were an economic affair as well as a social structure within which to produce children. A common method of protecting or increasing one's fortune was to marry one's daughter to a wealthy noble. A daughter's chastity was a marketable commodity, and a "loose" woman, whether in behavior or only in reputation, brought her parents less money from the marriage contract, if she managed to get a husband at all. A man, on the other hand, was not hindered socially or financially by acquiring a reputation as a Casanova.

Inheritance laws were, of course, also based on economic

necessity. The feudal economic system could survive only if landed estates were not broken up among the several children born to the lord. For this reason, the law required that the oldest lawful son take all the land and the lawful younger sons and all the daughters take nothing in the way of land. Under such a stark system of inheritance (primogeniture), a child who was born out of wedlock had almost no prospect of inheriting any land from his parents, even if his father acknowledged him as his bastard. (Shakespeare's plays are full of the flavor of this era.)

Although primogeniture was outlawed in the American colonies, some feudal family rules emigrated to North America, and continued to be followed after their economic basis had fallen into disuse in the urban, mercantile-capitalist era. The Puritan conscience also came over to the northern colonies and adultery by a woman continued to be a serious crime.

The South reverted back to the slave system in its drive for cheap agricultural and industrial labor. The slaveowner was encouraged by the economic system and permitted by law to ignore all relationships among the people who worked for him in the status of slaves. He had the authority to sell husband from wife and children from parents, making marriage and family meaningless. In addition, the double standard of morality for men and women, which had long existed in white society, became a quadruple standard: without ostracism, white men could have relations with both white women who were willing and black women who were slaves; however, white women were supposed to have relations only with their white husbands; black women were to have relations on demand with their white owners; and black men and women could have relations with each other, limited in duration by the master's plans to work them, or to sell them and the children produced by their union. The breeding of slaves was a profitable business in the South, particularly after 1808 when Article I, Section 9, of the Constitution permitted Congress to prohibit the importation of slaves.

All slave children could be considered illegitimate by the slaveowner. The Supreme Court, in the *Dred Scott* decision of 1857, held that slaves and their descendants had "had no rights which the white man was bound to respect" in 1787, when the Constitution was drafted, and therefore did not have any in 1857. Marriage and governmental recognition of marriage and family ties were among the rights denied to blacks.

Habits and customs beaten into a people by their slavemasters were not changed instantly when the economic relationship was changed from slavery to tenant farming and then to city work for wages. Men and women never allowed to marry legally or to raise children in a family setting did not all immediately adopt these social customs after emancipation. Nor did men, accustomed to demanding sexual favors from women of another race, suddenly stop their demands and treat all women on the same basis. Women had known for centuries that they must bear many children to be sure any would survive, and that more hands to work on the farm meant more income; they did not rush out to buy contraceptives when they became available. But as time passed, the customs that had been required for survival or had been taught by parents and ancestors were slowly reexamined by the next generations.

Thoughtful people looked at the reasons behind these old customs and found that some reasons had disappeared with time. The powers of ruler, church, and employer, formerly combined in the single person of the king or lord, were split in American society into separate entities. The United States developed a federal government to rule the citizenry; this government was separated from the church, which governed religion, and from the capitalist system, which governed the economic relationship between privately owned businesses and their employees.

The customs and rules of family life formerly ordained by the king, lord, or master, now sometimes fell into a no-man's land—the gaps or overlaps between the three separated functions, in which none had clear jurisdiction. Was government or church to regulate marriage? If the government recognized a marriage but the church did not, was it a valid marriage? In this no-man's land, people sometimes had to decide for themselves what was right, and sometimes did not agree with the laws, rules, or customs ordained by one or another institution. They ultimately came to change or discard some of the old rules, so that what was considered immoral or illegal in one era became acceptable in another. In the course of these changes people sometimes lived in open violation of an unwritten rule or even of a written statute.

In more recent times, the western world reexamined its views on family life following the defeat of Nazism in World War II. Hitler saw the family solely as a mechanism for producing more "Aryan" children who would rule all of Europe. Non-Aryan families were not to exist in Nazi Germany on an equal basis with Aryans and some were to be exterminated. The nations that fought this ideology were forced to think about the quality of life they were fighting for as well as against. After the war, when the United Nations was organized, it set up a Commission on Human Rights to discuss and formulate the tenets of this life. After months of debate, in 1948 the commission proposed a Universal Declaration of Human Rights. This document of thirty articles contains "a standard of achievement for all peoples and all nations," the best thinking to date on problems of human life and freedom, combining portions from basic documents in many countries, including the United States Bill of Rights, Reconstruction amendments, and New Deal legislation.

The U.N. Declaration of Human Rights contains seven articles dealing with family life and the rights of family members. In several ways they go beyond existing American law in spelling out the rights of children born out of wedlock and the responsibility of government to assist families.

Article 1. "All human beings are born free and equal in dignity and rights. . . ."

Article 2. "Everyone is entitled to all the rights and freedoms set forth in this Declaration, without distinction of any kind, such as race, colour, sex, language, religion, political or other opinion, national or social origin, property, birth or other status."

Article 6. "Everyone has the right to recognition everywhere as a person before the law."

Article 7. "All are equal before the law and are entitled without any discrimination to equal protection of the law. All are entitled to equal protection against any discrimination in violation of this Declaration and against any incitement to such discrimination."

Article 12. "No one shall be subjected to arbitrary interference with his privacy, family, home. . . . Everyone has the right to the protection of the law against such interference or attacks."

Article 16. "1. Men and women of full age, without any limitation due to race, nationality or religion, have the right to marry and to found a family. They are entitled to equal rights as to marriage, during marriage and at its dissolution."

"3. The family is the natural and fundamental group unit of society and is entitled to protection by society and the State."

Article 25. "1. Everyone has the right to . . . security in the event of . . . lack of livelihood in circumstances beyond his control."

"2. Motherhood and childhood are entitled to special care and assistance. All children, whether born in or out of wedlock, shall enjoy the same social protection."

Although an American, Eleanor Roosevelt, was chairman of the commission that drew up the declaration, and although the United States representatives to the General Assembly voted with forty-seven other nations in support of the declaration (ten abstained or were absent, none opposed), the declaration went further than many Americans were willing to go in the post-war era. However, when some Americans were denied rights listed in this U.N. document, they brought their complaints into the courts and eventually to the United States Supreme Court. Their lawyers occasionally referred to the language in the U.N. declaration, and always relied on the spirit of that document.

In 1964, in *McLaughlin* v. *Florida,* the Court ruled that a black and white couple who spent the night together could not be punished any differently from an all-white couple or an all-black couple who committed the same act. (This required overruling an 1883 decision, *Pace* v. *Alabama.*) Since the crime of interracial cohabitation would cease if the couple married, the Court was urged to decide in that case that laws in nineteen states making it a crime for a black and white couple to marry were unconstitutional. But the Court left that problem for another day, when it was raised directly.

A crime for black and white to marry

Loving v. Virginia (1967)
388 U.S. 1, 87 S. Ct. 1817, 18 L. Ed. 2d 1010

"But would you want your daughter to marry one?" became such a stereotype of racial prejudice in the 1960s that it was used as the punchline in jokes about various sorts of discrimination. The issue was no joke to a Virginia couple, appropriately named Mr. and Mrs. Loving.

Richard Loving and Mildred Jeter grew up together in the hill country north of Richmond, Virginia. The Jeters were black and the Lovings white. Their families were neighbors and friends. Richard and Mildred had a long, sometimes difficult, courtship and finally decided to marry. They went to Washington, D.C., on June 2, 1958, for the ceremony.

They soon returned to Virginia and set up housekeeping. About a month later, they were roused out of bed at 2:00 A.M. by the county sheriff, who insisted on taking them to jail. He said they were charged with the crime of miscegenation (marriage between a black and a white), prohibited by Virginia law. The county grand jury indicted them, and the Lovings pleaded guilty to the charge on January 6, 1959, before Judge Leon Bazile.

The judge said: "Almighty God created the races white, black, yellow, malay, and red, and he placed them on separate continents. And but for the interference with his arrangement there would be no cause for such marriages. The fact that he separated the races shows that he did not intend for the races to mix." He then sentenced the Lovings to a year in jail, but suspended the sentences if the couple would leave Virginia and not reenter for twenty-five years.

The Virginia statute was clear: It was a felony for "any white person" to "intermarry with a colored person," or vice versa. The Lovings could see they had violated this law, so the only thing for them to do was to move. They went to Washington. Mr. Loving was a construction worker and he had a hard time finding work in the nation's capitol. The Lovings also noticed that the cost of living was higher than at home. They had a son, a second son, and then a daughter, in successive years. With financial difficulties pressing them, and sorely missing their families and friends, the Lovings came back to Virginia for a visit in the summer of 1963. They were arrested again, but released on bail. Desperate to find a solution to their dilemma, they wrote to Attorney General Robert Kennedy asking for help. He passed the letter on to the Washington chapter of the American Civil Liberties Union.

The ACLU attorneys informed Mr. and Mrs. Loving that the antimiscegenation statute was probably unconstitutional, and the Lovings decided to fight for their right to live in Virginia as a married couple. As Richard Loving said in a *Life* interview, "We are not doing it just because somebody had to do it and we wanted to be the ones. We are doing it for *us*—because we want to live here."

On November 6, 1963, they filed a motion to vacate Judge Bazile's judgment and set aside the sentence he had imposed on them. The motion came before Judge Bazile himself, who took no action on it for months. On October 28, 1964, the Lovings therefore filed a class suit in federal district court in Virginia, asking that the antimiscegenation statutes be declared unconstitutional.

Before the three-judge federal court was convened, however, Judge Bazile ruled on the motion before him: he denied it. The federal court then told the Lovings to complete their proceedings in the state courts before pursuing their federal suit; but the federal court did issue an order announcing that it would free the Lovings on reasonable bail if the state authorities arrested or imprisoned them during the pendency of any court proceedings.

The Lovings appealed Judge Bazile's ruling to the Virginia Supreme Court of Appeals. They said the statute under which they had been convicted violated the due process and equal protection clauses of the Fourteenth Amendment because it was based on racial discrimination and denied the fundamental right of free people to marry as they chose. They also argued that Judge Bazile's sentence constituted banishment, a harsh violation of constitutional due process.

The Virginia appellate court upheld the statute as constitutional and affirmed the Lovings' convictions, but sent the case back to Judge Bazile for resentencing, because the condition he imposed in suspending the sentences was unreasonable and the offense (living together as man and wife in Virginia) could have been prohibited without banishing the Lovings from the state, the court said.

With the continuing help of the ACLU, the Lovings appealed to the United States Supreme Court. The state's attorney argued that marriage was a social contract subject to necessary state licensing and regulation, that the Virginia statute was applied equally to all white and all black persons wishing to intermarry, and that the state's legitimate purpose was "to preserve the racial integrity of its citizens."

Do you think the right to marry the person of your choice is protected by the federal Constitution? Is this a question of legitimate concern to the state, but not to the federal government? Or is this a personal matter of concern only to the individuals and protected from all government concern by the right of privacy and freedom of association? Is there a difference between statutes specifying the ages at which parties can marry and those specifying which race can marry which other race? If all parties are prohibited from interracial marriage and each race is subject to the same penalties, has anyone been denied equal protection of the law?

Chief Justice Warren delivered the Supreme Court's unanimous decision in June 1967. "Penalties for miscegenation arose as an incident to slavery and have been common in Virginia since the colonial period," he noted. In the present case, the justices rejected Virginia's "notion that the mere 'equal application' of a statute containing racial classifications" would satisfy the equal protection clause of the Fourteenth Amendment. The statute would have to meet "the very heavy burden of justification which the Fourteenth Amendment has traditionally required of state statutes drawn according to race," they said.

"There can be no question but that Virginia's miscegenation statutes rest solely upon distinctions drawn according to race. The statutes . . . [made] generally accepted conduct [illegal, if it was] engaged in by members of different races. Over the years, this Court has consistently repudiated 'distinctions between citizens solely because of their ancestry' as being 'odious to a free people whose institutions are founded upon the doctrine of equality.' . . . At the very least, the Equal Protection Clause demands that racial classifications, [which are] especially suspect in criminal statutes, be subjected to the 'most rigid scrutiny,' . . . and, if they are ever to be upheld, they must be shown to be necessary to the accomplishment of some permissible state objective, independent of the racial discrimination which it was the object of the Fourteenth Amendment to eliminate."

The Court found that the antimiscegenation law did not apply to marriages between blacks and people of Asian or

American Indian ancestry: "The fact that Virginia only prohibits interracial marriages involving white persons demonstrates that the racial classifications must stand on their own justification, as measures designed to maintain White Supremacy. We have consistently denied the constitutionality of measures which restrict the rights of citizens on account of race. There can be no doubt that restricting the freedom to marry solely because of racial classifications violates the central meaning of the Equal Protection Clause."

In addition, the Court held: "These statutes also deprive the Lovings of liberty without due process of law in violation of the Due Process Clause of the Fourteenth Amendment. The freedom to marry has long been recognized as one of the vital personal rights essential to the orderly pursuit of happiness by free men. . . . The Fourteenth Amendment requires that the freedom of choice to marry not be restricted by invidious racial discriminations. Under our Constitution, the freedom to marry, or not marry, a person of another race resides with the individual and cannot be infringed by the State."

Justice Stewart concurred, repeating his statement in *McLaughlin* v. *Florida* that "it is simply not possible for a state law to be valid under our Constitution which makes the criminality of an act depend upon the race of the actor."

Thus, nine years after their wedding, Mildred and Richard Loving were freed from the threat of imprisonment for the act of marrying and making their home in Virginia. *Life* magazine estimated that there were half a million black-white marriages in the United States when the Lovings presented their case to the Supreme Court. The Court's ruling invalidated the antimiscegenation laws in sixteen states, whether they forbade marriages between black and white only, or between members of other racial and national groups.

The rights of illegitimate children

Levy v. Louisiana (1968)
391 U.S. 68, 88 S. Ct. 1509, 20 L. Ed. 2d 436

Louise Levy was the mother of five children and their sole means of support. She took them to church every Sunday, and spent some of her earnings as a black domestic worker to send them to parochial schools in New Orleans.

In 1964, Ms. Levy became sick. On March 12, she went to Charity Hospital and saw Dr. Willard Wing, who was on duty that day. She complained of feeling dizzy, tired, weak, short of breath, and having a bad pain in her chest. Without ordering any laboratory tests, the doctor prescribed some tonic and tranquilizers, and sent her home.

A week later, on March 19, Ms. Levy came back to the hospital. She told Dr. Wing she was feeling much worse. The doctor quickly looked her over again, told her she wasn't taking the medicine, and made an appointment for her to see a psychiatrist two months later on May 14. Apparently he thought her complaints were psychosomatic, since he did not order the customary blood or urine tests.

On March 22, Ms. Levy was brought to the hospital semi-conscious. The staff conducted a series of tests and diagnosed her condition as hypertension uremia—a disease in which body wastes that normally go out in the urine are accumulated in the blood, poisoning the body. This diagnosis proved to be correct, but came too late. Louise Levy died on March 29.

The guardian appointed for her children filed suit on their behalf against the state hospital and the doctor for the wrongful death of their mother and to compensate for her pain and suffering before her death. Louisiana law provided that the husband or wife or children or parents or brothers and sisters of a person, in that order, could recover money to compensate for the injury and death of that person by the fault of someone else.

The attorneys for the state, the hospital, and Dr. Wing's insurance company asked the judge to dismiss the suit because the statute applied only to legitimate children and Ms. Levy's children were all born out of wedlock. The judge agreed, and the children's guardian appealed the dismissal. The Louisiana court of appeal said, "Our jurisprudence is well established that 'child' means legitimate child, and that recovery is denied . . . to illegitimate . . . children for the wrongful death of a parent." The three state judges explained: "Denying illegitimate children the right to recover in such a case is actually based on morals and general welfare because it discourages bringing children into the world out of wedlock."

The Louisiana Supreme Court refused to review the case, and the children appealed to the United States Supreme Court, with the help of attorneys for the American Civil Liberties Union. They used every precedent they could find, in and out of United States law. They argued that the Louisiana statute "contravenes the biblical injunction that 'the son shall not bear the iniquity of the father with him.' Ezekiel 18:23." They reminded the Court that Louisiana was the only jurisdiction that deprived an illegitimate child of an equal right to sue for the wrongful death of his mother. They might have been thinking of the Universal Declaration of Human Rights' provisions on illegitimacy. They argued that this distinction between legitimate and illegitimate children, all of whom were equally dependent on their mothers for care, love, and support, was one of those "invidious discriminations" forbidden by the equal protection clause of the Fourteenth Amendment.

The opposing attorneys maintained that the right to recover for wrongful death was created solely by the state legislature and made to apply only to certain clear classes of people—those named in the statute.

Has every human society classified its young as "legitimate" or "illegitimate"? Can a *child* be illegitimate, or is this a shorthand way of saying his *parents' relationship* was considered illegitimate by the government? Do you think laws discriminating against illegitimate children have been effective in discouraging people from bearing children out of wedlock? Is penalizing a person for his status rather than for his acts unconstitutional as a bill of attainder or as a violation of the due process or equal protection clause? What other kinds of people have suffered penalties because of their status? How has the Court regarded these penalties?

The Supreme Court split six to three. Justice Douglas wrote for the Court: "We start from the premise that illegitimate children are not 'nonpersons.' They are humans, live, and have their being. They are clearly 'persons' within the meaning of the Equal Protection Clause of the Fourteenth Amendment.

"While a State has broad power when it comes to making classifications. . . , it may not draw a line which constitutes an invidious discrimination against a particular class." The basic test is "whether the line drawn is a rational one."

"In applying the Equal Protection Clause to social and economic legislation, we give great latitude to the legislature in making classifications," the justices acknowledged. But, they went on, "we have been extremely sensitive when it comes to basic civil rights . . . and have not hesitated to strike down an invidious classification even though it had history and tradition on its side." Here the Court cited *Brown* v. *Board of Education* (see chapter 22).

"The rights asserted here involve the intimate, familial relationship between a child and his own mother. When the child's claim of damage for loss of his mother is in issue, why, in terms of 'equal protection,' should the tortfeasors [wrongdoers] go free merely because the child is illegitimate? Why should the illegitimate child be denied rights merely because of his birth out of wedlock? He certainly is subject to all the responsibilities of a citizen, including the payment of taxes and conscription under the Selective Service Act. How under our constitutional regime can he be denied correlative rights which other citizens enjoy?

"Legitimacy or illegitimacy of birth has no relation to the nature of the wrong allegedly inflicted on the mother. These children, though illegitimate, were dependent on her; she cared for them and nurtured them; they were indeed hers in the biological and in the spiritual sense; in her death they suffered wrong in the sense that any dependent would.

"We conclude that it is invidious to discriminate against them when no action, conduct, or demeanor of theirs is possibly relevant to the harm that was done the mother."

Justices Harlan, Black, and Stewart dissented from this and a companion decision announced the same day, in which the majority upheld the right of a mother to recover damages for the wrongful death of her illegitimate son. Justice Harlan wrote for the dissenters, "The only question . . . is whether the plaintiff falls within the classes of persons to whom the State has accorded a right of action for the death of another." He declared in plain language that showed his pique: "The

Court today, for some reason which I am at a loss to understand, rules that the State must base its arbitrary definition of the plaintiff class on biological rather than legal relationships. Exactly how this makes the Louisiana scheme even marginally more 'rational' is not clear, for neither a biological relationship nor legal acknowledgment is indicative of the love or economic dependence that may exist between two persons." He called the majority opinion "frankly . . . preposterous" for arguing that Louisiana might, by analogy, deny illegitimates constitutional rights. "The rights at issue here stem from the existence of a family relationship, and the State has decided only that it will not recognize the family relationship unless the formalities of marriage, or of the acknowledgment of children by the parent in question, have been complied with."

Justice Douglas answered in the majority opinion of the companion case, *Glona* v. *American Guarantee and Liability Insurance Company:* "To say that the test of equal protection should be the 'legal' rather than the biological relationship is to avoid the issue. For the Equal Protection Clause necessarily limits the authority of a State to draw such 'legal' lines as it chooses."

On remand of the *Levy* case, the Louisiana Supreme Court declared: "The members of this court may totally disagree with the reasoning and the result of the United States Supreme Court majority opinion and may agree with the dissent of Justice Harlan wherein it was said that the majority resolved the issue in this case '. . . by a process that can only be described as brute force.' Nevertheless it is our obligation to discharge our responsibility under constitutional authority and limitation." The court did not copy the massive, open violation of the United States Supreme Court's decision in *Brown* v. *Board of Education* (described in chapter 22). It found that Louise Levy's children had a right to recover for the wrongful death of their mother.

While these cases were wending their way to the Supreme Court, lower courts were struggling with cases in which white parents sought to adopt black children and Jewish parents sought to adopt Catholic children when no children of their own race or religion were available for adoption. Other cases arose when a white mother divorced her white husband, then married a black man, and had to fight to retain custody of her children. Still other cases involved a divorced or widowed parent fighting for custody of his or her natural children against grandparents who complained that the parent was too liberal in politics or religion. Frequently religious organizations in the local communities participated in these cases publicly, or behind the scenes. Many heartbreaking decisions were made, and only a Solomon could determine whether the best interests of the children were the paramount concern of the judges in such cases.

By 1970, race, religion, and legitimacy could be discussed more rationally in relation to cohabitation, marriage, divorce, and adoption. This was due, in part, to the Supreme Court decisions striking down the openly racist statute in *Loving,* the more subtly racist statute in *Levy,* and the contraception statute in *Griswold* v. *Connecticut* (discussed in chapter 7).

CHAPTER 28

Equal Protection for the Poor

Justice Black, in *Gideon* v. *Wainwright* (discussed in chapter 13) expressed the truism that anyone in a criminal case who had money hired a lawyer to represent his interests, which indicates that the assistance of lawyers is considered critical. While creditors and landlords have likewise hired lawyers for centuries, the recent work of poverty lawyers demonstrates this principle is valid for debtors and tenants in *civil* cases as well.

Until recently, few poor people could find lawyers to represent them against ghetto landlords, loan sharks, or corner businesses that frequently rooked them, especially if they knew little about their rights under the law. A lawyer in private practice would say he could not afford to handle cases that would take up his time and produce no income to help pay his overhead expenses (rent, phone, secretary's salary) even if he were willing to forgo payment of a fee to himself. It was a joke in the profession that lawyers who took too many poverty law cases became poverty cases themselves—although some got elected to public office because of the reputations they built for helping the poor, and others managed to combine some free work with much paying work.

The Equal Opportunity Act of 1964 authorized the federal

Office of Economic Opportunity (OEO) to establish a Legal Services Program. By July 1966, OEO had funded some 170 local legal services programs in 135 cities and towns across the country, and more were being planned. The government hired lawyers and legal staffs to work on the cases of poor people in offices in poor neighborhoods, and it footed all the bills—salaries, investigations, overhead, court costs, etc. The clients paid nothing for the service, but they had to be below a certain income level to qualify. Suddenly there were bright young lawyers with creative legal ideas who could afford to spend time fighting gouging landlords and unfair welfare regulations. In time, private agencies concerned with racial discrimination found they could get contributions to take poverty law cases as well. Law schools began to teach courses on poverty law and professors wrote useful articles on abuses of the welfare system long ignored by scholars and those with power to make changes.

Some legal service offices concentrated on helping individual clients with their individual problems, such as getting a divorce from an absent spouse or suing a landlord who refused to make repairs. Other offices decided to try a different tack. They kept statistics on which kinds of problems clients brought in most often and then tried to fashion lawsuits that would attack these problems at the root. Usually these were *class* suits, indicating that the plaintiffs were suing to protect not only their own rights but also the rights of everyone in the same situation.

Friendly critics argued that the OEO legal service programs contained two built-in weaknesses: there was no effort to combine older and younger lawyers on the staffs to obtain the advantages of both experience and freshness; and there was a rule prohibiting most offices from handling criminal cases, which meant that a major area of legal problems of the poor—arrests on criminal charges—was not touched, and that clients could not come to one law office for all the legal advice they needed.

Nonetheless, suits handled by the OEO lawyers made federal courts, and some state courts, face many problems that had never been litigated before, although the abuses complained of had long been with us. Legal service offices could afford to take appeals and they frequently did. Many of their cases reached the United States Supreme Court for decision. This chapter discusses only two landmark decisions out of a series of poverty law cases. Neither would have been filed by lawyers in private practice living from the fees paid by clients. The same constitutional principles were involved in most of these suits: (1) denials of equal treatment to people because they are poor—in violation of the equal protection clause of the Fourteenth Amendment, and (2) denials of fair treatment to the poor—in violation of the due process clauses in the Fifth and Fourteenth Amendments. Afro-Americans, Chicanos, Asian-Americans, Native Americans—sometimes called Third World people—constitute a larger segment of the poor population than of the population as a whole. As a result, poverty law also deals with (3) problems of equal protection regardless of race, creed, or color.

Freezing wages to pay creditors

Sniadach v. Family Finance Corporation of Bay View (1969)

395 U.S. 337, 89 S. Ct. 1820, 23 L. Ed. 2d 349

Christine Sniadach worked for the Miller Harris Instrument Company in Milwaukee, Wisconsin. In the 1960s, she borrowed money from the Family Finance Corporation and signed a note promising to repay with interest. When $420 was still owing on the note, the loan company filed a wage garnishment suit against Ms. Sniadach. Garnishment is a procedure by which a creditor files a lawsuit against a debtor, and then tells the debtor's employer to take money directly out of the debtor's wages or salary: the employer pays the creditor as the worker earns the money, and the worker never sees the money at all.

When Ms. Sniadach borrowed the money, she probably did not realize that her wages could be garnished if she failed to keep up her payments. However, Wisconsin law, like the laws of many states, provided for garnishment, and Wisconsin also provided that, during the garnishment period, the worker who was in debt should receive a "subsistence allowance" of $25 a week, or $40 if he had dependents, but never more than 50 percent of his wages. The remainder would go to the creditor.

Wisconsin also gave creditors the right to "freeze" the debtor's wages as soon as a garnishment suit was filed and long before a court decided that the money was really owed and that the debtor had no defense. The Family Finance Corporation proceeded to use this right. Its lawyer drew up a summons telling Ms. Sniadach's employer to withhold part of her wages until further orders from the court. The summons was signed by the court clerk and served on the Miller Harris Company on November 21, 1966. That same day Ms. Sniadach was served with a summons and complaint in the garnishment suit.

The Miller Harris Company answered the summons, stating that Ms. Sniadach had already earned $63.18, and it would freeze half, paying her the other half for subsistence.

On December 23, Ms. Sniadach filed a motion to dismiss the garnishment suit, claiming that the procedures used violated the due process and equal protection clauses of the Fourteenth Amendment. She had been given notice of the garnishment according to the law, her lawyer admitted, but she was then immediately deprived of her wages before she had an opportunity for a hearing or judgment by a court on the validity of the debt. Well-to-do defendants could post a bond to "unfreeze" their salaries while the case was pending, but workers were helpless if they did not have extra funds available for such a bond. Ms. Sniadach's lawyer argued that this was an improper or invidious discrimination between rich and poor.

The trial judge denied the motion to dismiss and the Wisconsin Supreme Court affirmed the judge's ruling. It pointed out that the wages were frozen only temporarily, and cited a 1929 United States Supreme Court decision upholding a similar procedure under Maine law by which a creditor could attach the land of a debtor before a court had ruled on the legality of the debt.

Ms. Sniadach, with legal assistance from the National Office for the Rights of Indigents and the NAACP Legal Defense and Educational Fund, asked the U.S. Supreme Court to review the decision.

Do you think it is unconstitutional to withhold a person's wages until a decision is reached on the legality of the creditor's claim? What can a creditor do if he wins the suit but then the debtor does not have the money to pay the debt and court costs? What can a debtor do if his wages are withheld on a false claim by a creditor? Are attachments of land and garnishments of wages comparable? Is it unequal treatment if workers' wages can be withheld to pay debts but doctors' or lawyers' fees cannot be withheld for that purpose?

Justice Douglas wrote the opinion for the seven-to-one majority in this case—one of the last to be decided under

Chief Justice Warren. "In this case the sole question is whether there has been a taking of property without that procedural due process that is required by the Fourteenth Amendment," he said. It was clear that, under the Wisconsin statute, from the time the summons was served until the trial court decision, "the wage earner is deprived of his enjoyment of earned wages without any opportunity to be heard and to tender any defense he may have," such as a claim that he doesn't owe the money or that the creditor defrauded him in some manner.

Justice Douglas then described the specific problems caused by wage garnishments, quoting from congressional debates and law review studies. "A prejudgment garnishment of the Wisconsin type is a taking which may impose tremendous hardship on wage earners with families to support. Until a recent Act of Congress, . . . which forbids discharge of employees on the ground that their wages have been garnished, garnishment often meant the loss of a job. Over and beyond that was the great drain on family income." A Wisconsin law journal had found that the subsistence allowance was "generally insufficient to support the debtor for any one week."

Creditors used the threat of these garnishments to coerce debtors into signing new "payment schedules" in which the original debt was increased by attorney's fees and other collection costs the loan company had incurred. "The result is that a prejudgment garnishment of the Wisconsin type may as a practical matter drive a wage-earning family to the wall."

The Court distinguished attachments of land, as in the 1929 Maine case, and garnishments of wages. A creditor under feudalism could "attach" the land of the debtor-landowner and the creditor would then have to be paid, either by the debtor, or by whoever bought the land from the debtor. The debtor could continue to live on the land, and could use the produce grown on the land, but he could not free the land of the debt—he could not leave the debt behind —because it was "attached" to the land.

When the feudal system gave way to the new economic system of capitalism, most workers left the land and went to cities to work for wages. Their creditors transplanted the idea of "attachments" from land to wages, the basic type of property that workers earned under capitalism. They got legislation passed permitting a creditor to attach or garnish wages. Theoretically, this kind of attachment was no harder on the debtor than attachment of real property. But in fact the results were very different. A worker could not "use" his wages when the creditor had garnished them, as a debtor could continue to use the products of his land after it was attached. And a debtor could not "sell" his wages to the grocer or landlord, subject to the debt, when the creditor had garnished them, as the land-debtor could sell his land subject to the debt. In other words, a wage earner under capitalism was in a worse situation if part of his wages were withheld than a landowner was under feudalism if all of his land was attached.

The Court explained, "the fact that a procedure would pass muster under a feudal regime does not mean it gives necessary protection to all property in its modern forms. We deal here with wages—a specialized type of property presenting distinct problems in our economic system." The Court concluded: "Where the taking of one's property is so obvious, it needs no extended argument to conclude that absent notice and a prior hearing . . . this prejudgment garnishment procedure violates the fundamental principles of due process."

Justice Black dissented, finding no constitutional basis in the Bill of Rights or the Fourteenth Amendment for the Court's holding, and deploring what he felt was a return to "the 'Natural Law,' 'Due Process,' 'Shock-the-conscience' test of what is constitutional." He and Justice Harlan argued the point back and forth in dissenting and concurring opinions.

The decision invalidated the Wisconsin procedure for freezing wages before trial of the garnishment suit. Similar procedures in sixteen other states were also voided by the ruling, affecting an estimated $250,000 in wages then being held under pending actions. Attorneys for the NAACP Legal Defense Fund commented: "The decision indicates that the Supreme Court intends to strike down those obsolete legal rules of consumer credit which victimize buyers and borrowers rather than serve them."

In an era when banks and other lending agencies advertise that it is easy to get credit and to pay in "low, easy installments," many people buy large appliances and other commodities on time without realizing how much interest they will have to pay—on top of the price—or figuring out how much income they will have left after the payments are taken out each month.

Despite outcries from many in the loan industry, Congress finally dealt with part of the problem that created the *Sniadach* case by passing the Truth in Lending Act of 1968. This statute requires all loan companies and others who sell goods on credit to make clear to borrowers exactly what interest they must pay on the money borrowed, and allows states to set limits on the interest rates.

While the Truth in Lending Act does not require a creditor to list all the steps he can take to collect his loan from the debtor, it does contain certain protections for the debtor. For example, the debtor must be told, before he signs the loan papers, that the creditor can go directly to the debtor's bank account and take out the money owed without prior notice to the debtor. In the past, it was common for a debtor to suddenly find he had no money in the bank because he had failed to make payments on his loan and the creditor had gotten an "undisclosed bank lien" for the money owed.

The *Sniadach* opinion gives poverty lawyers and clients a strong new weapon in their continuing battle against creditors and their garnishments, attachments, and repossessions based on loans and installment sales. It is being used against attachments on bank accounts, sheriffs' attachments on household goods, and repossession of automobiles without prior hearings. The loan industry has sponsored legislation to limit its scope, and some courts have found these new acts constitutional. State and federal legislators propose bills each year to prohibit the most flagrant abuses of sellers and lenders and to regulate their activities more closely in the interest of consumers, but few of these bills pass.

A blunderbuss method of denying welfare

Shapiro v. *Thompson* (1969)
394 U.S. 618, 89 S. Ct. 1322, 22 L. Ed. 2d 600

Miss Vivian Marie Thompson was nineteen years old in 1966. She had a baby son and was pregnant again. The father was not helping her support and raise the children. In June she moved from Massachusetts to Hartford, Connecticut, to live with her mother. By August, her mother could no longer support her. Miss Thompson moved to an apartment and applied for Aid to Families with Dependent Children (AFDC), an aid program jointly financed by the federal government and the states. In November, Connecticut denied her application because the Connecticut AFDC rules required applicants to live in the state for a year before they could receive benefits.

Miss Thompson went to an OEO Neighborhood Legal Services Office for help. There, lawyer Brian Hollander examined the facts and decided Miss Thompson's constitutional rights were at stake. He filed suit for Miss Thompson, as plaintiff, against Bernard Shapiro, the Commissioner of Welfare, as defendant, in federal district court, claiming that the Connecticut residence requirement was unconstitutional. It restricted the right to travel and it treated new and old residents unequally for no good reason, in violation of the Fourteenth Amendment.

The state's attorney argued that the restrictions on the right to travel were minimal and that there was good reason for the residence requirement: it discouraged welfare recipients from pouring into Connecticut from states that paid lower benefits. If all these people were allowed to come in and immediately get assistance, the state budget would soar to unmanageable proportions and Connecticut residents would have to pay higher taxes to support newcomers on welfare.

Two of the three federal judges agreed with Miss Thompson, holding the residence requirement unconstitutional, in June 1967. The state appealed this momentous decision directly to the United States Supreme Court (the same procedure used in *Dombrowski* v. *Pfister,* discussed at page 161).

The Supreme Court consolidated the Connecticut appeal with two others, from Pennsylvania and Washington, D.C., in which federal district courts had also invalidated residence requirements for AFDC and for Aid to the Permanently and Totally Disabled (blind, lame, mentally ill, etc.).

The government attorneys raised several further arguments. The residence requirements gave welfare departments a chance to check for welfare fraud and to predict the following year's welfare budget more accurately. They discouraged people on relief from "shopping around" for benefits and coming into a state solely to empty the public purse. The requirements were a means of distinguishing residents who had contributed to the state before taking its payments, from those who brought nothing to the state but expected immediate handouts. The attorneys also noted that the federal AFDC law specifically authorized federal funding of state programs that had residence requirements of a year or less—thus, by implication, authorizing residence periods of this length.

The lawyers for Miss Thompson and the other plaintiffs countered that each of these "reasons" was either not factually true or not sufficient grounds for upholding the residence requirement in the face of a constitutional challenge.

Do you think Miss Thompson moved to Connecticut because her mother lived there or because Connecticut had higher AFDC benefits? Should an unmarried mother be free to pick out and move to the state that pays the highest AFDC benefits? Should she be financially chained to her present location unless she can somehow guarantee a year's livelihood for her family in a new state? Or should AFDC payments be the same in every state? Why do some states have higher AFDC payments than other states? Does the cost of living have anything to do with these rates? Can a state pick and choose the poor it will assist, because it doesn't have the money to assist everyone? What standards are valid, if such a choice is permitted?

The Supreme Court heard argument in this weighty group of cases, and then asked the lawyers to come back for reargument, as in *Brown* v. *Board of Education,* discussed in chapter 22. Finally, in April 1969 it handed down its six-to-three decision, with Justice Brennan writing the majority opinion. "There is no dispute that the effect of the waiting-period requirement in each case is to create two classes of needy resident families indistinguishable from each other except that one is composed of residents who have resided a year or more, and the second of residents who have resided less than a year, in the jurisdiction. On the basis of this sole difference the first class is granted and the second class is denied welfare aid upon which may depend the ability of the families to obtain the very means to subsist—food, shelter, and other necessities of life."

The majority opinion noted the states' primary argument: "It is asserted that people who require welfare assistance during their first year of residence in a state are likely to become continuing burdens on state welfare programs. Therefore, the argument runs, if such people can be deterred from entering the jurisdiction by denying them welfare benefits during the first year, state programs to assist long-time residents will not be impaired by a substantial influx of indigent newcomers." The Court held: "We do not doubt that the one-year waiting period device is well suited to discourage the influx of poor families in need of assistance. . . . But the purpose of inhibiting migration by needy persons into the State is constitutionally impermissible.

"This Court long ago recognized that the nature of our Federal Union and our constitutional concepts of personal liberty unite to require that all citizens be free to travel throughout the length and breadth of our land uninhibited by statutes, rules, or regulations which unreasonably burden or restrict this movement." Justice Brennan was referring to *Edwards* v. *California,* a case from the Great Depression, in which the Court held unconstitutional a California statute aimed at forbidding Okies and Arkies to enter the "golden state" after the dust storms drove these farmers from their homes in the South and Southwest. The Court also cited the discussion on the right of every person to travel from state to state in *United States* v. *Guest* (the case discussed with *United States* v. *Price* in chapter 24).

The opinion then answered the other state arguments, finding that the statutes were not tailored to exclude only those shopping around for the highest benefits. "Rather, the class of barred newcomers is all-inclusive, lumping the great majority who come to the State for other purposes with those who come for the sole purpose of collecting higher benefits." The Court went further: "More fundamentally, a State may no more try to fence out those indigents who seek higher welfare benefits than it may try to fence out indigents generally. Implicit in any such distinction is the notion that indigents who enter a State with the hope of securing higher welfare benefits are somehow less deserving than indigents who do not take this consideration into account. But we do not perceive why a mother who is seeking to make a new life for herself and her children should be regarded as less deserving because she considers, among other factors, the level of a State's public assistance. Surely such a mother is no less deserving than a mother who moves into a particular State in order to take advantage of its better educational facilities."

The Court rejected the distinction between new and old residents on the basis of contributions to the state. "We have difficulty seeing how long-term residents who qualify for welfare are making a greater present contribution to the State in taxes than indigent residents who have recently arrived. If the argument is based on contributions made in the past by the long-term residents, there is some question, as a factual matter, whether this argument is applicable in Pennsylvania where the record suggests that some 40% of those denied public assistance because of the waiting period had lengthy prior residence in the State. But we need not rest on the particular facts of these cases." Arguing from parallel examples that would put the issue sharply before affluent Americans, Justice Brennan pointed out that the reasoning of the government attorneys "would logically permit the State to bar new residents from schools, parks, and libraries or deprive them of police and fire protection. Indeed it would permit the State to apportion all benefits and services according to the past tax contributions of its citizens. The Equal Protection Clause prohibits such an apportionment of state services."

Justice Brennan noted that, since the requirements had a chilling effect on the constitutional right to travel, using his famous phrase from a civil liberties case (*Dombrowski,* in chapter 6) in this poverty law case, therefore the requirements were invalid "unless shown to be necessary to promote a *compelling* governmental interest." The Court examined the remaining arguments in this light:

"The argument that the waiting-period requirement facilitates budget predictability is wholly unfounded. The records in all three cases are utterly devoid of evidence that either State or the District of Columbia in fact uses the one-year requirement as a means to predict the number of people who will require assistance in the budget year."

"The argument that the waiting period serves as an administratively efficient rule of thumb for determining residency similarly will not withstand scrutiny. . . . Before granting an application, the welfare authorities investigate the applicant's employment, housing, and family situation and in the course of the inquiry necessarily learn the facts upon which to determine whether the applicant is a resident."

"Similarly, there is no need for a State to use the one-year waiting period as a safeguard against fraudulent receipt of benefits; for less drastic means are available, and are employed, to minimize that hazard." Suspected double payments from two states to one indigent "can be prevented by a letter or a telephone call" to the other state's welfare department, said the Court. Therefore, "it is unreasonable to accomplish this objective by the blunderbuss method of denying assistance to all indigent newcomers for an entire year."

"Pennsylvania suggests that the one-year waiting period is justified as a means of encouraging new residents to join the labor force promptly. But this logic would also require a similar waiting period for long-term residents of the State."

The Court summed up, "We conclude therefore that appellants in these cases do not use and have no need to use the one-year requirement for the governmental purposes suggested."

The Court also rejected the argument that the federal statute implied Congressional approval of the one-year requirement. The legislative history indicated that Congress's intent was to reduce much more lengthy state requirements, not to "approve, much less prescribe, a one-year requirement."

Chief Justice Warren, joined by Justice Black, dissented. Examining the same legislative history of the federal act that the majority had looked at, he reached "the opposite conclusion, *i.e.*, Congress intended to authorize state residence requirements of up to one year." He balanced the burden the state placed on a person's right to travel against Congress's reason for enacting the restriction—which was to limit AFDC benefits so that more states would participate in the federal welfare program—and he concluded that restrictions on travel deterred few welfare recipients.

The Chief Justice foresaw additional problems created by the decision, which "reveals only the top of the iceberg. Lurking beneath are the multitude of situations in which States have imposed residence requirements including eligibility to vote, to engage in certain professions or occupations or to attend a state-supported university."

Justice Harlan dissented separately: "Today's decision, it seems to me, reflects to an unusual degree the current notion that this Court possesses a peculiar wisdom all of its own whose capacity to lead this Nation out of its present troubles is contained only by the limits of judicial ingenuity in contriving new constitutional principles to meet each problem as it arises."

Justice Stewart wrote a separate concurring opinion to refute Justice Harlan's dissent.

The majority's decision effectively removed residence requirements from the public assistance laws. According to *The New York Times*, government sources estimated that 100,000 to 200,000 people across the country were then being denied welfare benefits simply for failure to meet the residence requirements.

Several state welfare departments treated the *Thompson* decision as Alabama treated the Supreme Court decisions in the NAACP cases, described in chapter 6. For example, New York enacted a statute requiring a one-year residency, alleging a financial emergency would be created by obeying *Thompson*. A year later, the Supreme Court affirmed a three-judge court decision holding this statute unconstitutional.

Attacks on welfare recipients continued and have been intensified since the *Thompson* decision and other decisions favoring the welfare client. Critics imply that the rolls are swollen with able-bodied but lazy good-for-nothings who refuse to work and wax fat off the taxes of honest, hardworking Americans; they contend that there are numerous cases of welfare fraud. Welfare rights organizations, founded in the affluent sixties, have found they must wage a double campaign: against violations of law by welfare agencies and against adverse public opinion based on ignorance of the facts. Welfare mothers try to publicize the fact that the vast majority of welfare recipients are children and disabled persons, that most women who receive assistance are caring for preschool children, and that only a tiny fraction of those on welfare are physically able to work and not engaged in child care. Wherever white-collar unemployment goes up, it is easier to explain that people out of work are simply unable to find a job; they are not lazy.

The National Welfare Rights Organization and its local affiliates continue fighting on both these fronts. Politicians find welfare a convenient scapegoat—they blame this program for the taxpayers' heavy burden. (Others contend that war and inflation are the causes of high taxes.) Many say the entire welfare system should be revamped, and there have been several proposals to supplant it with a minimum annual family income or "negative income tax," under which each family below a specified income level (depending on family size) would receive payments from the government instead of receiving "welfare" or having to pay taxes. The Court's decisions in the area of welfare law created a controversy that has led to sharper questions about government assistance to other groups in society—the tax allowance to oil well owners because their wells ultimately run dry, and the payments to farmers for not growing crops, both paid regardless of need. A side effect of the *Thompson* decision, probably not anticipated by Vivian Thompson, has been a series of challenges to the residence requirements Chief Justice Warren mentioned—on out-of-state tuition rates at state-supported colleges, on voter registration in national elections, on eligibility for public housing, and on state licensing in many occupations, which restrict the movement of skilled workers and professionals in our jet-mobile age.

Much legal work has been started in the poverty law field; much remains to be done. The continued existence and expansion of the OEO Legal Services Program, and its continued freedom to innovate, are critical to this work, because other attorneys cannot afford to spend more than a small percentage of their time on nonpaying cases.

E. A. Dawley, attorney at the legal service office in the San Francisco ghetto at Hunter's Point, explains, in *The Relevant Lawyers* (1972), that the basic issue must be faced: "I don't think the problem of the poor is primarily law; it is primarily poverty, and I think you do a disservice when you try to pose it as something else. If a man doesn't have any money, he's in trouble. You can pass all the laws you want, but if he doesn't have any money he's in trouble."

This problem is not even touched by attacks on unfair legal procedures. Poverty lawyers may protect poor people from having to pay out more money than they should have to. But lawyers cannot improve their clients' income by filing lawsuits; they cannot increase the number of jobs in private industry or raise the wage rates. (Lawyers have won some additional income for their clients from government agencies, including food stamps and welfare payments.) *Congress* can pass laws providing more jobs by setting up government works programs financed by taxation. In 1946, Congress did pass the Full Employment Act requiring the President to use the services of his Council of Economic Advisers to come up with annual budgets and plans for full employment for all Americans. The *President* can encourage or discourage employment through the operation of the Federal Reserve System and other fiscal agencies. The *courts* can only rule that a particular economic practice of business or government violates some constitutional or legal principle.

Recognizing these basic rules, poverty lawyers began to expand their work to include proposals for legislation to alleviate their clients' worst problems. Some used their debating skills in appearances before legislative committees, as well as before judges and juries. Others started teaching courses on housing law and the rights of consumers to neighborhood people who want to be able to make their arguments more effectively in disputes with their landlords and creditors. Opposition to federal funding for poverty lawyers seemed to grow as the lawyers became more effective in winning cases for their clients. When they defeated regulations by other government agencies, there was grumbling: Why should taxpayers support lawyers who sue the Welfare Department, the housing agencies, and even the governor or board of supervisors?

The answer seemed clear to poverty lawyers: An injury to one is an injury to all. Unfairness by an agency dealing with the unemployed, the aged, and welfare recipients hurts all of society, and it paves the way for unfairness by agencies dealing with working people. The lawyers could point to many court victories that benefited both the lower and the middle classes, as in consumer protection cases.

Certainly the Warren Court issued several strong poverty law decisions opening up approaches to additional fields where the rights of the poor have long been ignored. But the relative powerlessness of the poor, in comparison with other groups in society, limits their ability to develop the law of human rights. And without the help of dedicated and skillful lawyers, no progress can be made in the courts. The future of poverty law, and related law for working people, depends on continuation of effective legal service programs at no or little cost to the clients. The answer for workers with steady jobs may be prepaid group legal service programs like those established by unions and finally approved by the Supreme Court in the *United Mine Workers* case described in chapter 6. But where can unemployed people, mothers on welfare, and pensioners with small incomes turn?

CHAPTER 29

Equality in Employment

The hardest part of most jobs is getting hired. It is easier to do the work than it is to get the job. There is usually a procedure for learning the specific tasks but there is no formal procedure that insures employment, no program of training to get a particular job or for finding any job at all.

The better the job is, the harder it is to get. For example, lawyers are considered to have good jobs. It takes them twelve years of public school, four years of college, three years of law school, and two months of review to pass a bar examination before they can start looking for a job in their profession. Architects, teachers, psychologists, nurses, librarians, engineers, and employees in many other fields have similarly long and expensive training programs. Doctors add to all of this formal training an internship—a period of apprenticeship, on-the-job training. Many trades have long training periods—for example, printers, carpenters, and steam fitters. It is almost a rule that the better the job, the longer the training period, the harder the entrance examination, and the higher the dues in a union or professional organization.

Getting the job is only part of the battle. The next step is to complete the probationary period so that the employer can't fire you without giving a reason. After a period, you may apply for on-the-job training in order to get a promotion. Meanwhile you are building your seniority so you can't get laid off, because the last hired is always the first fired.

But the hardest problems arise at an earlier stage. It is difficult to get admitted to a steam fitter apprenticeship program: you almost have to have a member of the union run interference for you, and it helps if this member is a relative with a good work record and many friends in the union. It is difficult to get admitted to law school: you almost have to have a college degree first, you must do well on the Law School Admissions Test, and it helps to have good references from lawyers and others. The easiest way to get a job anywhere is through someone who already has a job there. This is true in periods of full employment (like World War II) and in periods of high unemployment. But in periods of bad recession or depression, knowing someone is the *only* way to get a job or apprenticeship and being a member of a union may be the *only* way to keep a job or to get a promotion.

Under these conditions, how can a black high school graduate get a job or get signed up as an apprentice in a field that has always been closed to blacks? The same question applies to any Chicano, Puerto Rican, Native American, Asian, member of any other minority group, or to any woman seeking to enter a field that has traditionally hired only men.

Job discrimination lies at the heart of most of the other kinds of problems discussed in this book. If a person can get into a training program and then find a job for which he is qualified, he may get paid decent wages, get promoted when there is an opening, and join a union and seek improved working conditions for himself and others. He has a series of affirmative opportunities. His job enables him to find adequate housing at a price he can afford to pay. It permits him to send his children to a good neighborhood school (with an adequate tax base to provide quality education). It also makes it possible for him to build his savings so that he will never have to depend on government assistance during illness or old age. He can pay a lawyer to sue when his civil rights are violated. If anyone in his family is arrested, he can afford to bail him out of jail and to hire a lawyer to defend him. He, himself, is less likely to get arrested because he spends little time on the streets, where most arrests occur.

This list of opportunities does not mean that all of life's problems are solved by getting a decent job, but it does indicate that having a job makes it much easier to solve most other human rights problems.

Since this is so, and since everyone knows that this is so, why did the civil rights movement concentrate on every issue but employment? Why did Negro professionals sue for the right to use golf courses without segregation or harassment, instead of suing to end discrimination in their professional fields? Why did parents sue to get their children into desegregated schools instead of suing to get equal employment opportunities for themselves? Why are there more suits about fair housing than about fair employment practices? The answers begin to emerge from a study of the few job discrimination complaints that reached the Supreme Court, particularly those decided while Earl Warren was Chief Justice.

Racism on the railroads

Conley v. *Gibson* (1957)
355 U.S. 41, 78 S. Ct. 99, 2 L. Ed. 2d 80

Railroads early explained to the government and the people that they were a public utility, not an ordinary private business, and that they therefore were entitled to special concessions from the government. In the eighteenth century, this meant that railroads were given enough public land to build their lines from the East Coast all the way to California. This gift from the people through the United States government included enough land on each side of the tracks to make railroad stocks and bonds a first-class investment, as the roads sold off pieces of land to other industries and to settlers.

It also led the railroad magnates to gain enormous power in both the financial and the political world. Many a congressman and senator welcomed campaign contributions from railroad management. A rich employer is usually a tough employer, and the railroads, to make doubly sure their employees did not become united and powerful at the bargaining table, encouraged class or craft discrimination among the workers. A switchman was not as good as an engineer in pay or status, but he was way ahead of a carman. Workers accepted these distinctions and organized unions along craft lines. Railroad employers also practiced racial and nationality discrimination, hiring immigrants to build railroads (Irish in the East and Chinese in the West), hiring blacks as porters and whites as engineers. The railroad brotherhoods followed suit, refusing to admit black and yellow workers to their white locals.

The labor leader Eugene V. Debs tried to break these barriers between workers by organizing all employees in the industry into one union—the American Railway Union. Its initial success led to concerted employer resistance, and the union was smashed in 1894, along with its opposition to craft distinctions, which continued unbroken until the 1960s.

The struggle against racial discrimination was even more difficult than against segregation by craft. At a time when railroad jobs were numerous and secure, the struggle had to be waged both against the railroad employers and against the white workers and their craft unions. Judge Loren Miller reported, in *The Petitioners* (1966), that "no known Negro has ever been employed as a locomotive engineer, although many became qualified for the job through long training and experience as firemen. Barred from membership in the firemen's union, Negroes were extensively employed as firemen on southern railroads when their work was disagreeable and dirty. They were known as 'non-promotables' to distinguish them from white firemen who were styled 'promotables' to indicate that as whites they could win promotion to the rank of engineer. As the fireman's task became more desirable, white firemen set out to drive Negroes from the railroads. Violence and even murder were first used, but the provisions of the federal Railway Labor Act seemed to offer a more genteel and effective weapon."

Congress decided in 1890 that it had power to regulate the railroads because they are a public utility, a business "clothed with a public interest." It passed the Railway Labor Act in 1926 to establish a procedure for keeping the railroads running by preventing strikes and lawsuits. The act provided for the workers in each craft to choose a union to act as their bargaining agent with the company. This union then had the exclusive right to bargain with the railroad company concerning wages and other terms of employment for all workers. Disputes between the union and the company went before a National Railroad Adjustment Board.

The effect of the act was to give white-dominated unions exclusive bargaining power, and they used it to assist the railroad companies in discriminatory practices. For example, the all-white Brotherhood of Locomotive Firemen and Enginemen won the exclusive right to represent workers on the Louisville and Nashville Railroad. In the early 1940s, the company and the union signed a contract that sharply cut the number of black firemen, with the ultimate goal of completely excluding them from this work. Buster Steele, a Negro fireman with a long history of service for the company, was switched from a passenger run (considered highly desirable) to lower and lower positions, until he was finally assigned to a switch engine at much lower pay, while whites with less seniority got the better jobs. Steele took the case to state court, suing both the company and the union in a class suit on behalf of himself and all other Negroes discriminated against under the union contract. He argued that the union shouldn't be allowed to make a racially discriminatory contract, and the company should be prohibited from honoring such provisions.

The Alabama courts ruled against Steele, saying the union was a private organization and not subject to government control if it chose to favor its white members over blacks. But the United States Supreme Court ruled in *Steele* v. *Louisville and Nashville Railroad Company* in 1944 that the Railway Labor Act gave the union special powers, making it "comparable to a legislative body both to create and restrict the rights of those whom it represents." In return, the Act "also imposed a corresponding duty . . . to represent all the employees in the craft without discrimination because of their race." The high court got Steele his old job back.

Discrimination continued, however, and in cases throughout the 1940s and 1950s the Supreme Court ruled that federal courts could hear railroad cases and that railroad employers could be ordered to stop carrying out provisions of discriminatory bargaining agreements.

A new case began in May 1954, when the Texas and New Orleans Railroad said it was abolishing forty-five jobs held by black employees at the Houston freight house. The blacks were in an all-black local of the Brotherhood of Railway and Steamship Clerks. The contract between the union and the company covered an all-white local and this black local. The company discharged some blacks and demoted others. A few were later rehired but they lost their seniority—their job security based on length of service—and their pension rights. Meanwhile, the company hired white workers to fill the positions they said they had just abolished.

The ousted Negro employees asked and pleaded with the union to protect their right to their jobs. Finally they demanded that the union fight for their reinstatement. The union ignored them. Four of the men, J. D. Conley, Stanley Moore, Sr., George Carter, and B. A. Watson, got together and sought legal advice. They understood the principle that in union there is strength, and they needed all the strength they could muster to fight their union. Their lawyers explained that they could win more certainly and quickly in the federal courts than before the administrative agency governing railroad workers. A class suit was filed in federal district court against the white local, its officials, and the parent Brotherhood of Railway Clerks. The plaintiff workers charged that the union had discriminated against them because of their race, in violation of its duty under the Railway Labor Act.

The union moved to dismiss the complaint without answering the basic charge of racism. Union lawyers argued side issues: that disputes under the Railway Labor Act had to be heard by the National Railroad Adjustment Board, not the federal courts, and that the railroad company was a necessary party that should have been named as a defendant in the suit.

The district court ruled that the case should have gone to the adjustment board, and it dismissed the complaint. The federal court of appeals affirmed this decision, and the United States Supreme Court agreed to review the case.

Do you think a worker who alleges racial discrimination should be permitted to select the court or agency to hear his complaint? Should a union be permitted to defeat a charge of racism on technical grounds? Did it make sense for discharged employees to sue their union without suing the company as well? If they chose to sue only the union, did this make the case an internal dispute rather than a labor-management dispute?

Justice Black began the Court's unanimous opinion by noting: "Once again Negro employees are here under the Railway Labor Act asking that their collective bargaining agent be compelled to represent them fairly. In a series of cases beginning with Steele v. Louisville & Nashville R. Co., . . . this Court has emphatically and repeatedly ruled that an exclusive bargaining agent under the Railway Labor Act is obligated to represent all employees in the bargaining unit fairly and without discrimination because of race and has held that the courts have power to protect employees against such invidious discrimination."

The Court announced: "We hold that it was error for the courts below to dismiss the complaint for lack of jurisdiction. . . . This case involves no dispute between employee and employer but to the contrary is a suit by employees against the bargaining agent to enforce their statutory right not to be unfairly discriminated against by it in bargaining. The Adjustment Board has no power under . . . the [Railway Labor] Act to protect them from such discrimination."

The court went on, "Respondents contend that the Texas and New Orleans Railroad Company is an indispensable party which the petitioners have failed to join as a defendant. On the basis of the allegations made in the complaint and the relief demanded by petitioners we believe that contention is unjustifiable. We cannot see how the Railroad's rights or interests will be affected by this action to enforce the duty of the bargaining representative to represent petitioners fairly. . . . If an issue does develop which necessitates joining the Railroad either it or the respondents will then have an adequate opportunity to request joinder."

The Court repeated the old rule that a complaint should not be dismissed unless it is absolutely clear that the plaintiff cannot prove any set of facts that would entitle him to relief. Here the petitioners alleged they were discharged wrongfully by the railroad, and that the union deliberately refused to protect their jobs or to help them with their grievances because they were Negroes. "If these allegations are proven there has been a manifest breach of the Union's statutory duty to represent fairly and without hostile discrimination all of the employees in the bargaining unit. This Court squarely held in Steele and subsequent cases that discrimination in representation because of race is prohibited by the Railway Labor Act.

"The bargaining representative's duty not to draw 'irrelevant and invidious' distinctions among those it represents does not come to an abrupt end, as the respondents seem to contend, with the making of an agreement between union and employer. Collective bargaining is a continuing process. Among other things, it involves day-to-day adjustments in the contract and other working rules, resolution of new problems not covered by existing agreements, and the protection of employee rights already secured by contract. The bargaining representative can no more unfairly discriminate in carrying out these functions than it can in negotiating a collective agreement." The Court warned that "a contract may be fair and impartial on its face yet administered in such a way, with the active or tacit consent of the union, as to be flagrantly discriminatory against some members of the bargaining unit."

The union had pointed out that, under the Railway Labor Act, aggrieved employees could file their own grievances with the Adjustment Board, or could sue the employer for breach of contract. But the Court found that, even "granting this, it still furnishes no sanction for the Union's alleged discrimination in refusing to represent petitioners."

In November 1957, the Court sent the case back to the federal district court for trial of the facts. An employer can demand speedy court action when a strike shuts down his business, but no such procedure is available to an employee trying to get back his job. In this case, court delays held up the trial for three years. During this time, two of the plaintiffs, Moore and Carter, died. J. D. Conley had been rehired by the railroad while the suit was pending. He apparently walked off the job in January 1957, perhaps because of harassment, and returned to work that October, shortly before the Supreme Court opinion was handed down. A hearing was set to investigate his conduct, but Conley refused to appear and took off once more.

In December 1958, the union asked the remaining plaintiff, B. A. Watson, to answer its questions, under oath, in the presence of attorneys for each side in a deposition. The union tried to take Conley's deposition as well, but he did not appear. In order to show that Watson had not actually been harmed by the union actions charged in the complaint, the union attorney asked him: "You have already stated that you didn't lose any time?"

"I didn't lose any time," Watson replied.

"You didn't lose any pay?"

"I didn't lose any pay." . . .

"You didn't lose any seniority?"

"No, I didn't lose any seniority."

"So what you are complaining about is something that happened to somebody else; isn't that right?" the attorney asked.

In this duel of wits, the black railroad worker was at a serious disadvantage against the trained advocate from the union's law firm. But Mr. Watson had put too much into this fight to quit now. "Well," he said with dignity, "you can take it in that way, but I can consider that whatever happened to my fellow man, it happens to me as well."

The black railroad workers had charged from the beginning that the union's policy of maintaining two segregated locals (Lodge 6051 for blacks and Lodge 28 for whites) was illegal. On this issue, Watson was asked: "Have you ever filed any application with any lodge other than 6051?"

"Not in no labor organization, I haven't." . . .

"You never did file any application or attempt to become a member of Lodge #28?" the lawyer asked, knowing full well that such an application would have been rejected.

"Not to my knowing," said Watson.

The narrow questions and the truthful answers left out the critical facts and ended any chance of success for the workers. When the case came to trial, the federal district judge again granted the union's motion to dismiss the complaint, this time ruling that the deaths of Moore and Carter removed them as plaintiffs and that Conley and Watson, having failed to show that they had personally suffered harm from the union's actions, could not represent a class of persons who had been harmed. This freed the union and the railroad from having to disprove in court the charge that they had acted to deprive a class of workers of their jobs because of their race.

The black workers and the class they had tried to represent did not recover damages or regain their jobs, so it would be easy to say that they failed in their efforts. This would be inaccurate. The strong language used by the Supreme Court in *Conley* v. *Gibson* gave support to other employees seeking to use the courts to secure equality in employment and deterred other employers and unions from open discriminatory practices. The news coverage of the Court opinion paved the way for campaigns in Congress and in several states and cities for statutes guaranteeing fair employment practices and setting up agencies to hear job complaints.

Workers in many industries continue to file charges of discrimination by employers and trade unions similar to Mr. Conley's charges against the railroad industry. On the other hand, some unions have taken a strong stand to integrate their memberships and to force employers to stop discrimination. One of these, the United Packinghouse Workers, brought the National Labor Relations Board into court for failing to rule against discriminatory practices by an employer. Federal Judge J. Skelly Wright found that the union had a legitimate interest in stopping racism because it adversely affected union membership in two ways: "(1) Racial discrimination sets up an unjustified clash of interests between groups of workers which tends to reduce the likelihood and the effectiveness of their working in concert to achieve their legitimate goal under the Act; and (2) racial discrimination creates in its victims an apathy or docility which inhibits them from asserting their rights against the perpetrator of the discrimination."

Rank-and-file caucuses have developed in many unions around the country to find answers to the problems some union officials have ignored, particularly problems of alleged discrimination against black and other minority group members and against women. They have often turned to state commissions established in recent years to insure fair employment practices.

The year the Supreme Court ruled in favor of the black railway workers in the *Conley* case, the Colorado legislature passed its Anti-Discrimination Act of 1957, following a long campaign by civil rights organizations, Spanish-surname groups, and some unions. Soon afterward, a highly skilled black worker applied for a job in Colorado, leading to another key case. This time the employer challenged the new state fair employment practices commission.

A black pilot's slow takeoff

Colorado Anti-Discrimination Commission v. Continental Air Lines, Inc. (1963)

372 U.S. 714, 83 S. Ct. 1022, 10 L. Ed. 2d 84

"Join the Air Force; learn to fly." Marlon Green took them up on the offer in the early 1950s, not knowing any other employers who would train a young black man to be a pilot.

Shortly before leaving the service with the rank of captain, Green wrote to or called all the major airlines in the United States, looking for a commercial pilot's job. He applied to Continental Air Lines by mail on April 27, 1957, but did not answer the question on race or send a photograph as requested on the company form.

At that time, Continental was looking for about fourteen pilots. The personnel department called Green to come for an interview in Denver on June 19. The interviewer looked at the applicant and told him to fill in his race on the form.

Continental interviewed fourteen applicants in June. Only

six met the qualifications for age, experience, and physical fitness. Green not only was among the six, but also had logged more flight hours and more multi-engine experience than the other five.

When Continental selected four men for its July training class, Green was not among them. The vice-president in charge of personnel, Mr. Bell, called Green to say he had not been chosen but would be kept on the eligible list. Later the fifth qualified applicant was hired, and only Green remained.

Green had run into similar treatment at other airlines. He could see that if he really wanted to be a pilot he would have to fight for a job. He then filed complaints with the Michigan Fair Employment Practices Commission, the President's Committee on Government Contracts, and the Colorado Anti-Discrimination Commission, charging that he had suffered discrimination in hiring because of his race.

Green filed the Colorado complaint on August 3, 1957. During the rest of August and September, Continental hired seventeen more pilots, but not him.

After verifying the facts in Green's complaint, the Colorado Anti-Discrimination Commission contacted Continental and tried to settle the case. Most complaints to such commissions are settled through conciliation. In fact, a national study in 1955 found that of six thousand complaints of unfair employment practices filed with various commissions, only eight had reached the hearing stage. But Continental would not settle, and May 7, 1958, was set as the date for a full administrative hearing on the case before the Colorado commission.

Green didn't like his prominent position in this fight and at one point asked to withdraw his complaint, but once the hearing date had been set, withdrawal was allowed only by a majority vote of the commissioners, and they voted to pursue the complaint. The competent black pilot seeking to fly commercial planes had already become a significant symbol to them.

At the hearing, Vice-President Bell of Continental was questioned closely.

Why wasn't Green hired in July?

The company found it needed only four pilots then, Bell replied.

Why wasn't Green one of the four chosen, since he had the most experience?

The selection was made in a "haphazard" manner, Bell said, not according to who was most qualified.

Why wasn't Green hired in August or September, after he had been told he would be kept on the eligible list?

Continental had taken him off the eligible list when it learned of an Albuquerque newspaper article reporting on August 4 that Green had filed discrimination complaints. The company had a policy against hiring anyone to whom notoriety had attached, Bell testified. (Later federal court decisions held it is unconstitutional to penalize anyone for filing a complaint with a government agency alleging violations of law.)

On December 18, 1958, the Colorado commission issued its findings and orders. It found that "the only reason that the Complainant was not selected for the training school was because of his race," and that Continental's policy of asking an applicant for his race and photograph violated Colorado antidiscrimination regulations. The commission ordered Continental to hire Green, giving him the status he would have had if he had been hired on June 24, 1957.

Continental appealed the decision to the state courts. Like the railroad union in the *Conley* case, the employer here did not want to discuss the charge of racism. Instead it argued a jurisdictional question—that the state commission had no power to regulate it because it was an interstate transportation carrier coming under federal regulation. The company lawyers also argued that congressional power to regulate employment practices in interstate commerce preempted or covered the whole field, so that states could not regulate even if Congress then failed to act. The lawyers relied on two United States Supreme Court cases ruling that state laws requiring or forbidding segregated seating on steamboats and buses were void because they imposed an undue burden on interstate commerce.

The case came before the state court in Denver on June 11, 1959. For the next two and one-half years company lawyers were able to avoid decision by finding a variety of technical errors and partial rulings requiring further action by the courts and the commission. Ultimately the state court decided that Continental's status in interstate commerce *did* take it out of the jurisdiction of the Anti-Discrimination Commission and put it under federal jurisdiction, as the company had argued. The Colorado Supreme Court affirmed.

Five years after Marlon Green had qualified for a pilot's job at Continental, he asked the United States Supreme Court to hear his claim. The Colorado commission also asked the Court to decide that the commission had power to rule on his case. The Supreme Court announced that "the obvious importance of even partial invalidation of a state law designed to prevent the discriminatory denial of job opportunities prompted us to grant certiorari [hear the case]."

When Congress has failed to act to prohibit discrimination in employment, can a state act? Can a state pass a valid fair employment practices act to cover employers who could also be covered by a federal act? What factors made it possible for a state to pass fair employment practices legislation while congressmen from the North and West could not pass a federal act? Do you think interstate carriers should be subjected to *state* fair employment laws? Does it put an undue burden on the company to obey such laws if they are not the same in each state?

The Supreme Court's unanimous decision was delivered by Justice Black in April 1963. Black, who read the First Amendment broadly and strictly according to its language, came to read the Fourteenth Amendment narrowly in civil rights cases. His opinion discusses only the question of racial discrimination by interstate carriers and whether a state has power to pass legislation prohibiting certain personnel practices of such carriers. Justice Black apparently preferred that any federal legislation against racist practices be based on the power given Congress in the Constitution to regulate interstate commerce.

"The line separating the powers of a State from the exclusive power of Congress is not always distinctly marked," Justice Black noted; "courts must examine closely the facts of each case to determine whether the dangers and hardships of diverse regulation justify foreclosing a State from the exercise of its traditional powers." It might be proper to insist on uniform federal regulation of passenger seating rules (as in the steamboat and bus cases) so that passengers would not be forced to switch seats each time a state line was crossed.

But, the Court said, "we are not convinced that commerce will be unduly burdened if Continental is required by Colorado to refrain from racial discrimination in its hiring of pilots in that State. Not only is the hiring within a State of an employee, even for an interstate job, a much more localized matter than the transporting of passengers from State to State but more significantly the threat of diverse and conflicting regulation of hiring practices is virtually nonexistent. . . . Were there a possibility that a pilot hired in Colorado could be barred solely because of his color from serving a carrier in another State, then his case might well be controlled by our prior holdings. But under our more recent decisions [on segregation in schools and transportation] any state or federal law requiring applicants for any job to be turned away because of their color would be invalid under the Due Process Clause of the Fifth Amendment and the Due Process and Equal Protection Clauses of the Fourteenth Amendment." The Court concluded: "We hold that the Colorado statute as applied here to prevent discrimination in hiring on account of race does not impose a constitutionally prohibited burden upon interstate commerce."

Finally the Court considered whether federal preemption invalidated the state antidiscrimination law. Assuming that federal aviation laws "prohibit racial discrimination against passengers and other customers and that they protect job applicants or employees from discrimination on account of race," they still "had no express or implied intent to bar state legislation in this field," and the state laws "will not frustrate any part of the purpose of the federal legislation."

The Court reversed the Colorado Supreme Court decision and sent the case back for an order by the trial court based on the specific facts in the case. Before the trial court got around to making its decision, Congress, for the first time since 1866, passed a general law to discourage discrimination in employment on the basis of race.

In 1883, Congress had passed the Civil Service Act to prevent favoritism in federal employment based on political party affiliation. The regulations issued under the Act included a prohibition against religious discrimination, and, in 1940, the Ramspect Act broadened the principle of merit employment by prohibiting discrimination on account of race, creed, or color.

In 1941 the president established the first committee to hear complaints of job discrimination practiced by the federal government and by certain private employers with government contracts. This agency was killed in 1946 at the insistence of southern senators. Meanwhile, in 1942, Congressman Vito Marcantonio (American Labor Party, New York) proposed a broad federal fair employment practices act, and repeated his proposal unsuccessfully in each succeeding Congress during his tenure in the House. Each president since Franklin Roosevelt also issued one or more executive orders requiring fair employment practices in government employment and the armed forces and established one or more agencies to enforce these orders. Since the federal government has become the largest employer in the country, its action or inaction on employment discrimination affected the lives of many workers directly and its policies were copied by many private employers.

Then, on July 2, 1964, Congress passed a Civil Rights Act containing key provisions on employment in Title VII (other parts of the act are discussed in chapters 22, 23, and 25). It established a federal Commission on Equal Employment Opportunity and prohibited discrimination in all programs assisted with federal funds. The statute did not preempt (cover) the field even then, because it was limited to companies engaged in interstate commerce having twenty-five or more employees. However, the handwriting was on the wall for all employers to see, including Continental Air Lines of Colorado. With Congress joining the President and the Supreme Court in forbidding racial discrimination in employment, even delay in hiring qualified blacks would have its limits.

On October 8, 1964, the Denver court ordered Continental to offer Green a pilot's position at a salary equal to what he would be getting if the company had hired him seven years earlier in 1957. In many cases that take years to reach a final decision, the plaintiff or defendant has changed his circumstances so greatly that no reparation can really be made. Marlon Green had, of course, found other work during the seven intervening years. Nevertheless, although he was then flying for the Bureau of Reclamation, Green took the Continental job—becoming probably the best qualified, and certainly the highest paid, trainee the company had ever hired.

Passage of the federal act in 1964 did not solve the problem of job discrimination. It opened up an important avenue to process some complaints. It has been estimated that only 40 percent of American workers were covered by the act at the end of the Warren Court era. The act does not give the commission the power to order an employer to cease discrimination or segregation if an investigation shows that the employer is guilty. The individual must go to court and sue the employer, although the U.S. Attorney General can intervene in the case, giving the employee's claim added status in the eyes of the court. The act does contain an important feature—the court can order the company to pay a fee to the lawyer for the worker if his claim is successful.

After lengthy civil rights campaigns, cities and states also passed bills forbidding employment discrimination, until thirty-nine states and several key cities had fair employment laws and commissions similar to Colorado's. The Supreme Court decision in Green's case upheld the powers of all these commissions, and all are swamped with complaints.

Racism in employment is as widespread as racism in housing. Both touch basic areas of each person's life. Both were outlawed over one hundred years ago in acts of Congress passed in 1866 to end all discrimination on the basis of race or previous condition of servitude. The Civil Rights Act of 1866 declared that all citizens have the same right as white citizens not only to buy and sell real property, but also "to make and enforce contracts," including, of course, contracts for work. Although most employees today do not sign written agreements or contracts with their employers, and the "work contract" is seldom mentioned, the right to make a contract of employment is basic to a worker and in 1866 such contracts were often discussed. To be able to make a contract to work marked one a free man, not a slave, since it also carried with it the right to refuse to make a contract. Black workers had been born into slavery and had no freedom of contract. The end of the slave system meant that no worker could be required to work unless he made a contract with an employer, and more, that the employee, as well as the employer, could enforce the contract. (Persons convicted of crime were exempt from this concept.) The equal right to make contracts for employment is a critical part of equal protection of the laws. The 1866 act said this right applies to all jobs—those in intrastate, as well as interstate, commerce.

Americans looking for equal job opportunities in the 1970s and thereafter can find strong weapons in their arsenal: the Thirteenth, Fourteenth, and Fifteenth Amendments, the 1866 Civil Rights Act, the 1964 Civil Rights Act, the decisions of the Warren Court discussed in this chapter, and many decisions by state courts and commissions. However, it must be remembered that none of these enactments include the right to work when there is a shortage of jobs. They only cover the right not be discriminated against in the job market. Even under these laws, young people new to the labor market may have difficulty complaining about an employer's refusal to hire them, or to accept them in an apprenticeship program. When a person has never worked at a job, he may feel qualified to be hired, but it will be difficult for him to prove that the employer rejected him for discriminatory reasons. If he can find a lawyer to help prepare his case, they may be able to prove a pattern of refusal to hire members of minority groups, not just one isolated refusal. The same problems and possibilities exist as to acceptance in apprenticeship programs.

Not every employer, employment agency, union and apprenticeship program now covered by a state or federal fair employment statute is obeying the law. Complaints can be filed against them in fair employment practice agencies, and lawsuits can be brought. In the coming period, voters can insist that these statutes be broadened to cover more employers and employees, and that penalties for violation be increased. The fair employment practice agencies can be given more power to act quickly and decisively against violators.

However, these statutes and the Warren Court decisions do not provide the complete answer to problems of job discrimination. The decisions dealt with the problem of fair employment practices on the basis of race, and can easily be applied to prevent discrimination on the basis of religion, nationality, sex, and age. But efforts to achieve *fair* employment are undoubtedly doomed to failure unless efforts to approach *full* employment are successful.

Economists have pointed out that court decisions requiring nondiscriminatory hiring cannot solve the problems that arise in the economy when the number of available workers is expanding more rapidly than the Gross National Product and when, at the same time, automation techniques lead to extensive layoffs. At such a time, should employers be absolutely color blind, or should they give special consideration to members of minority groups who are qualified and have never had an equal chance before? (Some black militants insist that black Americans are entitled to some kind of reparations for the murders, mistreatment, and loss of income their race suffered under slavery, as the Israelis were paid reparations by the German government after Hitler's genocidal policies were defeated in World War II. Short of cash payments, they insist on preferential treatment when blacks apply for jobs.)

Other questions arise on another front. Should an employer hire a married man before a single woman, on the theory that the man has, or will have, more dependents? What if the single woman is the sole support of several children or a widowed mother, as is often the case? What about veterans of the Vietnam war, the physically handicapped, the very young, and the elderly? In other words, who should get preference, if anyone should? And how should decisions on preference be made?

These are not new questions, but they are new to the courts. In the past, employers made all of these decisions on their own and an employee had no forum in which to make a complaint. However, the passage of laws concerning the employment contract has changed the climate considerably from the early twentieth century when "freedom of contract" meant "no government interference." New Deal legislation required employers to bargain with their employees when they organized unions (Wagner or National Labor Relations Act), required employers to limit the hours of work, increase hourly wages, and stop child labor in many industries (Minimum Wage and Maximum Hours Act), forced employers to contribute to retirement funds for their workers (through Social Security) and to unemployment and workmen's compensation benefits.

Warren Court decisions further limited employer prerogatives in the civil liberties area. In the process of reopening the free marketplace of ideas (described in part I), the Court forbade many loyalty oaths previously required by employers, and reversed many firings based on the political beliefs or activities of employees. In the process of requiring fair procedures (described in part II), the Court said that fairness was also necessary in administrative proceedings, including disciplining and dismissal of employees of government and of some government contractors. In the process of opening the Pandora's box of poverty law problems, the Court faced the claim that an American has a right to live and therefore has a right to free medical care, free legal services, free food, and free lodging. These claims led to demands by middle-class Americans for inexpensive (if not free) housing, higher education, transportation, and cultural events.

Passage of fair employment practice legislation further restricted the absolute discretion of employers to hire, upgrade, and fire, opening up further questions on hiring practices. Warren Court decisions upholding this legislation made this a significant field for further action, and lower court decisions awarding fees to successful litigants ensured extensive use of the 1964 Civil Rights Act employment provisions.

By facing and settling the basic issues in fair employment litigation and in other fields that had been avoided in the 1940s and 1950s, the Warren Court made it possible for clients and lawyers to face new problems and to fashion litigation to test new theories of government responsibility. Concern for the rights of the unemployed and of welfare recipients led almost automatically to deeper concern for the rights of the *employed* (even though no new group of labor lawyers came to the Court with innovative ideas, as the new group of poverty lawyers had done).

Commentators noted that employment has taken on a new significance as fringe benefits have increased. Loss of employment means the loss of these benefits. Many workers earn not only wages or salary but also partial payment on their life, hospital, and medical insurance; contributions to a pension fund; the possibility of an annual bonus (and even the opportunity to participate in charter travel tours). When a worker is laid off, for any reason, he loses his ability to buy his immediate necessities (food, clothing, shelter), and he must suddenly pay all of his own health, accident, life insurance premiums, must find money to keep up his installment payments on appliances, and must make his own plans for retirement. These changes in life may force him to seek public assistance, and may also affect the operation of many public and private industries (insurance companies, hospitals, etc.).

Do all of these events mean that layoffs should be subject to government regulation? Should a worker be able to sue his boss, claiming his layoff was unfair? Should an employer in the Midwest be able to move his plant to the Philippines without notifying a government agency or making plans for alternative work for its employees? On the other side of the coin, can a public utility gain acceptance of its plans for a new power plant by arguing that the plant will create jobs, and thus defeat the arguments of conservationists concerned about the ecological effects?

Litigation raising such questions was just beginning to be planned and filed as the Warren Court ended its reign. Some lawyers feel that the Warren Court decisions on civil liberties, due process, and civil rights built the "on" ramps to a swiftly moving freeway of litigation on employment practices. They watch minority group students who got a better public school education (due to *Brown* v. *Board of Education*), who got into graduate schools and apprenticeship programs (due to other decisions and statutes), who moved to the suburbs with their families (due to *Jones* v. *Alfred H. Mayer Co.*), who became interested in government jobs when they were arrested and confronted by government officials in the civil rights movement. They see all of these individuals and groups converging on the job market, entering that employment freeway. When their interests collide with those of employees from old families who have had good jobs for generations, whose interests will win out? And what role will the courts play in making these decisions?

The only safe prediction is that the approach of the Warren Court, based on Reconstruction and New Deal legislation and attitudes, will prove helpful to clients, lawyers, and judges in these new, uncharted fields, and that future justices will have their hands full in dealing with restrictions on employment practices.

The Supreme Court will not weigh these conflicting interests alone. The outcome in each case will depend on the actions of all of the participants in the litigation: on the people who file the lawsuits, their lawyers and opponents, and on jurors, trial judges, and journalists. Everyone will be assisted in his efforts by decisions of the Warren Court. But we all have a long road to travel before our judicial system meets the needs of the people and their expectations under the United States Constitution, the Bill of Rights, and the Reconstruction Amendments.

GLOSSARY

The terms listed are defined in the senses in which they are used in this book. They may have additional meanings in other areas of law or subject matters.

abate: to put an end to, nullify, or make void.

abstention: the Supreme Court doctrine that federal courts are to "keep hands off" certain legal issues considered "state" issues to avoid unnecessary friction in federal-state relations, interference with important state functions, tentative decisions on questions of state law, and premature constitutional consideration. Abstention is appropriate only where the issue of law is uncertain, and justices disagree about its use even in such cases.

acquittal: decision by a jury or judge that a criminal accusation was not proved beyond a reasonable doubt.

administrative law: orders, regulations, and individual decisions by the administrative agencies that are part of the executive branch of government, often based on statutes (spelling out statutory requirements) and subject to court review.

admissible: pertinent and proper to be considered in reaching a decision. Admissible evidence is evidence that the judge must allow to be introduced at trial, not evidence that is irrelevant, immaterial, or obtained illegally.

affidavit: a written statement of facts that a person makes voluntarily and confirms by oath or affirmation before an officer having authority to administer the oath, such as a notary public.

affirm: to declare that a judgment, decree, or order by a lower court is valid and legally correct even if the reasoning behind the judgment is rejected.

allegation: an assertion or statement of fact made by a party to a lawsuit that he expects to prove in the case.

amicus curiae: a friend of the court. When a case raised questions of concern to people other than the parties, these organizations and individuals sometimes ask the court to permit them to file briefs and even to present oral arguments raising issues that are usually different from those raised by the parties; these are called friend of the court briefs and appearances because they enable the court to reach its decision on broader grounds or with a wider perspective than that presented by the parties. (The plural is "amici curiae.")

answer: the document filed by a defendant in a lawsuit either denying or admitting the plaintiff's allegations and sometimes presenting defenses by alleging additional facts.

antimiscegenation statute: law prohibiting racial intermarriage, especially between black and white. Often these laws imposed fines and/or jail sentences for the "crime" of marrying someone of another race.

apartheid: policy of rigid racial segregation and discrimination.

appellant: the party who loses his case in the trial or lower appeals court and takes the case to the next level of courts for review. The opposing party is called the "appellee" or "respondent."

appellate court (appeals court): three or more judges sitting to review decisions of lower courts by studying the records of the litigation, trial, and previous appeals, reading briefs, and hearing oral argument by the attorneys for the parties, but rarely hearing any live testimony themselves. The United States Supreme Court is the highest appellate court in both the state and the federal systems; there is one level of intermediate appellate courts in the federal system, and there are one or more levels of intermediate appellate courts in the fifty state systems.

appellee: the party who won his case in the trial of lower appeals court and is required to answer the loser's (appellants's) appeal to the next level of courts.

apportionment: division into proportionate districts for the election of congressmen, senators, or state legislators. *See also* malapportionment.

arraignment: appearance of a defendant before a criminal court judge or judicial officer to hear the charge against him and to make a plea.

attachment: the process of seizing property by means of a court order, so that the owner will have to act as security for a debt or costs or will have to notify a third person who has the property that he may become liable to pay the debt.

attainder: 1. extinction of a person's civil rights and capacities upon sentence of death or outlawry. 2. dishonor. *See also* bill of attainder.

bar: 1. lawyers as a group (distinguished from "the bench"—the judges). 2. the partition in a courtroom between the spectators and the lawyers.

bar: 1. to exclude or keep out. 2. to prevent or forbid.

barratry: the offense of persistently stirring up lawsuits and quarrels.

bill of attainder: a legislative act pronouncing a named person (or a group of readily identifiable persons) guilty of an alleged crime (usually treason) without court trial or conviction according to the recognized rules of procedure, and passing sentence of death and attainder on him (or the group); a feudal practice forbidden in the United States Constitution, Article I, Section 9.

binding: applicable and obligatory. A binding decision is a court ruling in one case that applies to or covers a later case and therefore must be followed or obeyed by the parties and the judge.

Black Codes: laws passed by southern legislatures after the Emancipation Proclamation, which sought to reverse the Proclamation and to deny the freedman all right of citizenship, returning him to virtual slavery.

booking: the police process of recording a person's arrest.

breach of the peace: the misdemeanor of disturbing the public peace by riotous, forcible, offensive, or threatening behavior.

brief: a booklet written by an attorney for one side (or by an amicus curiae) setting forth the facts and every argument on the law that could convince the judge or judges who read the document to decide in favor of his side. A brief may be short, but often it belies its name.

burden of proof: the duty of a party to present evidence that will create, in the mind of the judge or jury, a required degree of belief about a fact in order to win a lawsuit. The burden usually falls on the party asserting the affirmative side of an issue, rather than the negative. The law may require a party to establish a fact by a mere preponderance of the evidence or by clear and convincing proof, or it may require proof beyond a reasonable doubt—the degree of proof required is much higher in criminal cases and is specified for each type of case by precedent or statute.

capital crime or offense: a crime for which the punishment may be death.

capping: in some state statutes, the solicitation of clients and cases for a lawyer by a nonlawyer.

case law: the body of law developed by court decisions, as opposed to statutory or administrative law.

cause of action: a legal claim that contains all the elements necessary to file a successful lawsuit and to justify a court in passing judgment on the dispute.

certiorari: a proceeding (based on a petition to an appellate court) asking that court to review a lower court decision. The court may grant or deny certiorari (agree or refuse to review the case) as it sees fit, without stating reasons.

challenge for cause: the procedure by which the attorneys for each side in a jury trial may excuse a prospective juror from the jury by showing to the judge's satisfaction that the juror is biased against one side or in favor of the other. Unlike preemptory challenges, the number of challenges is unlimited.

change of venue: transfer of a trial to a different geographical location, by order of the trial judge, on a motion by the attorney for a party, usually because of the difficulty or impossibility of obtaining twelve jurors who have not made up their minds about the case before trial owing to extensive and biased media coverage or to the racial prejudices common in the area.

charge: 1. an accusation in a criminal case. 2. the judge's instructions to the jury on matters of law. *See also* instructions.

citation: court order to a person to appear at a certain place and time to show cause why he should not be punished, as for contempt.

citation notice: notice to appear before the police without a formal arrest.

civil suit: a legal proceeding started by one party against another to enforce a right, to protect property, or to redress or prevent a wrong. Judgment for the plaintiff requires the defendant to do an act or pay money in damages (rather than to be imprisoned or fined, as in a criminal case).

class action (class suit): a lawsuit filed by a plaintiff not only to right
a wrong done by the defendant to him individually but also on
behalf of everyone in the same situation or class as the plaintiff
in regard to the defendant and his actions. If the plaintiff wins,
everyone in the class benefits by the ruling (and, in some instances, can collect damages from the defendant—for instance
when a telephone company must pay rebates to all users as a
result of a suit by a few of them). A plaintiff may also file suit
against one named defendant and the class he represents, so
that if the plaintiff wins he can recover from the named defendant and all others in his group.

common law: 1. the body of law developed in England, which relied for its authority on previous court opinions and accepted
customs and usages, as well as on some basic statutes. 2. in the
United States, the parts of British common law adopted after
the Revolutionary War and not changed or overturned by later
statutes or regulations, plus the continually developing law
through court decisions as distinguished from statutes and
regulations. *Compare* equity.

companion cases: lawsuits raising one or more of the same or similar issues so that a court (usually an appellate court) hears all
of them argued together and often writes one opinion covering
all of them.

complainant: a party who applies to a court or administrative
agency for legal redress; one who instigates a prosecution or
accuses a suspected person.

complaint: 1. the first legal paper filed by the plaintiff in any civil
lawsuit, describing the facts requiring judicial decision. It must
state a cause of action or it is subject to demurrer. *See also*
demur. 2. the legal paper filed by a police officer or citizen
before a magistrate, describing the crime alleged to have been
committed and the person suspected of committing it.

concurring opinion: an opinion filed by an appellate judge or justice
that agrees with the conclusions or the result of another opinion
filed in the same case (either the majority opinion or a dissent)
but that states separate views on the case or different reasons
for reaching the same conclusion.

confession of error: an admission to the court by counsel for one
party that the position he has taken previously was not proper

(not good law), or was based on an inaccurate statement of the facts or on misconduct by his client (such as using evidence obtained illegally).

conflict of interest: a situation in which a person has two duties or obligations that require conflicting behavior from him. For example, when a lawyer in a criminal case is asked to represent two defendants whose stories contradict each other or whose interests otherwise differ, the lawyer has conflicting duties he cannot fulfill and must stop representing one (and sometimes both).

construe: to interpret or explain the meaning of. When a court construes a statute, regulation, or other document, it explains the intention of the framers and uses this interpretation to decide a case based on a particular set of facts.

construction: interpretation or explanation of.

contempt of court: any intentional act likely to embarrass, hinder, or obstruct a judge in the administration of justice or to lessen his authority or dignity. A contemptuous act may be committed in or out of the presence of the judge by a party, a witness, an attorney, a member of the audience, or some other person.

continuance: postponement of an action pending in court or a step to be taken in a case, usually until a specified date.

conviction: the judgment at the end of a criminal trial that the defendant is guilty.

counsel: the lawyer or lawyers.

court: the judge or judges. (The human beings who sit as judges are often spoken of as if they were the institution over which they preside.) "The court held" means "the majority opinion stated."

damages: the sum of money a plaintiff recovers from a defendant to compensate him for the physical injury, loss of rights, or property damage he suffered through the defendant's unlawful act or negligence.

de facto: a condition existing in fact; for example, racial segregation in public schools or other facilities that exists in fact (as in the North and West) although it is not required by law (as in parts of the South before 1954).

de jure: a condition existing by law; for example, racial segregation in public schools or other facilities that was required by statute, regulation, or court order (as in the southern and border states before 1954).

demur: to respond to the other side's allegations by arguing that, even if his statement of the facts is taken to be true, there is no legal basis for a suit. A "demurrer" is filed with the court instead of an "answer" to the complaint. *See also* dismiss.

deposition: testimony of a witness under oath, taken before trial and reduced to writing, after giving notice to the opposing party so that he (and/or his lawyer) can attend and enter objections, and cross-examine. A deposition is one form of discovery.

directed verdict: an instruction by the judge to the jury to return a verdict for one of the parties because the law of the case requires it and there are no questions of fact. The jury has no choice—it must obey this instruction.

discovery: the procedure by which one party to a lawsuit requires the other side to disclose, before trial, facts, documents, or other things in his exclusive knowledge or possession that are necessary to the first party in preparing his case; to take the surprise out of litigation by permitting both sides to prepare to prove their allegations in trial.

disfranchise: to deny or take away the right to vote.

dismiss: to dispose finally of a complaint, suit, motion, etc., without a trial of the issues involved. A court may dismiss a suit if, after assuming that all the plaintiff's allegations are true, the court finds that his complaint does not state a good cause of action or is not a case that the court has power to decide.

dissent: a judge's explicit disagreement with the decision of the majority of his court on a case before them. A dissent may or may not be accompanied by a dissenting or minority opinion. (Failure to vote is not a dissent.)

distinguish a case: to point out an essential difference between a previous case and the present case. A judge must decide whether to follow a previous decision in a case like the one he is hearing, thus following precedent, or whether to ignore the previous decision because of differences between the facts in that case and in the one before him. If he distinguishes the former case from the present one, he can ignore the earlier decision without overruling it.

due process of law: fair procedure; a series of steps in settling disputes that provide the protections guaranteed in the basic law (in the constitutions, statutes, regulations, court decisions, and customs). Due process is guaranteed in the Fifth and Fourteenth Amendments to the Constitution. Denial of due process at any stage in any civil, criminal, administrative, or legislative proceeding permits the parties to attack the decision, sometimes to get it reversed, and to have a new trial or hearing.

enjoin: to require or command a person by a court order to do or to not do or stop doing some act. (The order is called an injunction.)

entrap: for an agent or officer of the government to induce someone to commit a crime he had not intended to commit, in order to bring criminal charges against him. Entrapment is a defense to a criminal charge.

equity: historically, a separate court following principles of fairness and reason in reaching its decisions, as opposed to a law court following the common law or precedent. Equity courts never use juries; the judge or chancellor makes findings on the facts and affords relief by issuing an injunction or order based on moral or ethical fairness in the particular case rather than relying on legal precedents from previous cases or simply ordering the payment of money damages, for example. *Compare* common law.

establish: to prove beyond a reasonable doubt or by a lesser standard (*see* burden of proof); to convince the judge or jury of the truth of.

evidence: any kind of proof legally presented at trial; testimony of witnesses, records, documents, physical objects, etc., by which a party tries to convince the judge or jury that his description of the facts is accurate or that his opponent's description is inaccurate or insufficient.

examining trial: the name given to the preliminary examination in some jurisdictions.

exclusionary rule: the legal principle of excluding from a criminal trial any evidence that was secured illegally.

exhaust remedies: to use the grievance and appeal procedure of the administrative body, corporation, union, or other agency where the problem arose before going to court, or to go through all lower or all state court procedures before bringing the case to a higher or a federal court. The rule requiring a

complainant to exhaust his remedies is used by judges to limit
the number of cases filed in courts and to limit the issues raised
in court cases.

exhibits: documents or other things brought into court about which
a witness testifies, or documents attached to and referred to in
a pleading to support an allegation.

expunge: to destroy or obliterate a document or record by physical
annihilation. In some situations the document is not actually
destroyed, but it is labeled expunged.

ex rel.: abbreviation of "ex relatione," meaning "upon the relation
or information of." In a case name such as *Missouri ex rel.
Gaines* v. *Canada,* the term means that the suit is brought in
the name of the state at the instigation and on the information
of Gaines, the complainant, who has a personal interest in the
matter. Gaines is called the relator in such a case, Missouri is
the plaintiff, and Canada is the defendant.

extrajudicial statements: statements made outside the course of
regular court proceedings, or statements that are not founded
on or connected with the case in court.

extraordinary remedies: special procedures (such as habeas corpus)
for getting quick court action on an urgent problem (such as
release from prison) without waiting for a full court trial in
which both sides make formal presentations of evidence before
a jury.

F.2d: *Federal Reporter,* second series—the set of books containing
the published opinions of the federal courts of appeals. In citations to cases, the number before "F.2d" is the volume of the
series, and the number following is the page at which the case
begins. A first series (F.) ran until 1924; then the second series
began with volume 1 again.

federal (or United States) court of appeals: the first appellate court
for cases arising in the federal district court. (A few cases go
directly from a federal administrative agency to the federal
court of appeals.) The United States is divided into eleven cir-
cuits, each having a federal court of appeals. A circuit includes
several states. The full name of the court is, for example, United
States Court of Appeals for the Fifth Circuit.

federal (or United States) district court: the trial court for cases
arising under federal law or jurisdiction. The United States is
divided into districts each having its own federal district court.

A district may be a state or part of a state. The full name of the court is, for example, United States District Court for the Southern District of California.

felony: a serious crime that is punishable by incarceration in a state or federal prison (usually for more than one year) and/or a fine. Compare with misdemeanor.

finding: a determination of a question of fact. A court studies evidence on the facts in a case and makes a finding or decision on the facts. *See also* holding.

fine: a money penalty imposed on a party found guilty of an offense or wrong.

freehold: the right of title to real property (land).

fruits (of a search): papers, objects (such as illegal drugs), names and addresses of possible witnesses, and other leads to information obtained by the prosecution in the search of a person and his premises or in questioning him.

gag rule: an order of a judge to a lawyer, reporter, or other person not to discuss a case publicly during a certain period (such as prior to and during trial), with the threat of a contempt citation for disobedience.

garnishment: a procedure by which a creditor files a lawsuit against a debtor and then tells the debtor's employer to take money directly out of the debtor's wages or salary; the employer pays the creditor as the worker earns the money, and the worker never sees the money.

gerrymander: a method of drawing election districts solely in order to insure the election or defeat of a particular person or type of person, without following the customary rule that districts should be more or less uniform in size and shape. The word is derived from the name of Massachusetts Governor Elbridge Gerry and "salamander"; it was coined to describe an irregularly shaped election district in Massachusetts formed for partisan political purposes in 1812, which resembled a salamander.

ground: point relied on in a lawsuit; foundation, reason, or basis for an argument or a legal approach.

habeas corpus: "you have the body." The name of a court order (or writ) to a jailer, or other person having custody (such as a military officer), commanding him to bring a person before the court for a hearing on whether he is being detained illegally, usually because of a denial of due process of law somewhere in the proceedings. This procedure cannot be suspended except during a rebellion or invasion if the public safety requires suspension, according to Article I, Section 9, of the Constitution.

hearsay: evidence not coming from the witness's personal knowledge, but merely repeating what he has heard others say; such evidence is usually excluded.

holding: a determination of a question of law. A court studies the law applicable to a set of facts in a case and makes a holding or decision on the law. *See also* finding.

immunity: freedom from duty or penalty; protection from prosecution. When offered to compel a witness to waive his privilege against self-incrimination, the immunity must provide complete protection from all the perils against which the constitutional privilege was designed to guard. *See also* sovereign immunity.

impeach a witness: to produce evidence that calls in question a witness's truthfulness or proves that he is unworthy of belief.

inadmissable evidence: evidence that cannot be presented to the judge or jury for consideration in reaching a decision; for example, evidence that was obtained illegally, or is not pertinent.

incarceration: confinement in a jail or prison.

incorporation theory: the theory that the authors of the due process clause of the Fourteenth Amendment intended it to incorporate all of the guarantees in the Bill of Rights (the first ten amendments) and make them applicable to the states. Thus, a person would be entitled to the same protections in state proceedings as in federal proceedings, and would be guaranteed against state and local government interference with his freedoms, as he is against federal interference.

indictment: a written accusation presented by a grand jury to a court, charging a named person with a crime. The person accused is said to be "indicted." The grand jury holds hearings at which the prosecutor presents his evidence against the suspect. The suspect may or may not be called to appear before the grand jury. If the grand jurors decide that the prosecutor has sufficient evidence to warrant a trial, they issue the indictment. A prosecutor may file an "information" as an alternative method of charging a person with a crime.

indigent: a person who has insufficient funds to pay for legal services, and court costs, whether in civil or in criminal matters.

information: a formal accusation made by a prosecuting officer to a court, charging a named person with a crime.

injunction: a court order to a person, corporation, or government agency requiring him or it to do or refrain from doing a particular act. Failure to obey an injunction can lead to a citation for contempt of court.

in re: "in the matter of"; concerning. This is the usual method of entitling a case in which one party makes an application on his own behalf; such proceedings may also be entitled "ex parte" (by one party) rather than "in re."

instructions: directions given by the judge to the jury concerning the law to be applied once the jury has decided what facts were proved. The jurors are expected to accept and apply the instructions, also using their lay wisdom to achieve fairness and to express the community conscience on the issues in the case.

judicial notice: *see* take judicial notice.

jurisdiction: 1. the authority of a court to hear cases arising or brought by persons residing within a defined territory, such as a county or a judicial district. 2. the geographic area over which a court has authority. 3. the authority of a court to hear cases concerning particular subject matters or parties.

jurisprudence: the philosophy of law; the principles of law and legal relations; a body of law.

justiciability: the nature of a question that makes it proper for a court to decide it; a "political" question may have to be decided by the voters or legislators, while a justiciable issue can be decided by the courts.

lay a foundation: to establish beforehand; for example, before presenting evidence on point B, the attorney must present evidence on point A to explain why B is relevant to an issue before the court; or before presenting testimony by a witness on point B, the attorney must question the witness on point A to prove he is qualified to discuss point B.

L. Ed. 2d: *Lawyer's Edition, United States Supreme Court Reports,* second series—a set of books published commercially containing the Supreme Court opinions and decisions. In citations to cases, the number before "L. Ed. 2d" is the volume of the series and the number following is the page at which the case begins.

A first series (L. Ed.) ran to volume 100, ending in 1956; the second series then began with volume 1 again.

liable: responsible, chargeable, answerable, compellable to compensate or make restitution.

libel: an untrue statement deliberately made in print, writing, pictures, or signs that injures the reputation of another person.

litigant: a party to a lawsuit. *See also* parties.

litigation: a contest in court to enforce a right; a lawsuit.

magistrate: an officer with power to issue a warrant for the arrest of a person charged with a crime or offense. Every judge is a magistrate, but the term is generally used to refer to the inferior judicial officers, such as justices of the peace and police justices.

majority opinion: a statement of the reasons for a decision agreed to by a majority of the appellate court judges when the judges were not unanimous in their views. It becomes the court opinion and is used as precedent in other similar cases. When a majority of judges can agree on a decision but not on the underlying reasons for it, there will be a *decision* by the majority but no majority *opinion,* and no opinion can be used as precedent in another similar case.

malapportionment: division of a state into election districts of unequal numbers of people, for the election of congressmen, senators, or state legislators.

malice: the intentional doing of a wrongful act without just cause or excuse, and with an intent to inflict an injury or economic harm or with reckless disregard of the harmful effect.

materiality: relevance of evidence to a substantial matter in dispute; the quality of having a real bearing on the case.

memorandum decision: a brief unsigned note by a court telling its decision in a case without explaining the reasons in detail.

minority opinion: statement of the reasons a minority of appellate court judges do not agree with the majority (or court) decision and opinion. If the minority judges cannot agree on the reasons for their disapproval of the majority opinion, they may write several separate dissenting opinions.

miscegenation: marriage between persons of different races, especially a black and a white.

misdemeanor: a minor criminal charge punishable by incarceration in a city or county jail rather than a prison, usually for less than one year, and/or by a fine.

mistrial: an invalid, incomplete trial of an action because the court lacks jurisdiction or the jurors were not properly drawn or some other fundamental requirement was disregarded before trial began or a basic error occurred during trial that cannot be corrected by instructing the jurors to ignore it.

motion: a written or spoken request by a party for a ruling or order from the judge.

motion to dismiss: a request by a defendant that the judge dismiss the complaint. The defendant claims that, even if the plaintiff's statement of the facts is correct, the complaint does not state any claim for relief that the court can grant. *See also* demur.

objection: a statement by an attorney in court indicating formal disapproval of the admission of testimony or argument being presented by the opposition. The judge must rule on each objection; if he agrees, he says, "Objection sustained"; if he rejects the objection, he says, "Objection overruled," and, if the objector wants to be able to argue on appeal that the ruling was wrong, in many courts he must say, "Exception."

opinion: a judge's statement of the reasons for the decision in a case, based on the relevant and admissible facts, the legislative or social history, and the law. The opinion usually explains why the court applied particular statutes or legal principles and not others, or followed some previous decisions and distinguished others. It is usually written but may be delivered from the bench orally. *See also* concurring opinion, dissent, majority opinion, minority opinion.

own recognizance: *see* recognizance.

parens patriae: in the United States, the state playing the role of parent by exercising sovereign power of guardianship over persons under a legal disability, such as minors and insane persons.

parties: the persons actively concerned in filing or prosecuting and defending a lawsuit.

penal: criminal, punishable. The penal code is the compilation of statutes describing criminal acts and the punishments for committing them.

pending: started, but not yet decided or concluded.

per curiam: "by the court"; a phrase used in case reports to distinguish an unsigned opinion of the court from an opinion written by one judge and subscribed to by others.

peremptory challenge: the procedure by which the attorneys for each side in a lawsuit may excuse a prescribed number of prospective jurors from the jury without stating any reason (unlike challenges for cause).

perjury: a witness's willful assertion under oath of a material fact, opinion, or belief that he knows to be false.

per se: in itself; taken alone; inherently; without explanation.

personal injury litigation: a lawsuit charging that the defendant's negligence caused a hurt or damage to the plaintiff's person, such as a broken limb. (It may also include a claim for damage to the plaintiff's property by the same act of the defendant.)

petitioner: 1. a person who petitions a court, officer, or legislature. 2. the losing party at one stage of a lawsuit who petitions an appellate court to review his case. The opposing party is then called the "respondent." 3. a person seeking naturalization or other court action when there may not be an opposing party.

petit jury: the body of people, traditionally twelve, who hear and decide the factual issues in the trial of a civil or criminal action; the trial jury.

plea: in a criminal case, the answer of the defendant to the charges against him, such as "not guilty" or "guilty."

pleadings: formal written statements of charges or complaints and defenses presented by the parties alternately until all side issues are resolved or dropped and only the issues that one side affirms and the other side denies remain for trial.

precedent: a principle of law declared by a court in a written opinion to serve as a rule for guidance in future similar cases (not something mentioned in passing that was not decided). A court will follow the line of decisions of the past in deciding a case in the present unless it specifically overrules that line (stating its reasons), or distinguishes the present case by describing how it differs. Legislatures sometimes pass statutes explicitly changing a rule of law in order to stop courts from continuing to follow precedents the legislators feel are outmoded.

preempt the field: to assume authority over a subject area by legislating in that area. When a higher legislative body (such as Congress) preempts a field, a lower body (such as a state legislature) is prohibited from passing or enforcing contrary legislation of its own in that field.

prejudicial error: a mistake or incorrect ruling that substantially affects a party's legal rights and obligations, entitling him to relief such as a new trial.

preliminary examination: the short hearing given to a person accused of crime before a magistrate or judge to decide whether there is enough evidence to justify the charge and require the defendant to stand trial. If the defendant is in custody, the judge may decide at this point to release him, on bail or on his own recognizance, pending trial.

prima facie: at first sight; on the face of it; presumed to be true. When the plaintiff presents a prima facie case, he will win unless his allegations are disproved by evidence to the contrary.

primogeniture: the system of inheritance under which the oldest son of a family inherited all the family land and the younger sons and all daughters inherited none. It is prohibited in the United States.

prior restraint: action taken to prevent someone from exercising a liberty guaranteed in the First Amendment (such as speaking, publishing, collecting signatures on a petition, showing a movie, joining an organization, or hiring a hall). Most often the action taken is to arrest or fine him or require him to sign an oath of loyalty before he has done the act. The First Amendment is intended to prohibit advance censorship of expression; it requires the government to stop people (if at all) only after they have acted and then to try them in a court to determine whether their actions, or the government's restraints, were illegal.

privilege against self-incrimination: the right of a person not to be compelled by the government to be a witness against himself, that is, to give testimony that could lead to criminal charges being filed against him, even if he could defeat such charges in a trial. The privilege is guaranteed in the Fifth Amendment. *See also* immunity.

probable cause: facts that would lead a reasonably intelligent and prudent person (usually a police officer) to believe that a crime was committed and that the suspect committed it, therefore justifying an arrest or a search.

procedural law: that part of law that prescribes methods of determining facts and enforcing the rights and duties set forth in the substantive part of the law, or of obtaining damages for the invasion of those rights.

proscribe: to prohibit, forbid, or condemn as being harmful.

proscription: a prohibition or restriction.

punitive damages (exemplary damages): an amount of money awarded to an injured plaintiff in addition to compensation for his actual losses when the defendant's wrongdoing was not simply negligence but also included violence, oppression, malice, fraud, or wanton and wicked conduct. The extra penalty is intended to punish the defendant for his evil behavior or to make an example of him.

quash: to vacate, annul, or make void.

recognizance: a written promise by a prisoner that he will appear in court whenever ordered to do so, for example, to answer the charges against him. Criminal defendants in some jurisdictions are released on their own recognizance pending trial instead of being required to buy bail bonds or post bail (cash or securities) to secure their release.

record: the official, authentic, written history of the trial of a lawsuit. It includes the papers filed in the case by the parties, written rulings by the judge (these constitute the "clerk's transcript"), and sometimes the verbatim (word for word) transcript of the pretrial and trial proceedings (the "reporter's transcript"). In appealing from a judgment against his client, an attorney reads the entire record but uses in his argument to the appeals court only the parts showing that errors were made.

release on own recognizance: *see* recognizance.

relevant evidence: evidence relating to or bearing on the issue or tending to prove the point alleged. *See also* materiality.

relief: the specific remedies a complainant seeks from the court to recompense him for the wrongs done by the defendant, such as an order requiring payment of damages by the defendant or requiring him to stop doing an act.

remand: the action of an appellate court, after it has heard and decided a case, sending it back to the trial or lower appellate court it came from, for a trial, retrial, or other action on it.

remedy: the action a court requires of the losing party to enforce a right or prevent or redress the violation of a right of the winning party. Often it consists of payment of money by the wrongdoer to the wronged party, but it may take many other forms (such as a court order to rehire a worker, to stop polluting activities, to halt construction of a highway or structure, or to disclose information being withheld).

restitution: to restore something taken or to give compensation for its loss to the rightful owner; to pay damages for an injury or wrong.

restrictive covenant: a written agreement or contract made in a deed to a piece of real property (land) restricting its sale or use in a certain manner. So-called racial restrictive covenants prohibited members of certain racial, national, or religious groups from buying pieces of land. The agreements passed from each buyer to the next and thus were said to "run with the land." They have been declared unconstitutional by the Supreme Court.

retroactive application of a decision: a ruling by a court that a new decision on a point of law is to be applied not only to cases tried in the future (prospective application) but also to cases already concluded.

running: solicitation of clients and cases for a lawyer by a nonlawyer.

S. Ct.: *Supreme Court Reporter*—a set of books published commercially containing United States Supreme Court opinions and decisions. In citations to cases, the number before "S. Ct." is the volume of the series and the number following is the page at which the case begins.

sequester the jury: to order the trial jurors to be kept together in isolation from society during a trial, so that they do not go to their homes when court is not in session, in order to avoid all outside influences on them. The jury is always sequestered while it deliberates about the verdict.

sovereign immunity: a rule of law that protects government agencies and officials from suits for damages for their wrongful acts on the theory that "the king can do no wrong." Many states have passed statutes limiting sovereign immunity.

standing: the right to raise an issue in a lawsuit. A person does not have standing to sue if he was not personally damaged by the illegal or wrongful act of the defendant. The plaintiff's feeling that society in general has been damaged by the defendant's act does not give him standing to challenge it in court.

state action: action by an individual for which the state must take responsibility because the individual was acting as an employee, officer, or agent of the state or local government when he committed the act, and the state did not repudiate or cannot dissociate itself from the act or the actor.

statute of limitations: the limited period of time (set by statute) during which a lawsuit must be started or else the right to sue is lost. The statute of limitations is different for different civil and criminal wrongs, and varies from jurisdiction to jurisdiction. Some criminal charges, such as for murder, have no statute of limitations.

statutory law: laws enacted by the legislative branch of government (as opposed to case law, handed down by the judicial branch, and administrative law, issued by the executive branch). *See also* administrative law, case law, opinions, precedent.

stay: to stop or delay; to refrain from.

strike from the record: phrase used to indicate that the jury or judge is to disregard the material to be struck and pretend that the words were never spoken. The court reporter does not, however, actually take the words out of the transcript; they are preserved so that a party seeking to appeal the case can refer to them if he contends that the ruling to strike was in error.

subpoena: a command from a court or other body ordering a witness to appear and give testimony and imposing a penalty for refusal to obey. (It may include an order to bring certain documents into court.)

substantive law: that part of law that defines rights, duties, crimes, and torts (as opposed to procedural law). *See also* procedural law.

systematic exclusion: a methodical plan or procedure of keeping certain classes of people out (of a grand or petit jury panel). Defendants often allege systematic exclusion of blacks, women, young people, blue collar workers, or religious minorities.

take judicial notice: the act by which a court recognizes the existence and truth of certain facts bearing on the case without hearing evidence on them, such as indisputable geographical, astronomical, or historical facts.

test: a standard, rule, or criterion on a particular issue stated by a court to determine a specific case and all future cases on that issue.

test case: a suit designed to pose a general challenge to enforcement of a statute, regulation, or custom, as well as to determine the rights of the particular parties to the suit.

testator/testatrix: a man/woman who makes a will.

tort: a civil wrong or injury; a violation of a duty imposed by law.

tortfeasor: a wrongdoer; one who damages the person or property of another to whom he had a duty to be careful, thus committing a civil (not criminal) wrong.

transcript: 1. the word-for-word account of the oral proceedings in a case (also known as the "reporter's transcript"). 2. a copy of the documents in the record of a case (the "clerk's transcript"), which is sent to the appellate judges to review. *See also* record.

trespass: to enter another person's land without lawful authority.

trial de novo: a new trial of a case in a higher court, ordered after error was found in the original trial in the trial court; it is conducted as if no trial whatever had been held in the court below.

understanding statutes: laws requiring a person registering to vote to demonstrate his understanding of a section of the state constitution selected by the voting registrar. Typically these statutes were used by white southern registrars to reject blacks as voters, before passage of the 1965 Voting Rights Act.

undisclosed bank lien: a creditor's right to take payment of a debt directly from the debtor's bank account without notifying the debtor.

U.S.: *United States Supreme Court Reports*—set of books containing the official Supreme Court opinions and decisions. In citations to cases, the number before "U.S." is the volume of the series and the number following is the page at which the case begins.

U.S.C.: *United States Code*—the official set of books containing the federal statutes that have been arranged according to subject matter (codified). The codes are separated into titles, and each title is a subject area. In citations to statutes, the number before

"U.S.C." is the title number of the code and the number following is the section (§) number of the particular statute.

vacate: to annul, set aside, cancel, rescind, or render void.

venireman: a member of a panel of prospective jurors (subject to peremptory challenges or challenges for cause).

venue: the "neighborhood" (county or area) in which a wrongful act was done and from which the jury to try the case is chosen. *See also* change of venue.

waive a jury: to knowingly give up or renounce the right to be tried by a jury in a criminal case. (A plaintiff or defendant in a civil case will not have a jury trial unless he asks for one, and therefore he does not have occasion to "waive" a jury.)

warrant: an order from a magistrate or other authority requiring a police officer, sheriff, or other official to arrest a person or search specified premises.

wrongful death: the death of a person through the negligence or intentional act of someone else, which gives the deceased person's survivors a right to sue the wrongdoer for damages.

SOURCES AND SUGGESTED READINGS

I have found the books listed below to be useful or inspirational. They supply further information, background, or viewpoints on the subject matters covered in this book and contain references to additional materials.

GENERAL

Arnold, Thurmond. *The Folklore of Capitalism*. New Haven: Yale University Press, 1937.

Barnard, Harry. *Eagle Forgotten: The Life of John Peter Altgeld*. Indianapolis: Bobbs-Merrill Co., 1938.

Beard, Charles A. *An Economic Interpretation of the Constitution of the United States*. New York: Macmillan Co., 1956 reprint of 1913 edition.

Boudin, Louis. *Government by Judiciary*. 2 vols. New York: Russell and Russell, Publishers, 1968 reprint of 1932 edition.

Caughey, John W.; Franklin, John Hope; and May, Ernest R. *Land of the Free: A History of the United States*. Pasadena, Calif.: Franklin Publications, 1967.

Commager, Henry Steele, ed. *Documents of American History*. 8th ed. New York: F. S. Crofts and Co., 1968.

Cushman, Robert E. *Civil Liberties in the United States: A Guide to Current Problems and Experience*. Ithaca, N.Y.: Cornell University Press, 1956.

DeCaux, Len. *Labor Radical: From the Wobblies to CIO*. Boston: Beacon Press, 1970.

Dorsen, Norman. *The Rights of Americans: What They Are—What They Should Be*. New York: Random House, 1970; Vintage Books paperback edition, 1972.

Dunne, Finley Peter. *Mr. Dooley in Peace and in War*. Westport, Conn.: Greenwood, 1969 reprint of 1898 edition.

Emerson, Thomas I.; Haber, David; and Dorsen, Norman. *Political and Civil Rights in the United States.* 2 vols. 3rd ed. Boston: Little, Brown and Co., 1967.

Foner, Philip. *History of the Labor Movement in the United States.* 4 vols. New York: International Publishers Co., 1965 reprint of 1947 edition.

Foster, William Z. *Pages from a Worker's Life.* New York: International Publishers Co., 1970 reprint of 1939 edition.

Frank, John P. *Mr. Justice Black: The Man and His Opinions.* New York: Alfred A. Knopf, 1949.

Ginger, Ann Fagan, ed. *The Relevant Lawyers: Conversations Out of Court on Their Clients, Their Practice, Their Politics, Their Life Style.* New York: Simon and Schuster, 1972.

————, ed. *Civil Liberties Docket.* 14 vols. Berkeley, Calif.: Meiklejohn Civil Liberties Institute, 1955–69.

Ginger, Ray. *The Bending Cross: A Biography of Eugene Victor Debs.* New York: Russell, 1969 reprint of 1949 edition; Macmillan paperback edition entitled *Eugene V. Debs: A Biography,* 1962.

Goldberg, Arthur J. *Equal Justice: The Warren Era of the Supreme Court.* Chicago: Northwestern University Press, 1971.

Hamilton, Alexander; Jay, John; and Madison, James. *The Federalist.* New York: Random House, n.d., and various other editions.

Holmes, Oliver Wendell. *The Mind and Faith of Justice Holmes: His Speeches, Essays, Letters and Judicial Opinions.* Selected and edited by Max Lerner. Boston: Little, Brown and Co., 1943.

Human Rights: A Compilation of International Instruments of the United Nations. New York: United Nations, 1967.

International Juridical Association Bulletin. 1932–1942. New York: International Juridical Association.

Lockhart, William B.; Kamisar, Yale; and Choper, Jesse H. *Constitutional Law: Cases—Comments—Questions.* 2nd ed. St. Paul, Minn.: West Publishing Co., 1967.

Marcantonio, Vito. *I Vote My Conscience: Debates, Speeches and Writings, 1935–1950.* Selected and edited by Annette T. Rubinstein. New York: Vito Marcantonio Memorial, 1956.

Mason, Altheus T. *Brandeis: A Free Man's Life*. New York: Viking Press, 1956.

McKechnie, W. S. *Magna Carta*. 2nd ed. New York: Macmillan Co., 1914.

Myers, Gustavus. *History of the Supreme Court of the United States*. Chicago: Charles H. Kerr and Co., 1925.

National Lawyers Guild. *Law reviews* [under various titles] and materials. Berkeley, Calif.: National Lawyers Guild, Box 673, Berkeley, Ca. 94701 [issued periodically].

Parrington, Vernon L. *Maincurrents of American Thought*. 3 vols. New York: Harcourt, Brace and Co., 1927–30.

Smith, Bernard, ed. *The Democratic Spirit: A Collection of American Writings from the Earliest Times to the Present Day*. New York: Alfred A. Knopf, 1941.

Steffens, Lincoln. *The Autobiography of Lincoln Steffens*. 2 vols. New York: Harcourt, Brace and World, 1958 reprint of 1931 edition.

Stone, Irving. *Clarence Darrow for the Defense*. New York: New American Library, 1971 reprint of 1949 edition.

Swisher, Carl Brent. *American Constitutional Development*. Boston: Houghton Mifflin Co., 1943.

Terkel, Louis (Studs). *Hard Times: An Oral History of the Great Depression*. New York: Pantheon Books, 1970.

Wasserstein, Bruce, and Green, Mark J., eds. *With Justice for Some: An Indictment of the Law by Young Advocates*. Boston: Beacon Press, 1970.

Whipple, Leon. *The Story of Civil Liberty in the United States*. New York: Vanguard Press and the American Civil Liberties Union, 1927.

Warren, Earl. *Republic—If You Can Keep It*. New York: Quadrangle Publications, 1972.

Part I. Freedom

American Civil Liberties Union. *Newsletters and reports*. New York: American Civil Liberties Union [issued periodically].

Barth, Alan. *The Loyalty of Free Men.* New York: Viking Press, 1951.

Blanshard, Paul. *American Freedom and Catholic Power.* Boston: Beacon Press, 1949.

————. *The Right to Read.* Boston: Beacon Press, 1955.

Carr, Robert K. *The House Committee on Un-American Activities, 1949–1950.* Ithaca, N.Y.: Cornell University Press, 1952.

Chafee, Zechariah, Jr. *Free Speech in the United States.* Cambridge: Harvard University Press, 1946.

Commager, Henry Steele. *Freedom, Loyalty, Dissent.* New York: Oxford University Press, 1954.

Countryman, Vern. *Un-American Activities in the State of Washington.* Ithaca, N.Y.: Cornell University Press, 1951.

Davis, Elmer. *But We Were Born Free.* New York: Bobbs-Merrill Co., 1954.

Donner, Frank J. *The Un-Americans.* New York: Ballantine Books, 1961.

Douglas, William O. *An Almanac of Liberty.* Garden City, N.Y.: Doubleday and Co., 1954.

Emerson, Thomas I. *The System of Freedom of Expression.* New York: Random House, 1970.

Gellhorn, Walter. *Security, Loyalty, and Science.* Ithaca, N.Y.: Cornell University Press, 1950.

————. *Individual Freedom and Government Restraints.* Baton Rouge: Louisiana State University Press, 1958.

————, ed. *The States and Subversion.* Ithaca, N.Y.: Cornell University Press, 1952.

Gregory, Dick. *Nigger: An Autobiography.* With Robert Lipsyte. New York: E. P. Dutton and Co., 1964.

Jefferson, Thomas. *The Complete Jefferson.* Assembled and arranged by Saul K. Padover. New York: Duell, Sloan and Pearce, 1943.

Kahn, Gordon. *Hollywood on Trial: The Story of the 10 Who Were Indicted.* New York: Boni and Gaer, 1948.

Lamont, Corliss. *Freedom Is as Freedom Does: Civil Liberties Today.* New York: Da Capo Press, 1972.

MacIver, Robert M. *Academic Freedom in Our Time.* New York: Columbia University Press, 1955.

Meiklejohn, Alexander. *Political Freedom: The Constitutional Powers of the People.* New York: Harper and Brothers, Publishers, 1960.

Murry, Robert K. *Red Scare: A Study in National Hysteria, 1919–1920.* Minneapolis: University of Minnesota Press, 1955.

Nye, Russell. *Fettered Freedom: Civil Liberties and the Slavery Controversy 1830–1860.* Rev. ed. East Lansing: Michigan State University Press, 1963.

O'Brian, John Lord. *National Security and Individual Freedom.* Cambridge: Harvard University Press, 1955.

Preston, William, Jr. *Aliens and Dissenters.* Cambridge: Harvard University Press, 1963.

Richmond, Al. *A Long View from the Left: Memoirs of an American Revolutionary.* Boston: Houghton Mifflin Co., 1973.

Smith, Louise P. *Torch of Liberty.* New York: Dwight-King Publishing, Inc., 1959.

Taylor, Telford. *Grand Inquest. The Story of Congressional Investigations.* New York: Simon and Schuster, 1955.

Part II. Justice

Andrews, William. *Old-Time Punishments.* Detroit: Singing Tree Press, 1970 reprint of British 1890 edition.

Biberman, Herbert. *Salt of the Earth: The Story of a Film.* Boston: Beacon Press, 1965.

Frank, Jerome; Frank, Barbara; and Hoffman, Harold M. *Not Guilty.* New York: Doubleday and Co., 1957; Popular Library paperback edition, 1957.

Ginger, Ann Fagan, and Bell, Louis H. *Police Misconduct Litigation—Plaintiff's Remedies. American Jurisprudence Trials,* vol. 15. San Francisco: Bancroft-Whitney Co.; Rochester, N.Y.: Lawyers Co-operative Publishing Co., 1968.

Griswold, Erwin N. *The Fifth Amendment Today.* Cambridge: Harvard University Press, 1955.

Hall, Livingston; Kamisar, Yale; La Fave, Wayne R.; and Israel, Jerold H. *Modern Criminal Procedure: Cases, Comments and Questions.* 3rd ed. St. Paul, Minn.: West Publishing Co., 1969.

Joughin, G. Louis, and Morgan, Edmund M. *The Legacy of Sacco and Vanzetti.* New York: Harcourt, Brace and Co., 1948.

Lewis, Anthony. *Gideon's Trumpet.* New York: Random House, 1966.

Lowenthal, Max. *The Federal Bureau of Investigation.* New York: William Sloane Associates, 1950.

Matusow, Harvey. *False Witness.* New York: Cameron and Kahn, Publishers, 1955.

Packer, Herbert L. *Ex-Communist Witnesses: Four Studies in Fact Finding.* Stanford, Calif.: Stanford University Press, 1962.

Thompson, George. *Prison Life and Reflections.* Oberlin, Ohio: Printed for the author by James M. Fitch, 1847.

Triston, H. U. *Men in Cages.* Ann Arbor, Mich.: Gryphon Books, 1971 reprint of British 1938 edition.

Part III. Equality

Aptheker, Herbert, ed. *A Documentary History of the Negro People in the United States.* New York: Citadel Press, 1951.

Belfrage, Sally. *Freedom Summer.* New York: Viking Press, 1965; Fawcett Crest paperback edition, 1966.

Blaustein, Albert P., and Zangrando, Robert L., eds. *Civil Rights and the American Negro: A Documentary History.* New York: Washington Square Press, 1968.

Bontemps, Arna. *100 Years of Negro Freedom.* New York: Dodd, Mead and Co., 1961.

Braden, Anne. *The Wall Between.* New York: Monthly Review Press, 1958; Prometheus Books edition, 1959.

Civil Rights Congress. *We Charge Genocide: The Historic Petition to the United Nations for Relief from a Crime of the United States Government against the Negro People.* New York: Civil Rights Congress, 1951.

Denton, John H., ed. *Race and Property.* Berkeley, Calif.: Diablo Press, 1964.

DuBois, W. E. Burghardt. *The Autobiography of W. E. B. DuBois: A Soliloquy on Viewing My Life from the Last Decade of Its First Century.* New York: International Publishers, 1968.

———. *Black Reconstruction.* New York: Russell and Russell, 1935.

———. *John Brown.* New York: International Publishers, 1962 reprint of 1909 edition.

———. *The Souls of Black Folk: Essays and Sketches.* Chicago: A. C. McClurg and Co., 1903.

Flexner, Eleanor. *Century of Struggle: The Woman's Rights Movement in the United States.* Cambridge: Belknap Press, Harvard University Press, 1959.

Hansberry, Lorraine. *A Raisin in the Sun.* New York: Random House, 1959.

Higbee, Jay Anders. *Development and Administration of the New York State Law against Discrimination.* University, Ala.: University of Alabama Press, 1966.

Higginson, Thomas Wentworth. *Army Life in a Black Regiment.* New York: Collier Books, 1962.

Holt, Len. *An Act of Conscience.* Boston: Beacon Press, 1965.

———. *The Summer That Didn't End.* New York: William Morrow, 1965.

King, Martin Luther, Jr. *The Measure of a Man.* Philadelphia: Christian Education Press, 1959.

———. *Stride toward Freedom: The Montgomery Story.* New York: Harper and Brothers, Publishers, 1958.

———. *Why We Can't Wait.* New York: Harper and Row, 1964.

Korngold, Ralph. *Two Friends of Man: The Story of William Lloyd Garrison and Wendell Phillips and Their Relationship with Abraham Lincoln.* Boston: Little, Brown and Co., 1950.

Lerner, Gerda. *The Grimké Sisters from South Carolina: Pioneers for Woman's Rights and Abolition.* New York: Schocken Books, 1967.

Little, Malcolm. *The Autobiography of Malcolm X.* New York: Grove Press, 1965.

McCord, John H., ed. *With All Deliberate Speed: Civil Rights Theory and Reality.* Urbana: University of Illinois Press, 1969.

Miller, Loren. *The Petitioners: The Story of the Supreme Court of the United States and the Negro.* New York: Pantheon Books, Random House, 1966.

Morgan, Charles, Jr. *A Time to Speak.* New York: Harper and Row, Publishers, 1964.

Olshausen, George. "Rich and Poor in Civil Procedure." *Science and Society* 9 (1947): 11.

Record, Wilson, and Record, Jane Cassels. *Little Rock, U.S.A.: Materials for Analysis.* San Francisco: Chandler Publishing Co., 1960.

Schappes, Morris U., ed. *Documentary History of the Jews in the United States.* New York: Citadel Press, 1950.

Silberman, Charles E. *Crisis in Black and White.* New York: Random House, 1964.

Silver, James Wesley. *Mississippi the Closed Society.* New York: Harcourt, Brace and World, 1964.

Sutherland, Elizabeth, ed. *Letters from Mississippi.* New York: McGraw-Hill Book Co., 1965.

tenBroek, Jacobus. *The Antislavery Origins of the Fourteenth Amendment.* Berkeley and Los Angeles: University of California Press, 1951.

———; Barnhart, Edward N.; and Matson, Floyd W. *Prejudice, War and the Constitution.* Berkeley and Los Angeles: University of California Press, 1958.

———, and editors of *California Law Review,* eds. *The Law of the Poor.* San Francisco: Chandler Publishing Co., 1966.

U.S. Commission on Civil Rights. *Reports* [on various subject areas]. Washington, D.C.: Government Printing Office [issued periodically].

Warren, Robert Penn. *Who Speaks for the Negro?* New York: Random House, 1965.

Woodley, Thomas Frederick. *Thaddeus Stevens.* Harrisburg, Pa.: Telegraph Press, 1934.

Zinn, Howard. *SNCC, the New Abolitionists.* Boston: Beacon Press, 1964.

———. *The Southern Mystique.* New York: Alfred A. Knopf, 1968.

TABLE OF CASES

INDEX

RENNER LEARNING RESOURCE CENTER
ELGIN COMMUNITY COLLEGE
ELGIN, ILLINOIS 60123